DR. TONY HYMAN'S

I'll Buy That!

A GUIDE TO THE BEST BUYERS
OF ANTIQUES, COLLECTIBLES AND
OTHER UNDISCOVERED TREASURES
FOUND AROUND YOUR HOME & BUSINESS

by

H.A. Tony Hyman

Treasure Hunt Publications
Claremont, California

A Division of Collectors' Clearinghouse

© H. A. Tony Hyman

1989, 1990, 1991

All rights reserved.

Brief excerpts in reviews are encouraged if properly credited.
Names and addresses may not be printed without permission.

Treasure Hunt books are available at discount
with bulk purchase for business or promotional use.
Custom editions can be created to fill your specific needs.
Please call our Promotions Department at (714) 621-5952.

Previous books on buying and selling by Dr. Hyman:
The Where To Sell Anything and Everything Book
Where To Sell Anything and Everything by Mail
Cash For Your Undiscovered Treasures

**Treasure Hunt Publications
PO Box 3028,
Pismo Beach, CA 93448**
(new address)

Covers: Steve Gussman
Art Assistant: Daniel Hyman
Mechanicals: FullWrite Professional on Mac II
7 6

LC: 89-50578   ISBN: 0-937111-01-5

A note from the author

Dear Reader:

What can *I'll Buy That!* do for you?

I'll Buy That! can help you locate honest buyers for items you want to sell. Thanks to *I'll Buy That!*, more than 500 top buyers and experts are at your fingertips...only a phone call or letter away.

Many buyers also provide other services, including appraisals, auctions, brokering, newsletters, and price guides. Many of them also sell and rent. *I'll Buy That!* can also help you:

* Settle an estate for top dollar;
* Obtain insurance appraisals;
* Buy or rent antiques and collectibles;
* Make money buying at yard sales, antique shops, and secondhand stores, and reselling for profit;
* Have fun reading about unusual hobbies;
* Meet a great many interesting people;
* Find an unusual gift for a friend!

To get the most $$$ from *I'll Buy That!* read pages 2-11. They are crammed with inside tips on how to make money selling your castoffs....tips based on 25 years of experience buying and selling through the mail. Also read the valuable tips at the beginning of each chapter.

Since 1981, readers and book reviewers have praised our directories. Sellers say that following our suggestions and perseverance puts extra $$$ in their pocket time and again.

I'll Buy That! probably won't make you an instant millionaire, but readers have gotten thousands of dollars for items called "valueless" by local dealers. One reader recently found a buyer for a Japanese sword which had been hanging on her wall for 25 years. It looked ordinary, but our buyer informed the elderly widow she had a rare Oriental treasure made 250 years before Columbus, and paid her accordingly. You can imagine what that was worth!

Our books have brought good fortune to many. Whether you find treasures worth $50 or $50,000, our best wishes go with you.

Dr. H.A. Tony Hyman
July, 1989

Treasure Hunt Publications, Box 699, Claremont, CA 91711

HOW TO MAKE MONEY
WITH THIS BOOK

Six steps are required to make money by selling through the mail.

> Step 1: Find an item you'd like to sell;
> Step 2: Identify a buyer for it;
> Step 3: Contact the buyer;
> Step 4: Agree to a price;
> Step 5: Get $$$ in the mail;
> Step 6: Ship the item.

I'll Buy That! gives you inside tips on how to do each step easily and profitably. A few minutes reading about each step should put more $$$ in your pocket.

STEP 1 FIND AN ITEM

You may have bought *I'll Buy That!* with a specific item in mind...some thing you would like to sell. That's great! That's why this book was written.

I'll Buy That! will point out many other items that can put cash in your mailbox. Valuable items aren't always obvious. You may own something you think is worth nothing, that could prove to be worth hundreds of dollars. A briar pipe from 1950 recently sold for $875, a fishing plug for $9,000, an old tin can for $12,000, and a box of old letters for $500,000. Each of these items was originally purchased at a yard sale for less than $100 because their original owners didn't realize they could be valuable. You have the *I'll Buy That!* advantage.   You *know* what buyers want.

Almost anything can be valuable to someone. Read the Table of Contents and the Index, and you'll be amazed to recognize hundreds of things you own, or have seen at yard sales in your neighborhood. One Syracuse schoolteacher said,

> "Your book changed my life. I never paid attention to yard sales before. But I read your book cover to cover, like a novel, to get a sense of what people wanted. Then I went out looking. In just four weekends, I made over $1,800 buying things at yard sales, reselling to people in your book. And I never once paid over $5."

It is particularly important for senior citizens to be alert when settling estates. Items you take for granted because they have been part of your life for so long may be treasures to someone else. Read the Index!

$\overline{\underline{\text{STEP}}}$ **2** FIND A BUYER

If you have an item for which you'd like a buyer, start by skimming the Table of Contents. The 24 chapters are divided into broad categories, with dozens of sub-chapters. You may be able to spot the appropriate category right away. If you're still not certain where to begin, turn to the Index starting on page 286. Here you'll find more than 3,000 categories of items.

When looking for items in the Index, remember that people buy for many different reasons. People buy things because of:

What it is (a doll house, cigar box, doorstop, etc.);
Who manufactured it (*Coca-Cola, American Flyer, Colt,* etc.);
Where it was made (NY guns, Michigan art, Nevada bottles, etc.);
When it was made (books before 1700, art from 1930's, etc.);
What it is made of (plastic, glass, paper, etc.);
What it was used for (poker chips, prison money, Holy cards, etc.);
Where it was sold (Las Vegas souvenirs, Florida postcards, etc.);
What it is shaped like (cat figurines, motorcycle toys, etc.);
Who painted it (Rockwell paintings, comic art, prison art, etc.);
Who owned it (U.S. Presidents, movie stars, etc.).

It can be worth money in your pocket to look up your item in several categories. For example, an <u>ivory poker chip</u> covered with <u>advertising</u> for <u>patent medicine</u> used for <u>gambling</u> in a <u>prison</u> would be desirable to many buyers. When you consider all possibilities, *I'll Buy That!* can pay off for you.

When you've located an item in the Index, turn to the appropriate page(s) and read the entries to learn what those buyers are seeking. Entries vary from a few words to nearly half a page in length and contain more information than just name, address, and phone number.

Many entries also tell you what the buyer <u>doesn't</u> want, how much he* pays for some items, what books he's written, whether or not he makes offers, in what clubs he is an officer, and more. Many entries contain specific information regarding how to best sell to that particular buyer.

Before you contact your buyer, check the last page of *I'll Buy That!* Whenever we reprint, if we know of any buyers who have moved since the last printing, we put their new address on the back page. If *you* learn of a listee who has moved, please inform us. As a thank you, when we issue an update, we'll send you one free.

---

* "He" refers to men, women, and institutional buyers.

STEP 3 CONTACT YOUR BUYER

Most contacts are by letter or by phone, although a few buyers are open to FAX and computer modem contact as well. More than half our buyers have provided their phone number. **Never call collect** unless the buyer specifically authorized you to do so. Some buyers have a free 800 number. An 800 # is *not* an advice line and should be used *only* if you are selling.

> *INSIDE TIP: Phone calls are fast, easy, and able to get the most information to the buyer with the least effort. Selling something worth $50 up? Use the phone.*

Before you call, read the buyer's entry carefully. It sometimes tells you a great deal about the buyers wants. If a person's entry reads "No vibbles," don't inquire about selling your "vibble." An important reason for using the telephone is to let the buyer ask questions about your item(s), so call *only* when the item you wish to sell is right by the phone.

Some buyers, and many sellers, prefer not to use the phone. They like the slower pace and lower cost of writing. Contacting buyers by mail is as easy as filling in the blanks thanks to Dr. Hyman's exclusive SELL-A-GRAM.

Using a SELL-A-GRAM is self explanatory. Each section provides a set of reminders to make your selling experience effective and profitable. Using this handy form letter alerts buyers you are one of our readers. Some buyers provide readers with extra services at no charge. You may photocopy the SELL-A-GRAM as many times as you need to sell items to our buyers.

> *INSIDE TIP: If you have SELL-A-GRAMS made at a copy center, ask them to print on yellow paper. Marketing psychologists say colored paper gets faster attention. We think yellow works best.*

If you'd rather write a letter, make certain you include all information requested by the buyer. A good description, a photo or photocopy, and a Self Addressed Stamped Envelope (SASE) are three elements of successful selling by mail.

> *INSIDE TIP: Include your phone number in your letter. Many buyers prefer to call, especially on more valuable items. Others spend a great deal of time on the road and use the phone to answer quickly.*

How to describe things you sell

You must describe things well enough so that someone a thousand miles away understands exactly what you have. Start by telling what it is and, if necessary, what it was used for. Give its size, color, shape and identify the material from which it is made. Give any names, dates, model or serial numbers, makers' marks, signatures, and other characteristics which may be important. Provide as much much of an item's history as you know.

SELL-A-GRAM

from a reader of Hyman's *I'll Buy That!*

TO:
_____
_____
_____
_____

FROM:
_____
_____
_____

Phone: ( )

I have the following item:

Remember to include the (1) shape, (2) colors, (3) dimensions, and (4) all names, dates, and marks. Re-read pages 4-6 and Dr. Hyman's Prescription for selling what you have.

It's condition is:

List all chips, repairs, cracks, dents, fading, scratches, rips, tears, creases, holes, stains, and foxing. Note any missing pages, parts, or paint.

CHECK ONE

☐ The item is for sale for $_____ plus shipping.

☐ The item is for sale. I am an amateur seller and would like you to make an offer.

☐ The item may be for sale if the price is sufficient. Would you like to make an offer?

☐ The item is not for sale, but I am willing to pay a fee to learn its value.

To assist you to evaluate the item, I am enclosing a:

☐ Sample ☐ Photocopy ☐ Photo ☐ Tracing ☐ Sketch ☐ Rubbing ☐ Nothing

This is to certify that, to the best of my knowledge, the item is genuine and as described. Buyer has a 5 day examination period during which the item may be returned for any reason.

Signature: _____   Date: _____

☐ Answer Requested (SASE enclosed).   ☐ No answer needed.

BUYER'S RESPONSE:

©1986 Treasure Hunt Publications, Box 699, Claremont, CA 91711

TREASURE 🚃 HUNT

No matter what you sell, condition is important. Few people want to buy soiled, stained, damaged, or broken anything. Some items are *never* purchased damaged. But there are a few collectibles that can put money in your mailbox even if damaged or incomplete. These are usually mechanical devices such as phonographs or television sets that can be cannibalized for parts. Items in less than perfect condition will usually bring 50% or less of what items that are like new will bring.

> *INSIDE TIP: Describe condition accurately. If you don't, the buyer will return it, costing you and the buyer time, money, and wasted effort.*

Describing with photos and photocopies

Photocopy machines are a seller's best friend. Whenever possible, photocopy what you have to sell. It is the cheapest and easiest method of describing most items. Objects such as knives, small dolls, even pistols, will photocopy well. It is a particularly effective way to describe china patterns.

Some brands of photocopy machine make better copies of three dimensional objects than others. If yours doesn't make good copies, try a different brand or model. Copy machines are available in many businesses, banks, and libraries. Fees are a modest 4¢ to 25¢. Color photocopies are available at some copy centers, but for most items are an unnecessary expense.

Polaroid photos are not a good way to describe things. They are expensive, and the quality of print taken by amateurs usually lacks sufficient detail. If your item is worth more than $100 or so, the cost of taking (or having a friend take) a good slide or color print is usually worthwhile. Quilts, lamps, clocks, fine guns, scientific instruments, and cigar store figures are among the many items where photos are an important part of the description.

Self Addressed Stamped Envelopes....SASE

If you ask someone for information or an offer, take a long "business size" #10 envelope, address it to yourself, put a stamp in the corner, and include it with your **SELL-A-GRAM** or letter. If you ask for photos to be returned, put two stamps. Use a long envelope because many buyers will send you two or more pages of information, which won't fit well into smaller envelopes. When writing to Canada, send two loose U.S. stamps, instead of an SASE.

If you do not include an SASE, you are telling the buyer not to bother answering your letter if not interested in what you have to sell. "If my help isn't worth an envelope and stamp to the seller," said one expert, "it's not worth my time and money either."

Never ask for free information, appraisals, and the like without including an SASE. Our buyers have promised to answer your inquiries if you include an SASE. If an answer isn't important to you, please include a note saying "no reply needed." Otherwise, include an SASE.

STEP 4   SET A PRICE

When contacting a buyer, you can price the item you have for sale or you can ask the buyer to make a fair offer. If you are a professional full or part time antique dealer, or if you are selling something you know the value of, then you should set your price.

If, however, you are an amateur seller, offering items you know little about, asking for offers inevitably results in getting more money for what you have.

I'll Buy That! brings you many of the nation's top experts, men and women who write price guides, edit newsletters, or are officers in collectors' clubs. Many listees have been at their hobbies for 20 years or more, and keep up with daily market fluctuations. They, better than you, know what your item is worth.

So what's to keep them from cheating you...and telling you your $5,000 watch is worth $5? Honesty, for one thing. Reputation for another. The world of collectibles is a small one. Word gets around fast...and dishonest people don't stay in business long. You have the best defense of all, you can say no. Requesting an offer does not oblige you to sell at the price offered.

No reputable dealer is dishonest if he pays the price *you* set, but he can be at fault if you ask him for a fair price and he cheats you. Offers help protect you.

Even when dealing with experts, however, it is advisable when expensive items are involved to get more than one quotation. One buyer may offer you more because your item is less common in one part of the country than another, the buyer may want it for his own collection, or may have an immediate customer.

Naturally we can't guarantee private transactions between two people over whom we have no control. But hundreds of thousands of transactions have taken place based on our previous three books and we've received less than a dozen letters of complaint...most very minor, and none of the people involved are listed any more.

How much is something worth?

Strange as it seems, when selling old and used things, nothing has dollar value until you sell it. Only when a buyer and a seller agree to a price and money changes hands is value determined. Price guides, and one antiques columnist in particular, often cite very high prices for items, giving sellers false hopes. Although price guides are useful to antique dealers, they can be misleading. Price guides are usually based on the selling price of mint condition items sold by antique dealers to collectors. The likelihood that any guide will include the single item you have to sell is small. Seeing a blue vase listed as worth $40 tells you nothing about the value of your red vase, even if made by the same company. Expert dealers and collectors are usually more knowledgeable and hence better sources of information about specific items.

What you can expect a dealer or collector to pay

Generally, a dealer will pay from 30% to 80% of an item's full retail value. It depends on how much money the dealer has, how anxious he is to add your item to his inventory, how quickly he thinks your item will resell, and how valuable your item is. The more expensive the item you are selling, the higher percentage of retail value you're likely to get.

Collectors tend to pay more, 60% to 100% or more. They, too, pay more for expensive items. One collector explained:

> "If I'm offered a common item, worth only $5 or $6 dollars, I'm rarely interested in paying more than a dollar or two for it. I don't want to tie up my money or my space with minor items. When someone offers me a $100 item, I'm willing to pay full value or even more. If it's a very rare item, I'd rather overpay and make certain I get it."

Premium prices are paid by collectors and dealers for perfect condition items that are hot in the marketplace at that time. Antiques and collectibles, like other forms of entertainment and investment, undergo swings in popularity, hence in value.

Amateur sellers are notorious for overestimating the quality of condition. As a result, **some dealers and collectors will ask to see the item before they make a final offer.** This is particularly true of buyers of paper goods like post cards, trade cards, match covers, sheet music, and stamps. Paper dealers want to see what you have, because very small variations in condition can cause substantial difference in price. Paper money worth $50 in very fine condition might be worth only $5 in circulated condition. Post cards with rounded corners, or match covers with their strikers removed, are worth little or nothing.

A few other buyers, notably of watches, will also request an item be shipped prior to final payment. When you do this, protect yourself by insuring your package and sending it Registered Mail or "return receipt requested" which requires the recipient's signature.

INSIDE TIP: There are some excellent buyers in Canada. Make certain if you sell to a Canadian, however, that you require payment with a check in U.S. funds drawn on a U.S. bank. Many Canadians maintain accounts for this purpose. If they cannot write a check on a U.S. bank, request payment in U.S. funds by International Postal Money Order. These can be cashed at no charge at full value at any post office. Canadian bank checks can cost you as much as $7 in charges to cash at your bank. If drawn in Canadian funds, you will also lose on the exchange rate.

A few experts no longer make offers, even to amateur sellers. These are usually people who have been treated dishonestly by amateurs. They believe amateurs are "fishing for free information, don't really want to sell, and have outrageous expectations about the value of their objects."

Note to all sellers about honesty:

You expect honest information and fair prices from our buyers. It behooves you to follow the Golden Rule and do unto others. Be honest in *your* dealings with them.

Don't ask for offers when you are not planning to sell. If what you want is an appraisal, be honest and say you only want an appraisal. Many listees do free appraisals, others do it for a fee. Only a few buyers do not make offers or appraisals.

Don't ask for an offer, get it, and then sell your item locally or to a friend for the same amount. When you do that, it's a form of theft. You're taking someone's expertise that cost them thousands of hours and dollars to get, then depriving them of the opportunity to benefit from their work. That's dishonest.

These sentiments are often expressed by prominent dealers in expensive items. When knowledgeable and important people are forced to take this attitude to protect themselves from curiosity seekers, we all lose. These buyers are usually marked with NO OFFERS at the end of their entry.

I'll Buy That! gives you access to many of the most helpful, interesting, and knowledgeable people in the entire world of collectibles. Please don't abuse it.

There *are* dishonest dealers, referred to as "cheaters of old ladies," but none are knowingly included in this book. We want to provide people you can rely upon to treat you fairly. We urge you contact us if you ever have a problem with a listee.

Research about your object is always a good idea. It is essential when dealing with people who won't make offers.

> *INSIDE TIP: Dr. Hyman personally follows his own advice when selling and asks experts what he has, and whether they'd like to make an offer. During one month, he got (and accepted) offers from various buyers of $7, $65, $125, and $160 for items he purchased from antique dealers for $1, $2, $5, and $5. All four items went to collectors, who as a general rule, are in a position to pay more. He has sold to dealers on numerous occasions. On the whole, dealers are easier to sell to because they buy a wider range of items.*

STEP 5 GET $$$ IN THE MAIL

This is the best part of the transaction. If the funds involved are large, it's a good idea to wait for the check to clear before shipping. If you plan to do this, tell the buyer in advance. He/she may prefer to send you an immediately negotiable money order so you can send the item as soon as you receive payment.

STEP 6 PACK AND SHIP

The last step in most transactions is shipping the item you have sold. **What you ship belongs to you until the buyer agrees to accept it**. It if arrives broken, you've lost a sale and your item.

The buyer can often give you tips on packing. Chances are, many similar items have been shipped to him in the past. If your item is very heavy, bulky, or large, the buyer will often pick it up or make arrangements to have it professionally picked up and packed. This is usually true of items like jukeboxes, radios, television sets, slot machines, and the like. If your item proves to be worth thousands of dollars, the buyer may want to come and pick it up personally, unless it's small and easy to ship, like a watch.

Although we have confidence in our buyers, and know many of them personally, it is advisable to always be cautious about letting people you don't know into your home. This caution applies to salesmen, delivery men, and others as well.

Do not try to pack complicated and expensive items, such as lamps, yourself.

Many towns have franchised "packing stores" which can pack the more difficult items for you. They are convenient, but expensive. Since **the buyer normally pays for packing and shipping**, it is best to discuss this with the buyer before using professional services.

If you have a number of items, and will be packing more than one or two boxes, packing supplies, tape, boxes, styrofoam, and bubble wrap are all available from stores which sell these items to the commercial market. Depending upon the size of your town and its Yellow Pages, you find them listed under "Paper," "Packing Supplies," or "Boxes and Cartons." If it's hard for you to get around, you can often order these supplies with a credit card and they will ship them to you.

Guidelines for successful packing

When you pack, always use sturdy boxes. You can buy boxes at most post offices, stationery stores, and packing companies, but heavy duty boxes can often be obtained free from book stores. If an item is easily breakable, double boxing (one box inside another) is advised. Write your name and the addressee on the inside box as well. Don't ship anything, even shoes, in shoe boxes.

When packing breakables, never let two items touch. Wrap each breakable item separately, preferably in styrofoam sheeting or in bubble wrap. Don't leave lids on cookie jars, sugar bowls, and the like. They are very likely to chip if you do.

Never pack your item in direct contact with newsprint. Newsprint smears, and can damage clothing and ruin some other items like *Wedgwood* and other porous chinas. Wrap in tissue or plain paper, <u>then</u> use newspaper.

Flat items should be put between two sheets of cardboard approximately one inch bigger on all sides than what you're sending. Put the grain of the two pieces of cardboard at right angles. Your package will be less likely to bend.

Ship by First Class Mail or by private carrier. Do not use parcel post. The difference in price between parcel post and 1st class is so small, considering the extra risk and the handling delays, the few pennies you save aren't worth it. If your package weighs under two pounds, you can ship anywhere in the U.S. for less than $3.

Consider using Registered Mail. For between $5 and $10 in addition to postage your item receives special handling in transit, can be insured up to $25,000 and must be signed for by the addressee. All this for the one fee! Anything irreplaceable should be sent Registered Mail. There are some special rules for Registered Mail, however, so check with your Post Office, *before* you wrap. The most important differences are:

> You must use a clean box with no advertising printed on it. The box must show no signs of damage.
> The address and return address must be written directly on the box. you may not use labels.
> Each seam of the box (where it was assembled) must be covered with brown paper tape. Plastic tape, no matter how strong, is not OK.

Always insure what you mail. $500 worth of insurance on a 1st class package can be purchased for $5. The security on Registered Mail is so strict, the Post Office figures very little will get lost or damaged, so very expensive items can be insured very reasonably.

Care in packing can sometimes be the difference between a happy transaction and a disappointing one. Both you, the buyer, and history are better off for your care because your memento of the past is preserved for future generations to enjoy.

Table of Contents

Table of Contents

1
Big Things Around Home

Dr. Hyman's Prescription

Yes, you can sell furniture, lamps, rugs, and large heavy items through the mail. Top buyers are standing by ready to say "I'll Buy That!"

A photograph is essential. Furniture, lamps, rugs, and cast iron stoves, all exist in great variety. Each piece must be seen to be evaluated. Because these items can be worth hundreds, even thousands, or tens of thousands, of dollars, the fuss of taking a picture is usually justified.

Photos should be 35mm, either slides or prints. If you don't own a 35mm camera, ask a friend to take them for you. You want to send close ups of details, such as inlay and drawer pulls. If this is not possible, telephone the buyer and discuss your item over the phone. Be prepared to answer specific questions about colors, dimensions, type of wood, etc.

IMPORTANT: Make certain when selling large or heavy items that both you and the buyer agree on who has responsibility for shipping. This cost is normally born by the buyer.

If you are aged, or have trouble getting around, or live outside a big city, request the buyer agree to have large items picked up as part of the sale.

In many cities there are "packing stores" who can ship almost anything. Most packer/shippers will come pick up items for a fee. Look under "Packing Services" in the local Yellow Pages.

tony hyman

Furniture

◆ **Entire estates including furniture and accessories from the American colonial period**, art, or important collections of toys, dolls, guns, decoys, miniature lamps, or other specialties. Your estate or collection must have a value in excess of $50,000 to be handled by this important firm. No interest in minor collectibles, limited edition plates, or common items.
James D. Julia Auctioneers,
Rt. 201,
Fairfield, ME 04937
(207) 453-9725

◆ **Heavily carved or decorated American furniture made between 1820-80** including fancy Empire, Gothic revival, American Renaissance, rococo, etc., especially furniture made by Belter, Roux, or Meeks. Also **gas chandeliers and Argand Astral lamps.** This prestigious dealer does not make offers so research is in order since many of these pieces can be very valuable. Send her a photo of the furniture plus a copy of every label or maker's mark you can find. She will help an amateur seller if you're really *selling* and not fishing for free appraisals.
Joan Bogart,
Box 265,
Rockville Centre, NY 11571
(516) 764-0529

◆ **Mission oak or Arts & Crafts furniture** by Stickley, Limbert, Rohlfs, and Roycroft of any type or size from letter boxes to giant refectory tables. Especially hexagonal tables, folding screens, copper faced clocks, and bedroom furniture. All pieces considered including badly damaged, but prefers original finish furniture and unpolished metalwork. Inlaid pieces and those with small square spindles are best.
Harvey Kaplan,
40 First St.,
Troy, NY 12180
(518) 272-3456 eves

◆ **Prairie style furniture from the Midwest,** 1890-1920. Look for straight line design oak pieces with small straight applied moldings, seldom pegged, usually of a lighter construction than mission oak. These seldom signed pieces have finish ranging from very dark to fairly light. Also **mission oak furniture** made by Gustav Stickley, 1901-16. Look for plain oak pieces (never carved) with pegged or wedged construction at the joints. Often signed with a joiner's compass mark burned in or with a decal, but many fine pieces are unsigned. "I prefer pieces with original finish and original upholstery, if any, no matter how abused."
William Porter,
908 Pierce,
Birmingham, MI 48009
(313) 647-3876

◆ **Roycroft furniture and accessories** including lamps, wastebaskets, clocks, frames, art, pottery, china, glassware, and all books and paper ephemera associated with the Roycroft company or its founder, Elbert Hubbard. When you write, make certain to honestly state whether the item is for sale or whether you are seeking identification and appraisal. Please give the source of the item for sale and include any stories or history. The Knopkes publish *The Wee Willy Fra* newsletter and offer a primer on Hubbard for $1.
Tom Knopke, House of Roycroft,
1430 E. Brookdale Pl.,
Fullerton, CA 92631
(714) 526-1749

◆ **Furniture and accessories from the Mission or Arts & Crafts period.** Oak furniture, light fixtures, and metalwork by L& J.G. Stickley, Gustav Stickley, Roycroft, Limberts, Lifetime, Charles Stickley, Rohlfs, Stickley Brothers, and Dirk Van Erp, especially unusual pieces, custom made pieces, and items inlaid with silver pewter or copper. Also textiles, various publications and catalogs from these firms. "If you have any doubts, please call. I will be glad to help."
Robert Berman,
Le Poulaille,
5313 Baynton St.,
Philadelphia, PA 19144
(215) 843-1516

◆ **Small Victorian furniture** like music stands, dictionary stands, coal hods, pants presses, candlestands, sewing tables, small accessory furniture, especially a Victorian shaving stand with mirror and candleholder. Always want things for child's room (especially 1860-90) like small rocking chairs, sample stoves, and children's books. No dolls.
Ginger Carver Daily,
Box 33862,
San Antonio, TX 78265
(512) 657-3242

◆ **Twig furniture.** "I'm interested in any type of rustic or Adirondack furniture. This includes pieces by Old Hickory and Twig furniture. The wilder the style, the more I will want it. As always the better the condition, the more I will pay. If you have any doubts, call."
Robert Berman,
Le Poulaille,
5313 Baynton St.,
Philadelphia, PA 19144
(215) 843-1516

◆ **Wicker furniture and luggage.** Also buys **brass beds.**
Joan Brady,
834 Central Ave.,
Pawtucket, RI   02863
(401) 723-4693 or 725-5753

◆ **Folding chairs.** "I'm interested in everything dealing with folding chairs, including photographs of chairs, chairs in use in lodges, churches, picnics and other events. Interested in some chairs only to add to collection. Must have a photo or photocopy of offered photos, catalogs, or chairs. Particularly want folding chairs with advertising on the back.
Richard Bueschel,
414 N. Prospect Manor Ave.,
Mt. Prospect, IL 60056
(312) 253-0791

Rugs

◆ **Oriental, Indian, and South American rugs, tapestries, textiles.** Also all fine folk rugs from any culture worldwide. Want Coptic, Turkish, Greek, Persian, Russian, Balkan, and Egyptian rugs. Will also purchase some US and European art deco and art nouveau textiles and rugs. A good clear color photograph is important. Make certain to mention wear or stains. Does not want items made after 1900. Appraisals and/or offers are made *only* after actually seeing your rug.
Renate Halpern Galleries,
325 E. 79th Street,
New York, NY 10021
(212) 988-9316

◆ **Oriental rugs.** Claims "highest prices paid" for Oriental rugs of all types: Antique, used, old.
David Tiftickjian, Jr.,
260 Delaware Ave.,
Buffalo, NY 14202
(716) 852-0556

Lamps

◆ **Lamps and lamp parts of all types from all periods.** Buys a wide range of wall, floor, and table lamps from the Betty lamps of the 1700's right through to the 1950's. Will buy kerosene whale oil, electric, Aladdin, organ, marriage, student, desk, and other lamps. Also interested in *Tiffany* and other high quality leaded and painted lamps. This major Western dealer can be very helpful to amateurs with just about any type of lamp to sell. **Especially wants Aladdin lamps and parts** including galleries, chimney cleaners, bug screens, flame spreaders, wick cleaners, wick raisers, finials, and anything else made by *Aladdin*. Also buys parts from other lamp makers. If you have lamps or parts for sale, please note whether they are brass or nickel plated and give all numbers and wording. A photo is very helpful if asking for an offer.
    Richard Melcher,
    1206 Okanogan St.,
    Wenatchee, WA 98807
      (509) 662-0386

◆ **Light fixtures made of brass or cast iron-** between 1850-1915. They can be gas or electric or a combination of both and can be wall, floor, ceiling, or table style. Also glass shades for lighting fixtures. No oil or kerosene lamps. "I'll probably pay more than anyone for what I want."
    Mike Leonard, Antique Lighting,
    2215 Market St.,
    San Francisco, CA 94114
      (415) 863-9466

◆ **Lamps and light fixtures from the Mission or Arts & Crafts period.** Anything signed by L& J.G. Stickley, Gustav Stickley, Roycroft, Limberts, Lifetime, Charles Stickley, Rohlfs, Stickley Brothers, and Dirk Van Erp, especially unusual pieces, custom made pieces, and items inlaid with silver pewter or copper. Also catalogs from these firms. "If you have any doubts, please call. I will be glad to help."
    Robert Berman,
    Le Poulaille,
    5313 Baynton St.,
    Philadelphia, PA 19144
      (215) 843-1516

◆ **Tiffany and other quality antique lamps,** including
    (1) Signed Handel, Pairpoint, Duffner/ Kimberly, Moe Bridges, Steuben;
    (2) **Art glass lamps and shades;**
    (3) **Leaded table lamps** and domes;
    (4) **Lithopane shaded lamps;**
    (5) **Cranberry lamps;**
    (6) **Student lamps,** all types including table, hanging, wall, miniature and full size, single or double shade.
Also shades and parts for all good antique lamps. No new or reproduction items or parts. Dan and Dottie say *you* must price your lamp, so **research is essential before selling** since some of these lamps can be quite valuable.
    Dottie & Dan Besant,
    Besantiques,
    60 Meaford Rd.,
    Buffalo, NY 14215
      (716) 833-8138

EDITOR'S NOTE: Lamp collectors want to know if your lamp is original and complete. You should mention if it shows signs of repair or being a marriage of parts from different lamps.

Describe the quality of the finish on the base and whether the glass shows any cracks or chips. What's wrong with it?

A signature on the base or shade usually makes a lamp worth more. It can be very hard to find on some valuable lamps.

◆ **Reverse painted, leaded glass, or art glass lamps** including table lamps, boudoir lamps, and floor lamps. "I am interested in buying shades, bases or parts for lamps of these types. I have a special interest in Moe-Bridges, Classique Studios, or Phoenix Light Co. I am also interested in buying catalogs from lamp and lighting fixture manufacturers (not retailers) before 1935." Does **not want** oil lamps, hurricane lamps, Gone With the Wind lamps, etc. No lamps after 1920's. Give all names and numbers found anywhere on the lamp or shade, and all dimensions. This long time collector prefers you to set your own price, but will make offers.
  Merlin Merline,
  Box 16265,
  Milwaukee, WI 53216
    (414) 871-6261

◆ **Tiffany lamps and grapevine picture frames.** Frames are worth from $300 - $1,500 depending upon their size and condition. Lamps bring from $2,500 up. Dawson requests a complete description of condition and return privileges if judged not to be as described. He prefers you to set the price, but will help amateur sellers if their item is for sale. No appraisals.
  T.O. Dawson,
  2110 Noel Dr.,
  Champaign, IL 61821
    (217) 352-7373 eves

◆ **Emeralite and Bellova lamps, 1909-40s,** wall or desk models, either green-shaded, acid etched or reversed painting models. These can be found with brass and with metal bases. Prefers signed pieces. Unsigned pieces must be heavily decorated to be of interest. Photo essential.
  Bruce Bleier,
  73 Riverdale Rd.,
  Valley Stream, NY 11581
    (516) 791-4353

◆ **Oil lamps made in the shape of any figure,** especially those made of colored glass.
  Tom Burns,
  109 E. Steuben St.,
  Bath, NY 14810
    (607) 776-7942

◆ **Miniature oil lamps, fairy lamps, peg lamps, and Galle and Daum art glass lamps.** Claims she pays the highest prices around. Prefers you to price your lamps but amateurs who are serious about selling may request help in determining the value. Wants a photo of your lamp.
  Celeste Leone,
  Box 10819,
  Stamford, CT 06904
    (203) 323-7322

◆ **Lamp cord (electric wire).** "I'll buy 16 or 18 gauge, single strand or double braided, fabric covered electrical wire suitable for use in lamp restoration. How much can you supply?"
  X. Young,
  4200 Sunshine Rd.,
  Miami, FL 33133

◆ **Small bedroom lamps made of art glass.**
  Madeleine France,
  Antiques,
  Box 15555,
  Plantation, FL 33316

2
Little Things
Around Home

Dr. Hyman's Prescription

Read this chapter, and a few others, like a novel. Become familiar with the wide range of items that can have value.

Small household items are among the many items which can be purchased from yard sales and antique dealers and sold for profit. The key is learning what you're doing, and working closely with your buyer.

If you plan to "pick for profit" for various buyers, you should familiarize yourself with what the person wants and what he's willing to pay. Don't buy items for resale until you are certain you can turn a profit.

Inquire as to the availability of wants lists and the buyer's suggestions for books to read on the topic.

Pocket knives are one of the collectibles with great profit potential. One Southern disk jockey keeps five or six shiny new multi-blade pocket knives in his glove compartment. Whenever he stops at a gas station or other place where knives are used, he offers to trade new knives for old. He then resells the knives to collectors. He claims to make at least $500 a month. Pocket knives are surprisingly valuable, with many that look ordinary bringing $100 or more.

Fountain pens are another collectible often greatly undervalued by amateurs. There is great profit in buying them at 25¢ to a few dollars and reselling to expert buyers at five to ten times as much or more. Watch fobs, canes, Stanhopes, and matchsafes are also items to learn about if you plan to pick for profit.

tony hyman

Kitchen Tools

◆ **Iron, tin, or wooden tools used in food preparation or household cleaning.** This nationally known expert on kitchens of yesteryear wants *19th century* handmade tools, homemade modifications of factory tools, one-of-a-kind creations, odd and unusual kitchen devices, or folk carved and decorated kitchen items. "If you think it's too old or odd for anyone to want, you may have found just the person who's interested." No junk or 20th century tools.
> Linda Franklin,
> Box 383 Murray Hill Sta,
> New York, NY 10156
>> (804) 973-3238

◆ **Victorian gadgets and kitchen accessories** such as napkin rings, spice boxes and chests, spooners (other than glass), and anything else **that's small, useful, and Victorian** if it's made of wood or metal (cast iron to silver). Wants multi-drawer wooden spice cabinets that hung on a kitchen or store wall. "These are often erroniously called apothecary cabinets". Does not buy pottery, dishes, or glassware. A photocopy or photo is suggested.
> Ginger Carver Daily,
> Box 33862,
> San Antonio, TX 78265
>> (512) 657-3242

◆ **Cast iron muffin pans**, gem pans, popover pans, and maple sugar molds in unusual patterns and shapes. Also interested in old catalogs, etc., which list multi-sectioned baking or muffin pans. Will pay $200+ for Griswold #13, 50, and 2800 pans. If you're a dealer, send for his wants list.
> David Smith,
> Box B,
> Perrysburg, NY 14129
>> (716) 532-5154

◆ **Kitchen utensils and implements.**
> Vernon Ward,
> Rt. 2,
> Poultney, VT 05764

◆ **Early kitchen items made of cast iron** or which are folk carved or decorated.
> Louis Picek,
> Box 340,
> West Branch, IA 52358
>> (319) 643-2065

◆ **Iron pans and broilers in odd or decorative shapes,** including pans for muffins, popovers, rolls, and maple sugar molds. Roll pans shaped like hearts bring $50 and up, while those like fruits and vegetables are worth $150. Pans made by GF Filley start at $40. Cast iron broilers look like strange frying pans with grid work, slots, and holes. Not interested in reproductions (detectable by rough surface and grind marks) or in tin pans of any type. Trace or photocopy.
> David Smith,
> Box B,
> Perrysburg, NY 14129
>> (716) 532-5154

◆ **Fancy or unusual nutcrackers,** big or small, made of iron, brass, wood, or any other material. A sketch or photocopy is suggested. Include dimensions, colors, and all writing or marks.
> Hal Davis,
> 1815 West 18th Street,
> Santa Ana, CA 92706

◆ **Novelty figural salt and papper shakers related to water.** She'll buy fish, frogs, ducks, penguins, seals, umbrellas, bridges, mermaids, sailors, firemen, fishermen, pirates, boats, lighthouses, shells, lobsters, crabs, alligators, seagulls, pelicans, dinosaurs, watermelons, sea serpents, and more! Generally doesn't want sets with chips or repairs, unless they are very rare. "Pictures are the only way to describe things. I have several thousand sets and it's impossible to know whether I have it without seeing a picture." (Photocopies would probably be fine). Likes you to set the price, but will make offers. Editor of the quarterly news letter of the Novelty Salt &Pepper Shakers Club, she also issues catalogs of salt and peppers.
> Sylvia Tompkins,
> 25C Center Drive,
> Lancaster, PA 17601
>> (717) 569-9788

◆ **Russian samovars.** Please send picture with descriptive information and a statement of condition. He prefers that you price what you have. Also interested in any written material on samovars, especially catalogs.
Jerome Marks,
962 Sibley Tower Bldg.,
Rochester, NY 14604
(716) 546-2017

◆ **Salt and pepper shakers.** He'll buy salt and peppers that are marked as souvenirs, that feature Blacks/Negros, and those that are marked as from a World's Fair.
Larry Carey,
Box 2284,
Arlington, VA 22202

◆ **Unusual condiment sets.** These combination salt, pepper, and mustard sets are wanted if they are unusual and figural. Wants pieces without chips or repairs, but will consider them if the piece is extremely unusual. Especially likes German sets, and those related to water. A picture is important.
Sylvia Tompkins,
25C Center Drive,
Lancaster, PA 17601
(717) 569-9788

◆ **Toasters.** Old or unusual electric toasters are bought if in good condition.
Joe Lukach,
7111 Deframe Ct.,
Arvada, CO 80004

◆ **Ceramic or chalk figural string holders,** in wall or counter style. Wants figures of fruits or people (full figure or face) including Indians, Chinamen, Black mammys, Black men, animals, cows, dogs, cats, or birds. Does not want apples, pears, Dutch girls, or chefs.
Emmy Kretchek,
5726 Terrace Park Dr.,
Dayton, OH 45429
(513) 434-9126

◆ **Wall type stringholders** in either china or chalkware.
John Reece,
1426 Turnesa Dr.,
Titusville, FL 32780

◆ **Coffee grinders.** Both lap or wall models are wanted. Please send a photo or good sketch.
Coffee Grinder,
5753 Marlin Dr.,
Byron, CA 94514

◆ **Pie birds.** "I'll buy, sell, or trade pie birds."
Connie Soost,
1331 Weverton Rd.,
Knoxville, MO 21758
(301) 694-7325

◆ **Kitchens, restaurants, and food.** "I'll buy trade cards, quality postcards, and pre 1940's magazine ads that feature kitchens, restaurants, and food." No recipe booklets, please.
Kitchen Arts & Letters,
1435 Lexington Ave,
New York, NY 10128

◆ **Fruit and cake knives made of *colored* glass,** especially the Jackson Sanitary Knife (J.G.W.), Westmoreland Sanitary knife (ribbed handle), and an Imperial glass knife in Candlewick Design. He pays $20-$45 for knives.
Gary Crabtree,
Box 3843,
San Bernardino, CA 92413

◆ **Tunbridge ware** is attractive woodware with geometric or mosaic designs, or with embedded pictures created with cut woods of different colors. She buys boxes, candlestick holders, tea caddies, etc. made in Tunbridge. These pieces are rarely marked. If in doubt, send a good photo or a Xerox© copy of the patterned portion of the item.
Lucille Malitz,
Lucid Antiques,
Box KH,
Scarsdale, NY 10583
(914) 636-3367

Cookbooks

◆ **Cookbooks and related pamphlets** from before 1950. State condition and price or just ship for immediate offer.
Alan Levine,
Box 1577,
Bloomfield, NJ 07003

◆ **Cookbooks published as advertising** by various companies pre 1930, especially those from before 1900. Love to find pre 1920 *JELLO* cookbooks. Also **fund raising cookbooks** from before 1940. Also buys pre 1920 grocer's catalogs, pre 1920 cooking magazines, reference books and bibliog-raphies of cookbooks. Unusual cookbooks of any vintage including those assembled by movie stars, famous artists, etc., are also sought. Also wants historical information about commercial food companies.
Roberta Deal,
Box 17,
Mecklenburg, NY 14863

◆ **Handwritten cookbooks from 1920 or before.** They may be hard or soft cover, or one of the blank 19th century books designed for cooks to fill in their favorite recipes. Prefer those which are signed and dated between 1860-80, but buy older and newer. "Please send me a photocopy of a page or two and if I'm interested I'll ask you to send it to me for inspection. **No printed cookbooks!**
Ginger Carver Daily,
Box 33862,
San Antonio, TX 78265
(512) 657-3242

◆ **Cookbooks and commercial booklets in any language.** Especially wants early out-of-print items, including **hand written cookbooks**. Also wine, candy, chocolate, baking and specialty cooking books and booklets. Special interest in Yugoslavian cooking.
Kay Caughren,
284 Purdue Ave.,
Kensington, CA 94708
(415) 524-8859

Knives

◆ **Pocket, hunting, and military knives.** Brands to look for include: New York Knife, Canastota, Remington, Wabash, Winchester, Honk Falls, Napanoch, Schatt & Morgan, Schrade, Henry Sears, Shapleigh, Union Cut, Keen Kutter, Bingham, American Knife, Bridge, Capitol, Case, Cattaraugus, Phoenix, James Price, Platts, Press Button, India Steel Works, Wallkill, Walden, Van Camp, Union Razon, Standard, Zenith, Northfield, Crandall, and others. "This is only a small listing of the many good brands to be found. I love large bone handled US made knives." **Non collectible knives include** Ambassador, Atco, Camco, Colonial, Executive, Frontier, Hit, Ideal, Klien, Richards, U.S.A., Pakistan, and Sabre. It is best to photocopy any knives with the blade(s) open. Write down everything found on the blades and handles. Describe the handle material as best you can. Stapp is an advisor on knives for one of the popular price guides.
  Charles Stapp,
  Rt. 2, 10 Haynes Rd.,
  New Albany, IN 47150
  (812) 923-3483

◆ **Knives less than 1" long,** especially multi-bladed with pearl, sterling, stag, or horn handles. As much information as possible, including number of blades, maker, condition, etc.
  Jim Kegebein,
  Box 60669,
  Sunnyvale, CA 94088
  (408) 749-9175

◆ **Knives.** "I'll buy mint and near-mint old knives. Brands names are unimportant to me, but I pay more for better ones. Also want original **cutlery advertising** from boxes, to signs, to catalogs. Photocopies will save us both a lot of time." This co-author of 12 books on knives is willing to help beginning collectors and amateurs, but "I am not in the free appraisal business."
  Bruce Voyles,
  Box 22171,
  Chattanooga, TN 37421

◆ **Unusually shaped figural pocket knives** shaped like objects such as dogs, cats, hats, baseball bats, lady's legs, etc., from the late 1800's or early 1900's. Value depends upon the shape, condition and manufacturer. "Knives in unusual shapes made by Remington, Winchester, and Case may be worth several hundreds of dollars. I am also interested in any old advertising signs, pinbacks, postcards, etc., related to the cutlery industry. Please phone or write." When you do, give the shape, the name of the maker, number of blades, and material from which handles are made.
  John Baron,
  2928 Marshall Ave.,
  Cincinnati, OH 45220
  (513) 751-6631

Cast Iron

◆ **Cast iron doorstops and windmill weights.** No reproductions or modern pieces.
  Louis Picek,
  ain Street Antiques,
  Box 340,
  West Branch, IA 52358
  (319) 643-2065

◆ **Cast iron doorstops and other cast iron:** figural bottle openers, figural lawn sprinklers, figural paperweights, figural pencil holders, match holders, string holders, windmill weights, horse weights, shooting gallery targets, and firemarks. Include your phone number when you write.
  Craig Dinner,
  Box 45,
  Valley Stream, NY 11582
  (516) 825-0145

◆ **Pencil sharpeners, Xmas tree stands, and other useful household items made of cast iron.** Will consider anything except apple corers.
  George Walsh,
  RFD #2 Box 145,
  Epsom, NH 03234
  (603) 798-5200

◆ **Antique pressing irons of all kinds** including sad irons, polishing irons, hat irons, fluters, goffering irons, charcoal irons, alcohol irons, gasoline irons, boxed sets of irons, miniature and toy irons, and all iron related items such as postcards, trade cards, advertising giveaways by iron companies, and the like. Single items or entire collections wanted. "Condition is very important. I am not interested in broken irons, repaired irons, or irons with missing pieces. I do not want reproductions. A photo is a good idea. Trace your iron and give the height.
    Carol Walker, The Iron Lady,
    100 NE 5th St.,
    Waelder, TX 78959
        (512) 665-7166

◆ **Miniature sad (flat) irons.** Wants irons smaller than 4", nothing bigger. No electric iron, no matter how early.
    George Fougere,
    67 East St.,
    North Grafton, MA 01536
        (508) 839-2701

Accessories

◆ **Accessories from the Mission or Arts & Crafts period** including light fixtures or metalwork by L& J.G. Stickley, Gustav Stickley, Roycroft, Limberts, Lifetime, Charles Stickley, Rohlfs, Stickley Brothers, and Dirk Van Erp, especially unusual pieces, custom made pieces, and items inlaid with silver pewter or copper. Also catalogs from these firms. "If you have any doubts, please call. I will be glad to help."
    Robert Berman,
    Le Poulaille,
    5313 Baynton,
    Philadelphia, PA 19144
        (215) 843-1516

◆ **Hammered copper light fixtures and accessories** by Stickley, Limbert, Rohlfs, Dirk Van Erp, and other Arts and Crafts and Mission style manufacturers. Also wants catalogs and other paper ephemera from these makers and others working in this style.
    Harvy Kaplan,
    40 First St.,
    Troy, NY 12180
        (518) 272-3456 eves

◆ **Items of banded agate.** Will purchase pens, button hooks, snuff boxes, and small decorative items made entirely or mostly of banded agate. Give dimensions and condition.
    Stanley Block,
    Box 51,
    Trumbull, CT 06611
        (203) 261-3223

◆ **Art deco accessories** "that compliment my collection of radios." Ed is interested in a wide range of distinctive deco items, so give him a try for everything from ashtrys to lamps. If you are the original owner, he'd appreciate the item's history. He prefers you to set your price but will make offers *if* you intend to sell.
    Edward Sage,
    Box 1234,
    Benicia, CA 94510
        (707) 746-5659

◆ **Metal wall hangings** with color picture of lady or child with rolled corners. Also **sachet shakers** in the shape of a lady.
    Mike Newell,
    2113 Nottingham,
    Cape Girardeau, MO 63701
        (314) 334-5153

◆ **Small handpainted American boxes.**
    Louis Picek,
    Main Street Antiques,
    Box 340,
    West Branch, IA 52358
        (319) 643-2065

Pens & pencils

◆ **Unusual quality fountain pens,** pre 1940, by makers such as *Eversharp, Waterman, Swan, Dunn, MacKinnon, Laughlin, Shaeffer, Chilton, Wahl, Moore, Camel* and many others. Some of these can be worth several hundred dollars. She also buys old quill cutters, stylus pens, and glass pens. **Advertising related to pens** is also wanted, including signs, trade catalogs, repair manuals, and spare parts. Also wants packaged powdered ink. Give maker's name, model, color, and measurements of your pen. Describe the pen point and all decorations on the pen. Best to photocopy. Pens will have to be inspected before final price offered. No unbranded pens, *Wearever, Esterbrook,* ball points, or magazine ads. She will send you a guide to help you describe pens.
Mrs. Ky,
Box J,
Port Jefferson Station, NY 11776

◆ **Fountain pens.** "Quality old pens, not junk or common stuff," says this 22 year veteran.
C. Ray Erler,
Box 140, Miles Run Road,
Spring Creek, PA 16436
(814) 563-7287

◆ **Pencil sharpeners.** Wants small hand held figural pencil sharpeners made of metal, celluloid or bakelite in Germany or Japan during the 1930's and 40's. No sharpeners from Hong Kong; these are usually a bronze color metal depicting antiques. In describing your sharpener, give the shape, condition, country of origin, size, condition of the blade, and price.
Martha Crouse,
4516 Brandon Lane,
Beltsville, MD 20705

◆ **Inkwells,** either U.S. or foreign, figural or traveling, whether made of pottery, glass, or wood. Especially would like one made by *Tiffany.* No desk sets or fountain pens.
Eli Hecht,
19 Evelyn Lane,
Syosset, NY 11791

◆ **Pencils with advertising.** Prefers unusual and older unsharpened pencils. No pens.
Susan Cox,
800 Murray Dr.,
El Cajon, CA 92020
(619) 447-0800 days,   697-5922 eves

Pest traps

◆ **Mouse, rat, and fly traps** are bought, as are **tinder pistols** used to light fire places. Bob also buys pocket and desk style **pencil sharpeners** that are unusual, **traveling ink wells, gadget canes,** and **early lighting devices.** Bob prefers you to set the price, but makes some exceptions.
Robert Kwalwasser,
168 Camp Fatima Rd.,
Renfrew, PA 16053

◆ **Traps of all types and sizes from fly to grizzly bear.** Wants fly, mouse, rat, mole, gopher, glass minnow traps, and spring operated fish traps. Wants anything unusual in any material including plastic, wood, wire, cast iron, glass, cardboard, and tin. Is especially fond of old and unusual mouse traps. He also buys patent models, books, catalogs, and advertising (pre 1940) related to traps. Does not want rusty or broken traps unless odd 19th century items. Send a picture or drawing, a good description, and an SASE and he promises to answer your letter.
Boyd Nedry,
728 Buth Dr. NE,
Comstock Park, MI 49321
(616) 784-1513

◆ **Glass flytraps or flycatchers,** especially early or unusual ones. Will consider interesting traps in other materials. Also advertising and paper ephemera related to early flytraps.
Maris Zuika,
Box 175,
Kalamazoo, MI 49004
(616) 344-7473

Personal items

◆ **Canes and walking sticks** that are carved into figures, in either wood or ivory.
Bruce Thalberg,
23 Mountain View Dr.,
Weston, CT 06883
(203) 227-8175

◆ **Canes, canes, canes.** Especially likes dual purpose, container, weapon, gadget, and fancy carved canes made with ivory, gold, or silver. "Any cane or walking stick that does something, or has something enclosed or attached to the shaft for purposes other than support is of interest, as are well executed hand-carved canes." Describe the tip of the cane and indicate whether it gives any evidence of having been shortened. Is there a hole in the shaft? What materials?
Arnold Scher,
1637 Market St.,
San Francisco, CA 94103
(415) 863-4344

◆ **Strap type watch fobs picturing machinery or advertising products.** No lodge, American Legion, or VFW, and similar fobs. He'd like you to tell him how much wear it shows and the name of the stamper, usually found at the bottom. No fakes or modern fobs.
Albert Goetz,
1763 Poplar Ave.,
South Milwaukee, WI 53172
(414) 762-4111

◆ **Stanhope viewers** are small objects with a peep hole and tiny pictures inside. They come in a wide variety of shapes and materials including alabaster urns, crucifixes, pens, and letter openers and Don will consider all types. **Lithopanes** are figures and scenes viewed through transparent porcelain. They, too, are found in many objects. Don wants them all *except* steins or cups.
Donald Gorlick,
Box 24541,
Seattle, WA 98124
(206) 824-0508

◆ **Unusual Stanhopes**. Stanhopes are objects with tiny holes which show a picture when you look inside. Wants rings, sewing items, figurals, pipes, and naughty ones. Does not want Stanhopes in crucifixes, rosaries, or pens.
Lucille Malitz,
Lucid Antiques,
Box KH,
Scarsdale, NY 10583
(914) 636-3367

◆ **Matchsafes.** "I'll buy small pocket matchsafes, 1850-1920, in silver, brass, nickle plate, or other materials. Especially want interesting figurals or those advertising tobacco products or outlets. Make a photocopy of what you have. Price it, or I'll make an offer."
Tony Hyman,
Box 699,
Claremont, CA 91711

◆ **Eyeglasses, spectacles, and lorngnettes,** but only old, rare, and unusual. You'd be surprised how well a photocopy machine works on most glasses.
W.H. Marshall
727 SW 27th St.,
Gainesville, FL 32607
(904) 373-0556

Dr. Hyman's Prescription

When describing a camera, give the brand and model name, as well as any numbers which appear on the body of the camera.

Most camera buyers want information about the lens. Give the maker's name and all numbers and other information that is printed around the front circumference of the lens.

It is helpful to answer the following:

(1) Does the camera have a folding cloth or leather bellows? If so, what color is it?

(2) Is the case and camera covered with wood, metal, leather, or cloth? What condition is the covering?

(3) Does the camera work?

(4) Does it seem to be complete?

(5) What accessories come with the camera, such as lenses, instructions, boxes, etc.

Provide this information in your first letter.

Remember, that camera buyers generally want the odd and the unusual. Hidden ("detective") cameras were popular in the late 1800's and bring premium prices today, as do panorama cameras, multi lens cameras, and other early oddities. It is hard to recognize the earliest Daguerreotype cameras because they often do not have a lens. They can be quite valuable.

tony hyman

Cameras

◆ **Unusual and early cameras** including panorama cameras, wide angles, sub miniatures, hidden cameras, and oddly shaped or novelty cameras such as those shaped like cartoon or advertising characters. When writing, include all names and numbers found on the lens. If the camera is unusual, make certain to take a picture of it or make a good sketch. Jim is author of *Collectors Guide to Kodak Cameras* and *Price Guide to Antique and Classic Cameras*.
  Jim Mc Keown,
  Centennial Photo,
  PO Box 3605,
  Grantsburg, WI 54840
    (715) 689-2153

◆ **Pre 1948 cameras of brass, chrome, or wood** but anything interesting photographic, be it camera, book, or what have you, will be considered, including pre 1930 **photo magazines**, pre 1948 catalogs, and other ephemera. *No Polaroids.* Provide any numbers or names anywhere on the object. Describe condition of wood, leather, or metal. *Must* include SASE.
  Alan Voorhees, Cameras & Such,
  492 Breesport Rd.,
  Horseheads, NY 14845

◆ **Quality cameras such as Leitz, Zeiss, Nikon, and Canon.** Particularly interested in German cameras. Also buys old wooden cameras, tri-color cameras, and other older oddities.
  Harry Poster,
  Box 1883,
  South Hackensack, NJ 07606
    (201) 794-9606

◆ *Kodak* **cameras** including *Bantam Special, Super-620, Chevron,* colored cameras including those for Boy and Girl Scouts, vest pocket cameras, and petite cameras.
  Harry Poster,
  Box 1883,
  South Hackensack, NJ 07606
    (201) 794-9606

◆ *Kodak* **publications,** especially *Kodak* catalogues before 1950, *Kodak* advertisements in color prior to 1900, *Kodak Salesman* magazine, *Kodak* trade circulars, *Kodak* display counter cards, *Kodak* advertising novelties, and *Kodak* postcards. He does not want cameras or equipment.
  Wayne Ellis,
  754 Bob-Bea Lane,
  Harleysville, PA 19438
    (215) 256-6888

◆ *Kodak* **cameras, advertising, and memorabilia.** "I'll buy only pre 1930 cameras in near mint condition, especially those with original cardboard or wooden cartons. I'll also buy just the empty cartons!" Frank's list of cameras he seeks is too long to print here, but if you regularly deal in cameras or if you have an old *Kodak*, it might be worth picking up his wants list. He also wants a **Kodiopticon slide projector,** and cameras made by companies absorbed by Kodak including *Poco, Columbus, Ludigraph, Kameret* and **Rochester Optical's** *Empire State View* camera. *Kodak* newspaper and magazine advertising before 1930 may also find a buyer, as will countertop advertising, posters, signs, wooden framed pictures of people using *Kodaks,* and any of the the literally hundreds of items with the *Kodak* logo. "If it says '*Kodak*' on it, I want to know about it. That includes books which use *Kodak* as part of the title, advertising in foreign languages, instruction books, stock certificates from any camera company, *Kodak* annual reports, and anything else that is old and in fine condition."
  Frank Storey,
  8700 Calmont Ave., #29,
  Fort Worth, TX 76116
    (817) 560-1940 eves

◆ **Cameras, accessories, and photographic literature.** Wants early or unusual cameras and photo accessories, photography books, catalogs of photo equipment, advertising for cameras and film, and miscellaneous photographic ephemera such as lapel pins, buttons, and *Kodak* items.
  Nicholas Graver,
  276 Brooklawn Drive,
  Rochester, NY 14618
    (716) 244-4818

◆ **UNIVEX photo equipment.** Wants to buy photo equipment, advertising displays, binoculars, and literature from Universal Camera Corp.

Repinski,
N80 W13004 Fondulac #24,
Menomonee Falls, WI 53051
(414) 251-4253

◆ *View-Master* **reels and equipment** made by *Sawyers* or *GAF*, the companies that owned *View-Master* before 1980. Will buy single reels, 3-pack reels, cameras, Stereomatic 500 projectors, and the blue Model B viewer. Also buys some *Tru-Vue* and other 3-D items. Does not want any cartoon reels or any damaged, broken, or worn items. Give numbers and condition.

Walter Sigg,
Box 208,
Swartswood, NJ 07877
(201) 383-2437

◆ **3-D stereoscopic cameras and accessories** including viewers, projectors, manuals, books, by *Airequipt, Realist, Kodak, TDC, Wollensak, Busch, Radex, Brumbnerger,* and other makers. He also wants anglyph (red/blue) photographic items. Harry is one of the few buyers of *Polaroid* camers, but only wants models 180, 190, and 195.

Harry Poster,
Box 1883,
South Hackensack, NJ 07606

◆ *View Master* **cameras, reels, and dealer displays.** Wants military, advertising, and other less common reels, 3-Packs, film punches, close-up lenses, focusing viewers, and dealer displays. Also wants *Tru-Vue, Novelview,* and similar 3D items.

Harry Poster,
Box 1883,
South Hackensack, NJ 07606
(201) 794-9606

◆ **3-D cameras, reels, and other** *View-Master* **equipment,** including flash, close up lenses, cases, film cutters, 3-D projector, library boxes, adjustable viewer, and old order lists from *Sawyers* or *GAF*, the manufacturers of *View Master*. Want early views with blue backs, view reels that look like they're hand printed, Belgian made scenic views, pre 1970 US scenics of other continents. "I don't want children's cartoon reels made after 1950 or any scratched or damaged reels." The reel number and © date are more important information than the title.

Robert Gill,
3934 Fulton Ave.,
Seaford, NY 11783
(516) 781-8741

EDITOR'S NOTE: Most *Kodak* and *Polaroid* still cameras and 16mm home movie equipment has little if any value. Colored, commemorative, and very early *Kodak* cameras are worth inquiry.

Toilette

◆ **Perfume bottles with glass stoppers.** Wants art glass bottles, large department store display bottles, and samples. Give the brand of perfume and photocopy the bottle. No *Avon*.
   A.M. Chaussee,
   1530 Kenland Ct.,
   Colorado Springs, CO 80915
      (719) 597-4000

◆ **Chamber pots, slop jars, foot baths, and other 19th c. bathroom accessories** including covered toothbrush holders, and whatever else you might have made of porcelain from early baths. Examine the piece(s) carefully, and provide a statement of condition noting all chips, cracks, and crazing. If decorated, give all colors. Photos are very helpful. Price if you can.
   B. Bronzoulis,
   KouKla,
   1931 Laurel Hill,
   Kingwood, TX 77339

EDITOR'S NOTE: Many perfume bottles are worth over $100, so research is suggested before you price these.

◆ **Perfume bottles made of blown or cut art glass,** singles or matching sets. Wants fine beautiful bottles including those with atomizers. Some important makers include DeVilbiss, Daum Nancy, Galle, Baccarat, Webb, Moser, Czechoslovakian, Lalique, and Steuben. Also English scents, bottles with sterling overlay, and figurals. Also **Sterling silver dresser sets, hair brushes, mirrors and other boudoir items.** NO OFFERS. No *Avon*.
   Madeleine France,
   Past Pleasures for the 20th Century Woman,
   Box 15555,
   Plantation, FL 33316
      (305) 584-0009

◆ *Avon* **bottles** remain a popular collectible, but there are few people buying *Avons* except rarities through the mail. Western World Publishing offers six bi-monthly issues of *Avon Collectors Newsletter*, 20 pages of articles and "For Sale" ads for $13.50. Your subscription includes club membership and free classified advertising for a year. They also publish *Avon 8,* the lavishly illustrated basic price guide to *Avon* collectibles for $17.95.
   Western World Publishing,
   Box 23785,
   Pleasant Hill, CA 94523

◆ **California Perfume Company (CPC) products made between 1886 and 1929,** especially *Natoma Rose* fragrances. He also wants CPC products marketed as *Goetting and Company, Savoi Et Cie, Gertrude Recordon, Marvel Electric Silver Cleaner,* and the *Easy Day Automatic Clothes Washer.* Dick **does not want anything with** *Avon* **on the label,** although he will answer specific questions about *Avon* if you include a Self Addressed Stamped Envelope. Please give a complete description of the item you have for sale, including its condition and whether or not it has its original box. Is there a label and/or a neck band? Are there cracks or chips? Photocopy is helpful. Dick's collection is open to the public by arrangement.
   Dick Pardini,
   3107 N. El Dorado St.,
   Stockton, CA 95204
      (209) 466-5550 7am to 11pm

◆ **Unusual eye cups.**
   W.T. Atkinson,
   Route #1, Box 71,
   Wilmington, NC 28405

◆ **Powder compacts,** especially precious metals, unusual, art deco, etc. Wants *you* to price.
   June,
   270 No. Canon Dr.,
   Beverly Hills, CA 90212

Shaving

◆ **Straight razors with fancy handles** made of gold or sterling silver. Also razors with figural handles, multiple blades, fancy etching on the blade, or with fraternal emblems or advertising on the handle. Handles may be made of horn, mother of pearl, or multi-colored celluloid. Rare razors will be considered even if damaged. Also razor and cutlery advertising and memorabilia, catalogs, trade cards, etc., including oversize displays.
  William Campesi,
  Box 140,
  Merrick, NY 11566
    (516) 546-9630

◆ **Straight razors with handles of sterling, rough bone, mother of pearl, or aluminum.** Celluloid or pressed horn razors with several characters are also wanted. Good razors generally bring from $50-75, with some higher, some less. Please provide all information found on the blade or handle. He does not want plain handled razors from Solingen, Germany. Make photo-copies with the blade(s) open. Indicate the material from which the handle is made.
  Charles Stapp, Rt. 2,
  10 Haynes Rd.,
  New Albany, IN 47150
    (812) 923-3483

◆ **Safety razors and accessories.** This 20 year veteran collector wants to buy odd safety razors and advertising for razors including posters, magazine ads, and signs. He'd love to find more oversize store display razors. He's not interested in shaving mugs or brushes if they're normal size, but would like oversize display ones. Give all colors and metals and note "all writing on the items. A good clear photo is best," he says, but photocopies will suffice.
  Cary Basse,
  6927 Forbes Ave.,
  Van Nuys, CA 91406
    (818) 781-4856

◆ *Ever-Ready* **shaving memorabilia.**
  Michael Blankenship,
  5320 Spencer Drive SW,
  Roanoke, VA 24018
    (703) 989-0402 eves

◆ **Razor blades and blade sharpeners.** "I'll buy U.S. or foreign blades, in singles, packages, or on cards as well as interesting advertising signs, posters, and displays related to razor blades." Describe your sharpener carefully, noting all damage, and any words or numbers on it.
  Cary Basse,
  6927 Forbes Ave.,
  Van Nuys, CA 91406
    (818) 781-4856

◆ **Razor blade banks** are small figural depositories for double edge razor blades, popular from 1925-60. They can be made of ceramic, tin, metal, paper, wood, glass or plastic. Herb would like to make an offer for yours. Herb especially seeks a ceramic bank shaped like a barber chair.
  Herb Shearer,
  904 La Puente Dr.,
  Bakersfield, CA 93309
    (805) 831-1778

Useful Miscellany

◆ **Thermometers and thermostats**, pre 1940, especially ornate Victorian desk or mantle types. "I buy just about every *non advertising* one I can locate," but railroad and European models are particularly prized, and can bring more than $100 each. "I have the largest antique poultry thermometer collection in the world but am always looking for more." Thermometer ephemera and catalogs are also sought. No commercial, industrial, clinical, advertising, or "cutsey" thermometers are wanted. Give the maker, condition and whether it has mercury or red liquid in the bulb.
  Warren Harris,
  4555 Auburn Blvd. #11,
  Sacramento, CA 95841
    (916) 487-6964

◆ **Flashlights.** Antique flashlights, advertising, and catalogs are wanted, especially anything early marked *Eveready*.
  Bill Utley,
  7616 Brookmill,
  Downey, CA 90241
    (213) 861-6247

◆ **Alligator suitcases.** Also doctor's bags and overnight cases made of alligator. Must be in fine condition for resale. Please describe giving condition of the interior and exterior. Please price.
  Newman's,
  149 Arkansas St.,
  San Francisco, CA 94107

◆ **Antique and unusual padlocks.** "We'll buy padlocks of all kinds and types, odd shaped, cast iron, brass, figural, Wells Fargo, Winchester, railroad, miniature, and many others." Photocopy will be helpful. Indicate whether it has a key.
  Joe and Pam Tanner,
  Tanner Escapes,
  Box 349,
  Great Falls, MT 59403
    (406) 453-4961

◆ **Human hair wreaths.** Serious collector wants to buy wreaths made of human hair, either framed or unframed. Send photograph and / or description with your asking price.
  Savannah's,
  4758 Cedar Pass #B,
  Corpus Christi, TX 78413
    (512) 850-9040

◆ **Vacuum cleaners** that are hand powered. "I pay well for information leading to the location of unusual and scarce items, and am prepared to travel anywhere. I pay in cash immediately without fuss or bother for the right items. I am happy to buy single items or entire collections."
  Peter Frei,
  Box 500,
  Brimfield, MA 01010
    (800) 942-8968   (413) 245-4660 in MA

◆ **Glass fire grenade bottles** in any color if embossed with a brand name and "fire grenade." He is particularly interested in finding those with the name of a railroad. He does not want glass bulb grenades from the 1940's filled with carbon tet. List the color, size, and all defects.
  Larry Meyer,
  4001 Elmwood,
  Stickney, IL 60402
    (312) 749-1564

◆ *Weller* **flower frogs.** "I buy *Weller* frogs. How do you tell a *Weller* frog? Pottery flower frogs with bees, butterflies, frogs, fish, women, lily pads, etc. sitting on top a base are probably *Weller* if they are colored with greens, beiges, white, and muted orange, basic *Weller* colors."
  Susan Cox,
  800 Murray Dr.,
  El Cajon, CA 92020
    (619) 697-5922 eves

◆ *Cowan* **ceramic flower frogs** in art deco style, featuring dancing ladies. Values range from $100-$500 depending on the figure, colors, condition. Note the manufacturer is you can.
  William Sommer,
  9 West Tenth St.,
  New York, NY 10011
    (212) 260-0999

Quilts

◆ **Graphically artistic pre 1940 quilts** especially those pre 1900. Cotton, wool, and silk quilts all have value if made well. Solid color materials and small calico patterns are the most desirable. Large patterns cut into small pieces usually make the quilt of no interest. Most desirable colors are blue/white, red/white, red/white/blue, red/green, and pre 1900 earth tones. Yellow, orange, hot pink, and purple usually make a quilt less desirable. Children's size quilts are best if they do not have children's subject matter. All quilts should be in mint condition, with at least six stitches per inch, preferably more. No holes, tears, stains, thin spots when held to light, fading, soft from too much washing, and no patched repairs. A photo is very desirable. Herb says he will pay $5,000 for an 1840-60 album quilt, $15,000 for an 1840-60 Baltimore album quilt, and $600 up for navy blue and white quilts in excellent condition. **Herb does not make offers.**
   Herbert Wallerstein Jr.,
   Calico Antiques,
   2163 San Ysidro Dr.,
   Beverly Hills, CA 90210
        (213) 273-4194   FAX: (213) 273-1921

◆ **Quilting and patchwork patterns, books, and tools** from before 1950. Also vintage fabric, cloth scraps, patterned feed sacks, and **material useful for old style quilting.**
   Judy Speezak,
   Box 2528, Rockefeller Center Sta.,
   New York, NY 10185

◆ **Quilts** from before 1940. "I'll buy graphically interesting patchwork and applique quilts in excellent condition only, preferably that have never been used of have had minimal use. I prefer quilts that are made with solid color fabrics or old calico. I'm particularly interested in schoolhouse quilts ($400+), Amish quilts from Pennsylvania or Ohio ($300+), floral appliques ($300+) and quilts that are signed and dated. Photograph please.   No inferior, dull, or damaged quilts.
   Bob Carr,
   7325 Cornell Ave.,
   St. Louis, MO 63130
        (314) 721-8232 eves

◆ **Patchwork quilts made by African-Americans,** especially unusual or improvisational quilts. Provide a full photo of the quilt, a statement of condition, and all the details you can provide about its history. It is probably a good idea to discuss the value of the item with Eli before setting a price. "I'll also buy **fabric sample books,** especially of printed cottons.
   Eli Leon,
   5663 Dover St.,
   Oakland, CA 94609

EDITOR'S NOTE: Use caution when pricing quilts, especially those made before 1900. Prices over $50,000 have been paid. Although most quilts sell for under $500, a little research could be worth a great deal.

Clothing & Accessories

◆ **Women's vintage clothing, accessories, and jewelry** pre 1950. Wants hats, belts, purses, and other, but in excellent reusable condition only. Nothing stained or soiled.
Clark St. Waltz,
2360 N. Lincoln Ave.,
Chicago, IL 60614
(312) 472-5559

◆ **Vintage Hawaiian shirts, 1930-1955.** The label, size, coloration, and pattern are important, as is the material, so include all that when you write. Shirts can be made of cotton, rayon, or silk. A silk shirt with a fish pattern (his personal favorite) could bring as high as $100. Most are considerably less, but well worth your time. "I'm willing to answer questions and provide information to people who are not sure if their shirts are old enough." A photo or photocopy is helpful.
Evan Olins,
Flamingo's,
75-5744 Alii Drive,
Kailau-Kona, HI 96740
(808) 329-4122

◆ **Panties and bloomers.** A lingerie collector is willing to buy pretty ladies' silk or rayon panties and bloomers from the 1930's and 40's.
Lingerie,
Box 91272,
Atlanta, GA 30364

◆ **Vintage clothes made before 1950** such as beaded sweaters, evening gowns, prom dresses, men's tuxedos and hats, etc. Does not want damaged or stained items. Purchased for resale.
Bird In the Cage,
201 King St.,
Alexandria, VA 22314
(703) 549-5114

◆ **Men's and ladies suits from the 1940's.** Want men's double breasted wool or gabardine suits in fine condition. Also ladies' fitted gabardine (Joan Crawford style) suits. Must be in fine condition, priced to resell. Also **wide and wild jacquard print neckties.**
Retro Image Co.,
13908 Michigan Ave.,
Dearborn, MI 48126
(313) 582-3074

◆ **Handmade lace from 1500-1900.** Does not want Batterberg, lace known to be machine made, ordinary crochet and tatting. Unless you are a lace scholar or have access to important reference books on lace, the best thing is to Xerox© as much of the piece as possible. From that I can often tell whether a full appraisal is warranted or if it is a piece I might like to buy. She prefers sellers to set the price, but will assist genuine amateurs to identify what they have if it's for sale.
Elizabeth Kurella,
Lace Merchant,
Box 222,
Plainwell, MI 49080
(616) 685-9792

◆ **Linens from grandma's attic** including:
(1) **Table linens** especially with large napkins, lace, or handwork;
(2) **Lace hankies;**
(3) **Embroidered pictures, samplers,** etc.;
(4) **Lace curtains** or panels, of fine quality;
(5) **Lace collars and lace yardage** from before 1940;
(6) **Pillow cases or sheets** with hand embellishment or lace before 1925;
(7) **American arts & crafts** embroideries or printed fabrics
(8) **Anything unusual** from before 1930 in weaving, embroidery, or lace.
No hand towels, plain linen or Damask, damaged goods, or items made after 1960. If interested in buying your items, he will request you ship on approval. Photos or photocopies useful.
Paul Freeman,
Box 2251,
13 Circular Ave.,
Pittsfield, MA 01201
(413) 442-1854

◆ **Clothing worn by famous people, US Presidents, first ladies, and entertainers.**
Paul Hartunian,
Autographs,
127B East Bradford Ave.,
Cedar Grove, NJ 07009
(201) 857-7275

◆ **High quality hand woven textiles and tapestries** from anywhere in the world.
Renate Halpern Galleries,
325 E. 79th Street,
New York, NY 10021
(212) 988-9316

◆ **Antique fancy buttons.** Please price your buttons for resale. Photocopy is helpful.
B. Bronzoulis,
KouKla,
1931 Laurel Hill,
Kingwood, TX 77339

◆ **Lucite or plastic purses from the 1950's.**
Kevin Prediger,
120 Pierce St. #5,
San Francisco, CA 94117
(415) 863-7284

Sewing & Textiles

◆ **American sewing machines from before 1875,** especially rare early treadle machines with low serial numbers for which he will pay from $1,000-$10,000. Small hand operated machines in the shape of animals are of particular interest. Also photographs of sewing machines, in use, before 1890. Tell him the maker and the serial number as well as the condition. If there is no name, send a photograph. No *Wheeler & Wilson, Willcox & Gibbs*, or machines which you recognize. No oak-cased treadle machines. No machines with chrome or nickle plated fly wheels or high serial numbers.
Carter Bays,
135 Springlake Rd.,
Columbia, SC 29206
(800) 332-2297

◆ **Sewing related collectibles,** ordinary to obscure, one item or a whole collection. "I'll consider anything, including toy and mini-sewing machines. Price what you offer."
Joann,
15934 Wyandotte St.,
Van Nuys, CA 91406

◆ **Fabrics from the 1940's and 1950's.** If you have at least three yards of any floral or tropical patterned fabric, and it's in perfect condition, it could find a buyer here.
Swan & Unicorn,
515 Flemming St.,
Key West, FL 33040

EDITOR'S NOTE: Clothing is bought for resale. Stained or torn clothes are <u>not</u> wanted. Describe the style, color, material, size, and label. Photocopy lace and unusual patterns. Designer labeled clothes are particularly desirable.

3
China &
Breakables

Dr. Hyman's Prescription

When selling china, the first step is to ask yourself, "Would I want to buy this china and use it?" No one wants chipped, stained, or damaged items.

Our buyers are pattern matching services who buy for resale. From their point of view, the best china was bought by your great grandmother, packed away, and never used. That's what brings the most money when they sell it...and when you sell it to them.

When offering china for sale, you must make an inventory of how many pieces you have. List how many of each type item (plates, cups, saucers, etc.) you have.

Unless your china dates before 1860, do not list any pieces that have cracks or chips. You should note all crazing, knife scratches and pattern wear on listed pieces.

Some pieces are harder to find and as a result worth more. Serving pieces always bring more than ordinary table settings, especially pieces with lids.

If you don't know the pattern name, send a photocopy of the front and back of a small plate and indicate the color of the maker's marks. Most photocopy machines will take excellent pictures of china. Photocopies are better than photographs for describing what you have unless you can send close-up slides.

Do not overlook the colored glassware of 1920-1940. A few pieces have substantial value. Covered butter dishes in most depression glass patterns, for example, are worth $75 to $200 each. Carnival glass will shock you with its value. A carnival punch bowl and cup set can go to $10,000.

tony hyman

China

◆ *Wedgwood, Royal Doulton, Lenox* china. Also wants *Castleton, Coalport, Franciscan, Spode, Gorham, Minton, Pickard, Royal Worcester*, and *Flintridge* china. No giftware. Ives offers a free pamphlet *On Caring for your China* if you send her a business size SASE.
  Jacquelynn Ives, China Match,
  219 N. Milwaukee St.,
  Milwaukee, WI 53202
    (414) 272-8880

◆ Discontinued patterns of English and American china in perfect condition, produced by *Castleton, Franciscan, French Haviland, Lenox, Spode, Minton, Pickard, Royal Doulton, Royal Worcester, Syracuse, Wedgwoo*, etc.
  "We buy sets or incomplete sets consisting of ten pieces or more. For patterns in demand we buy outright; others are listed in our computer system and customers notified as to availability and prices. They do not want to buy Asian (Japanese) china or *anything* that is imperfect. Roundhill personally collects 100+ year old museum quality *Worcester* products. He prefers you to set the selling price, but will make offers.
  J.Warren Roundhill,
  Patterns Unlimited WTS,
  Box 15238,
  Seattle, WA 98115

◆ *Royal Doulton* "logo china" from hotels, restaurants, ships, railroads, airlines, and private companies of all types.
  Diane Alexamder,
  1700 1/2 Jefferson Ave.,
  Miami Beach, FL 33139
    (305) 673-8280

◆ *Royal Doulton, Royal Worcester, Minton* and other fine china and stoneware. This 12 year veteran matching service also buys most fine crystal in popular patterns.
  Freda Bell, China Match,
  9 Elmford Rd.,
  Rochester, NY 14606
    (716) 426-2783

◆ Haviland china for resale. Buys sets or single unusual pieces, especially wants jardiniers, claret jugs, unusual tea or toast sets, free form salads, syrup jugs, spoon trays, tea caddys, lemonade sets, and other unusual pieces. She does not want Limoge china that is not marked *Haviland* nor does she want individual saucers. Pieces must be in mint condition with no worn or scratched china. Give the pattern name in backstamp, a Xerox© copy, and note the colors. Eleanor has 22,000 pieces in stock and has a computerized search service to help customers find others.
  Eleanor Thomas, Auld Lang Syne,
  7600 Hwy 120,
  Jamestown, CA 95327
    (209) 984-DISH

EDITOR'S NOTE: Learn how to date your *Haviland* china.
See page 223.

Information courtesy of Eleanor Thomas and a good example
of the helpful material some buyers include when you send an SASE.

◆ *Noritake* china in *Azalea* pattern. Also *Noritake* scenic *Tree in the Meadow* and all raised gold patterns by *Noritake*. No chips, cracks, or worn gold or paint. Provide all info on back of pieces.
> Ken Kipp,
> Box 116,
> Allenwood, PA 17810
> (717) 538-1440

◆ **Haviland china in Butterfly pattern**, especially unusual pieces for a personal collection. Must have fluted edge. Also, all types of **oyster plates**. Nothing damaged, please.
> Sheldon Katz,
> 211 Roanoke Ave.,
> Riverhead, NY 11901
> (516) 369-1100

◆ **Wedgwood china in discontinued patterns**. Buys sets or individual pieces, but only in mint condition. "I don't give appraisals on other people's china, so please set the price you want." Include a photocopy if you don't know the name of your pattern.
> Rosemary Evans, Vintage Patterns,
> 9303 Mc Kinney Rd.,
> Loveland, OH 45140
> (513) 489-6247

◆ **Sets or pieces of French, American, or English china and stemware** especially pieces by Haviland, Castleton, Franciscan, Oxford, Royal Doulton, Lenox, Spode, Syracuse, and Wedgwood. Wants **stemware** by Cambridge, Duncan, Fostoria, Heisey, Imperial, Lenox, Gorham, Rock Sharp, and Tiffin. She does not buy German or Japanese china. Medley has been a dealer for 18 years.
> Laura Medley, China & Crystal,
> 2625 W. Britton Rd.,
> Okla. City, OK 73120
> (405) 755-0582

◆ **Pottery by the Buffalo Pottery Company.** Also Company ephemera.
> Thomas Knopke,
> 1430 E. Brookdale Pl.,
> Fullerton, CA 92631
> (714) 526-1749

◆ **Obsolete sets and pieces of fine English dinner china** including *Aynsley, Coalport, Lenox, Minton, Oxford, Paragon, Rosenthal, Spode, Royal Albert, Royal Crown Derby, Royal Doulton, Royal Worcester, Shelley, Wedgwood,* and some patterns in *Elite* and *Haviland*. **Also buys and sells other popular patterns made by American, French, and German makers.** Margaret does business worldwide and will make offers for items she can use. Items *must* be in excellent condition. If you wish things appraised, their appraisal fee is refundable if they buy your dishes.
> Margaret Roe,
> Old China Patterns Unlimited
> 1560 Brimley Rd.,
> Scarborough, Ontario M1P 3G9, CANADA
> (416) 299-8880

◆ **Buffalo Pottery or Buffalo china.** "I'll buy almost any marked piece."
> Seymour Altman,
> 8970 Main St.,
> Clarence, NY 14031
> (716) 634-4488

◆ *Warwick* **china, especially portrait items.** Include a photo with your complete description, and he'll return it. Promises to answer every letter regarding the work of this fine American china maker. Prefers you to set the price wanted, but amateurs should still write.
> Jeff Mauck,
> 142 N. 19th St.,
> Wheeling WV 26003
> (304) 277-2356

◆ **Shawnee Pottery Co.** wanted, but only their gold trimmed cooking jars, creamers, pitchers, and teapots. This small popular company operated between 1937 and 1961.
> Van Stueart,
> Rt. 3 Box 272,
> Nashville, AR 71852
> (501) 845-4864

◆ **Eggcups.** If you have a fine eggcup to sell, the *Eggcup Collectors Corner* may be your best source of information. Sample copies cost only $3 and will give you insights into cups and their prices, a bibliography, and twenty or more classified ads of people looking for egg cups. When you order your sample, tell Joan why you want one and she'll pick an appropriate issue.
Joan George, Pastimes,
67 Stevens Ave.,
Old Bridge, NJ 08857

◆ **Goss china** especially pictorials, cottages, busts, animals, military commemoratives and foreign crests.
Jeanne Goss Spaulding,
1325 West Avel,
Hilton, NY 14468

◆ **Any piece marked** *Clarus Ware* . "We also buy old pieces of **Pope Gosser China Ware.**"
C.W. & Hilda Roderick,
27858 TR 31,
Warsaw, OH 43844
(614) 824-3083

◆ **White House china** and other items from the White House, including Presidential Christmas cards and gifts given as souvenirs of a White House visit.
H. Joseph Levine,
6550-I Little River Turnpike,
Alexandria, VA 22312
(703) 354-5454

◆ **Official china from the White House.**
Raleigh DeGeer Amyx,
Box 465,
Vienna, VA 22183
(703) 938-1956

◆ **China from bus lines, fast food chains, diners,** restaurants, and lunch counters, as long as it is in fine condition and "top marked" with the name of the place that used it.
Dale Falk,
5622 Evars Rd. #1792,
San Antonio, TX 78238

◆ **Westmoreland milk glass** in grape pattern.
Jay Ketelle,
3721 Farwell,
Amarillo, TX 79109
(806) 355-3456

◆ **Pictorial Souvenir china** with views of various towns, streets, and places of interest. Especially interested in pictorial china with New England views, but all are considered. Indicate what the scene is, where the item was made, and whether there are any cracks or chips. Gary publishes *Antique Souvenir Collectots News,* the marketplace for antique souvenirs.
Gary Leveille,
Box 562,
Great Barrington, MA 01230
(413) 528-5490

◆ **Souvenir china** plates, cups, and saucers picturing local pictures and inscriptions.
David Sloane,
4 Edgehill Terrace,
Hamden, CT 06517
(203) 624-4206

◆ **G.A.R. china, mugs, and spoons.** Any pieces marked G.A.R. (Grand Army of the Republic).
Don McMahon,
385 Thorpe Ave.,
Meriden, CT 06450

◆ **Miniature teapots or cups and saucers** marked with the name of any state or tourist attraction.
T.M. Carter,
882 So. Mollison,
El Cajon, CA 92020
(619) 440-5043

◆ **Wheelock souvenir china.** Bill buys this German-made blue and green scenic souvenir china.
Bill Copeland,
2 Clifton Park Court,
Melrose, MA 02176

Silverware

◆ **Silverplated dinnerware, serving pieces, and carving sets.** "I will also buy worn items and hollow knives with bad blades. I will pay return postage if items are sent in for offer, and offer is not accepted." Write before shipping anything. Photocopies are helpful.
  Grace Friar,
  The Silver Chest,
  415 Tangerine Dr.,
  Olsmar, FL 34677
      (813) 855-0132

◆ **Sterling and silver plated flatware,** especially made by 1847 Rogers, Community, and Holmes & Edwards. Also all old "grape" patterns. Send a photocopy, the information on the back of your silver, and a photocopy if you don't know the name of the pattern. An SASE will get you a pattern guide. Particularly interested in more unusual pieces such as pie forks, punch ladles, ice tongs, sardine forks, etc. "We do not want monogrammed, damaged, or worn silver except large serving pieces or very rare patterns." A 30 year veteran of buying through the mail.
  L.C. Fisher,
  Silver Exchange,
  Box 680042,
  Houston, TX 77268
      (713) 353-4167

◆ **Sterling and silver plated flatware** in active, inactive, and obsolete patterns, especially ornate and "grape" patterns. "I maintain over 900 patterns in stock." No silver with monograms or with worn heels or tines. Must look almost like new. Include the company and pattern name, number of pieces, and condition if you wish to sell. Photocopies helpful.
  Carol Bennett's Antiques,
  825 Texas St.,
  Fairfield, CA 94533
      (707) 426-4815

◆ **Napkin rings,** new, used, or antique. Send description, photos, and price, please.
  S. Andrusier,
  3550 Lake Shore Drive,
  Rochester, NY 14625

◆ **Sterling silver flatware, holloware, and silver table service.**
  Helen Cox,
  As You Like It,
  3025 Magazine St.,
  New Orleans, LA 70115
      (504) 897-6915

◆ **Silver spoons with advertising** on them. Either sterling or plate.
  W.T. Atkinson,
  Route #1 Box 71,
  Wilmington, NC 28405

◆ **Souvenir spoons** from before 1930, especially those with hand engraving.
  T.K. Treadwell,
  Tower House Antiques,
  4201 Nagle Rd.,
  Bryan, TX 77801
      (409) 846-0209

◆ **Sterling silver souvenir spoons of Cuba or Puerto Rico,** especially with enameled bowls. "Will pay well" for a spoon from Tampa with cigar shaped handle. Please photocopy. NO OFFERS.
  Frank Garcia,
  8963 SW 34th Street,
  Miami, FL 33165

```
                                    ▓
   Your Name
   Your Address

```

Don't forget an SASE

Glass

◆ **Many kinds of glassware and china** are sought by Tom, a veteran collector and one of the country's largest auction firms specializing in post-Victorian glass. He buys outright or accepts on consignment for auction:

(1) **Carnival glass** especially pitcher sets, tumblers, whimsies, opalescent pieces, and common items in rare patterns and colors. He encourages you to contact him with one item or a giant collection since there are many valuable pieces that only an expert will recognize;

(2) **Victorian pattern glass** in a variety of pieces, colors, and patterns;

(3) **Cameo glass vases,** plates, urns, other items made by *Phoenix Glass Co.*;

(4) **RS Prussia china** decorated with scenes, portraits, or pearlized florals;

(5) **Noritake china** with geometric designs;

(6) **Nippon china humidors** and large high relief "blown out" vases depicting birds, animals, or figures;

(7) **Mandarin red glassware** by *Fenton Glass Company.*

Include your phone number if the piece is for sale. Tom has a reputation for being a bit slow to respond, but *very* helpful with amateur sellers nationwide.
Tom Burns Auction Service,
109 E. Steuben St.,
Bath, NY 14810
(607) 776-7942

◆ **Glass toothpick holders** in mint conditions. There are numerous patterns she is still seeking, so make a photocopy of your holder if you don't know the pattern name. Describe the color as best you can. There are lots of reproduction holders, so he'll have to examine it. Judy is founder of the Nation Toothpick Holder Collectors Society and publisher of their newsletter for 17 years.
Judy Knauer,
1224 Spring Valley Lane,
West Chester, PA 19380
(215) 431-3477

◆ **Antique glass items** including paperweights, art glass, glass pens, canes, and whimsies.
Stanley Block,
Box 51,
Trumbull, CT 06611
(203) 261-3223

◆ **American and European open salt dishes** if rare and unusual. No common or repro salts are wanted. Johnson is author of *5000 Open Salts*, available for $40 with price guide.
Patricia Johnson,
Box 1221,
Torrance, CA 90505

◆ *Willow Oak* **pattern glass** in amber, blue, or Vaseline colors.
Audrey Buffington,
2 Old Farm Rd.,
Wayland, MA 01778
(508) 358-2644

◆ **Dorflinger Glass.** Wants Kalahua pattern glass and glass items signed "Honesdale," particularly cameo cuts with gold decoration intact. Give condition, color, dimensions, and price.
Seymour Gross,
615 Kings Highway,
Middletown, NJ 07748
(201) 615-0252

◆ **Depression glass** in various makers, colors, and patterns.
Nadine Pankow,
207 S. Oakwood,
Willow Springs, IL 60480
(312) 839-5231

◆ **Fine crystal.** Known for his restoration service which repairs glass, crystal, porcelain, bisque and figurines, David also buys damaged and undamaged figurines, *Hummels*, china and crystal.
David Jasper,
Box 46,
Lennox, SD 57039

Orientalia

◆ **Fine quality Oriental antiques** with special emphasis on Japanese netsuke, inro, lacquer, and fine Chinese porcelains. Marsha buys, sells, and collects all types of Oriental antiques from early ceramics to late 19th century items including furniture, Japanese swords, sword fittings, jade carvings, and jewelry. Many small ivory carvings are worth between $1,000 and $10,000. Modern or reproduction items are not wanted, nor is anything imported since 1960. Marsha is a senior member of the American Society of Appraisers, specializing in Oriental art, and will appraise for a fee. She will also help amateur sellers with fine items genuinely for sale if you make a good photo, give the measurements, and draw or photocopy all markings or signatures.
  Marsha Vargas,
  The Oriental Corner,
  280 Main St.,
  Los Altos, CA 94022
    (415) 941-3207

◆ **Japanese fancy handled metal letter openers** with raised designs of faces, animals, insects, mythological characters, people, etc. Although made of many materials, they are usually copper. Please photocopy both sides for this 30 year veteran collector.
  Lawrence Gichner,
  3405 Woodley Road NW,
  Washington, DC, 20016
    (202) 362-4393

◆ **Antique Japanese netsuke, inro, and other art** including pouches, pipes and pipe cases, ivory and wooden statues, Japanese lacquer, metalwork, cloisonne, paintings, and ceramics. Will pay $10,000 up for ivory and wood 18th and 19th century netsuke and $500 for netsuke inlaid in various materials. No roughly carved pieces, man made materials, or factory pieces bought in hotel lobbies, airports or gift shops. If you provide clear close up photographs of your netsuke from all angles and an exact drawing of the signature, Denis will make an offer. He is member of the Appraisers Association of America and does formal appraisals for a fee.
  Denis Szeszler,
  Antique Oriental Art,
  Box 714,
  New York, NY 10028
    (212) 427-4682

Earthenware

◆ **American art pottery of all types.** "I'll buy pottery from *Fulper, Paul Revere, Rookwood, Grueby, Dedham, Teco, Tiffany, Clewell, Marblehead, Saturday Evening Girls, Newcomb College, George Ohr, Van Briggle, Cowan, Grand Feu, Losanti, New Orleans Art Pottery, Robineau,* and other quality American art pottery. I'll **also buy good quality European pottery** such as *Martin Bros, Moorcroft,* and others." Especially likes large and unusual pieces, and has been known to consider damaged pieces if they are important. "If you have any doubts, phone me and I will be glad to be of assistance."
Robert Berman, Le Poulaille,
5313 Baynton St.,
Philadelphia, PA 19144
(215) 843-1516

◆ *Weller* **sculptural vases with raised figures** such as nudes, snakes, frogs, insects, and the like. Also *Weller* pieces with strong organic or geometric forms in either matte or glossy finish. Buys **other art pottery** as well, especially TECO, Jervis, SEG, UND, Marblehead, Overbeck, NC, and Rookwood. Give all markings and colors. No damaged pieces.
Gary Struncius,
Box 1374,
Lakewood, NJ 08701
(201) 364-7580

◆ **China, pottery, and other art objects featuring automobiles.** Pre 1920 depictions of cars or airplanes are wanted, especially on *Royal Doulton* and *Nippon* pitchers and china.
David Bausch,
252 North 7th St.,
Allentown, PA 18102
(215) 432-3355

◆ *Royal Doulton* **figurines, character jugs, and coaching ware.**
Pascoe & Co.,
545 Michigan Ave.,
Miami Beach, FL 33139
(800) 872-0195

◆ *Roseville* **pottery Juvenile line dishes.** "I'll buy all fine condition juvenile *Roseville* with decals of Santas, chickens, ducks, dogs, pigs, sunbonnet girls, etc., if you send a photocopy and describe the marks." Susan is a regular writer for *The Antique TraderWeekly* and is publisher of *The American Clay Exchange,* a magazine devoted to pottery and its collectors.
Susan Cox,
800 Murray Dr.,
El Cajon, CA 92020
(619) 447-0800

◆ **Stoneware crocks and jugs with blue decorations.** Especially likes pottery with clear incised markings from NY, NJ, OH, PA, and New England. "I'll pay top dollar for unusual forms decorated with people, animals, ships, trees, houses, strong blue florals, etc. Dated pieces are particularly desirable. I pay from $100 to as much as $10,000 for the right items." He emphasizes that he is interested **only** in stoneware that is blue decorated. No browns or whites. Needs to know the size of the piece in quarts or gallons if marked, in inches if not. Take a photo or make a good sketch of the decoration because the more unusual the decoration, the more he pays. Mention the darkness of the blue. Also buys inkwells, flasks, and unusual small items made of blue decorated stoneware. He will help amateur sellers determine what they have.
Richard C. Hume,
1300 Northstream Parkway,
Point Pleasant, NJ 08742
(201) 899-8707 eves

◆ **Stoneware crocks and jugs** in all sizes and shapes, signed and unsigned. Blue decorated preferred. Please give size, shape, and a description of the decoration. Nothing damaged. Also buys "quality glassware," **art glass, depression glass, carnival glass,** and **pressed glass.** Will consider some "Occupied Japan" if you give size, color, pattern, and number of pieces. Photos are preferred, photocopies OK.
Loren Ladd,
21 Bostwick Rd.,
Shelburne, VT 05482

◆ **Majolica.**
Joan Bogart,
Box 265,
Rockville Centre, NY 11571

◆ **Spongeware, stoneware, and redware pottery and crockery.**

> Louis Picek,
> Main Street Antiques and Art,
> Box 340,
> West Branch, IA 52358

◆ **Blue decorated stoneware.** "We will buy Pennsylvania, Maryland, Virginia, New Jersey, New York, and New England stoneware, especially Pennsylvania pitchers and batter pails or crocks signed either "Baltimore" or "Alexandria, Va." Call today or send photos."

> Anthony & Barbara Zipp's Antiques,
> Box 11277,
> Baltimore, MD 21239
> (301) 337-5090

◆ *Stangl* **Pottery.** "We especially want *Stangl* stubby mugs with ashtray hats, Stangl birds and animals, and the following dinnerware patterns: Fruit, Fruit and Flowers, Country Gardens, Country Life, Blueberry, Garden Flower, Thistle, Town and Country, Chicory, Star Flower, and all Christmas patterns. We don't want brown stains, chips, or cracks."

> Bob and Nancy Perzel, Popkorn,
> PO Box 1057,
> Flemington, NJ 08822
> (201) 782-9631

◆ **Presidential and patriotic English urns, vases, mugs, etc.,** with American historical motifs, pictures of political figures, battles, or famous events. May be any type of china by any maker. A delft teapot advocating "No Stamp Act" would bring $5-6,000.

> Rex Stark,
> 49 Wethersfield Rd.,
> Bellingham, MA 02019
> (508) 966-0994

◆ **Lithopanes (porcelain transparencies)** in any size or shape, colored or uncolored, used as a lamp, plaque, stein, cup, etc. Give the size, description of the picture, and any letters or numbers appearing on the object.

> Laurel Blair,
> Box 4557,
> Toledo, OH 43620
> (419) 243-4115

◆ *Clarice Cliff Bizzare Ware.* This English hand painted pottery is decorated with fanciful, geometric, and floral themes. Most pieces are marked, often with the name of the artist, but usually "Clarice Cliff" or "Bizzare." Does not want transfer patterns, only painted ones such as Crocus, Fantasque, Delecia, Caprice, Ravel, and many others. A photo or Xerox© is very important as the company made so many patterns, they're almost impossible to know which you have without seeing it.

> Darryl Rehr,
> 11433 Rochester Ave. #303,
> Los Angeles, CA 90025
> (213) 559-2368

◆ *Wedgwood* **commemorative ware transfer print china.** Earthenware or bone china plates, trivets, tiles, etc., with American scenes, calendars, historic places, children's topics, literature, any topic. "We mainly want items of American interest, but will also buy some Canadian and Australian scenes." These pieces almost always bear backstamps marked Josiah Wedgwood & Sons, Wedgwood, Etruria, or Etruria & Barlaston. Calendar tiles from the 1870's and 80's are worth up to $200, and tiles honoring the Washington Light infantry and President Garfield are worth in excess of $400 each. "It's hard to give advice as to what we don't want. People are better off to inquire by giving a good description, photo, description of the back markings. Some items will have to be seen before we can make an offer."

> Benton & Beverly Rosen,
> Manion House,
> 9 Kenilworth Way,
> Pawtucket, RI 02860
> (401) 722-2927 winters
> (508) 759-4303 summers

◆ **Redware plates, bowls, and other pieces.** When describing, mention all marks on the bottom and take a photo or make a sketch of the pattern, indicating what part of the pattern is yellow or green. Make certain you note if there are any cracks or chips.

> Richard C. Hume,
> 1300 Northstream Parkway,
> Point Pleasant, NJ 08742
> (201) 899-8707 eves

4
Watches, Clocks & Jewelry

Dr. Hyman's Prescription

If you want to sell your clock or watch, you must provide the information a buyer needs so he will know exactly what you have. It's not hard to describe a watch or clock, but it may mean opening up the back of your timepiece. If you can not do this, perhaps a friend can open it for you.

When describing a watch or clock, answer the following:

(1) What does it look like?

(2) What name is on the dial?

(3) What name is on the movement (works)?

(4) Does it say how many jewels?

(5) What is the size of the case?

(6) What is the case made of?

(7) Is the case decorated or engraved?

(8) Is there a label inside the case?

(9) Is there a serial number?

(10) How is it wound or activated?

(11) Do you have the key and weights?

(12) Is it presently running?

Be especially cautious about selling watches to local jewelers. The fact that he sells expensive new watches does not make your local jeweler expert in collectible watches. There can be a great deal of money at stake, perhaps five or ten times as much, when you deal with international experts.

tony hyman

Watches

◆ **Vintage wristwatches and better antique pocket watches,** especially *Patek Philippe, Cartier, Rolex, Vacheron & Constantin, Audemars Piguet, E. Howard, Hamilton, Illinois,* and *Reed.* Also wants chronographs, watches that chime, enamels, phases of the moon, calendar watches, historical watches, gold cases, character watches, sports watches, oddly shaped watches, both U.S. and foreign. Exceptional prices paid for fine and rare vintage wristwatches and pocket watches, running or not. Call toll free if you have a watch to sell or know someone who does. "We pay a $signifi-cant finder$ fee for leads on large collections, estates, or accumulations." Not buying *Timex,* electronic, or inexpensive watches made after 1965. Describe your watch according to instruc-tions on previous page. Ask for his wants list.
Miles Sandler,
Maundy International,
PO Box 13028TH,
Overland Park, KS 66212
(913) 383-2880 for info about watches;
(800) 235-2866 toll free for selling

◆ **High quality and collectable watches** by *Patek Phillipe, Rolex, Cartier, Tiffany, Audemars* and types of watches like chrono-graphs, repeaters, alarm, doctor's watches, two time zone, and rectangular faces made between 1870 and 1960. **Also advertising items relat-ing to watches.** Irv deals in watches from rare to common. Buys parts, cases, boxes, move-ments, dials, bands, from all *Rolex, Patek* or *Cartier* watches. If you are thinking of auction, Irv says, "We will buy any piece of interest at 95% of anticipated net sellers hammer pro-ceeds." Irv promises: "Fair prices, next day payment, postage refunded, and free appraisals" adding "I will travel for large purchases."
Describe metal, shape, details, all names and numbers. Priced wants list.
Irv Temes,
American Int'l Watch Exchange,
Box 28461,
Baltimore, MD 21234
(301) 882-0580 for info about watches;

◆ **Racing stopwatches, pocket watches, dashboard clocks, and schoolhouse clocks** with the name of a horse, horse race, carriage company, or automobile manufacturer on the face. Also sterling silver clock cases, with or without clocks. Also leather cases for car clocks that clip over the dashboard of a carriage. "When in doubt, please write, or send on approval for an immediate response."
Donald Sawyer,
40 Bachelor St.,
West Newbury, MA 01985
(508) 346-4724 days

◆ **Watches and clocks with cartoon charac-ters or product advertising on the face.** Any pre 1975 items that are mint in their original box are particularly desirable. "I'll pay $1,000 for a mint in the box 1934 Ingersoll Tom Mix pocket or wrist watch." Wants to know whether the face is round or rectangular, any wording on the face or back of the watch, defects (including scratches), the condition of the box (if any), and whether or not it is working. Don't overwind!
Maggie Kenyon,
Maggie's Place,
One Christopher #14G,
New York, NY 10013
(212) 675-3213

◆ *Hamilton* "electric" wristwatches. "I'm particularly interested in those with odd and asymmetrical shaped cases. Also want parts, movements, **advertising materials, catalogs,** and most anything else related to the Hamilton Electric watch, particularly early prototypes, cal-endar models. No Hamilton *Electronic* watches, only American made pre-1970 electric watches. **Also Electronic LED watches from the 1970's** with red or blue dials and faces that are always blank until a button is pressed. Prefers "big awkward clumsy models" from major makers such as *Pulsar, Elgin, Bulova,* etc. Not interest-ed in any by *Timex, Texas Instruments,* or made in Hong Kong or Taiwan. No LCD watches with grey dials and numbers always visible. "I don't want anyone expecting riches for a 10 year old watch. These aren't worth that much."
Rene Rondeau,
120 Harbor Dr.,
Corte Madera, CA 94925

Clocks

◆ **American wall and mantle clocks** from the 1700's through the arts and crafts movement of the early 20th century. "I'll buy, sell, or trade a wide range of clocks, but my specialties are weight driven calendar and regulator clocks that hang on a wall. I also buy interesting, unusual, and better grades of shelf (mantle) and other wall clocks of the 1800's. Especially like to find clocks with multiple dials or faces, in either plain or fancy cases." Some of the many names to look for include Simon-Willard, E.N. Welch, Howard, Ithaca, Waterbury, Seth Thomas, New Haven, and other early Connecticut makers. Bruce is well versed in clocks of all types so can be helpful to the amateur seller. "If I'm offered something I can't use, I try to refer folks to someone who might like to buy it. Early electric clocks don't interest me much, but I may be able to give readers some help in identifying or evaluating them." Provide a full description (see the notice to your right). Bruce says, "For my own collection, I like to find things that are a little out of the ordinary." Minor interest in **European clocks, with porcelain dials, or fine cases with gilt, inlay, or marble.**
 Bruce Austin,
 RIT, College of Liberal Arts,
 Rochester, NY 14623
  (716) 223-0711 eves

◆ **Grandfather clocks made in America.** Wants tall floor clocks made in the United States, especially in Pennsylvania. "I generally don't buy them myself, but I screen clocks for one of the world's expert buyers of good clocks. If you have something good in the way of an old tall case clock, I'll put you in touch with the buyer. **No European tall clocks.**
 Old Timers,
 Box 392,
 Camp Hill, PA 17001-0392
  (717) 761-1908

◆ **Advertising clocks** made by Baird.
 Jerry Phelps,
 6013 Innes Trace Rd.,
 Louisville, KY 40222
  (502) 425-4765

◆ *Lux, Keebler,* **and German animated clocks.** These are the clocks with swinging cats tails, rolling eyes, and the like. Describe fully, noting any damage. Picture helpful.
 Ed Kazemekas,
 35 Riverview Circle,
 Wolcott, CT 06716
  (203) 879-1814

◆ **Meissen and Dresden porcelain and** *Royal Bonn Ansonia* **clocks.**
 L. Fraser,
 Box 27162,
 Minneapolis, MN 55427
  (612) 937-0477

◆ **Clocks, pocket watches** and better quality wristwatches.
 Robert Kolbe's Clock Repair,
 1301 So. Duluth,
 Sioux Falls, SD 57105
  (605) 332-9662

```
                        ▨

       Your Name
       Your Address


```

**If you want an answer
Don't forget your SASE.**

EDITOR'S NOTE: Watch buyers will often wish to see your watch before making final offer. Send it Registered Mail and insured. That will require the recipient to sign for the package and cover you for loss in transit.

◆ **Old wall and shelf clocks.** This husband - wife team buy a wide range of 18th and 19th century shelf and wall clocks, but are especially interested in the following:
  (1) **Victorian shelf clocks.** Want ornate ones, with hanging teardrops, busts (such as Jenny Lind), cherubs, side mirrors, etc.;
  (2) **Reverse painting on glass pillar and scroll clocks** about 36" high with free standing wooden pillars and curved scroll ("swan's neck") tops;
  (3) **Steeple or beehive shelf clocks,** *but only if the veneer is nearly perfect.* "These are plentiful with poor veneer. I want those in beautiful condition."
  (4) **Any American carved clocks.** "I'm a pushover for clocks with carved columns or splats, with eagles, fruit baskets, etc.," says Ken.
  (5) **Clocks by Eli Terry or any of his sons.**
  (6) **Seth Thomas clocks.**
  (7) **French, German, and English clocks from the 18th and 19th century.** "Some excellent 20th century German clocks were made in Mission style, but no matter how good the clock, we don't buy 20th century."
  (8) **Coo-coo clocks if very old, very heavily carved, and in perfect condition.** "I'm afraid I'll open a floodgate if I mention I'm interested in coo-coos, because there are so many junk ones around. I only want those that are very early, and very ornate...no souvenir clocks. Sending a photo a must."

(9) **Black Forest trumpeter clocks.** These are chiming clocks, like coo-coos, but instead of a bird have a man who plays a tune on a trumpet. "These are valuable, and we'll travel to pick yours up if it's a nice one."

"We buy clocks with walnut or cherry cases. We buy spring driven clocks but especially like to find older weight driven clocks. We buy clocks with wooden works only if in running condition," say the owners, "but there are a few exceptions, so it's worth inquiring."

"We are *not* interested in oak clocks or metal figural clocks, no matter who is depicted. We don't buy any 20th century clocks, oak gingerbread kitchen clocks, electric clocks, or mission (arts and crafts) clocks. Nor do we buy *Lux* or *Keebler* novelty clocks with rolling eyes or swinging tails. We also do not buy plain ogee clocks (rectangular veneered clocks with fronts that look like picture frames). We almost never buy clocks that have undergone restoration or modification".

"My wife and I think of ourselves as a clock adoption agency. We look for nice items in need of a good new home. We don't want to spend lots of time with the clocks. We prefer to buy them in nearly perfect condition."
Old Timers,
Box 392,
Camp Hill, PA 17001-0392
  (717) 761-1908

EDITOR'S NOTE: See p. 52 A for pictures of various clocks sought by Old Timers' Clock Shop.

EDITOR'S NOTE: Jewelry can often be photocopied.

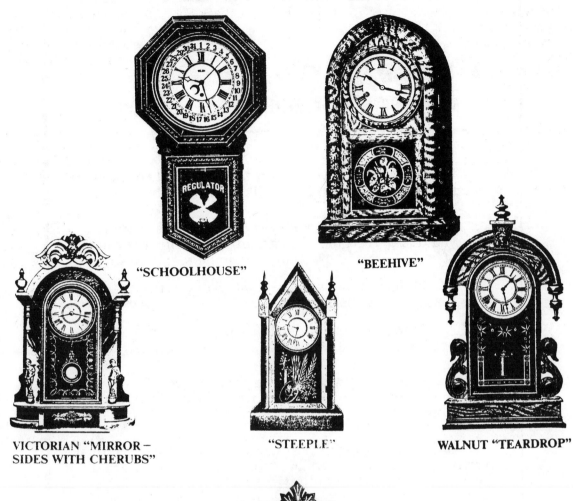

"SCHOOLHOUSE"   "BEEHIVE"

VICTORIAN "MIRROR –   "STEEPLE"   WALNUT "TEARDROP"
SIDES WITH CHERUBS"

"CARVED COLUMN"   "GINGERBREAD"   "PILLAR AND SCROLL"

Dr. Hyman's Prescription

People who buy jewelry want to know what your item is made from and what it looks like. Provide the following:

(1) Is it silver, gold, brass, plastic, or a material you do not recognize for certain?   Describe the color of your item and any names, numbers, or markings.

(2) If there are stones, what color are they? How many of them are there?

(3) Dimensions are helpful, especially on hatpins bracelets, and larger pieces.

Many items of jewelry can be photocopied. It is a particularly good way of doing pins, brooches, hatpins, and some bracelets.

Be prepared to ship your jewelry with a five day return privilege. Buyers will undoubtedly want to inspect what you own prior to committing to buy. Get payment first, before you send, but be willing to give the money back if they are not happy for any reason with what you send.

When mailing jewelry that is valuable, send it Registered Mail. For between $5-$10 (plus postage) you can mail it anywhere in the U.S. with insurance as high as $25,000. The recipient signs for Registered Mail. Read more about this valuable service on page 11.

Be cautious when selling old jewelry. Diamonds and other fine gems were not cut the same way 100 years ago, and the untrained eye can easily mistake them for glass. I saw a 2.5 carat diamond sold for 25¢ at a yard sale.

tony hyman

Jewelry

◆ **Hatpins and hatpin holders** and related objects such as pincushion dolls from before 1930. "Especially interested in plique-a-jour hatpins for which I'll pay up to $350 or more if artist signed. I also like sterling hatpins marked "C.H." and will pay $45-$110. Always interested in vanity or figural hatpins such as compacts, pin-holders, perfume tops, thimble with needle, etc., especially if Art Nouveau design atop 12" pin stems. My special want is a hatpin hinged on the top ornament which opens to reveal a teeny nude baby and I would pay as much as $500 for a perfect one on a long pin. I also want to buy **figural hatpin holders** by *Royal Bayreuth, RS Prussia* (red mark only), *Oriental, Schafer & Vater* (S&V), others." Mrs. Baker is the author of books on jewelry and a limited edition encyclopedia of hatpins available for $79 postpaid. She founded the International Club for Hatpin Collectors. An SASE brings information about the club or available books. She wants to know the history of your hatpin, where you acquired it, and whether it has any flaws. Will make offers to amateurs only after inspection.
  Lillian Baker,
  The Hatpin Lady,
  15237 Chanera Ave.,
  Gardena, CA 90249
    (213) 329-2619

◆ **"Good looking costume jewelry,"** 1860-1940. Make a photocopy.
  Clark St. Waltz,
  2360 N. Lincoln Ave.,
  Chicago, IL 60614
    (312) 472-5559

◆ **Celluloid bracelets.** "I'll pay $12 to $25 for multicolored carved bracelets made of celluloid, usually marked "Japan" on the inside. No solid colored bracelets.
  Mike Newell,
  2113 Nottingham,
  Cape Girardeau, MO 63701
    (314) 334-5153

◆ **Various pieces of good jewelry** made of precious metals, including:
  (1) **Enamel on gold jewelry** (will consider damaged pieces);
  (2) **Georg Jensen's Danish sterling** silver jewelry;
  (3) **Puffed heart charms** in sterling silver;
  (4) **Cuff link and shirt stud sets** if made of gold;
  (5) **Moonstone jewelry**.
Photocopy with description. Prices preferred, but may make offers for amateur sellers.
  Timepiece Antiques,
  Box 26416,
  Baltimore, MD 21207
    (301) 944-6414

◆ **Gold scrap.** "I buy all marked and unmarked gold and silver rings, wedding bands, and scrap" says this giant dealer in medals.
  Rich Hartzog,
  World Exonumia,
  Box 4143 BBL,
  Rockford, IL 61110
    (815) 226-0771

◆ **Bakelite polka dot bracelets and jewelry.** "I'll pay $100 each for old Bakelite polka dot bracelets and other unusual Bakelite jewelry."
  Irene Kaufman,
  1913 Hyde St.,
  San Francisco, CA 94109
    (415) 776-8865

◆ **Costume jewelry fur clips** in good condition. Describe or photocopy. Please price.
  Kevin Prediger,
  120 Pierce St. #5,
  San Francisco, CA 94117

◆ **Plastic *Hummel* jewelry** from 1940's in shapes similar to their figurines. She buys both painted and unpainted jewelry.
  Sharon Vohs-Mohammed,
  Box 822,
  Auburn, IN 46706

5
Toys, Dolls, & Pop Culture

Dr. Hyman's Prescription

"Pop culture" describes a broad range of toys and advertising ephemera, usually associated with the world of cartoons, comics, the movies, television, and other popular entertainment. Do not overlook small items, such as cereal premiums from your childhood. A few are worth $100 or more!

To sell toys and other pop culture, you need to provide the following information:

(1) What it is, including its size, color, and the material from which it is made;

(2) Names, dates, and numbers embossed, stamped, or labeled on the toy;

(3) The condition, including mention of any missing parts, pieces, or paint. Be certain to describe all repairs or repainting;

(4) Whether it has the box and instructions.

Some potential buyers want additional info. Bank buyers, for example want you to trace around the base of the bank, and to be extra careful in describing the colors and condition of paint.

Vehicle buyers want to know the size, color, and the material from which the tires and wheels are made. Electric train buyers want the serial numbers of engines, and the color, name, and stock number of cars you have.

Photographs and photocopies are important since a great many of these banks, vehicles, dolls, robots, and other toys are worth $100+ and a surprising number can bring you $1,000 or more.

tony hyman

Games

◆ **Board games pre 1930**, especially large size McLaughlin Bros. Wants fancy games with elaborate lithographed boxes, preferably complete with all rules and pieces. Doesn't want chess, checkers, *Pit, Rook, Flinch, Authors,* or other common games. NO OFFERS.
   Lee and Rally Dennis,
   110 Spring Rd.,
   Peterborough, NH 03458
      (603) 924-6710

◆ **Adult and children's card and board games.** Should be complete with rules in original box. No *Pit, Rook, Authors, Flinch, Touring,* and other common card games. Also unusual decks of cards, odd domino sets, patriotic games, and original strategy games. Pre 1940 items preferred.
   Dave Galt,
   302 W 78th Street,
   New York, NY 10024
      (212) 769-2514

◆ **Antique and collectible board and card games** made in the US from 1840-1960's. Any game before 1860 is wanted, especially those made by Ives, Crosby, Magnus, or Adams, for which they will pay $500 and up. Other items of particular interest are baseball games before WWI, and games about TV shows, cartoon characters, space exploration and pop culture (including movies) of the 1930-1970's. They also bus **wooden jigsaw puzzles, blocks, and paper toys.** They *do not want* checkers, *Lotto,* anagrams, *Rook, Pit, Flinch,* chess, autobridge, *Parcheesi, Touring,* variants of Bingo, TV "Game show" games, or "kiddie" games like *Chutes and Ladders.* Give name, condition, size, maker, copyright date, and the degree of completeness.
   Dave Oglesby & Sue Stock,
   57 Lakeshore Dr.,
   Marlborough, MA 01752
      (508) 481-1087

◆ **Almost any complete playable game,** especially out-of-print titles by Avalon Hill, 3M, SPI, pre 1964 Parker Bros., war games, sports games, political games, and TV related games. Include the name of the manufacturer and copyright date. Please thoroughly check the contents and note whether *anything* is missing, and how much wear is evident on the box and pieces. Also buys gaming magazines such as *The General, The Wargamer, The Dragon, Games & Puzzles,* and others. Please, no checkers, chess, or common children's games like *Authors.*
   H.M. Levy,
   Box 197CC,
   East Meadow, NY 11554
      (516) 485-0877

◆ **Unusual theme chess sets.** Dennis buys rare and unusual chess sets of all sorts, but particularly likes those with themes such as Disneyania, Watergate, etc. Will buy historical, literary, fictional, mythological, geographical...if it's out of the ordinary in theme, design, material, or whatever, give him a call. He would especially like to find the 3-D chess set from *Star Trek* which was marketed in the late 1960's. No plastic or "typical wooden sets," he warns, "I'm looking for works of art or imagination." Describe board if one accompanies your set. Provide whatever background you can about the history of both the board and pieces. Describe condition of both.
   Dennis Horwitz,
   425 Short Trail,
   Topanga, CA 90290
      (213) 455-4002 eves

◆ **Figural European chess sets** with playing pieces shaped like actual people or animals. Also antique chess boards. This 30 year veteran collector also wants porcelain or bronze figurines as well as paintings and other original artwork depicting chess players.
   David Hafler,
   11 Merion Road,
   Merion Station, PA 19066
      (215) 839-7171

◆ **Checkers ephemera**, primarily books about checkers or draughts, but also early handmade boards or anything unusual related to checkers. If offering a book, in addition to standard bibliographic information, Don would like you to photocopy or any advertising in the book.
Don Deweber, Checker Book World,
3520 Hillcrest #4,
Dubuque, IA 52001

◆ **Better quality marbles.** Stan publishes *Marble Mania Quarterly i* and is willing to make offers.
Stanley Block,
Box 51,
Trumbull, CT 06611
(203) 261-3223

◆ **Marbles and marble related items.** "I'll buy marbles with pontil marks (from where they were made), toys and games using marbles, marble bags, tournament pins and medals, boxes of marbles, and pictures, magazine ads, and postcards which depict children playing marbles." He does not buy beat-up or chipped marbles, machine made marbles, homemade games, or Chinese Checkers. When selling marbles, give the diameter as part of your description.
Larry Svacina,
2822 Tennyson,
Denver, CO 80212
(303) 477-9203

◆ **Mah Jongg sets, racks, and accessories,** pre 1930. Tiles may be made of bone, bamboo, celluloid, jade, or ivory. Especially interested in jade, ivory, gold, or fine inlaid tiles and boxes. Pays $500-$1,000 and up. Generally does not buy partial sets unless unusual. Mah jongg is also called Ma Chuck, Pung Chow, Sparrows, Game of China, etc. Joe also wants Mah Jongg books and magazines. Also old **domino sets** made of ivory or ebony. Also **ebony Pai Gow games.** For his offer, mail him two typical tiles (insured), a count of how many pieces you have, and a listing of other items present.
Joe Scales,
3827 Los Santos Dr.,
Cameron Park, CA 95682
(916) 677-0262

Banks

◆ **Cast iron mechanical banks,** 1870-1920, **and Japanese tin battery operated banks,** 1946-1960. Include a bottom tracing. To sell a battery toy, indicate whether it works or not and if you still have the original box. Battery banks *must* be in near mint condition. No plastic banks.
Rick Mihlheim,
Box 128,
Allegan, MI 49010
(616) 673-4509

◆ **Still banks made of cast iron or metal** with special emphasis on unusual or rare examples in excellent to near-mint condition. Letters should include an accurate description including an estimate of how much of the original paint is still there. Accurately measure the length, width, and height. Photos are appreciated. Private collector answers all letters which include SASE.
Ralph Berman,
3524 Largo Lane,
Annandale, VA 22003
(703) 560-5439

◆ **Mechanical banks made of cast iron, tin, or wood** with no repairs or repainting. Also trade cards, catalogs, and other advertising depicting mechanical banks. Also painted and stenciled cast iron or tin still banks shaped like buildings. Especially any mechanical bank with its original box, packing, and receipt. Greg is VP of the bank collectors' club.
Gregory Zemenick,
763 Pilgrim,
Birmingham, MI 48009
(313) 642-8129

◆ **Cast iron or tin banks, still or mechanical.** Also buys original boxes and color trade cards for mechanical banks. "Girls like old banks and toys, too!" No banks after 1950. Please indicate any repairs, repaints, and give the dimensions. Prefers you to set the price you want.
Virginia Jensen, c/o GI School,
23270 E. River Rd.,
Grosse Ile, MI 48138
(313) 561-9259 eves

Misc. toys

◆ **Fine old kaleidoscopes** made of wood and/or brass especially elaborate inlaid or complex instruments from the mid 19th century. No cardboard toys.
Lucille Malitz, Lucid Antiques,
Box KH,
Scarsdale, NY 10583
(914) 636-3367

◆ **High quality kaleidoscopes** from the 1800's, made of wood and/or brass by makers such as Bush, Brewster, Carpenter, or Leach. Prefer perfect original condition brass instruments in wooden cases with the Royal seal, but will consider less. No inexpensive cardboard or 1900's kaleidoscopes. Include your phone number and time you're home so he can phone.
Martin Roenigk, Grand Illusions,
26 Barton Hill,
East Hampton, CT 06424
(203) 267-8682

◆ **Antique toys** in excellent condition, including cars, carousels, and character and comic wind-ups. German and American tin toys, penny toys, nested blocks, and pop-up books. No interest in dolls or trains. List manufacturer, size, and condition. Picture desirable.
James Conley,
2405 Brentwood Rd., NW,
Canton, OH 44708
(216) 477-7725

◆ **Polyramapanoptique and megalethescopes.** If you have to ask what they are, you probably don't have one. The former are early 19th century cardboard or wooden boxes with flaps for slides, which permit viewing of hand painted or pin-pricked scenes. Megalethescopes, invented in 1860, are large wooden cabinets, often heavily carved, also devices for slides, usually seen as day/night views of the same scene in 3D. Also wants slides for them.
Lucille Malitz, Lucid Antiques,
Box KH,
Scarsdale, NY 10583
(914) 636-3367

◆ **Collections of fine tin and iron toys** are sought for auction by this well known New England auctioneer. No junk, reproductions or items made after 1940.
James D. Julia Auctioneer,
Rt. 201, Skowhegan Rd.,
Fairfield, ME 04937
(207) 453-9493

◆ **Old one of a kind kites from before 1940** especially those made by important inventors. Names on desirable kites include *Hargrave, Lecornu, Saconney, Conyne, Perkins, Bell,* and many others including *Barrage Kite, Target Kite,* and the *U.S. Weather Bureau.* Also wants prototype models of production kites. Also traditional kites of Europe, the Orient, Malaysia, or South America. If it's old, interesting, or unusual, she'd like to hear about it. As publisher of *Kite Lines,* Valerie says she can act as a contact person to help you sell your kite if it's something she doesn't want. Rare and important kites are scarce but the market is small. They bring from $100 to $500. Give the history of your kite if you can.
Valerie Govig, Kite Lines,
Box 446,
Randallstown, MD 21133
(301) 922-1212

◆ **Early miniature outboard marine motors** used on model boats. Wants fuel type motors only. No electrics. Condition should be described carefully.
Sven Stau,
Box 1135,
Buffalo, NY 14211
(716) 825-5448

◆ **Toy outboard motors,** either battery or wind up, alone on mounted on toy boats. "I'll buy motors by *K&O Fleetline* between 1952-1962 with names of popular manufacturers of real outboard motors. Will pay $75-$400 for your toy depending on the model. Describe decals and color.
Jack Browning,
214 16th St. NW,
Roanoke, VA 24017
(703) 890-5083 eves

◆ **Toys run by live steam or hot air.** Also wants accessories and catalogs related to steam and hot air toys. "I'll pay from $100 to several thousand dollars for boats and tractors run by live steam, whether American, German, or British made. I don't want modern steam toys made by Wilesco, Mamod, or Jansen." Give dimensions and markings. A good clear photo or two or, in many cases, a personal inspection is needed to determine value.

Lowell Wagner,
5492 Feltl Rd.,
Minnetonka, MN 55343
    (612) 442-4036

◆ **Model airplane engines,** 1930-1955 that used a miniature spark plug (usually a Champion). These engines also had a coil, condenser, batteries, and incorporate a moveable timer for spark advancement. Later engines use a glow plug and do not requre electrical support once running. Also want **model race cars from the 1940's using these engines.** Indicate the brand name and if the engine is complete. "It is usually necessary to see the engine to assess its condition."

Bruce Pike,
RD #1, Box 291, Lot 92,
Aliquippa, PA 15001
    (412) 378-0449

◆ **Any sand-operated self contained toys,** including the "not very old" enclosed boxes with figures set in motion by flipping over the box. Also **small toy scales** made of tin.

Donald Gorlick,
Box 24541,
Seattle, WA 98124
    (206) 824-0508

◆ **Building kits such as** *Erector Sets, Lincoln Logs,* etc. Buys *Marlin, Sterling, Structator, Wright blocks,* European building blocks, *Lincoln Log* figures, and other sets for building things, especially buildings, bridges, and other engineered items.

Coffman,
1035 17th St.,
Santa Monica, CA 90403
    (213) 828-4727

◆ **Yo-Yo items** including displays, boxes, awards, patches, and pins.

John Fawcett,
Art Dept. U-99,
University of Conn.,
Storrs, CT 06268
    (203) 429-9228 eves

◆ **Fisher-Price items.**

Bill Bege,
7925 Tropicana St.,
Miramar, FL 33023
    (305) 962-9282

◆ **Mechanical puzzles.** Wants all types including trick locks, trick matchsafes, etc.

Slocum,
Box 1635,
Beverly Hills, CA 90213

Toy Vehicles

◆   **All sorts of metal vehicles and toys,** pre1959, including cars, trucks, airplanes, trains, boats, and construction equipment:

(1) **Large steel toys** by *Buddy-L, Sturditoy, Turner, Kingsbury, Sonny, Keystone*, and *Structo*. Will pay $800 for 14" *Ford Buddy-L* delivery truck;

(2) *Tootsietoys* with white rubber tires or all metal wheels, pre 1940;

(3) **Old tin toy boats,** the larger the better;

(4) **Children's pedal cars** and trucks made pre 1940;

(5) **Large steel *Smith-Miller* or *M-I-C* trucks** made in California 1945-57;

(6) **Tin windup automotive, aviation, or comic toys,** U.S. or European, working or not. Pays $2,500 for an 8" Aunt Eppie Hogg truck in perfect condition;

(7) **English and French *Dinky* toys,** pre 1964;

(8) **Any metal motorcycle** longer than 8", especially a *Hubley Indian* delivery cycle worth $1,500 in original condition;

(9) **Wind up or battery robots** especially *Mr. Atomic* worth $1,000 in original box and *Robby Space Patrol* vehicle worth $750;

(10) **Japanese scale models of U.S. cars;**

(11) **Cast iron toys** by *Hubley, Arcade, Kilgore*, and *Williams*.

Plastic, rubber, or wood vehicles are not wanted.
Larry Bruch,
Box 121,
Mountaintop, PA 18707
(717) 474-9202 eves

◆   **Hard rubber toy vehicles,** motorcycles, trains, airplanes, ships, animals, soldiers, football and baseball players, especially by Rainbow Rubber Co. Hard rubber toys only. No Vinyl. Hard rubber is painted. Vinyl is made in the color of the toy and is the same color throughout. Give the maker, size, colors, condition, and description of features. "Photos are best."
K.S. Kelley,
Box 695,
Desert Hot Springs, CA 92240
(619) 329-3206

◆   *Kelmet* **toy trucks,** especially the *Trumodel* tank truck, as well as *Kelmet* sales literature. Also wants **truck parts from Erector sets (#7 1/2 size)**. No tin toys.   NO OFFERS.
William Hall,
15 Conard Dr.,
West Hartford, CT 06107
(203) 521-8169

◆   **Toy motorcycles** made in the US, Japan, Germany, France, or England of tin, cast iron, hard plastic, or rubber that function by means of wind-up, friction, or batteries, especially by *I-Y*. Also other **vehicle and comic character toys** from Japan and Germany, especially *Lehmann*.
Chris Savino,
Box 419,
Breesport, NY 14816
(607) 739-3106

◆   **Toy motorcycles of all types** made of cast iron, tin, die cast metal, early plastic, iron ride-on pedal cars, cycles, etc. Michael does not want vinyl toys by *Auburn* and warns that cast iron cycles with cast iron wheels are almost always fakes as are most two-toned ones. Pays $500+ for pre-war Japanese tin cycles.
Michael Nelson,
Box 1303,
Laguna Beach, CA 92652

◆   **Toy farm tractors and equipment** from 1970 or older. "I'll buy the ones with real farm equipment company names like *John Deere, Farmall, Oliver, Ford, Allis-Chalmers* and the like, in plastic or metal, and will pay over $100 for some tractors. A *John Deere* Model 430 is worth $750+ in its original box and an *Oliver* Super 55 is worth $500+ in its box.   Also buys other scale model toys, like outboard motors, with tractor company names, and is interested in all scale *Caterpillar* tractor and heavy equipment toys. Does not want repros or anything made after 1975. Give the color, size, brand, model, condition, and status of original box.
Dave Nolt,
Box 422,
New Holland, PA 17557
(717) 768-3554

◆ **Toy airplanes.** Especially wants to find **large pedal-car airplanes** and cast iron planes.
Perry Eichor,
703 N. Almond Dr.,
Simpsonville, SC 29681
(803) 967-8770

◆ **Toy firetrucks and fire related toys.** This veteran collector-dealer wants U.S. made fire toys made prior to 1960. Buys all types, all sizes, all styles as long as they are in good condition. Is particularly interested in finding *Ahrens Fox* and *Bulldog Macks* and other large steel firetruck toys, some of which can be worth $700 or more. Buys toy fire stations, firemen, and other toys and games that are fire related. Requests color photos, the price you'd like, and a statement of condition. Include your phone number. Will assist amateurs to set price. No Japanese tin toys or anything made after 1965.
Luke Casbar,
Toys for Boys,
22 Garden St.,
Lodi, NJ 07644
(201) 478-5535

◆ **Larger pressed steel toy cars and trucks** are wanted by this ten year veteran collector-dealer. "I'll buy *Smith Miller, Doepke, Tonka, Buddy-L, Keystone, Arcade* and other makes of toy vehicle including construction types, boats, airplanes, and farm tractors." To sell your vehicles, tell him [1] the maker if you can, [2] what it looks like, including what type of vehicle it is, [3] how many you have, [4] and its condition. Make an estimate of what percentage of the original paint is left. "I prefer not to buy rusty or damaged vehicles, but this policy is not written in stone."
Jay Robinson
The Chicago Kid
PO Box 529
Deerfield, IL 60015
(708) 945-8691 or 945-1965

Plastic Model Kits

◆ **Plastic model kits** especially from the 1950's made by *Aurora, Bachman, Comet, Hawk, ITC, Frog, Allyn, Monogram, Revell, Strombecker*, and others. Models can be airliners, commercial ships, space, science fiction, TV and movie subjects, cars, and figures. Also manufacturers catalogs and store display models. Kits must be complete and unbuilt, with minimal damage to the box. Sealed unopened kits are best. He offers to send a copy of the grading system used by kit collectors for an SASE. He'll pay $100 for a perfect condition Athearn gas-powered flying model of the Convair XFY-1 Pogo. Bob publishes *Vintage Plastic*, the Journal for Kit Collectors International and produces *The Model Club*, a public access TV show on model building (which you can order).
Bob Keller,
Starline Hobbies,
Box 38,
Stanton, CA 90680
(714) 826-5218 days

◆ **Plastic model kits** of airplanes, tanks, ships, figures, cars, buildings, or what have you *if complete, unbuilt, and in original box*. When writing, include the manufacturer and kit number. John publishes *Kit Collector's Clearinghouse*, a bi-monthly newsletter for kit collectors and is the author of *Value Guide for Scale Model Plastic Kits*, available for $24, and other model books.
John Burns,
3213 Hardy Dr.,
Edmond, OK 73013

◆ **Plastic model car kits depicting antique cars.** Unbuilt kits from before 1970 only, please.
Henry Winningham,
3205 S. Morgan St.,
Chicago, IL 60608
(312) 847-1672

Electric Trains

◆ **All types of old electric trains** including *Lionel, American Flyer, Ives, Marklin, Bing, Carette, Howard*, and other U.S. and foreign brands in "any amount, any condition, working or not." Is particularly interested in *Lionel* trains from the 40's and 50's, espcially the pink *Lionel* trains made for girls. Give the number on the body of the engine, the color of the engines and cars, the condition, and whether or not you have the box. "I would be glad to help anybody interested in the hobby of collecting old toy trains."
> Tom Ryan,
> 234-04 Bay Ave.,
> Douglaston, NY 11363
>   (718) 423-3732

◆ **Toy trains and accessories, U.S. or foreign, made between 1900-1970.** Will buy any maker and gauge except HO gauge trains. Items do not have to be in perfect condition to be considered. **Also buys train literature.** A wind-up *American Flyer* train with cars marked *Coca-Cola* is worth $350 in mint condition.This 40 year veteran will make offers only if you're serious about selling. Lazarus is past president of the Toy Train Operating Society and publisher of its attractive monthly newsletter. He will accept donations for the Society's exhibit at the California State Railroad Museum in Sacramento.
> Hillel Don Lazarus,
> 14547 Titus St., #207,
> Panorama City, CA 91402
>   (818) 762-3652 eves

◆ **All makes of old toy trains except HO gauge and hand made scale models.** Buys Lionel, *American Flyer, Ives, Marx* and all foreign trains larger than HO. "I'll buy engines, cars, accessories, signals, and incomplete sets that are new, like new, used, and even incomplete but useful for parts, but no layouts, transformers, track, rusty junk, or other toys. This 37 year veteran hobby shop operator offers a very large price guide to trains for only $6.
> Allison Cox,
> 18025 8th Ave., N.W.,
> Seattle, WA 98177
>   (206) 546-2230

◆ **Electric trains by Marx** with cars with eight wheels, especially sets in original boxes. Cars can be either metal or plastic. "I'll pay $100 for Marx Pennsylvania RR car #53941. I also buy **American Flyer standard gauge** (large) freight cars, and pre-war American Flyer three-rail trains and sets (1938-1942). Not interested in plastic engines #400 or #490 or cars with only four wheels. When writing, give numbers on boxes or cars.
> Robert Owen,
> Box 204,
> Fairborn, OH 45324

◆ **Marklin and other European toy trains and metal toys.** Trains can be powered by clockwork, electricity, or live steam. Other Marklin toys (airplains, boats, circus toys, and many others) were usually clockwork or live steam. The name *Marklin* appears on many; others are marked with an entwined GM. "I want anything by Marklin before 1950 in decent condition." Also want **Bing, Schuco, Carlyle & Finch, Carette,** and **Bassett-Lowke** trains and metal toys in very good or better condition. Marklin trains from the 1930's are worth from $500 to $10,000 to Ron so check carefully. "I will buy common items in excellent condition, but don't want repros, fakes, or toys with pieces missing. I'm a collector so prefer people not contact me unless they actually want to sell or trade what they have, but if they do, I pay fair prices and am willing to travel to inspect collections."
> Ron Wiener,
> Packard Bldg #1200,
> 111 S. 15th St.,
> Philadelphia, PA 19102
>   (215) 977-2266

EDITOR'S NOTE: If you have an interest in toy trains
you should join the *Toy Train Operating Society.*
Their bimonthly *Bulletin* is one of the fine club publications.
Information: 25 W. Walnut St., #408, Pasadena, CA 91103.

◆ **Trains and other vehicles.** Will offer on trains in any gauge, especially HO, standard, and O. Also any fine old toys, but especially steam engines, tin plate toys, and airplanes. Color photo is a must to sell to this long time dealer.
Heinz Mueller, Continental Hobby,
Box 193,
Sheboygan, WI 53082
(414) 693-3371

◆ **Electric trains** of all types, made before 1940. This 30 year veteran collector-dealer says "I'll buy trains in all gauges, including electric, wind-up, push-pull, etc. I buy whatever strikes my fancy. I especially like to buy large collections but will buy smaller units as well." To sell your trains, you must list [1] whether it is HO, O, S, N, or some other guage, [2] the maker, [3] quantity, [4] the numbers on engines and cars, [5] condition, and [6] whether you have the original boxes. He usually does not buy rusty items or those with missing parts.
Jay Robinson, "The Chicago Kid"
PO Box 529
Deerfield, IL 60015
(708) 945-8691 or 945-1965

Toy Soldiers & Guns

◆ **All toy pistols, rifles, capshooters, and BB guns made before 1900.** He will buy unusual toy pistols and air guns as late as 1955, especially cast iron. If a magnet sticks, he may be interested. Also wants "Boys' Brigade Rifles" and accessories. Offers to pay a premium for any authentic 19th century patent models of early toy pistols. Send a detailed sketch, noting all defects. Best wrote the book on toy pistols and co-authored books on collecting other toys.
Charles Best,
6288 So. Pontiac,
Englewood, CO 80111
(303) 771-3153

◆ **Cast iron cap guns, bombs, cannons, and caps.** Also catalogs about them, 1870-1940.
Bob Williamson,
190 Washington St.,
East Stroudsburg, PA 18301
(717) 421-6957

◆ **Cap pistols made of cast iron,** especially animated guns from 1800's or guns featuring movie cowboys and other pop culture heroes before 1940. A magnet *must* stick to your gun or he's not interested.
George Fougere,
67 East St.,
North Grafton, MA 01536
(508) 839-2701

◆ **Fine quality European lead toy soldiers,** especially early boxed sets. A photocopy is the best way to describe them to this nationally known dealer in fine antiques.
Samuel Lowe Jr.,
80 Charles St.,
Boston, MA 02114
(617) 742-0845

◆ **Repairable lead soldiers.** "I'll buy them if you have the pieces and set price wanted."
Ken Cross,
6003 Putnam Ave.,
Ridgewood, NY 11385

◆ **Toy soldiers of all types** including: (1) dime store soldiers, 1930-50, made in the USA of painted lead (usually painted khaki); (2) German composition soldiers of WWII; and (3) boxed sets of fine British soldiers. Make photocopies of your soldiers for free appraisals.
Larry Bruch,
Box 121,
Mountain Top, PA 18707
(717) 474-9202

Dr. Hyman's Prescription

Dolls can be treasures to find. High quality French dolls, mechanical dolls, and a few others can be worth $10,000 and many dolls, including U.S. made, are worth $100 or more.

Doll buyers want to know:

(1) Length of the doll, and on older dolls, the circumference (how big around) of the doll's head;

(2) Material from which the head, hair, hands, feet and body are made;

(3) Type and color of eyes (painted, button, glass) and whether they move;

(4) Whether the mouth is open and whether teeth (molded, painted, or attached) show;

(5) Marks incised into the scalp, nape of the neck, shoulders, or back of the doll;

(6) How the doll is dressed and whether the clothes appear to be original;

(7) Any chips, cracks, repainting, or other repairs;

(8) History of your doll.

A photograph is extremely helpful, but you can often get better results faster, easier, and cheaper with a photo-copy machine.

There are many fine books on dolls which can help you identify what you have. You should be able to get these through your public library. If they don't have any, ask the help of the reference librarian.

tony hyman

Dolls

◆ **Antique and collectible dolls.** "We are constantly looking for fine antique and collectible dolls for future auctions. If you are considering the liquidation of all or part of your collection, we can be of assistance. We are happy to visit with you to discuss packing, pricing, shipping, and selling dolls. We know how to make the sale easy, comfortable, private, and profitable for you." There is no obligation and all inquiries are handled personally and confidentially by Barbara.

Barbara Frasher's Doll Auctions,
RD #1 Box 142,
Oak Grove, MO 64075
(816) 625-3786

◆ **Old dolls and their parts.** "I buy both as a collector and as a dealer, a large variety of old dolls and their parts. I will also buy any **damaged dolls** if priced reasonably. I'm always looking for accessories for old dolls, such as shoes, clothing, wigs, purses, **doll carriages,** etc. I'm interested in old wooden creche-type jointed dolls for display at Christmas. Also any cloth comic characters such as Lulu, Tubby, Alwin, Nancy, or Sluggo and *old* Raggedy Ann or Andy dolls. I am most interested in adding to my colelction of old German dolls, bisque snowbabies, and Buster Brown china dishes but I have no interest at all in Japanese bisque or currently made dolls.

Patricia Snyder,
My Dear Dolly,
Box 303,
Sparta, NJ 07871
(201) 729-8087

◆ **Dolls and doll accessories.** This doll museum owner buys better and unusual dolls, both antique and modern. Also buys old cotton lace, costumes, trim and material for dressing old dolls. Also wants doll props like shoes, purses, combs, opera glasses, furniture, buggies, etc.

Madalaine Selfridge,
Forgotten Magic,
Box 413,
Norco, CA 91760
(714) 735-6242

◆ **Schoenhut circus animals, games and dolls.** "I'll pay $150+ for each glass eyed animal in original or near original condition. Also want circus wagons, tents, comic characters. No pianos.

Harry McKeon Jr.,
18 Rose Lane,
Flourtown, PA 19031
(215) 233-4094

◆ **Renwal plastic dolls and furnitures.** They are jointed dolls ranging in height from a few inches to more than two feet. They are embossed "Renwall USA" and a number. The furniture is very hard plastic, and made by Ideal and Acme. No foreign plastic furniture.

Growing hair dolls are also bought. Look for Crissy (common) and six others, especially black haired Tressy in a yellow Hawaiian dress for which she'll pay $50. "I don't buy naked dolls with cut up hair."

Judaline McNece,
1823 Santa Ysabela Dr.,
Rowland Heights, CA 91748

◆ **Modern collectible dolls** including Nancy Ann Storybook, Miss Revlon, Miss Toni, Bonnie Braids, Madame Alexander, Hollywood dolls, from 1920-65, especially black or Indian Nancy Ann in bisque or plastic. Give length, description, and whether clothes are original. Photocopy.

Sharon Vohs-Mohammed,
Box 822,
Auburn, IN 46706
(219) 925-5756

◆ *Barbie* **Dolls.** Wants to buy all 1960's Barbie dolls and accessories. It's worth your time to look, especially for clothes and accessories in original boxes, because some are hot items with collectors. Describe fully or make a photocopy. Buys for her collection and resale.

Marl Davidson, IBT,
5707 39th Street Circle E.,
Bradenton, FL 34203
(813) 751-6275

◆ **Madame Alexander dolls.** Buys dolls in all sizes and series made by this famous nonagenerian as long as they are not currently available from the factory. Indicate whether you have the original box (and paperwork?). Describe the size, series, and costume colors. Does not want dolls that have been heavily played with or are missing their costume.

Lia Sargent,
74 The Oaks,
Roslyn Estates, NY 11576
(516) 621-4883

◆ **Chinese "Door of Hope" dolls** sold by Christian missionaries to raise funds between 1909 and 1947. **Also china/bisque headed dolls** made before 1925. Will buy doll parts, bodies, heads, and old clothes. NO OFFERS.

Marjorie Gewalt,
94 E. Parkfield Ct.,
Racine WI 53402
(414) 639-2346

◆ **Realistic ethnic costume dolls,** 6"-14" tall, with nicely sculpted adult faces only. Faces may be composition, clay, wax, or wood but bodies can be of any materials. Asian, Mid-Eastern, and Eastern European dolls *only*, especially representing peasants, dancers, musicians, and theatrical characters such as Japanese Kabuki dolls. No baby dolls, cute dolls, homemade dolls, or dolls from Western Europe, Tropical Africa, or South America. Whether old or new, high quality is a must. If you wish to sell to her, a photograph is essential. Pays $50-$200.

Karen Kuykendall,
Box 845,
Casa Grande, AZ 85222
(602) 836-2066

◆ **Dolls made to promote a product or event.**
Maggie Kenyon,
Maggie's Place,
One Christopher #14G,
New York, NY 10013
(212) 675-3213

Soft dolls & Teddies

◆ **Teddy bears that are fully jointed with glass or shoebutton eyes.** Wants pre 1920 Steiff bears in any condition and will pay $1,000+ for those larger than 20" long. Not interested in any non-jointed bears or bears made after 1940. Also Teddy Bear books, postcards, photos, trays, etc. Polly also buys **stuffed animal toys on cast iron wheels.**

Polly Zarneski,
5803 N. Fleming,
Spokane, WA 99205
(509) 327-7622

◆ **Mohair teddy bears with long arms and big feet** made between 1903-1915 are wanted in all sizes as long as they are fully jointed. Also wants perfume and compact bears in various colors and any unusual mohair teddy or teddy related items. Also **Billy Possum stuffed dolls with shoebutton eyes,** President Taft's answer to Roosevelt's Teddies. All Billy Possum related items are also wanted including doll dishes and silverware, banks, and postcards. Mimi wants us to assure you that your dolls are going to a "loving home, not a dealer."

Mimi Hiscox,
12291 St. Mark,
Garden Grove, CA 92645
(213) 598-5450

◆ **Raggedy Ann and Andy dolls and other ephemera.** Also dolls of other characters by Johnny Gruelle, 1918-45, either homemade or commercial. They usually have shoebutton or printed eyes, and many early ones have a black outline around a red triangular nose. Raggedy Ann dolls from the 20's with wooden hearts are wanted in any condition. Other characters include Beloved Belindy, Johnny Mouse, Little Brown Bear, Eddie Elephant. This collector will pay $400 for iron bookends or doorstops of Ann and Andy marked "PF Volland," and wants a great deal of other Ann and Andy merchandise. Also a Schoenhut Danny Daddles, 12" tall, with top hat will bring to $200 if in fine condition.

Andrew Tabbat,
66 Cumberland St.,
San Francisco, CA 94110
(415) 641-8532

◆ **Troll dolls from 6" to 12" high, dressed or undressed,** as long as they are in good condition. Especially 1964 12" Dam Trolls which are worth $40-$45 if in original costume in excellent condition. Trolls are usually marked "Dam," "Wishnik," or "Lucky Schnook." Will pay $30 for any nude 12" troll, $20 for seated trolls, $15 for 2 headed trolls, and $10 tops for six to eight inch trolls. Six inch trolls wanted only in large quantities. No ceramic trolls or animal trolls.
> Karen Dellinger,
> Rt. 6, Box 19,
> Harrisonburg, VA 22801

◆ **Troll dolls from the 1960's.**
> Kevin Prediger,
> 120 Pierce St. #5,
> San Francisco, CA 94117
>   (415) 863-7284

◆ *Cabbage Patch Kids.* They can be any color or have any name. As long as they're from the 1983 *Coleco* issue and have freckles, she's interested in buying them. This widely advertised dealer issues frequent catalogs of these and similar dolls for sale.
> Marl Davidson, IBT,
> 5707 39th Street Circle E.,
> Bradenton, FL 34203
>   (813) 751-6275

Doll houses

◆ **Doll houses and miniatures,** especially Schoenhut and Bliss houses for which he will pay $500-$1,500. "We are one of the oldest and most experienced companies in the dollhouse and miniatures industry," Bob says, "and we will consider buying anything in miniatures that is old and in good condition." Their catalog of new doll house parts is fascinating!
> Robert Dankanics,
> The Dollhouse Factory,
> Box 456,
> Lebanon, NJ 08833
>   (201) 236-6404

◆ **Doll houses and furniture circa 1900,** but *only* wooden houses covered with colorfully lithographed paper. Especially wants houses made by *Bliss.*
> Jerry Phelps,
> 6013 Innes Trace Rd.,
> Louisville, KY 40222

◆ **Victorian doll and children's furniture.** Only wants original unaltered pieces.
> Ken Nordquist,
> 4233 Meridian Ave. N.,
> Seattle, WA 98103
>   (206) 634-3131

EDITOR'S NOTE: Original boxes can add substantial value to toys and dolls.

Pop Culture

◆ **Americana and pop culture of all sorts** is wanted by Ted Hake the longest established mail dealer and auctioneer of pop collectibles. Ted buys:

 (1) **Political and other pin back buttons;**
 (2) **Premiums from radio/TV or cereal;**
 (3) **Disney** characters pre 1970;
 (4) **Animation art** from Disney and other cartoons;
 (5) **Battery or wind up toys** especially those related to pop culture characters;
 (6) **Television related toys**, games, lunch boxes, etc. from 1950's and 60's;
 (7) **Singing cowboys** and other western film heroes memorabilia;
 (8) **Robots and space toys;**
 (9) Items directly related to the **U.S. Space Program;**
 (10) **Elvis Presley** pre-death items;
 (11) **Beatles** and other famous rock and roll personalities;
 (12) **Movie posters**, lobby cards, etc.;
 (13) **Toys of the 1960's** like *GI Joe, Capt. Action, Batman*, etc.;
 (14) "Just about any item from a famous character or personality."

Wants to know the material your item is made from, its size, any dates you can provide, and general condition. Offers made only after inspection. Hake has written four books on pin back buttons. No reproductions and no political items after 1968.

 Ted Hake,
 Hake's Americana,
 Box 1444,
 York, PA 17405
  (717) 848-1333 days

◆ **Comic character pin back buttons,** 1896-1966, from the earliest Yellow Kid character to all comic strip and comic book characters since. This Star Trek actor (Chekov) will pay as much as $500 for rare buttons like the Flash Gordon Movie Club or *Washington Herald* Mickey Mouse. Upon request he'll send you an illustrated wants list. Include your phone number.

 Walter Koenig,
 Box 4395,
 North Hollywood, CA 91607

◆ **Items depicting pre 1960 comic characters, superheroes, fictional detectives, movie heroes** and villains are purchased by this well known dealer:

 (1) **Toys and pin back buttons;**
 (2) **TV games, premiums, and ephemera;**
 (3) **Radio and cereal premiums;**
 (4) **Buttons from various radio "clubs",** worth up to $500;
 (5) **Movie Posters**, especially from serials, cartoons, and adventure movies;
 (6) **Disneyana** of all types, toys, books, posters, etc;
 (7) **Store stand-up figural displays;**
 (8) **Memorabilia associated with heroic characters** such as Tarzan, Batman, Superman, Flash Gordon, Captain Midnight, and the Lone Ranger.

"I want a very wide range of pop culture toys and pay more than anyone for the top range items." He warns, "There are so many repros and fakes now that I will no longer buy something sight unseen. Unmarked rings worth 2¢ and $1,500 can look quite similar to the inexperienced. I pay more! If you want to sell to me it has to be on my terms. You must write first, providing a full description of the item and its condition." If Rex is interested he will request that you ship for his inspection. Rex pays postage both ways on items he does not buy. "I have bought and sold this way for 18 years," he adds, pointing out numerous awards he has won for dealer integrity. Rex **does not want** Hopalong Cassidy and other 1950's cowboys, nor does he buy lunchboxes, common items, or anything damaged.

 Rex Miller,
 Rte. 1 Box 457D,
 East Prairie, MO 63845
  (314) 649-5048 (10 to 10)

◆ **All comic character toys and collectibles from the 1930's and 40's,** made of any material from cardboard to cast iron, especially Disneyana, radio premiums, and all **children's play suits** from western heroes to sailor suits. No Halloween costumes. There are also many pieces of **comic character related sheet music** Ralph is seeking.

 Ralph Eodice,
 Nevermore,
 161 Valley Rd.,
 Clifton, NJ 07013
  (201) 742-8278

◆ **Robots and space toys** made of tin before 1965, either windup or battery operated. "I'll pay $2,000 for Mr. Atomic and $750 for the Robby Space Patrol vehicle. Condition is important with these toys, so I'll pay an extra 10% for any toy in its original box." Also buys tin wind-up **comic character toys** made in the USA or Europe, whether working or not, and any **Disney toys** especially celluloid toys from the 1930's. **Santa Claus toys** are also of interest.

Larry Bruch,
Box 121,
Mountaintop, PA 18707
(717) 474-9202 eves

◆ **Pop culture treasures**, especially made of paper, including:
(1) **Comic books** 1890's-1980's, but only hero comics after 1963;
(2) **Sunday comics** 1890's-1959;
(3) **Original comic strip art**;
(4) **Walt Disney** books and anything else pre 1960;
(5) **Big Little Books** 1933-1950;
(6) **Movie magazines** 1920-1945;
(7) **Television collectibles** 1948-1970;
(8) **Radio and cereal premiums** and giveaways pre 1960;
(9) **Song magazines** 1929-1959 such as *Hit Parader* and *400 Songs*;
(10) **Popular music magazines** 1920-1959 including *Downbeat* and *Billboard*;
(11) **Pulp magazines** 1930-49 except love, Westerns, and crime magazines.

Wants nothing in poor condition. Ken has been in business 25 years, and pays Americans in U.S. dollars and drafts for quick payment.

Ken Mitchell,
710 Concacher Dr.,
Willowdale, Ontario M2M 3N6,
CANADA
(416) 222-5808

◆ **Political and advertising pinback buttons** from North Carolina and South Carolina. Also early buttons advertising newspapers or magazines from any location. Also buys **panorama photos** of groups in North Carolina or South Carolina.

Lew Powell,
700 E. Park Ave.,
Charlotte, NC 28203
(704) 334-0902

◆ **Radio premiums from children's adventure programs** such as The Lone Ranger, Jack Armstrong, Tom Mix, Sky King, Sgt. Preston, The Shadow, Doc Savage, Buck Rogers, Dick Tracy, Radio Orphan Annie, etc. Also **cereal boxes offering premiums** from the 30's through the 60's. Tom is author of the four volume book on Disney collectibles and will buy *anything related to Disney* that is not pictured in one of his price guides, especially Mickey Mouse items from the 1930's including Mickey with teeth, celluloid Mickey, wood and bisque Mickeys and any Disney wind-up toy. He also wants glossy Disney Studio Xmas cards, **character watches other than Mickey** (especially in gold), items in original boxes, and odd items. If your item is for sale, Tom says "I will not jeopardize my reputation by underpaying and making someone mad. But sellers must understand how much even small blemishes reduce the value of an item." Tom makes offers only on items he can see in person or in close up color slide.

Tom Tumbusch,
Box 292102,
Dayton, OH 45429
(513) 294-2250

◆ **Pop culture toys** including :
(1) **Disney and other comic character toys**;
(2) **Toys from radio, television, and movie characters**;
(3) **Beatles** and Elvis memorabilia;
(4) **G.I. Joe** dolls, accessories, pre 1970, in 12" size;
(5) *Renwall* plastic **doll house dolls** and accessories;
(6) **Toy vehicles** by *Smith Miller, Tonka, Doepke, Dinky, Renwal* (plastic), *Auburn* (rubber), *Arcade, Marx*, and *Wyandotte*;
(7) Superheroes, including **James Bond** and the **Man from U.N.C.L.E.**;
(8) **Cap guns** from the late 19th century;
(9) **Cap guns** from western movie or TV characters.

Detailed description including dimensions is required. Will make offers only on items he personally inspects.

William Hamburg,
Box 1305,
Woodland Hills, CA 91365
(818) 346-9884

◆ **Wind-up and battery operated toys** made in Germany, Japan, or the US, including comic characters, carnival items like merry-go-rounds, airplanes (no jets), and space toys. "I'll pay over $1,000 for Mr. Atomic robot or Mickey the Magician, two battery toys." He doesn't want common items like Charlie Weaver bartender, plastic toys, wind up dogs, trains, dolls, items with missing parts, or toys made in the third world. Don is a toy consultant and restorer. Indicate the condition of the item and box, and whether there is any restoration or repainting.

Don Hultzman,
5026 Sleepy Hollow Rd.,
Medina, OH 44256
(216) 225-2668

◆ **Toy robots from 1950-1972.** Wants Mr. Atomic, Robby the Robot, and the Robby Space Patrol vehicle among others. Especially in original boxes! Also buys other **German and Japanese wind-up, friction, and battery operated toys**, vehicles, and comic characters.

Chris Savino,
Box 419,
Breesport, NY 14816
(607) 739-3106

◆ **Cereal boxes with advertisements for giveaways or premiums**, or the premiums themselves, before 1970. Jerry also buys radio, TV, and movie cowboy and space premiums and pre 1960 *Crackerjack* boxes, premiums, and signs. Send for his wants list of other pop culture ephemera. No Orphan Annie decoders or manuals. NO OFFERS.

Jerry Doxey,
HCR#1, Box 343,
Sciota, PA 18354
(717) 992-7477

◆ **Badges, buttons, and pins:** "I'll buy all good pins, buttons, or badges, including Disney, movie, TV, political, protest, railroad, Scout, automotive, police, fraternal order, you name it. I will consider any button, badge or pin collection earlier than 1968. Make a photocopy of what you have, since written descriptions aren't adequate for these items."

Fred Swindall,
111 NW 2nd Ave.,
Portland, OR 97209
(503) 234-0678

◆ **Cereal boxes depicting comic characters or radio show giveaways.** Wants 1930-1959 boxes and the premiums they offered. Also wants a wide range of 1930-59 **Lone Ranger** items including dolls, games, posters, premiums, gun sets, carnival plaster figures, and autographs. Also buys **comic book subscription giveaway premiums**, membership cards, pins, photos, and comic character pictures. In general, John is interested in most **comic and pop culture figures** from the 1930's and 40's, including Felix and Betty Boop. A series of 1940's *Cheerios* boxes featuring Disney characters is particularly desirable as is the 1946 Atom Bomb ring box of *Kix*.

John Fawcett,
Art Dept. U-99, U of Conn.,
Storrs, CT 06268
(203) 429-9228 eves

◆ **TV related memorabilia.** "I'll buy books, games, gum cards, lunch boxes, soundtrack albums, theme songs, toys, and especially TV fan type magazines like *TV-Radio Mirron, TV Fan, TV Carnival, TV Western* and the like as well as paperback books spun off from TV series. Items from before 1970 are preferred. Examine your fan magazines carefully and note if they have had pictures clipped. No movie fan mags.

Ross Hartsough,
Psych Dept, U of Manitoba,
Winnipeg, R3T 2N2
CANADA

◆ **Yellow Kid character items.** Wants tins, buttons, dolls, paper items, *anything*.

Craig Koste,
RD #2 Box 194,
Morrisonville, NY 12962
(518) 643-8173

◆ **Hopalong Cassidy collectibles.**
Ron Pieczkowski,
1707 Orange Hill Drive,
Brandon, FL 33511

◆ **Lone Ranger items.** Posters, cereal boxes, dolls, books with dust jackets, paper, radios, and premiums, among other items.

John Fawcett, RR #2,
720 Middle Turnpike,
Storrs, CT 06268

◆ **Smokey the Bear ephemera.**
Thomas McKinnon,
Box 86,
Wagram, NC 28396

◆ **Disneyana pre 1946**, especially: (1) Mickey and Donald painted plaster lamps, (2) Waddle Books from the 1930's, (3) animation cels and original art for WWII combat insignia, (4) Mickey, Minnie, and Donald costume dolls, (5) *Vernon Kilns* ceramic statues, (6) tin and celluloid toys of Disney characters, and (7) wood or porcelain figurines. Art from the 1950's is of interest, but nothing newer. Include dimensions, color, manufacturer's markings, condition (including all damage or missing parts. Dennis will make offers for items "only when I'm holding it in my hand," preferring you to set the price. Include your phone number when you write.
Dennis Books, Comic Characters,
Box 99142,
Seattle, WA 98199
(206) 283-0532

◆ **Captain Marvel, Captain Marvel Jr., and Mary Marvel memorabilia** including toys, buttons, posters, comic books, mechanical items, and statues. Also items related to similar Fawcett characters.
Michael Gronsky,
9833 Meadowcroft Lane,
Gaithersburg, MD 20879

◆ **Batman.** "I'll buy Batman toys, games, figures, paper, etc., especially from the 60's."
Ed Osepowicz,
43 Lincoln Ave.,
Northampton, MA 01060

◆ **Dick Tracy collectibles.** "I'm buying premiums, toys, books, paper, figures...anything!"
Larry Doucet,
2351 Sultana Dr.,
Yorktown Heights, NY 10598

◆ **Howdy Doody memorabilia.**
John Andreae,
51122 Mill Run,
Granger, IN 46530
(219) 272-2337

◆ **Snoopy and Peanuts toys and memorabilia** such as tin items made by *Chein*, wooden items by *ANRI*, papier mache statues by Determined, and a variety of toys by *AVIVA*. Also plaster or composition statues, pin back buttons, rubber dolls, wooden music boxes, and many other items. Prefer items in original boxes but will consider all (and only) items which have a United Features Syndicate or UFS mark. No ceramic music boxes, plates, or toys made after 1972.
Michael Dyer,
230 Eldon Dr. N.W.,
Warren, OH 44483
(216) 847-9044

◆ *Snoopy* and *Peanuts* **toys and memorabilia** such as ceramics, music boxes, advertising, pins, buttons, books, magazines, toys. Especially wants a *Snoopy Says* See and Say game, *Charlie Brown's Talking Book*, and wooden Snoopy music boxes, pianos, etc. Boxes are needed for many of his toys, so don't throw one away. All items *must* be marked United Features (UFS). **Does not want** plush dogs, lunchboxes, school bags, or kiddie clothing.
Freddi Margolin,
12 Lawrence Lane,
Bay Shore, NY 11706
(516) 666-6861

◆ **Uncle Wiggily items** including books, sunday comics, puzzles, toys, mugs, dishes, games, and "all other memorabilia." Especially Uncle Wiggley's hollow stump bungalow and stand-up figures, *Put-Together* puzzles, Marx *Crazy Car* wind-up, and decorated tin Uncle Wiggily cup.
Martin Mc Caw,
1124 School Avenue,
Walla Walla, WA 99362
(509) 525-6257

◆ **Uncle Wiggily items** including toys, paper dolls, 1st edition books, comics, etc.
Audrey Buffington,
2 Old Farm Rd.,
Wayland, MA 01778

◆ **Alice In Wonderland illustrated books and memorabilia** including films, figurines, tins, toys, games, puzzles, posters, greeting cards, dolls, etc. Especially wants a Beswick china figurine of the Cheshire Cat, but encourages all inquiries. Also wants other Lewis Carroll items, including **books, letters, and personal articles associated with Carroll.** No books published by Whit-man or illustrated by John Tenniel but would love the Appleton Alice of 1866 $1,000 worth!
Joel Birenbaum,
2486 Brunswick Circle #A1,
Woodridge, IL 60517
(312) 968-0664

◆ **Beany & Cecil memorabilia,** not only from the old *Time for Beany* of the 1950's but also from the animated TV series of the 60's. Wants a Beany cookie jar from with Beany's face, a plaster Cecil the Sea-Sick Sea Serpent lamp, program scripts and cels, kinescopes, and other items associated with the show and its creator, Bob Clampett. The Felasca's have started a Beany club for $15 and will soon have a book out on Beany memorabilia.
Jeff and Maria Falasca
20159 Cohasset Street #5,
Canoga Park, CA 91306
(818) 718-8202

◆ **Alice In Wonderland memorabilia** including dolls, figurines, tins, cookie jars, coffee mugs, and "anything else." Especially editions of **books in obscure languages,** or editions with lesser known illustrators (Allen, Adams, Appleton, McEune, Norfield, or Sinclair). Alice encourages you to quote all Alice items.
Alice Berkey,
127 Alleyne Dr.,
Pittsburgh, PA 15215
(412) 782-2686

◆ **Tarzan and Edgar Rice Burroughs memorabilia** including books, magazines, and collectibles. This enormous Library collection still seeks items, such as the 1915 edition of *Return of Tarzan* with a dust jacket for which they'll pay well over $1,000. Also seeking early Tarzan movies, foreign editions, Armed Services Editions and many smaller items associated with Burroughs or any of his characters. George advises, "Don't waste your time if your items aren't in fine to mint condition, including dust jackets." Please describe what you have carefully, give a guarantee, and tell what form you'd like payment.
George McWhorter,
Burroughs Memorial Collection,
University of Louisville,
Louisville, KY 40292
(502) 588-8729

EDITOR'S NOTE: Some of these "pop culture" toys can be surprisingly valuable, so be careful about setting prices if you don't know what you're doing.

Dr. Hyman's Prescription

Collectors tend to be fussy about condition. Comic collectors are among the fussiest. What you think looks "pretty good" might be graded fair or poor by experts.

Every tiny crease, tear, wrinkle, misprint, and off center or rusty staple affects the value of comic books. Severe grading standards are suggested in comic book price guides, and collectors follow them religiously.

If you have comics for sale, it will be worth your while to read Overstreet's *The Comic Book Price Guide.* It is comprehensive, easy to use, and the reference used by nearly all collector's and dealers. You can purchase the latest edition through any bookstore ($15-20) . Most libraries can obtain it for you through interlibrary loan.

The Comic Book Price Guide contains current "prices" for nearly every American comic book. You will also find pages of ads from comic dealers. Dealers, and our buyers, generally pay from 30% - 70% of prices quoted, depending on dealer's finances, customer wants, and that month's market.

Comic collectors and dealers will usually request that you send your items for inspection prior to payment. Since the value of comics is so tightly linked to condition, this is a reasonable request.

Ask your post office for "return receipt requested" service which costs under $1 and requires the recipient to sign for the package. Always include a list of what you are sending and keep a copy of the list for yourself. Cautious sellers photocopy the covers of what they send, since the creases on the cover are like a fingerprint and can identify *your* comic should it be necessary.

tony hyman

Comic Books

◆ **All comic books in fine condition 1900-69,** *Big Little Books* 1932-1950, and Sunday comics 1929-59 *but nothing brittle or damaged.* Also original comic book or comic strip art. Pays in U.S. dollars and bank drafts.
Ken Mitchell,
710 Concacher Dr.,
Willowdale, Ontario M2M 3N6,
CANADA

◆ **All 10¢ comic books.** I'll pay 50%-100% of price guide figures. No comics which sold for more than a dime originally. Also **comic strip original art** for daily or Sunday strips.
Gary Colabuono,
Moondog's,
301 Lively Blvd.,
Elk Grove Village, IL 60007
(800) 344-6060

◆ **Comic books featuring movie cowboys** especially John Wayne, Roy Rogers, Sunset Carson, and Lash LaRue. All must be complete and in sound condition. Also **pre 1960 comic books based on television shows.** Generally pays approximately 50% of Overstreet.
Larry Maddy,
Rt. 4, Box 147,
Ironton, OH 45638

◆ **Pre 1968 comic books,** *Better Little Books* and *Big Little Books.* Twenty year vet dealer.
Hugh O'Kennon,
2204 Haviland Dr.,
Richmond, VA 23229
(804) 270-2465

◆ *MAD* **Magazine and associated memorabilia** including *MAD* Specials, annuals, posters, bumper stickers, and other items originally sold by *MAD.* Especially wants small plaster busts and the *MAD* straight jacket. Also all Alfred E. Neuman memorabilia. Buys *MAD's* under number 150 only.
Claude Held,
Box 218,
Buffalo, NY 14225

◆ **Full color comic sections from Sunday newspapers,** 1900-1940 in good or better condition. Value depends on several factors. Write or phone giving the city, newspaper, date, number of pages, and comics included. Free appraisals.
Al Felden,
8945 Fairfield St.,
Philadelphia, PA 19152
(215) 677-0657

◆ **Sunday comic sections,** 1930-60. Prefers to purchase runs of several years. "A few odd sections are not needed." He especially wants the color comics from the Saturday issues of the Chicago or the NY *Journal American,* 1934-64.
Claude Held,
Box 218,
Buffalo, NY 14225

◆ **Sunday and daily adventure comic strips, 1930-60** such as *Tarzan, Prince Valiant, Flash Gordon, Terry and the Pirates, Steve Canyon, Casey Ruggles, Lance, Captain Easy,* and *Dick Tracy.* No single dailies. No humor strips. No torn strips.
Carl Horak,
1319 108th Ave.,
SW Calgary, Alberta T2W 0C6,
CANADA

Comic Art

◆ **Original American comic art, 1860 - 1950,** from Nast to comic books, strips, and movies.
   Ron Graham,
   8167 Park Ave.,
   Forestville, CA 95436
      (707) 887-2856

◆ **Original artwork for comic strips and cartoons, 1920-1950,** especially animation cels from Disney, Warner Bros, etc., for which this 25 year veteran has paid as much as $12,000. Jerry also buys original art from comic strips and magazines cartoons. Information he wants includes title, artist, description, the year, and any documentation you might have. In your description of condition, note any yellowing, folds, tears, cracked or missing paint, paste overs, etc. He does not want reproductions from newspapers or magazines; nor does he buy posters or prints of any type. Museum Graphics publishes a bimonthly newsletter and price list, available for $2 a year.
   Jerry Muller,
   Museum Graphics,
   Box 10743,
   Costa Mesa, CA 92627
      (714) 540-0808

◆ **Original comic strip, caricature, or editorial cartoon art.** Any era, any country.
   Bill the Booky,
   PO Box 6228,
   Long Island City, NY 11106
      (718) 728-4791

◆ **Original comic art by Carl Barks and others.** "Although I'll buy cels, paintings, and drawings of many different cartoonists, I am particularly interested in Barks, one of Disney's top artists. If I don't buy what you have, there's a good chance I know people who will."
   Michael Autrey, Bookseller,
   13624 Franklin St. #5,
   Whittier, CA 90602
      (213) 945-6719

◆ **Comic strip art by any noted cartoonist.** Dennis issues an illustrated annual catalog.
   Dennis Books,
   Comic Character Shop,
   Box 99142,
   Seattle, WA 98199
      (206) 283-0532 eves

EDITOR'S NOTE: Drawings signed by Walt Disney have sold for more than $100,000. Most comic art sells for $50-$2,000. Value depends on the artist, the subject matter, the age, and the condition. R. Outcault's work is particularly valuable.

6
Entertainment

Dr. Hyman's Prescription

As you'll learn when reading this chapter, almost anything associated with entertainment is collected by someone.

If you don't find a listing in the Index for the item you would like to sell, there are many general dealers in pop culture who might help you, so check Chapter 5 as well.

Although highly valued movie memorabilia does continue to surface, most star photos and production stills from films are of limited value.

Posters from popular stars and important or cult films can bring in the hundreds of dollars and on rare occasion a great deal more.

Sadly, many of the movie star autographs and signed photos are not genuine, but signed by secretaries and machines. Their signatures on handwritten letters and on scripts are of more interest. Stars to watch for include female stars, cult comedians (Laurel & Hardy, Three Stooges, etc.), and those who seldom signed autographs such as James Dean or Mick Jagger.

Follow general guidelines for describing the type of item you have to sell. Whenever possible, it's to your advantage to send photocopies.

tony hyman

Movies

◆ **Kinetoscopes and peep machines from old arcades and amusement parks.** He does not buy a great many machines, instead is selectively looking for a few fine examples with historical or intrinsic value. "Amateurs can't tell one machine from another. An expert should look at all old arcade machines." Pays $7,500 for an Edison Kinetoscope from 1894. He suggests you shoot a roll of high speed 35mm film, covering all aspects of whatever machine you might wish to sell. Send him the roll and he'll process it and reimburse you for your film. That's a good deal so it's not fair to waste his time with junk or late model machines. *"It is very important for me to know where you got your machine."* Richard is author of numerous books on slot machines, trade stimulators, pinball, and arcade machines and is historical editor of *The Coin Slot*, the quarterly magazine for people who collect coin operated machines.

Richard Bueschel,
414 N. Prospect Manor Ave.,
Mt. Prospect, IL 60056
(312) 498-9300 days

◆ **Professional motion picture cameras from the silent era,** 1900-1927, especially with wooden bodies and hand cranks, although some desirable cameras have metal bodies and electric motors. They range in size from small hand held to as large as suitcases. When describing, pay particular attention to the size, finish, and whether the film magazine is square or round, inside or outside the camera. There are a number of cameras that can be worth more than $1,000 to him, including the Bell & Howell #2709 and machines by Mitchell or Gaumont. No home movie or 16mm. No motion picture projectors. Wes is a member of numerous clubs, and is publisher of *Sixteen Frames*, a quarterly bulletin for collectors of early cine equipment.

Wes Lambert,
1568 Dapple Ave.,
Camarillo, CA 93010
(805) 482-5331

◆ **Movie projectors and films pre 1960** in all gauges including kinescopes, Hollywood theatrical films, Castle, Official and others. Also some good 16mm home movies from the 1930's and 40's. Also old projectors, mutoscopes, and any other machines having to do with the viewing of motion pictures, including toy projectors designed to run movies. Also wants film catalogs from Castle and others. Wants a flawless mint *Mills* **Pan-O-Ram machine** which showed 3 minute movies for a dime.

Phil Johnson,
Box 2508,
Texas City, TX 77590
(409) 935-6539

◆ **Anything depicting silent movie stars** including coming attraction slides, posters, lobby cards, figurines, sheet music, pin back buttons, paper dolls, plates, especially a Star Players photo plate of Bryant Washburn and anything featuring Our Gang or Jackie Coogan. Nothing from the talkies or from later stars. No autographs or photographs from any period.

Richard Davis,
9500 Old Georgetown Rd.,
Bethesda, MD 20814
(301) 530-5904

◆ **Paper movie ephemera 1925-1950** including movie heralds, posters, sheet music, photographs, and studio disks of film music. **Studio disks** were 78rpm for studio use only. Also interested in movie magazines 1930-1944 and in trade journals sent to theater owners.

Buddy McDaniel,
2802 West 18th St.,
Wichita, KS 67203
(316) 942-3561

◆ **Original studio production movie scripts** with original binders or covers whenever possible. Not interested in Xerox© copies, TV scripts, or unproduced scripts unless by very important writers. When describing your script, indicate whether it has its cover, what draft (or the date), whether all pages are present, whether there are notations, the name of the author.

Grayson Cook,
367 W. Avenue 42,
Los Angeles, CA 90065
(213) 227-8899

◆ **Cartoon posters from silent movies.** "I buy posters featuring cartoon characters like Felix the Cat, Out of the Inkwell, and other silents, but will consider other silent movie posters as well."
Richard Davis,
9500 Old Georgetown Rd.,
Bethesda, MD 20814
(301) 530-5904

◆ **Movie memorabilia about cowboy heroes, especially John Wayne** 1930-55. Buys and sells comic books, posters, lobby cards, photos, etc. "Almost any material on this subject is wanted."
Larry Maddy,
2529 S. 12th Street,
Ironton, OH 45638

◆ **B Western cowboy star memorabilia** from Hopalong Cassidy, Tom Mix, Ken Maynard, Roy Rogers, Tex Ritter and especially Gene Autry. "I'll buy buttons, photos, games, toy guns, radio giveaways, autographs, books, and anything else that has to do with these stars of yesteryear." Dennis is interested only in the ephemera of B westerns, not epics, and does not buy damaged or overpriced items.
Dennis Schulte,
8th Ave., NW,
Waukon, IA 52172

◆ *Gone With the Wind* **items** associated with the film, the book, or its author. Wants book and Mitchell related items 1936-1965, foreign language editions of the book, movie scripts, movie posters, banners, props from the film, and all the promotional items such as dolls, games, scarfs, book ends, figurines, jewelry, nail polish, paint books, paper dolls, and more. Nothing printed after 1965.
Herb Bridges,
Box 192,
Sharpsburg, GA 30277
(404) 253-4934

◆ *Gone with the Wind* **memorabilia from 1939 only** including jewelry, games, posters, music, paper dolls, press books, and the like. No reproductions, story books, fakes, copies, or junk. NO OFFERS.
Frank Garcia,
8963 SW 34th Street,
Miami, FL 33165

◆ **Comedy movie posters (and a few others).** Dennis wants original posters from movies by The Marx Brothers, W.C. Fields, The Three Stooges, Laurel and Hardy, Buster Keaton, Charlie Chaplin, and Woody Allen. He **also** wants movie material from specific films: *Psycho, Bedtime for Bonzo, 2001: A Space Odyssey, Some Like It Hot, Midnight Cowboy, Clockwork Orange,* and *The Kid From Cleveland.* Prefers American posters but will consider foreign editions. When describing posters, mention [1] folds, tears, and stains, [2] whether rolled or linen backed, [3] if it is an original release poster, and [4] how you came to own the poster. Photo desirable.
Dennis Horwitz,
425 Short Trail,
Topanga, CA 90290

◆ **Movie glossies** (8 x 10 publicity photos) pre 1960 and **casting directories** pre 1960. No other movie items, please.
Ken Jones,
100 Manor Dr.,
Columbia, MO 65203

◆ **Movie memorabilia** including autographs of stars, promotional stills, lobby cards, and posters. This dealer is **primarily interested in buying in bulk** rather than in buying single items from private parties, unless, of course, the items were unusually good. Everything is purchased for resale.
Ralph Bowman,
Paper Gallery,
5349 Wheaton Street,
La Mesa, CA 92042
(619) 462-6268

◆ **Movie memorabilia** 1920-59, including posters of all sizes, inserts, lobby cards. Also wants movie autographs and magazines. Stars of particular interest include Jean Harlow, Marlene Dietrich, Bette Davis, Errol Flynn, James Cagney, Humphrey Bogart, James Dean, and Marilyn Monroe. Condition on all material is important. Seller must give phone number.
Gary Vaughn,
Box 954,
Clarksville, TN 37041
(615) 552-7852 eves

◆ *E.T. (The Extra Terrestrial)* ephemera. Has been collecting since the movie first came out sohe owns all the common stuff. Is very interested in larger pieces such as the blanket and sleeping bag, and would especially like to get point of purchase displays used in stores for *Reese's Pieces, Budweiser* beer, *Texas Instruments Speak n Spell,* and other *E.T.* endorsed products. Will consider any *E.T.* item if you send a photocopy and SASE.
> Cliff DeManty,
> 9300 Santa Fe Springs Rd.,
> Santa Fe Springs, CA 90670
> (213) 946-2511

◆ **Movie posters, lobby cards, and still photos** pre 1950 especially from major stars like Jean Harlow, Boris Karloff, Laurel and Hardy, etc. Will buy 1950's posters from Monroe, James Dean, and John Wayne movies only. All types of films (comedies, Westerns, Sci-fi, etc.) are wanted. No reprints, reissues, or magazine ads. Prefer to buy in quantity. Give title of movie, releasing company, major star, size, and condition of poster.
> Gene Arnold,
> 2234 South Blvd.,
> Houston, TX 77098
> (713) 528-1880

◆ **Castle newsreels,** 1937-1975, sound or silent, 16mm or 8mm, as long as they are complete. No shortened 50' or 100' versions are wanted. Will also buy selected titles of Castle space and moon flight films, and 200' or longer 8mm comedies by Laurel and Hardy or Our Gang if made before 1935. Please list film number if possible.
> Newsreels,
> Box 295,
> Cliffside Park, NJ 07010

◆ **Selected 16mm home movies from the 1930's and 40's.** Write about what you have.
> Phil Johnson,
> Box 2508,
> Texas City, TX 77590
> (409) 935-6539

Movie stars

◆ **Shirley Temple memorabilia** especially sheet music and "unusual stuff" including paper dolls and jewelry. Pays $50 for early press books featuring Shirley.
> Frank Garcia,
> 8963 SW 34th Street,
> Miami, FL 33165

◆ **Shirley Temple items** from her child star days. No paper.
> Jack Matlack,
> Box 14067,
> Portland, OR 97214

◆ **Humphrey Bogart and Woody Allen memorabilia.** "I want anything of interest about these two personalities." Among special wants, Dennis lists film or video copies of early Bogart films: *Broadway's Like That, A Devil with Women, Body and Soul, Bad Sister, A Holy Terror,* and *Women of all Nations.*
> Dennis Horwitz,
> 425 Short Trail,
> Topanga, CA 90290

◆ **James Dean memorabilia** including books, magazines, photos, records, sheet music, lobby cards, film programs and posters, gum cards, scrapbooks, novelty items, plates, etc. Description should include size, year, condition, and how much you want for it.
> David Loehr,
> JADE,
> GPO Box 7961,
> New York, NY 10116

◆ **Jeanette MacDonald and Nelson Eddy memorabilia.** Wants scrapbooks and original material. Send description and asking price.
> IBT Hanson,
> Box 1222,
> Edgewood, MD 21040

◆ **Ruth Etting anything.** "I'll buy anything pertaining to and picturing Ruth Etting that I don't already own. Seeking musical short subjects, photographs, sheet music, radio magazines, theater playbills, posters, stereoviews, etc., that feature her."
Russell Wilson,
14 Reynolds Drive,
Wallingford, CT 06492

◆ **Rudolph Valentino.** Anything on this silent star: books, magazines, photos, etc.
Stella Grace,
Box 683,
Coventry, RI 02816
(401) 828-0463

◆ **Three Stooges and other comedy team memorabilia.** Frank buys and sells.
Frank Reighter,
10220 Calera Rd.,
Philadelphia, PA 19114
(215) 637-5744

◆ **Claudia Cardinale, Catherine Deneuve, Rosanna Schiaffino, and Maria Michi** photos (both glossies and clippings) and other items.
Taylor Warren,
7713 Enfield Ave., #102,
Norfolk, VA 23505

Amusements

◆ **Carnegie Hall memorabilia.** Seeking relics of its own past, the Carnegie Hall Corporation wants especially to find programs and stagebills from 1892-98, 1929-31, and 1944-45. Also photos of the building in construction, or any interior shots of performers or speakers on stage. Also recordings, films, and posters of events as well as any administrative records of Hall history. Any type performances wanted.
Gino Francesconi, Archivist
Carnegie Hall Corporation
881 Seventh Ave.,
New York, NY 10019
(212) 903-9629

◆ **Ferris Wheel memorabilia** related to the Columbian Expo (1893) and the St. Louis World's Fair (1904), including folders, guide books, photos of the wheel (even in the background), sheet music, drawings, newspaper or diary accounts of first time riders. This serious historian will pay $1,500 for blueprints of the wheel.
Richard Bueschel,
414 N. Prospect Manor Ave.,
Mt. Prospect, IL 60056

◆ **Amusement park memorabilia:** catalogs, brochures, photos, tickets, stationery, sheet music, letterheads, pennants, tokens, advertisements, books, postcards, and anything else.
Jim Abbate,
1005 Hyde Park Lane,
Naperville, IL 60565

◆ **Roller coaster and amusement park memorabilia** including official or amateur photos, prints, blueprints, postcards, souvenirs, home movies, and *anything* else, no matter how small or odd that is remotely related to roller coasters or amusement parks. This long time veteran collector has ridden 230 different roller coasters, once for 9 hours straight!
Thomas Keefe,
161 Forest St.,
New Lenox, IL 60451

◆ **Mardi Gras souvenirs, tokens, and other ephemera** are wanted, especially pre 1900 ball invitations and colorful Carnival Bulletins originally printed in local newspapers. Hardy and his wife are always looking for photographs, postcards, early magazine articles, and other items from before 1940 which they can reproduce in their annual *Mardi Gras Guide*. Please inquire about all illustrated items and this prominent New Orleans collector will help you with pricing.
Arthur Hardy,
Box 8058,
New Orleans, LA 70182
(504) 282-2326

◆ **Disneyland souvenirs.** Dean will buy all types including ceramic figurines, guidebooks, maps, buttons, pins, coins, postcards, employee materials,etc. Items **must** be marked 'Disneyland.' Also will buy **Disneykins,** plastic figurines of Disney characters sold by *Marx* in the 1950's and 60's. Also will buy anything related to **Tinkerbell.** Would love to get Walt's autograph, Disneyland items from 1955, and a Tinkerbell glow-in-the-dark wand. Everything must be in excellent condition. Items may be sent on approval. Edits a Disney button newsletter.

Dean Mancina,
Box 2274,
Seal Beach, CA 90740
(213) 431-5671

◆ **Disneyland souvenirs and memorabilia** "from the California park" pre 1980, including maps, guidebooks, tickets, food wrappers, brochures, parking tickets, special event programs, posters, passes, postcards, and what have you. This serious collector has been to Disneyland more than once a month for thirty years! No DisneyWorld (Florida). Especially wants 1961 Marx playset.

Linda Cervon,
443 N. Gardner,
Hollywood, CA 90036

◆ **Minstrel memorabilia of all sorts.** "I'll buy playbills, autographs, letters written by minstrels, news clippings, postcards, posters, radio and TV programs, rare book and magazine articles, recordings, and miscellaneous artifacts. I'm particularly interested in Bert Williams, Al Jolson, Eddie Cantor, Sophie Tucker, and Jimmy Durante. Has a lengthy multi-part wants list which details books, TV shows, movies, phonograph records, and other items he seeks. If you have *anything* related to minstrels or minstrel shows, give Norm a call. Norm is a professional recreator of minstrel shows and serious researcher of that entertainment.

Norman Conrad,
Box 184,
East Walpole, MA 02032
(508) 668-6926 eves

◆ **Harry Houdini memorabilia** including books, magazines and newspaper articles, photos, handbills, pamphlets, autographs, posters, personal apparatus and belongings. Anything relating to Houdini will probably be of interest. He especially wants to find a voice recording of Houdini or copies of any of his silent movies (including home movies) except *The Man From Beyond.* If you are offering personal apparatus of effects you must explain why you know it is from Houdini. You may price or he will make offer. Standard bibliographic information when offering books. Art is a 15 year veteran collector and happy to provide free appraisals and make offers.

Arthur Moses,
3512 Wosley,
Ft. Worth, TX 76133
(817) 294-2494

◆ **Magic apparatus of all sorts** including all paraphernalia and props, escape devices, tokens, programs, books, and other ephemera. Has a particular interest in pre 1900 posters, original photos of Houdini, and a complete set of Houdini letters, one on each of his twelve letterheads (worth $5,000 if you have it). A complete set of Thayer Manufacturing's wooden turned devices (1910-20) would be worth $12,000 to some lucky seller. No items after 1950, newspaper clippings, radio premiums, or pulp books issued by Wehman Bros. An illustrated catalog of magic books and devices is available for $5 from this 18 year veteran collector dealer.

Mario Carrandi Jr.,
122 Monroe Ave.,
Belle Mead, NJ 08502
(201) 874-0630

◆ **Magic posters and memorabilia.**
Ken Trombly,
5131 Massachusetts Ave.,
Bethesda, MD 20816
(301) 320-2360 eves

◆ **Broadway theater ephemera** including photos, posters, programs, etc., **except** postcards. Describe or photocopy.
C. Meunier,
498 Lakeview Ave.,
Clifton, NJ 07011

◆ **Theatrical lighting from the gas-light era.** "I'll buy anything you have dealing with theatrical lighting, particularly gas and limelighting. I want spotlights themselves, stage lights, footlights, parts, manuals, patents, manuals, and catalogs. I will even buy photocopies of documents related to the history of their development and use." A good description includes how complete the item is, any maker's information, and a good sketch or photo. No magic lantern or cinema projectors as a rule but Lindsay will buy projector literature that has information about limelight that he can use in his research. "I would be grateful if people set the price they want." Lindsay would pay as much as $400 for a perfect condition complete spotlight from the mid 1800's.

    Lindsay Lambert,
    324-B Somerset St. W.,
    Ottawa, Ontario K2P 0J9, Canada

◆ **Broadway theater playbills,** posters, programs, and memorabilia, from any era. Buys and sells.

    P. Newman,
    2714 Webster,
    San Francisco, CA 94123

◆ **Can-Can dancers.** Primarily interested in movie and TV portrayals in B-Westerns and musicals rather than in actual French can-can. Especially wants film clips and costumes, but will buy glossies, clippings, posters, prints, dolls, and just about anything else with traditional froufrou dresses and ruffled underskirts. Photocopy or color photo requested. Will reimburse expenses upon request. Please tell him where you got any print material.

    Taylor Warren,
    7713 Enfield Ave., #102,
    Norfolk, VA 23505

◆ **Theater programs and souvenirs** especially items related to an anniversary such as 50th performance, 100th performance, etc. Wants pre 1920 items mostly.

    D. Eliot,
    529 W. 42nd St. #5R,
    New York, NY 10036
    (212) 563-5444

◆ **Circus ephemera** is sought, including real photos, posters, programs, prints, route cards, books, toys, postcards, and painted sideshow banners.

    Ross Wandrey,
    1603 Morse,
    Houston, TX 77109

◆ **Circus ephemera.** "I'll buy anything directly related to circuses, especially Barnum's. Includes posters, programs, couriers, bills, photos, route books, etc.

    Al Mordas,
    66 Surrey Drive,
    Bristol, CT 06010

◆ **Buffalo Bill's Wild West Show.** Wants all ephemera including programs, photos, business forms, advertising, pre 1918 clippings, and miscellany of all kinds. No books. Send Xerox©.

    Melvin Schulte,
    211 Fourth Ave., SW,
    Pocahontas, IA 50574

◆ **The National Orange Show, San Bernardino, CA,** 1911-1920, souvenirs and paper ephemera.

    Gary Crabtree,
    Box 3843,
    San Bernardino, CA 92413

◆ **Chalk carnival prizes,** especially cartoon and movie characters or figures marked *Jenkins, Rainwater, Venice Dolls,* or *Gittins.* No animals[except movie or comic characters. The earliest figures were not painted on the back and have a pink cast to the plaster. When describing what you have, mention whether or not is has glitter highlights.

    Thomas Morris,
    49 Monterey Dr.,
    Medford, OR 97504
      (503) 779-3164

World's Fair

◆ **International Expositions and Fairs, 1851-1940.** The library buys print and photographic materials including reports from various governmental and official bodies relating to the construction, exhibits, awards, and demolition of expositions. Also interested in letters, sheet music, tickets, passes, award medals, maps, and photos (both commercial and non commercial). The library does not collect exposition artifacts or souvenirs. "Purchase offers are made based on the value to the collection rather than on any other consideration."
Ron Mahoney,
Head of Special Collections,
Madden Library,
Calif. State University,
Fresno, CA 93740
(209) 294-2595

◆ **1851 Crystal Palace memorabilia** including books, engravings, stereo cards, photos, newspapers, tickets, guidebooks, awards, and miscellaneous artifacts made of paper, glass, porcelain, metal, or something else. Ron wants **all material on the building's history (1851-1937),** but is especially interested in early years.
Ronald Lowden, Jr.,
314 Chestnut Ave.,
Narberth, PA 19072
(215) 667-0257

◆ **1876 Centennial** and other 19th century fairs. Wants all types of items, including souvenirs, china, glassware, textiles, and items of metal.
Andy Rudoff,
Box 111,
Oceanport, NJ 07757
(201) 542-3712

◆ **1876 Centennial** collectibles.
Robert Cohen,
3217 Polk Road,
Norristown, PA 19403

◆ **1895 Atlanta Cotton States Exposition** memorabilia, especially medals, tokens, and postcards. Also **agriculture medals from Georgia state fairs.**
R.W. Colbert,
4156 Livsey Rd.,
Tucker, GA 30084

◆ **1904 World's Fair in St. Louis** and other US expositions from 1876 to 1939. Especially *Ingersoll* souvenir watches, clocks, banks, lamps, steins, lithopanes, hold to light postcards, large china souvenirs picturing fair scenes, ribbons, badges from judges and officials, full sets of stereo cards, photographs, complete decks of playing cards, and much more. Only "very rare and unusual items" from fairs after 1939.
Doug Woollard, Jr.,
11614 Old St. Charles Rd,
Bridgeton, MO 63044
(314) 739-4662

◆ **1904 St. Louis World's Fair** china, mugs, tumblers, etc.
William Crowl,
2302 N. Vermont St.,
Arlington, VA 22207

◆ **1905 Lewis and Clark Exposition** held in Portland, Oregon. All memorabilia wanted. Also wants brochure or program from **Sally Rand's** act at the 1939 NY World's Fair.
Jack Matlack,
Box 14067,
Portland, OR 97214

◆ **1907 Jamestown Exposition memorabilia** except no postcards.
W.T. Atkinson, Jr.,
Route #1 Box 71,
Wilmington, NC 28405

◆ **1909 Alaska-Yukon-Pacific Exposition** in Seattle. "Postcards and memorabilia."
   W.E. Nickell,
   102 People's Wharf,
   Juneau, AK 99801
      (907) 586-1733

◆ **Worlds Fair ephemera from before 1935**. "I'll buy pre-1935 tickets, official and unofficial stationery, postcard sets, badges, pin back buttons, tokens, medals, enongated coins, toys, and souvenirs. Please write or ship for offer." One of the world's biggest dealers of tokens, Hartzog does not buy single items after 1935 except unusual items. Newer pieces are wanted only in large collections.
   Rich Hartzog, Exonumia,
   Box 4143 BBL,
   Rockford, IL 61110
      (815) 226-0771

◆ **1939-40 New York World's Fair memorabilia** especially the rare scale models of the Fair worth up to $10,000. Despite the fact he began collecting in 1939, Ed still actively buys almost anything associated with the Fair, including magazine articles, amateur photographs, exhibitor's literature, and just about anything else you can think of. No items with World's Fair decals. A photograph or photocopy is urged. Ed is editor of the newsletter of ECHO, the collector's organization for expo fans. A wants list is available.
   Ed Orth,
   1436 Killarney Ave.,
   Los Angeles, CA 90065

◆ **Paper ephemera picturing the trylon and perisphere at the 1939-40 NY World's Fair** is sought by this major NY stamp dealer, in business for 50 years. Send a Xerox of what you have.
   Harvey Dolin,
   5 Beekman St. #406,
   New York, NY 10038

◆ **1964 New York World's Fair.** Especially want fabrics, jewelry, toys, and unusual items.
   Dave Oglesby ,
   57 Lakeshore Drive,
   Marlborough, MA 01752

◆ **Paper ephemera from World's Fairs** including award and attendance certificates, honorable mention diplomas, admission or concession tickets, invitations, ·letterhead stationary, employee badges, passes, and playing cards from any fair before WWII.
   William Lipsky,
   1800 Market St. #260,
   San Francisco, CA 94102
      (415) 821-6017

◆ **All sorts of World's Fair memorabilia suitable for resale or auction.** All Fairs are wanted, especially the early ones. Rex is one of the largest mail order dealer/auctioneers in the country. He offers a large quarterly auction catalog, and constantly needs new items. No items under $20.
   Rex Stark, Americana,
   49 Wethersfield Rd.,
   Bellingham, MA 02019
      (508) 966-0994

◆ **Memorabilia of the 1962 Seattle World's Fair** but only small memorabilia including buttons, postcards, and programs.
   Reed Fitzpatrick,
   Box 369,
   Vashon, WA 98070

◆ **Atlanta Cotton States Exposition memorabilia**, including postcards and envelopes.
   Gordon Mc Henry,
   Box 117,
   Osprey, FL 33559

Dr. Hyman's Prescription

Collectors of radios and television sets like to know the maker, the model name and/or number, the serial number, and its cosmetic condition. Describe whether it is scratched, faded, dented, chipped, cracked, or the paint or veneer is peeled, etc.

Do not test very old equipment. Plugging it in may cause damage because insulation around wires deteriorates over time, resulting in short circuits or fires, neither of which will make your set more valuable.

Examine the chassis carefully for missing parts or damage. If the chassis has blank spots where a tube or component might have originally been, add that information to your basic description.

When describing early radios and televisions, include the numbers on the tubes if you can remove and read them easily. It always makes a set more valuable to have the original instruction papers.

Radios and television sets are among those few collectible items that don't have to be in perfect condition to find a buyer. Certainly, the better the condition, the better the price, but scarce radios and television sets will find buyers in almost any condition, because parts are always in demand by people who enjoy rebuilding them.

Note that two of our buyers produce periodicals which contain advertising for radios.

tony hyman

Radios

◆ **Radios of many types** including crystal sets, battery operated, wireless sets and parts, cathedral, grandfather clock style, odd shapes, and all luxury models like *Zenith* Stratosphere (pays $2,000+). Other names and models to watch for are *Marconi* (pays $1,200 for model #106), *De Forest, Leutz, Wireless Specialty, EICO, Norden Hauck, E.H. Scott, Grebe,* and *RCA Radiolas* #1, VI, and VII. Also novelty radios shaped like Peter Pan, Charlie McCarthy, or Mickey Mouse. Also radio dealer indoor and outdoor **advertising signs,** point of purchase displays, brochures, instruction books, and service manuals prior to 1940. Don is editor of the monthly *Radio Age* for collectors of vintage electronics. No rectangular table radios of the 30's, Bakelite radios of the 40's, or transister radios of the 50's. Don is a collector rather than a dealer, but does have excess items, and does buy large collections.

Donald Patterson,
636 Cambridge Rd.,
Augusta, GA 30909
(404) 738-7227

◆ **Radios of many types 1905-40,** including crystal sets, wireless receivers and transmitters, battery operated radios 1914-1928, and small electric table models 1928-35. Buys radios in wood, metal, or plastic cabinets. Especially interested in large collections of usable speakers, **tubes and parts** for radios from this period. No large console models of the 30's except those with chrome plated interiors. Also radio **magazines, catalogs, service manuals, sales literature, and advertising,** pre 1935, including novelties and radio dealer **promotional items** such as banks, toys, pin back buttons, games, postcards, and dealer promotional items. Gary publishes *Antique Radio Classified*, a monthly digest for electronic collectors.

Gary Schneider,
14310 Ordner Dr.,
Cleveland,OH 44136
(216) 582-3094

◆ **Antique radios.** Wants WWI equipment, fancy horn speakers, crystal sets, *Atwater Kent* breadboards, *Radiola, Kennedy, Federal,* the older and the more primitive the better, working or not. Will buy **art deco and novelty radios of the 1930's.** Also wants all **WWI wireless communications equipment** from ships, planes, and ground forces, either complete or for parts (worth from $200-$1,000 and up). Especially looking for old US Navy equipment with CN prefixes. Also **pre World War II television sets** and sports transmitting equipment. No floor model radios.

Mel Rosenthal,
507 S. Maryland Ave.,
Wilmington, DE 19804
(302) 322-8944

◆ **Pre 1930 wireless, crystal sets, and battery radios** such as *Atwater Kent, Crosley, Amrad, Deforest, Federal, Grebe, Kennedy, Firth, Paragon, Marconi, R.C.A.,* and *Zenith.* Also early vacuum tubes with brass or Bakelite base. Also *Jenkins* **scanning disc television.** Also all wireless and radio books and magazines printed before 1930. Also radio advertising, parts, relays, ear phones, horn speakers, amplifiers, batteries, meters, etc. Will pay $500 for a *Marconi* CA294, $600 for a *Marconi* 106, $800+ for a *Pacific Wireless Specialty* audio reciever, and some others to $2,000. Nothing made after 1940. No consol or floor model radios. No transisters.

David Shanks,
115 Baldwin St.,
Bloomfield, NJ 07003
(201) 748-8820

◆ **Unusual radios.** "I buy unusual radios, 1930-50, of wood, metal, chrome, mirror, or Bakelite. Especially novelty radios like Mickey Mouse or Charlie McCarthy, **blue mirrored radios,** black and chrome radios, or tombstone-shaped *Bakelite* (for which he will pay from $1,000-$3,000). Prefers unusual styling with rounded corners and clean lines, but will consider most radios for parts. Will also buy **some large special floor models.** I'll also buy **early transistors and transistor radios.** Also **repair manuals, dealer advertising, and radio-shaped novelties.** No poor condition wooden sets. No radios made after 1955." Harry wrote *Modern Stereo Equipment 1940-80*, available for $10.

Harry Poster,
Box 1883,
South Hackensack, NJ 07606
(201) 794-9606

◆ **Mirrored glass radios.** "I'm especially fond of green mirrored glass radios and forever trying to acquire Spartan floor model mirrored glass radios (model 1186). I'll pay through the nose if I have to." That translates to as much as $7,000 for a perfect condition peach colored glass. Glass covered radios do not have to work and the glass may be cracked as "I don't turn down mirrored glass radios offered to me." He claims to outbid anybody, and points out that he will either come pick up any radio or have it professionally moved so you don't have to worry about shipping. He also buys **colorful plastic radios** of the 1930's and 40's. If you are the original owner, he'd appreciate the item's history. He prefers you to set your price but will make offers if you intend to sell.
  Edward Sage,
  Box 1234,
  Benicia, CA 94510
    (707) 746-5659

◆ **Radio manuals, handbooks, and sales literature** pre 1970.
  Alan C. King,
  PO Box 86,
  Radnor, OH 43066

◆ **Radios with wood cabinets.** No offers. Give make and model number, condition, price.
  Alvin Heckard,
  RD 1, Box 88,
  Lewistown, PA 17044
    (717) 248-7071

◆ **Radios, tubes, test equipment, open frame motors, generators** and other electrical apparatus, switch board meters, knife switches, **neon signs, fans,** Tesla coils, **quack medical devices** (Violet Ray, etc.), **unusual clocks,** etc., as well as books on radio and electrical theory and practice. Give info from the items ID plate, and include a sketch or photo.
  Hank Andreoni,
  2650 Alessandro,
  Riverside, CA 92008
    (714) 849-7539

Auto radios: see Automobiles in chapter 13, Transportation

Microphones

◆ **Pre 1940 microphones and related equipment** including call letter plates which were attached to mics. Also catalogs, sales literature, parts, repairman's tools, broadcast mixers, and anything else reated to the early history of microphones. See his illustrated wants list for $100-$400 mics. Nothing newer than 1940. No home broadcast mics. Does not want to buy mics used by famous people.
  Bob Paquette,
  Microphone Museum,
  107 E. National Ave.,
  Milwaukee, WI 53204
    (414) 344-5631 eves

Hi-fi

◆ **Early tube high fidelity equipment** 1947-1960 especially monaural but also some early stereo from companies such as Dynaco, Marantz, Fisher, McIntosh, Scott, Eico, Altec Lansing, JBL, etc. Most makes and models are wanted, working or not, complete or for parts, as well as tubes, loudspeakers, literature, schematics, manuals, and hi-fi magazines. Among items of particular interest are all early McIntosh amps. Nothing after 1970, "But I'll buy anything relating to early audio, from broadcast equipment to home systems."
  Jack Smith,
  288 Winter St.,
  North Andover, MA 01845
    (508) 686-7250

Televisions

◆ **Television sets made before 1941** are sought by Chase, one of the country's biggest buyers of memorabilia from TV's earliest years. "Mechanical TV's are often mistaken for early electronic junk," he cautions, "so look for 12" metal disks containing tiny holes that spin in front of a neon glow lamp. These early TV's drew their sound from radio sets, and most had no cabinets. Look for names like *Daven, Insuline, ICA, Jenkins, See-All, Western Television,* and *Shortwave Television.* The electronic era sets from 1938-41 used picture tubes and were often combined in consoles with radios. One popular early style was the "mirror in the lid" which reflected the picture from a vertical picture tube. Brands to look for include *Andrea, GE, Philco, RCA, Stewart-Warner,* and *Westinghouse.* Minimum value for an early set is $500 with many of them a great deal more. A 1939 *Zenith* television would be worth about $10,000 to me, regardless of condition," says Chase. He will also buy selected sets made from 1941-1948 which can be recognized by having a Chanel 1. He will also buy early giant screen 30" sets made by *Dumont* and *CBS-Columbia's* sets with a spinning color wheel. Readers are encouraged to send for his large and informative wants list.
Arnold Chase
9 Rushleigh Rd.,
West Hartford, CT 06117
(203) 521-5280

◆ **Early television items.**
Gary Schneider,
14310 Ordner Drive,
Cleveland, OH 44136
(216) 582-3094

◆ **Television sets** with a reflective mirror in the lid and other small screen television sets such as the RCA TRK-9 or TRK-12 ($2,000+ each), and the GE HM 171 (worth $750). Only wants sets dating from before 1940.
Donald Patterson,
636 Cambridge Rd.,
Augusta, GA 30909
(404) 738-7227

◆ **Early television sets.** "I'll buy antique and unusual TV's, and will pay more than $1,000 for any TV sold before 1942. Names to look for includ *Baird, Western, Empire,* and other mechanical disc Televisions. I buy all mirror-in-the-lid sets by *Pilot, Philco, Garod, General Electric, Zenith,* and *RCA RR* and *RCA TRK* series. Also *Fada* and *Meissner* kits with 5" screens. Also want *Dumont 180* series, and others. I pay from $20 to $200 for post WWII TV's which are unusual such as many 3", 7", and 10" screens plus built-in magnifier sets plus *Philco Predictas.* I also pay from $200 to $2,000 for early (1950-55) color TV's, color wheels, sets with color drums, and early 30" TV's. I also buy TV books and magazines before 1944, TV and radio signs, and **dealer promotional material** before 1970." Has particular interest in televisions and television promotions associated with the 1939 World's Fair. Harry publishes a quarterly journal for collectors of old televisions.
Harry Poster,
Box 1883,
South Hackensack, NJ 07606
(201) 794-9606

◆ **Television literature,** including books, catalogs, and company pamphlets (whether internal or intended for the public) from before 1940.
Harold Layer,
SFSU-AV,
1600 Holloway Ave,
San Francisco, CA 94132

EDITOR'S NOTE: Cities where early TV's are most likely: Schenectady, Philadelphia, Los Angeles, New York, Chicago.

7
Music & Song

Dr. Hyman's Prescription

When describing musical instruments, begin by identifying what the instrument is (if you can) and what it is made of.

Many instruments will indicate a manufacturer, and a few will have model names or numbers. Include all wording on any paper labels inside string instruments.

Your condition statement should include mention of all cracks, dents, and the like. If it is something unusual, make a sketch or take a photograph.

Make certain to check out stringed instruments. Do not underestimate the value of early electrical guitars.

If you have phonograph records to sell, it is important to list the artist, song, record label, and the catalog number. Note the condition of the record, the record jacket, and its paper sleeve. Mention any tears, scuffs, owner's names, cracks, chips, or scratches on the record or the cover. Damaged records aren't worth anyone's time.

Most later pop records are of little value, but some rock and show tune albums are considered scarce by collectors and bring $50 or more.

Condition of records is of prime importance. Even slight damage to the track reduces value substantially.

tony hyman

Musical Instruments

◆ **Most string, wood, and brass musical instruments** are of interest for trade or resale. For his own collection he wants instruments that are rare, very old, pretty, unique, or hand crafted. He especially wants trumpets or cornets that have extra keys, fewer keys, or keys that are in unusual positions or shapes. He buys *any* museum quality instrument. Also instruments of other cultures including African, Asian, Pacific, etc. No pianos or organs. A photo should go with a complete description, including all labels or markings.

Sid Glickman,
42 Butterwood Lane E.,
Irvington, NY 10533
(914) 591-5371

◆ **Stringed musical instruments** including banjos, electric and acoustic guitars, mandolins, ukes, and violins. No ukelins or Mandolin-Harps, please. He'll buy banjos by *Fairbanks, Cole, Vega, Stewart, Epiphone, Stromberg, Gibson, Leedy, Ludwig, Baystate, Haynes, Lyon & Healy, Bacon, B&D, Studio King, Recording King,* or *Paramount.* Will buy the following brands of guitar in any condition: *D'Angelico, Gibson, Martin, Epiphone, Fender, Gretsch,* and *Rickenbacker.* "There are lots of guitars purchased for $100-$300 in the 1950's that are worth five to ten times as much today. I'll pay $1,500+ for a *Gretsch* White Falcon guitar, $2,000+ for a *Gretsch* Chet Atkins, $5,000+ for a *Gibson* Flying V electric guitar, and up to $10,000 for a mint *Gibson* Les Paul with the sunburst finish. We will consider all violins offered to us, especially those with carvings or inlaid work, no matter what its country of origin." Photos of the front and back of any instrument are requested.

Steve Senerchia, The Music Man,
87 Tillinghast Ave.,
West Warwick, RI 02893
(401) 821-2865

◆ **American Guitars, banjos, and mandolins** by the following makers: *C.F. Martin, Gibson, Fender* (older models), *Dobro, National, D'Angelico, B&D* (Bacon & Day), *Epiphone* (older), *Paramount, Vega, Fairbanks, SS*

Stewart, Washburn, Lyon & Healy, Stromberg, Gretsch, and *Rickenbacker.* "If you have fine condition instruments for sale **by these makers** *only* you may call us collect for an offer. Have your instrument in your hand. Be prepared to answer specific questions about condition, originality, serial number, color, and the type of case it has. Without this information, we cannot provide meaningful evaluation. *Sellers only may call collect.* All others are welcome to call for advice or information." Among instruments Jay and his team would most like to find are the *Martin* D-45 with abalone inlay, the electric *Gibson* Les Paul Standard made in 1958-59, a *Gibson* F-5 mandolin made between 1922-24 signed by Lloyd Loar, and *Gibson* Mastertone banjos made during the late 1930's. Dates and models are very important. "Another model made at the same time might be worth only 1/20 as much as these key pieces. But *all* instruments made by these makers can be worth your inquiry. Original condition matters a lot." Offers an interesting catalog of high quality new and used instruments. Wants list available.

Stan Jay, Mandolin Bros.,
629 Forest Ave.,
Staten Island, NY 10310
(718) 981-3226

◆ **High quality Italian violins and some of their imitators** are the prime interest of this 15 year veteran west coast dealer. Cremona school violins 1650-1750 can be worth from $2,500 to $100,000 or more, but many copies exist. Jones will also consider your fake "Stradivarius" violins as well as better French instruments. German violins 1850-1920 seldom bring much but there are many **guitars, banjos, basses, violas, mandolins,** and other stringed instruments that can be fairly valuable if you have one of better quality. Jones also buys books on identification of musical instruments and catalogs of collections, auctions, and sales, as well as old violin maker's tools. "It takes years of handling violins to be able to recognize originals or instruments of value. For this reason it is difficult to buy through the mail, but not impossible." Describe all damage, the finish, the bow, and give every word on label. No Oriental instruments.

David N. Jones' Violin Shop,
3411 Ray St.,
San Diego, CA 92104
(619) 584-1505

◆ **Fretted stringed musical instruments** such as banjos, guitars, mandolins, ukuleles, and the like. "A *Martin* D-45 guitar made prior to 1942 could be worth as much as $20,000," so instruments are worth selling properly. **Also** related memorabilia such as manufacturer's catalogs, old photos of guitar shops and players, accessories, etc. State the preservation of your instrument. Examine carefully for repairs. Look for any signs that it might not be original. Mention the type of case. Offers a monthly 8pp catalog of new and used instruments for $4 per year.
Stan Werbin,
Elderly instruments,
Box 14210,
Lansing, MI 48901
(517) 372-7890

◆ **French and Italian violins, violas, and cellos.** "I'll pay high prices for high grade quality instruments, both commercial and hand-made from anywhere in the world, but especially France and Italy. I don't want children's or school violins nor any imitations of Stradivarius, Guarnerius, or other masters." Describe the label inside the instrument. Appraisal services available.
Robert Portukalian, Violin Shop,
1279 North Main St.,
Providence, RI 02904
(401) 521-5145

◆ **Rare and unusual musical instruments** including harps, bagpipes, hurdi-gurdies, wooden flutes, concertinas, ethnic instruments, and all manner of brass and woodwinds, stringed instruments, and others. No keyboards. Mickie repairs instruments and will purchase good ones in "any restorable condition." Can make arrangements for consignment selling of instruments he doesn't wish to buy. This 20 year veteran conducts annual seminars on musical instrument history and performance and is available for insurance appraisals and offers. An extensive illustrated catalog may be ordered for $2.50.
Mickie Zekley,
Lark in the Morning,
Box 1176,
Mendocino, CA 95460
(707) 964-5569

◆ **Old Jew's harps** (also called jaw harps, juice harps), especially those that are hand-forged or made of ivory, bone, silver, or gold. They must me in good condition, complete with the tongue ("twanger"). "I'll buy Jew's harp cases in any material and want literature, instruction books, etc., and would love to find instruments composed of several harps joined together."
Leonard Fox,
278-A Meeting St.,
Charleston, SC 29401
(803) 722-2531

◆ **Cigar box musical instruments.** "I'll buy any realistically priced musical instrument made out of a cigar box. Send description and a sketch or photo. If interested (I usually am) I'll request to see the instrument and will pay you for shipping it whether I buy it or not." If you know any of the instrument's history, please include that information." Mention type of instrument, whether strings and pegs are present, type and condition of finish, and any applied or painted decorations.
Tony Hyman,
Box 699,
Claremont, CA 91711
(714) 621-5952

◆ **Brass musical instruments,** especially the unusual and obsolete. He wants "to know about all your old brass instruments since they all look the same to the untrained" and he hopes to assemble a representative collection of the hundreds of brass instruments. Among other things, he especially wants a B-flat cornet with the bell pointing over the shoulder and a Schreiber horn with a straight up bell. If you regularly sell musical instruments, his informative illustrated wants list is a must.
Jonathan Korzun,
1201 Williamson Rd.,
North Brunswick, NJ 08902
(201) 297-0308 eves

Sheet Music & Books

◆ **Sheet music in bound volumes,** 1700-1900. Also scarce or high quality individual sheets from the same period. Please describe contents and condition of the material when inquiring. Not interested in "run of the mill piano music" of the 20th century, but does want early sheet music with brightly lithographed covers. Also want **singing school song books,** 1700-1900 (oblong and open-enders), especially collections by Lowell Mason, Thomas Hastings, William Walker, Andrew Law, William Bradbury, and others. Top money for 18th century books compiled by Billings, Lyons, and others. **Song books with shaped notes** are always of interest. Follow standard procedure for describing books. Indicate whether sheet music is instrumental or vocal.
Carl Shull,
436 N. Mt. Joy St.,
Elizabethtown, PA 17022
(717) 367-5346

◆ **Songbooks with oddly shaped notes.** "I'll buy singing school books with oblong, triangular, rectangular, pictorial or other shaped notes, especially pre 1860, for $25 and up in good condition. Authors of these books include Funk, Carden, Davisson, Swan, and others."
Jim Presgraves,
Box 639,
Wytheville, VA 24382
(703) 686-5813

◆ **Songbooks and sheets:**
(1) American and British **topical song books** 1700-1900 in paper, leather, or hard covers, such as political, temperance, medicine show, vaudeville, etc.;
(2) American and British song **broadsides and ballad sheets,** 1500-1900;
(3) Hillbilly and **Country and Western song folios** before 1946;
(4) **Song books of occupational groups,** miners, sailors, cowboys, pre 1946;
(5) **Regional collections,** American, Indian, Irish, West Indian, etc., any period.
Full bibliographic information is required. **No religious collections** are wanted by this widely acclaimed folk music author and authority.
Kenneth Goldstein,
4840 Cedar Ave.,
Philadelphia, PA 19143
(215) 476-5857

◆ **Sheet music illustrated by E.H. Pfeiffer.** They are signed in a variety of ways including EHP, Fifer, Pfeiffer Illustrating Co., Pfeiffer Publishing Co. Has a lengthy wants list. Also buys other items illustrated by Pfeiffer. Please describe things carefully, noting all damage, tears, creases, stains, tape, etc.
Ann Pfeiffer Latella,
70 Mariposa Dr.,
Rochester, NY 14624
(716) 247-2823

EDITOR'S NOTE: People usually collect sheet music for the illustrations on the front cover. Give a good description of what is pictured.

Include information you find on the front or back about the publisher, the cover artist, featured musical artists, and the composer/arranger.

Most important, mention all chips, creases, tears, wear, or handwriting, information critical to determine value.

◆ **Old popular sheet music** from 1820-1970, with pictorial covers, especially movie and show song sheets, WWI, WWII, ragtime, blues, Negro, ethnic, baseball, cartoons, musical comedy, fire, aviation, and automobile songs especially with illustrations by Homer or Nathaniel Currier. No classical or religious. Also buys *Downbeat, Metronome, Billboard* and movie magazines.
Beverly Hamer,
Box 75,
E. Derry, NH 03041
(603) 432-3528

◆ **Sheet music** in small or large collections or accumulations. Primary interest is in popular music of the 20th century (1890-1970). Movie and show tunes are of primary interest, but "also any music that falls into any of the main collectible categories, like presidential, political, patriotic, war, transportation, cartoon, baseball, *Coca-Cola,* advertising, historical, Black related, and others with interesting cover art." Particularly likes to find music published by the ET Paull Music Company, and will pay from $10 to $300, depending upon the title and condition. Does **not** want to buy classical music or sheet music designed for teaching. "If the person wants to sell the music as a lot, I need to know quantity, condition, and the rough percentage of movie, show, and pop tunes. I also want to know the percentage of large format (11" x 14") and small format (9" x 12") music.
Wayland Bunnell,
Clean Sheets,
199 Tarrytown Rd.,
Manchester, NH 03103
(603) 668-5466

◆ **Bound volumes of sheet music from before 1900.** Pays $1 or more per title for illustrated ones, those by rare publishers bring more. Prefers books with no titles removed.
Jim Presgraves, Bookworm & Silverfish,
Box 639,
Wytheville, VA 24382
(703) 686-5813

◆ **Sheet music about WWI and WWII** in very good to mint condition *only*.
Herman Rush,
10773 Ojai-Santa Paula Rd.,
Ojai, CA 93023

"Please don't describe sheet music as 'good for its age.' Collectors and dealers take that to mean fair or poor condition.

'Excellent' and 'mint' are terms reserved for music that has almost never seen the light of day, music store stock or publisher's remainder."

Wayland Bunnell

EDITOR'S NOTE: All collectors are fussy. Sheet music collectors are among the most fussy. Don't waste their time and yours by offering items in poor condition.

Phonograph Records

◆ **Jazz, blues, big band, hillbilly, rock and roll, rhythm and blues, rockabilly, and celebrity records,** including 78's, 45's, and LP's. Especially jazz and dance bands from the 1920's and 30's and jug and washboard bands. Also radio transcription disks. He buys many rare, obscure, and scarce but unpopular records and will buy anything recorded on the following labels: *Autograph, Black Patti, Bluebird, Broadway, Brunswick*, and 50 others. Also most records which are marked "fox trot," "stomp," or "for dancing." No easy listening, hit records, or pop recording stars like Jolson or Crosby. If you have 78's to sell, send $2 for the *Shellac Shack's Wants List*, a 72 page booklet listing the prices they pay for thousands of records. Les is author of *American Premium Record Guide*, a popular reference work available for $16.95.
Les Docks,
The Shellac Shack,
Box 691035,
San Antonio, TX 78269
(512) 492-6021

◆ **78 rpm recordings, 1900-1940,** including popular, classical, jazz, country and Western, and personality. Also catalogs and sheet music in those areas of interest. David especially likes to buy entire collections and will travel anywhere in the East.
David Alan Reiss,
3920 Eve Drive,
Seaford, NY 11783
(516) 785-8336

◆ **Pop American 78 rpm records, 1888-1949,** especially in quantity. Pays 10¢ - $1 apiece, less if records are not in fine condition. Buys disks, cylinders, and sapphire ball recordings at higher prices. He'll pay $100 for *Where Did Robinson Crusoe Go With Friday on Saturday Night?* Some interest in **sheet music for pop music** from 1890-1925.
Ron Graham,
8167 Park Ave.,
Forestville, CA 95436
(707) 887-2856

◆ **Country and western phonograph records.** "I'll buy LP's, 45's, and 78's. Also country music song books, sheet music, and fan magazines. Also anything related to the singing cowboys like Gene Autry, Roy Rogers, etc."
Dave Cook
303 Elm St.,
Crawford, NE 69339
(308) 665-2242

◆ **Jazz LP's from the 1950's and 60's.** No 45's or 78's. No music other than jazz. No records with poor condition covers. Also **jazz literature of all kinds,** any years, and "some other materials associated with jazz" such as magazines. Please include your phone number.
Gary Alderman, G's Jazz,
Box 9164,
Madison, WI 53715
(608) 274-3527

◆ **Rock and roll, rhythm and blues, and country music records.** Wants 45 and 33 rpm, especially 45's with picture sleeves, odd ball items, and disc jockey radio promos. Also rock, blues, or country sheet music and magazines. No classical, big bands, opera, or polka.
Cliff Robnett,
7804 NW 27th,
Bethany, OK 73008
(405) 787-6703

◆ **45 rpm records in quantity** in unplayed or nearly unused condition. Looking for store stock or radio station collections, but will also buy small collections if they contain desirable records. Nothing worn or scratched. Phone.
Ken Clee,
PO Box 11412,
Philadelphia, PA 19111
(215) 722-1979

◆ **Spoken word, historical, and satire records** about famous statesmen or historical news events such as the Kennedy assassination, the moon landing, Viet Nam, Watergate, Black history, etc. "Must be in original jacket sleeves, but may be 33, 45, or 78 rpm. They may be produced for limited or mass distribution."
Richard Harrow,
85-23 210th St.,
Hollis Hills, NY 11427

◆ **Transcription discs of old radio programs** such as *Suspense, Jack Benny, Lux Radio Theater, Bing Crosby*, newscasts, the big bands, musical, dramas, mysteries, detective shows, kids shows, "most all categories." Discs are typically 16" and aluminum based, but may also be 10" or 12" and can be found single and double sided. Glass disks from WWII years are extremely fragile and desirable. Not interested in dubs of originals or in disks of advertising, public service spots, or promotions. "Generally not interested in most library type disks but will consider if asking price not too high." Larry prefers not to make offers.
Larry Kiner,
Box 724,
Redmond, WA 98073-0724

Singers & Musicians

◆ **Eubie Blake or Sissle & Blake records and other memorabilia**, especially 10" recording *Jammin' at Rudi's*.
Steven Ramm,
420 Fitzwater St.,
Philadelphia, PA 19147

◆ **Big Band memorabilia from the 1930's and 40's** especially of Glenn Miller or Bunny Berigan. John buys phonograph records, home recordings, tapes of concerts or radio performances, transcription disks, autographs, photographs, newspaper articles, magazine articles, movie short subjects, home movies, posters, and sheet music if it has to do with big bands. This 30 year veteran collector will negotiate an item's value with you.
John Mickolas,
172 Liberty Street,
Trenton, NJ 08611
(609) 599-9672

◆ **Al Jolson ephemera.** "Anything and everything pertaining to Jolson. Mail on approval."
Rick Hoffman,
4615 Silverwood St.,
Philadelphia, PA 19128

◆ **Al Jolson and his brother Harry.** "I have an extensive collection of items and music sheets, so am mostly looking for unusual items and in novelty song sheets. No common well known songs. Please, no *Mammy*."
J. Markowitz
139-12 84th Drive,
Briarwood, NY 11435
(212) 512-5281

◆ **Frank Sinatra records and memorabilia.**
Stan Komorowski,
1089 Toll House Rd.,
Warminster, PA 18974
(215) 675-1452

◆ **Elvis Presley memorabilia** from before his death, including all marked "E.P. Enter 1956" such as lipsticks, skirts, perfume, gloves, etc. Also lobby cards and posters from Elvis movies, and promotional items from his records, appearances, and movies. Seeks a plastic guitar with pictures on it, and issues of 1950's magazines such as *Dig* and *Teen Stories* with all Elvis features. Also interested in The **Beatles, Kiss, Monkee,** and other rock memorabilia. Autographs are especially desired. No phonograph records except promotional copies.
Robert Urmanic, Bob's Nostalgia,
199 Brookvalley Dr.,
Elyria, OH 44035
(216) 365-3550

```
┌─────────────────────────────┐
│                        ▨     │
│                              │
│   Your Name                  │
│   Your Address               │
│                              │
└─────────────────────────────┘
```

SASE's bring faster checks.

◆ **Beatles memorabilia** from before their 1970 breakup. Everything is wanted, including games, toys, dolls, posters, movie related items, candid photos, concert posters and programs, tickets, and ads for merchandise or concerts. Would love to find any Beatles toy musical instruments, such as guitars and drums picturing the group, and will pay from $200-$500 for Beatles bongos and banjo. Will buy common items as long as they are old and original. Wants to know where you got your item, and asks you to include your phone number.
    Jeff Augsburger,
    507 Normal Ave.,
    Normal, IL 61761
        (309) 452-9376

◆ **Beatles memorabilia** including toys, buttons, clothing, lunch boxes, etc. No paper.
    Cliff DeManty,
    9300 Santa Fe Springs Rd.,
    Santa Fe Springs, CA 90670
        (213) 946-2511

◆ **Janet Lynn memorabilia.** "I buy photos, articles, and books, from 1970 to the present."
    Alberic Gerard,
    Box 97,
    Lafayette, OR 97127

◆ **Beatles memorabilia** of all sorts including toys, dolls, games, tickets, cartoon kit, model kits, *Yellow Submarine*, Halloween costumes, wall paper, talcum powder, shampoo, ice cream wrappers, blankets, jewelry, china, toy musical instruments, fan club items, etc., especially items sealed in their original factory cartons. Also hard to find Beatles albums such as *Beatles vs the 4 Seasons* or *Yesterday & Today* with the butcher cover. "I'll pay $800 for a mint record player, and up to $500 for an unopened bottle of pomade, and $250 for a mint Kaboodle Kit." Rick also buys **Monkees!** ephemera of all types.
    Rick Rann,
    Box 877,
    Oak Park, IL 60303
        (312) 442-7907

◆ **Bobby Breen phonograph records and song sheets** from the late 1930's.
    Ralph Eodice, Nevermore,
    161 Valley Rd.,
    Clifton, NJ 07013

EDITOR'S NOTE: Watch for these things at local yard sales and second hand stores. Many people throw them away.

Dr. Hyman's Prescription

"Coin-ops" is what collectors call slot machines, juke-boxes, arcade games, trade stimulators (games you play for product prizes), kinetoscopes (early flip-card "movie" machines), and other machines which are put into play by dropping a coin into a slot.

Coin-ops are made of cast iron, aluminum, plastic and wood. The oldest machines not always the most valuable.

Coin-ops are among those few collectibles which do not need to be in perfect condition to sell readily. Most collectors and dealers restore them.

If you give the make, model, and serial number, most dealers will know exactly what machine you mean. You can find this information on an identification plate along with the address of the manufacturer, patent dates, and (sometimes) the operating instructions.

Almost all collectors want a photo of older items, especially pin ball games, arcade and vending machines, and trade stimulators since unfamiliar models turn up regularly. When photographing pinball machines, include the play field in one picture and the back glass in another.

When writing about a coin-op, make certain to indicate whether it works and whether or not parts are missing or broken. When describing pinball machines, it is important to note whether paint is peeling off the back board illustration, and, if so, how much.

Because the machines are large, heavy, and valuable, shipping can be a problem. If you have a good machine, the buyer will make shipping arrangements.

tony hyman

Mechanical Music

◆ **Any pre 1930 device that plays music mechanically** including disk and cylinder music boxes, clocks and watches that play tunes, disk players, automata dolls, player organs, monkey organs, nickelodeons, horn phonographs in any condition from perfect to incomplete. Especially a barrel operated monkey organ with pipes ($2,000-$4,000), large disc music boxes that play more than one disc at a time ($10-$12,000), and cylinder music boxes with more than 175 teeth, and early musical watches. No player pianos, but most other mechanical music brings $300 up. Give measurements of any disk or cylinder. Please include your phone number with correspondence.
 Martin Roenigk,
 Grand Illusions,
 26 Barton Hill,
 East Hampton, CT 06424
    (203) 267-8682

◆ **Musical instruments "that play themselves"** by motor, springs, pneumatics, or other means, including **music boxes**, roller organs, cylinder music boxes, musical bird cages, nickelodeons, and organettes. Will buy rough condition items for parts or repair. Also musical disks, cylinders, piano rolls, old photos, postcards or paper ephemera depicting anything in mechanical music. NO OFFERS.
 Doug Negus,
 Phonograph Phunatic,
 215 Mason St.,
 Sutherland, IA 51058
    (712) 446-2270

◆ **Anything that makes music automatically or mechanically** such as phonographs, music boxes, player pianos, nickelodeons, organettes, and others. Also the records, discs, rolls, cobs, and anything else that plays these instruments. Also any catalog, magazine, bulletin, book, literature or advertising pertaining to these items.
 Seymour Altman,
 Vi & Si's,
 8970 Main St.,
 Clarence, NY 14031
    (716) 634-4488

◆ **Antique music boxes and phonographs.** Want all types, 1850-1920, including cylinder, disc, paper roll, and cob organs. Brands like *Regina, Mira, Stella, Symphonian,* and *Kalliope* are sought. Especially interested in a *Regina Changer,* a 15 1/2 upright music box which changes automatically. He'd pay $12,000 for a nice one. Is not interested in "late miniature music boxes." He needs the brand, model, size, and condition. Pictures are most helpful.
 Chet Ramsay,
 RD #1 Box 383,
 Coatesville, PA 19320
    (215) 384-0514

◆ **Phonographs and related memorabilia pre 1930** including cylinder and disc records, signs and other advertising except magazine ads, catalogs, needle tins, postcards and stereoviews depicting phonographs. Also cylinder records of speeches by Taft, Roosevelt, and other famous people, for which he pays $10-$50. Also all material related to Thomas Edison. Also toy phonographs. List make, model, and condition. Include label, artist, and title of records. SASE for offer.
 Steven Ramm,
 420 Fitzwater St.,
 Philadelphia, PA 19147
    (215) 922-7050

◆ **Horn phonographs in any condition** or parts from machines made by the following companies: Berliner Gramophone, National Gramophone, Universal Talking Machine, or Zonophone.
 Charlie Stewart,
 900 Grandview Ave.,
 Reno, NV 89503
    (702) 747-1439 days

◆ **Phonographs with outside horns**, complete or for parts. No Victrolas. Alvin doesn't want to be bothered unless you're serious about selling. NO OFFERS.

Alvin Heckard,
RD 1, Box 88,
Lewistown, PA 17044
(717) 248-7071

◆ *RCA* or *Capehart* **radio-phonographs that automatically flip records over** to play the other side. Pays $500-$700 for these large complicated machines from the 1930's. "If your machine weighs less than 75 pounds, I'm probably not interested." Take a photo of the record changing mechanism or give him a call.

Joseph Weber,
604 Centre St.,
Ashland, PA 17921
(717) 875-4401 3-5 pm

◆ **Catalogs, repair manuals, and advertising for phonographs and piano rolls** published by the record and piano roll companies between 1890 and 1960. Prefers to buy collections or very early pieces. No records, magazine ads, or damaged items. Tim is past president of the Association for Recorded Sound Collections, a national club for recording historians. He is also author of three books on television.

Tim Brooks,
Box 41, Greenway Drive,
Greenwich, CT 06831

◆ **Telegraphones and other unusual magnetic recorders, especially wire.**

Harold Layer,
SFSU-AV,
1600 Holloway Ave.,
San Francisco, CA 94132

EDITOR'S NOTE: Be certain to see Dr. Hyman's Prescription for selling mechanical music and coin-operated machines.

Coin-ops

◆ **Select coin-op machines** especially early wood cabinet and cast iron machines 1885-1912, very rare pin ball machines, kinetoscopes, and 1888-1905 peep machines. Offers $20,000 for the *Fey* 1906 Liberty Bell slot machine but has only minor interest in most other slots. Pays $7,500 for an *Edison* Kinetoscope from 1894. Particularly interested in paper ephemera about coin op machines including catalogs, brochures, advertising, letterheads, and anything else historical related to coin-ops. Also photographs of store or saloon interiors which depict the machines in place, in use, or ready for use. Also *The Coin Machine Journal, Automatic Age, Automatic World, The Pacific Coin Machine Review, Spinning Reels, The Billboard* (pre 1932), and other trade magazines devoted to coin op machines. Bueschel is an editor of the quarterly *The Coin Slot* and author or publisher of more than three dozen books and guides to coin operated machines. Since thousands of dollars are sometimes involved, he wants you to shoot a roll of 1000 ASA 35mm film of your coin op, including all details and ship the undeveloped roll to him. He'll reimburse. You *must* tell him where you got your machines.
   Richard Bueschel,
   414 N. Prospect Manor Ave.,
   Mt. Prospect, IL 60056
      (312) 498-9300 days

◆ **Coin-ops** including jukeboxes, nickelodeons, arcade devices such as diggers and claws, view machines, coin op fans and radios, and gum, prophylactic and other vending machines. Has particular interest in **slot machines and gambling devices that pay cash rewards.** These have a minimum value of $500 with the more exotic and unusual machines bringing considerably more. Pre 1910 gambling machines made on the West coast are very desirable. Also **paper ephemera** about coin op machines including catalogs, brochures, advertising, letterheads, and anything historical. No pin ball, video arcade, or service machines like washers.
   Fred Ryan, Slot Closet,
   7217 N. Jersey,
   Portland, OR 97203
      (503) 286-3597

◆ **Coin-op machines** especially pre 1940 slots and jukeboxes. No solid state pinball machines. Ted publishes the monthly *Coin Machine Trader* devoted to ads and information about coin ops.
   Ted Salveson,
   PO Box 602,
   Huron, SD 57350
      (605) 352-3870

◆ *Gottlieb* **pinball machines,** 1948-58. He explains that most of the games from this period have wooden cabinets, trim, and legs, except those made after 1956 which have metal legs. Machines before 1948 don't have flippers and are not of interest. Will buy *Gottlieb* machines in any condition, but premium prices are paid for fine condition working machines. The backglass must me present and in good condition with little or no chipping, cracking, or paint flaking. Cabinets that have been repainted are undesirable but acceptable. Normal wear on the playing surface is expected, but severely damaged playfields make a game uncollectible. Damaged machines have some value for parts but their value is a fraction of what collectible games in fine condition command. Pays $500 for *Gin Rummy* or *Mystic Marvel* games by *Gottlieb*. "I will consider games by other manufacturers, but only if they are in very good condition. No games which have revolving reels to record scores or that have metal cabinets. "If you are in doubt, call and I will try my best to identify your game. When you describe your game, pay attention to cosmetics, missing bumper caps, lights shields missing, cracks, etc." He prefers amateurs to set the price wanted, but he will make offers if you are serious about selling.
   Gordon Hasse, Jr.,
   Box 1543 GCS,
   New York, NY 10163
      (212) 996-3825 eves

◆ **Table model jukeboxes.** Only buys the small ones if they have to be shipped. He will buy *all* pre 1960 jukeboxes if you live close enough for pick up. Also jukebox literature, ads and parts.
   Alvin Heckard,
   RD 1, Box 88,
   Lewistown, PA 17044
      (717) 248-7071

◆ *Wurlitzer* and *Rock Ola* jukeboxes, working or not, especially *Wurlitzer* model 42 (worth up to $1,800) and model numbers 500 or above (which begin at $450 for a #500 and can go to nearly $12,000 for a nice condition model #950). Also **all slot machines, in any condition,** complete or not, working or not. All but the most common working machines will bring $500, many over $1,000. He advertises widely that $50,000 is waiting for the finder of a working *Fey* Liberty Bell slot machine. Will pick up machines anywhere in the U.S.

    Frank Zygmunt,
    Antique Slot Machine Co.,
    Box 542,
    Westmont, IL 60559
        (312) 985-2742

◆ Coin op machines including 78rpm *Wurlitzer* jukeboxes from 1938-48, pre 1920 penny arcade machines, pre 1910 vending machines, and all slot machines.

    Martin Roenigk,
    Grand Illusions,
    26 Barton Hill,
    East Hampton, CT 06424
        (203) 267-8682

◆ Pre 1940 *Wurlitzer* jukeboxes with model numbers lower than 500. These machines pre-date the plastic-and-bright-lights era of Wurlitzer that is favored by most collectors. Also *Capehart* radio-phonographs **and jukeboxes from the 1930's that flip records over.** Pays $500-$700 for *Wurlitzer* 416 or *Capehart* C20-30. He'll buy these in any condition, but condition does affect value. Will pick up anything east of the Mississippi and arrange for shipments in the West.

    Joseph Weber,
    604 Centre St.,
    Ashland, PA 17921
        (717) 875-4401 3-5 pm

◆ **Penny arcade games** such as grip tests, target games, kicker and catcher, Pike's Peak, and the like. Prefers penny machines.

    James Conley,
    2405 Brentwood Rd.NW,
    Canton, OH 44708
        (216) 477-7725

◆ *Wurlitzer* jukeboxes from the 1940's. Also **paper ephemera, service manuals, and advertising related to jukeboxes** of all types. Rick publishes the monthly *Jukebox Collector Newsletter* and is author of three books about jukeboxes, including *A Complete Identification Guide to the Wurlitzer Jukebox* available from him for $15.

    Rick Botts,
    2545 SE 60th Court,
    Des Moines, IA 50317
        (515) 265-8324

◆ **All types of coin-op machines,** especially unusual.

    Marvin Yagoda,
    28585 So. Harwich Dr.,
    Farmington Hills, MI 48018
        (313) 851-8158

◆ **Pinball machines and coin op kiddie ride animals** pre 1965.

    Don Olson,
    Box 311,
    Humboldt, IA 50548

8
Vices & Pleasures

Dr. Hyman's Prescription

Liquor, gambling, sex, and tobacco have been part of our culture for centuries. Nearly everything associated with these somewhat forbidden pleasures is collectible.

The best advice I can give you is to check out everything, especially older advertising, pre WWI cigarette packages and cigar boxes, liquor bottles with the label embedded in the glass, and all mechanical devices having to do with smoking, gambling, liquor, and sex.

Collecting briar pipes is one of the faster growing hobbies and an area with many possibilities for profit. Don't ever throw out (or pass by) briar pipes without looking to see if you have found one of the more collectible brands. Valuable briar pipes ($25 - $100) are often bought for pennies at yard sales and secondhand stores.

Cigar boxes, too, are often overlooked. Collectors want fine condition pre 1920 boxes, preferably with their inside paper liners. The value of boxes is $5-$75 for most, although a few can bring more.

Many collectors of tobacciana, breweriana, gambling and saloon paraphernalia are interested only in brightly colored items to decorate their walls. Others are serious historians, seeking every photograph, catalog, and scrap of historical information.

tony hyman

Beer

◆ **Anything with the name of a beer on it.**
It's called *breweriana*, and includes glasses,
coasters, trays, calendars, label collections,
signs, mugs, and anything else used to promote
beer. Lynn particularly wants tin signs and
other display advertising from around the turn of
the century. Lynn is one of the nation's fore-
most authorities on beer collectibles, and operator of an auction service exclusively devoted to
items associated with beer. No *Billy Beer* or
J.R. Beer.
Lynn Geyer,
The Brewery,
329 W. Butler,
Phoenix, AZ 85021
(602) 943-2283

◆ **Beer uniform sew-on patches from anywhere in the world.** Jim wants any patches,
arm, cap, shirt, all ages, all sizes, all breweries...any sewn patch naming a brewery. He isn't
interested in beer club patches. Please describe
condition noting whether it is used or unused,
clean or not, and indicate whether it is a "second" or has been cut from a larger patch.
Photocopy helpful.
Jim O'Brien,
Box 551,
Aurora, IL 60507
(312) 892-8535 eves/ weekends

◆ **Beer bottles with painted labels.** American
breweries only. Most of these are 6,7, or 8
ounce size, but some older ones from the 1930's
are 12 oz. There are a few, very desirable, larger bottles with painted labels. He is particularly
interested in finding New York bottles, especially from Buffalo, Rochester, Utica, Syracuse,
Troy, Tonawanda, and New York City.
Describe condition of the paint. No soft drink
bottles, please, even if from breweries.
Jim O'Brien,
Box 551,
Aurora, IL 60507
(312) 892-8535 eves/some days

◆ *Hamm's* **brewery memorabilia** including
advertising, packaging and bottles, souvenirs,
foam scrapers, coasters, bottle caps, kegs,
glasses, signs, and so on for all of Hamm's
brands. These include *Buckhorn, Velvet Glove,
Matterhorn, Burgie, Right Time, Old Bru*, and
Waldech. When selling glasses or cans, it is important to include *all* writing that appears on the
object. Pete wants everything he doesn't already
have and says that the areas around Los
Angeles, San Francisco, Houston, St. Paul, and
Baltimore "are particularly saturated with
Hamm's breweriana."
Peter Nowicki,
1531 39th Ave.,
San Francisco, CA 94122
(415) 566-7506

◆ **Pre 1965 beer and soda cans from small
regional companies.** Prefers cone topped cans
but also buys flat topped cans. Also buys brewery advertising, signs, trays, statues, glasses,
from the same period. Especially likes to find
items from the Manhattan Brewing Company
owned by Al Capone and the Grace Bros.
Brewing Company in California. Prices on cans
from these two companies tend to start at $500.
No rusty cans are wanted by this ten year
veteran collector-dealer, but "some light spotting
and aging is natural. I do require cans be sent
before a final purchase offer is made because
condition so greatly affects the value and I need
to examine cans closely."
Tony Steffens,
615 Chester,
Elgin, IL 60120
(800) 443-8712

◆ **New Jersey breweriana** from the 1930's or
older including calendars, signs, trays, tap knobs
and inserts, coasters, labels, cans, books and
misc. "I would buy some collections of general
breweriana if they contained some NJ items I
want." He warns amateurs not to guess at age of
items, that it's better to ask and urges you not to
"buy breweriana items with the thought of reselling them to make money, since the chances are
you won't." This 17 year veteran collector requests that you make it clear whether you are
seeking information or have the item for sale.
Paul Brady,
Box 811,
Newton, NJ 07860
(201) 383-7204

◆ **Near beer advertising from the days of prohibition in Chicago** and items related to Chicago pre-prohibition beers and breweries like *Budweiser, Schlitz, Blatz, Old Milwaukee, Atlas, Keely, Schoenhoffen, Sieben's,* and *Manhattan.* Wants signs, beer barrels, bottles, etc.
  Michael Graham, Roaring 20's,
  345 Cleveland Ave.,
  Libertyville, IL 60048
      (312) 362-4808 days

◆ **Beer coasters.** Want any coasters containing advertising, especially for beer. Send any quantity for my offer by return check.
  Art Landino,
  88 Centerbrook Rd.,
  Hamden, CT 06518

◆ **Pottery ginger beer bottles** and associated paper ephemera. Sven has an illustrated wants list of these bottles, some of which can be worth $150!   He is author of *The Illustrated Stone Ginger Beer*, a limited edition available for $12.50.
  Sven Stau,
  Box 1135,
  Buffalo, NY 14211
      (716) 825-5448

◆ **American and foreign miniature beer bottles** especially pre-prohibition 1880-1920. The earliest are about 5" tall, filled with beer, and have a cork stopper. These are desirable if they have complete labels or the bottles are embossed. Post-prohibition bottles are smaller and of interest only if all labels are complete and in good condition. Foreign bottles must be in mint condition to be of interest. Also bottle openers with handles in the shape of mini beer bottles, wood or metal. There is a small group of post prohibition mini beers which can be worth to $100 each. They include *Old Glory, Royal Pilsen, Wagner, Spearman, Ambrosia, Nectar, Frederick's 4 Crown, Citizens, Manro, Atlantic, Pennsy* and others. Alex will pay top price for sets of mini bottles in their original box. Condition of the label is crucial so describe every scratch or discoloration. Measure exact height. Also buys bottle shaped bottle openers. No Taiwan bottles.
  Alexander Mullin,
  915 Lincoln Ave.,
  Springfield, PA 19064

Beer Steins

◆ **Steins.** "I buy etched and print Mettlachs, colored glass steins with pewter casings/lids or fine enameling, milk.glass, early blue-gray Westerwald, faience, figural steins or plain gray steins with painted decorations of brewery logos, any Muenchen, and anything unusual. All must have lids and be before 1920. I do not want gaudy low relief pottery souvenir steins either cream colored or gray-blue. Photo is essential, as is a complete description including any cracks, hairlines, dents chips, or color wear. Lotti is a private collector and prolific writer about steins.
  Lottie Lopez,
  Box 885,
  Santa Paula, CA 93060

◆ **Steins** including fine early *Mettlach*, regimental, faience, stoneware, glass, porcelain, occupational, *Royal Vienna, Meissin,* or wooden. Gary has written two books on steins.
  Gary Kirsner,
  Box 8807,
  Coral Springs, FL 33075

◆ **Antique beer steins of all types,** from $10 to $10,000 except those made after WWII. A photo is helpful, as are all markings, materials, and a description of what is portrayed. Free appraisal.
  Les Paul,
  2615 Magnolia St. #A,
  Oakland, CA 94607
      (415) 832-2615

Whiskey

◆ **Advertising for whiskey and beer.** Also enameled back bar bottles for which he pays to $125.
   Charlie Smith,
   1006 NE 4th St.,
   Milton-Freewater, OR 97862

◆ *Jack Daniels, Green River Whiskey,* **and Lem Motlow memorabilia,** including crockery jugs, embossed bottles, cork screws, shot glasses, lighters, and old paper advertising. Older items only.
   Don Cauwels,
   3947 Old South Road,
   Murfreesboro, TN 37129
   (615) 896-3614

◆ *Green River Whiskey* **advertising and promotional materials,** including paper, magazine ads, signs, display bottles, "give-aways," counter displays, and company receipts, letterheads, etc. Will pay $100-300 for warehouse receipts and stocks. No Green River soft drink please.
   Elijah Singley,
   2301 Noble Ave.,
   Springfield, IL 62704
   (217) 546-5143 eves

◆ **Ceramic** *Jim Beam* **type figural liquor bottles.** The bottle *must* have its original stopper. Your description should include the brand name, the figure, all marks on the bottom, the dimensions, and all colors. Fred offers a price guide containing values of 1,500+ figural bottles for only $3.
   Fred Runkewich,
   Box 1423,
   Cheyenne, WY 82003
   (307) 632-1462

◆ **Shot glasses with advertising,** especially for brands of whiskey.
   Charlie Smith,
   1006 NE 4th St.,
   Milton-Freewater, OR 97862

◆ **Souvenir shot glasses.** The inscription on the glasses is vital, for this buyer and seller. No interest in home painted shot glasses. Correspondence with other collectors welcome.
   Kensil,
   241 Riviera Drive W.,
   Massapequa, NY 11758

◆ **Swizzle sticks** and picks made of any material, as long as the stick has a three dimensional or cut-out design, either letters, people, buildings, etc. Collections of at least 100 sticks are preferred. Sticks *must* advertise a product, place, or service. Generally, pays a dime each.
   Edy Chandler,
   Box 20664,
   Houston, TX 77225
   (713) 531-9615 eves

◆ **Advertising swizzle sticks.** "I'll buy or trade advertising swizzle sticks made of any material including plastic, metal, glass, wood, or laminated cardboard." Photocopy helpful.
   Joe Smith,
   4407 Seminole,
   Pasadena, TX 77504

Wine

◆ **Wine bottles with embossed oval or circular seals on the shoulder** of the bottle marked with the name and vintage, especially fine wineries and vintages. "The more crude the bottle, the better." No beer, whiskey, or wine bottles that do not have shoulder ovals. Also **pre WWII paper wine labels** especially 19th century European and pre-prohibition California companies. Prefers loose labels but will buy important ones that are still on the bottle. Rene notes that values are still relatively low for most labels yet finding them can be tough.
> Rene Rondeau,
> 120 Harbor Dr.,
> Corte Madera, CA 94925

◆ **Corkscrews and wine-related artifacts** from before WWII. Buys wine tasters, wine funnels, silver and porcelain wine labels, silver coolers, coasters, decanter wagons, and the like. Will also buy unusual drinking vessels, but **does not want to buy** glassware or cut glass decanters. Corenman is a **leading buyer of corkscrews** from 18th and 19th century who is seeking mechanical types, bar mounted types, and those with ivory silver, bone, or pearl handles. Modern post war types are not needed, nor does he want anything that is broken, missing parts, or has repairs. This 25 year veteran expert offers a catalog and illustrated wants list. Please give your phone number.
> Aaron Corenman,
> Box 747,
> Los Altos, CA 94023
> (415) 948-6174

Saloons & Prohibition

◆ **Anything associated with saloons and speakeasies** including photos of interiors and exteriors, advertising, saloon equipment catalogs, letterheads, etc. Also trade magazines such as *the National Police Gazette* pre 1919, *Fair Play, Brewers Gazette,* and others.
> Richard Bueschel,
> 414 N. Prospect Manor Ave.,
> Mt. Prospect, IL 60065

◆ **Prohibition artifacts of all kinds,** 1919-1933, especially as they relate to the gangster activity in Chicago and environs. Seeks relics from famous speakeasies such as *Colosimo's Cafe, Four Dueces, Red Lantern, Pony Inn, Cotton Club*, and *The Green Mill.* Also pamphlets, posters, and the like from the Anti-Saloon League, WCTU, the Prohibition Party, and other organizations for and against prohibition.
> Michael Graham, Roaring 20's,
> 345 Cleveland Ave.,
> Libertyville, IL 60048
> (312) 362-8531 eves

◆ **Prohibition and the manufacture, smuggling, and drinking of illegal booze,** with particular interest in rum running from Canada. Want all ephemera including handbills and advertising for speakeasies and private clubs, photos of speakeasies, and the like.
> Bob Buckie,
> 107 Sandwich Street So.,
> Amherstburg, Ontario N9V 1Z5,
> CANADA

Pipes

◆ **Pipes of many types** including carved meerschaums, Oriental opium pipes, water pipes, rare porcelain figural pipes, early bas- and high-relief wood pipes, and selected clays. A 20+ year veteran, Ben is author of *A Complete Guide To Collecting Antique Pipes*, available for $20. Ben is also a leading specialist in the literature of tobacco, and buys **books and pamphlets** on all aspects of tobacco culture and use, in any language, from any period.
Ben Rapaport,
11505 Turnbridge Lane,
Reston, VA 22094
   (703) 435-8133 eves

◆ **Name brand pre-smoked (used) briar pipes.** Especially wants *Dunhill, Barling, Castello, Charatan* and other top European brands from the 1900's. Among special wants, Barry lists *Barling* pipes with bent stems in any finish. When describing a pipe, include the brand name, its dimensions, shape, finish and all stampings on the pipe. If you are not familiar with standard pipe shapes, make a photocopy. Barry does **not** buy antique pipes, meerschaums, or tobacciana. Barry is a popular dealer who produces 6-8 color sales catalogs a year of used briar pipes.
Barry Levin,
Levin Pipes International,
RFD #1, Box 83,
Craftsbury, VT 05826
   (802) 586-7744

◆ **Antique meerschaum pipes, carved briar, and quality English briars** by *Charitan, Barling,* or *Frieborg & Treyer.* This 25 year collector also buys American Indian pipes.
Lee Pattison,
Box 24,
Franklinville, NY 14737
   (716) 676-2562

◆ **Clay pipes and clay pipe ephemera.** Especially wants faces, figurals, or political clay pipes. Prefers American pipes, but buys others. This author-historian also buys pipe molds, presses, or anything else involved in the making of clay pipes. Also wants billheads, letterheads, checks, catalogs, and other advertising before 1950 for any clay pipe maker. Has a particular interest in William Kelman, a Baltimore pipe manufacturer. Generally not interested in plain white clay pipes with no markings or decoration. Please make a photocopy of your items, indicating any markings, and tell what you know about its origin or background. Paul has produced a giant limited edition book on 19th century pipe patents which he sells for $55.
S. Paul Jung,
Box 817,
Bel Air, MD 21014
   (301) 676-2194

◆ **Antique smoking pipes and pipe parts.** Also buys books and other publications on pipes, tobacco, and related items. Will purchase complete collections as well as individual pipes. Not interested in damaged pipes or reproductions. Give size (length and width), condition, and all other information you can provide. Primary interest is in meerschaums, but also other antique pipes, especially porcelains, and any historical or unusual items.
Frank Burla,
23 West 311 Wedgewood,
Napierville, IL 60540
(312) 961-0156

Smoking tobacco

◆ **Pocket tobacco tins**, but only rare ones. No *Prince Albert, Kentucky Club, Velvet, Edgeworth, Dial,* or other common tins. Selected tin signs advertising smoking or chewing tobacco.
Ken Jones,
100 Manor Dr.,
Columbia, MO 65203

◆ **Tin tobacco cans** from before 1940, especially pocket tins, lunchboxes, and cigar cans. Wants mint or very fine condition items only. Save yourself time and effort by sending a photocopy of the top or front of your tin, give dimensions, and describe colors and condition.
Tony Hyman,
Box 699,
Claremont, CA 91711
(714) 621-5952

◆ *Mail Pouch Tobacco.* "I'll buy anything and everything, in any size and in any condition.
Mike Boggs,
4022 Farnham,
Dayton, OH 45420
(513) 252-4839 eves

◆ **All Tobacco related collectibles:** "We accept tins, pipes, cigar labels, catalogs, books, cigar boxes, posters, advertising, and other tobacco related ephemera for auction. Prefer collections, but will accept individual items if value or collectible interest is sufficiently high. Fees are 10%-20% depending upon item's value. Phone with your items in front of you."
Collectors' Clearinghouse
Tobacciana Auctions
1947 Chapman Rd.,
Claremont, CA 91711
(714) 621-5952

Cigars

◆ **Cigar boxes and all other cigar industry ephemera** including labels, advertising, photographs, counter top lighters, cigar store figures, and everything else related to cigar making, selling, and smoking before WWII. Especially want trade directories (1865-1940) listing cigar and tobacco factories. Want all materials relevant to the Cigar Maker's International Union or Samuel Gompers, former CMIU officer. Condition is important. Tony requests you photocopy the inside lid. Pays from $5 to $50+ for cigar boxes. Send an SASE for informative priced wants list. Tony is author of *Handbook Of American Cigar Boxes,* an illustrated hardback available with a *Price Guide* for $29.95. No cigar bands or items covered with cigar bands, please, except as a donation.
Tony Hyman,
Box 699,
Claremont, CA 91711
(714) 621-5952

◆ **Cigar band collections** especially U.S. bands prior to 1920. Good or mint condition, only.
Joseph Hruby,
1511 Lyndhurst Rd.,
Lyndhurst, OH 44124
(216) 449-0977

◆ **Pre 1941 cigar bands** especially older European and Cuban bands or bands with pictures of people, animals, places, etc. No common, current, or damaged bands. Not interested in incomplete sets or large accumulations of similar bands. "I will accept receipt of the bands by mail for an appraisal with an option to purchase. It is next to impossible for a seller to list all the required data. I will not make or accept an offer without seeing them or having *every* band described individually," says this 40 year veteran.
Paul Krantz,
356 Delaware Avenue NE,
Massillon, OH 44646
(216) 833-5429

Cigarettes

◆ **Cigarette packs, tins, and cardboard boxes** from obsolete U.S. brands of cigarettes. No cards, premiums, silks, flat 50's tins, or cigar or tobacco items. Give the Series Number found on the tax stamp. Dick is President of the Cigarette Pack Collector's Assn and editor of *Brandstand*, a monthly newsletter for cigarette collectors.
> Richard Elliott,
> 61 Searle St.,
> Georgetown, MA 01833
> > (508) 352-7377

◆ **Cigarette packs of discontinued brands.** Including tins, boxes, labels, etc. Wants U.S. brands only.
> David Brame,
> 5405 Vicksburg Lane,
> Durham, NC 27712

◆ *Lucky Strike* **collectibles of any kind.** "I'll buy bridge hand cards, favors, celebrity ads, pre 1930 magazine ads, and LS/MFT marked items."
> John Van Alstyne,
> 466 South Goodman St.,
> Rochester, NY 14607

◆ **Cigarette and tobacco insert cards, silks, and flannels.** Wants American 19th century items primarily, such as cards by *Allen & Ginter*, but will buy more scarce 20th century pieces. Does not want flannel flags.
> William Nielsen
> PO Box W
> Brewster, MA 02631
> > (508) 896-7389

Accessories

◆ **Smoking accessories and other objects** marked *Dunhill* including pipes, cigarette holders, cigarette lighters, pens, etc. This disabled combat vet says, "I prefer items to be sent to me for my offer. I will refund shipping costs if my purchase price is rejected. But I would like to stress *that I do not need common items, junk, or damaged goods.* I buy only for my own collection and will pay fair prices."
> C. Ray Erler,
> Box 140 Miles Run Road,
> Spring Creek, PA 16436
> > (814) 563-7287

◆ **Humidors** made of fine glass, china, or copper.
> Lee Pattison,
> Box 24,
> Franklinville, NY 14737
> > (716) 676-2562

◆ **Snuff boxes** including early American, Civil War period, and Oriental.
> Eli Hecht,
> 19 Evelyn Lane,
> Syosset, NY 11791

◆ **Cigarette lighters.** Will buy old or new, books, catalogs, brochures, pictures, advertising, parts lists, instruction sheets, boxes, counter displays, etc. Will pay cash, trade for other lighters, or borrow for inspection and research. "All material guaranteed safe return." Send Xerox© copy.
> Jack Seiderman,
> 1050 NE 120th St.,
> Miami, FL 33161
> > (305) 893-6847

Matches

◆ **Matchcover collections,** match boxes, salesman's sample books, pamphlets, and other match industry ephemera. Send brief description and SASE.
Bill Retskin,
3417-A Clayborne Ave.,
Alexandria, VA 22306-1410
(703) 768-3932

◆ **Matchcovers and matchboxes,** foreign or domestic. "I don't want damaged covers generally, but will consider those with *minor* damage if they're from the early 1930's or before." Wants to know approximately how many items, whether they are U.S. or foreign, whether they are used or unused, whether the covers are in an album or loose, and whether the matches are present. John is Secretary of the Rathkamp Matchcover Society.
John Williams,
1359 Surrey Rd., Dept. TH,
Vandalia, OH 45377
(513) 890-8684

EDITOR'S NOTE: Matchcovers are considered damaged if they are torn or dirty, or if their striker has been cut off. Collectors do not want covers that have been glued, taped, or stapled into a book.

◆ **Paper matchcover collections.** Dave is a long time collector of matchcovers and president of the Sierra Diablo Matchcover Club. He collects many different types of matchcovers and will help amateur sellers to auction their collection through his club affiliations. Individual matchcovers are not worth a great deal, but collections of early covers are worth finding out about. Dave is happy to hear from folks with questions or collections.
David Hampton,
1395 Springhill Dr.,
Pittsburg, CA 94565
(415) 432-6980

◆ **Matchsafes.** "I'll buy small pocket matchsafes, 1850-1920, in silver, brass, nickel plate, or other materials. Especially want interesting figurals or those advertising tobacco products or outlets. Make a photocopy of what you have. Price it, or I'll make an offer."
Tony Hyman,
Box 699,
Claremont, CA 91711

◆ **Matchcovers and matchboxes.** Wants interesting singles or entire estates. Hiller is a West Coast auctioneer who can handle large collections. The ideal condition for matchcovers is - unused, open, with the staples carefully removed. No "grocery store" covers, Thank You's, or covers not identified as to origin (like *Holiday Inn* covers that don't give a location). His favorite find would be a matchcover from the Lindbergh welcome home dinner.
Robert Hiller,
2501 W. Sunflower, #H5,
Santa Ana, CA 92704
(714) 540-8220

◆ **Wall model match safes made of cast iron.** No others.
George Fougere,
67 East St.,
North Grafton, MA 01536
(508) 839-2701

Sexy stuff

◆ **Most erotica.** Old or recent girlie magazines including newsstand, hardcore, nudist, "arty," cheesecake, etc. Also boxes of cut girlie magazine pages, photos, calendars, cards, movies, videos, art, and nude photo books.
    Antiquarian Bookstore,
    1070 Lafayette Rd.,
    Portsmouth, NH 03801
        (603) 436-7250

◆ **Erotica of all types, all languages, all eras,** including girlie and pornographic magazines, hard and soft cover books, sex newspapers, typescripts and mimeos, sex comics, original erotic art, films, photos, statuary, and sexually explicit objects of all types.
    C.J. Scheiner Books,
    275 Linden Blvd. B2,
    Brooklyn, NY 11226
        (718) 469-1089

◆ **Girlie magazines published by Parliament** from the 1950's, 60's, and 70's. Also *Playboy* from the 1950's only. Buys related girlie material, calendars, and paperbacks, but nothing from the 1980's. Fine condition items only. Warren offers an extensive magazine catalog for $3.
    Warren Nussbaum,
    29-10 137th Street,
    Flushing, NY 11354
        (718) 886-0558

◆ **Girlie magazines,** 1945-80, especially nudist magazines and adult store type issues from the 1960's including titles like *Tip Top, Nylon Jungle,* and *Leg Show,* tame by today's standards, but are worth $2 apiece to Michael. Fine or better condition only. No *Nugget, Dude, Swank, Mr., Cheri, Hustler, Chic,* or *Velvet.* A catalog of some of his 25,000 magazines is available for $2.
    Michael Blessing,
    A.R.S., Box 882,
    El Sobrante, CA 94803
        (415) 234-2636

◆ **Erotic art in all forms and formats** including statues, paintings, prints, post cards, photography, and three dimensional objects of all kinds from the days of the Roman empire up to the present. Especially seeks Oriental and European erotic bisque/porcelain figures. Also **original art for pin up calendars** or illustrations 1920-1970, especially work by Alberto Vargas and George Petty, but including Earl Moran, Gil Elvgren, Zoe Mozert, Armstrong, Alk Buell, Al Moore, and others. Also Vargas *Esquire* calendars and prints, other calendar pin ups, and some homemade erotica.
    Charles Martignette,
    455 Paradise Isle #306,
    Hallandale, FL 33007
        (305) 454-3474

◆ **Prostitution in the U.S.** and around the world. No surprise that he is particularly interested in items from Nevada, but he buys a wide variety of ephemera from anywhere. What have you?
    Douglas McDonald,
    Box 20443,
    Reno, NV 89515

◆ **Burlesque items** such as posters, photos, magazines, autographs etc., with emphasis on Tempest Storm, Betty Page, Blaze Starr, Irma the Body, Lili St. Cyr, Virginia Bell, and other headliners.
    John Fawcett,
    Art Dept. U-99,
    University of Conn.,
    Storrs, CT 06268
        (203) 429-9228 eves

◆ **Books about the gay lifestyle** (hard and soft cover) pre 1910 and some paper ephemera.
    Ed Drucker, Elysian Fields,
    80-50 Baxter Ave. #339,
    Elmhurst, NY 11373
        (718) 424-2789

◆ **Prophylactic (condom) and feminine hygiene** vending equipment, tins, and advertising.
    Mr. Condom,
    11417 271st Ave.,
    Trevor, WI 53179
        (414) 862-6797

Gambling

◆ **Clay, ivory, or mother-of-pearl gambling chips** and selected other memorabilia. No plain, paper, or interlocking chips. Send a sample, rubbing or photocopy. Tell how many chips of each color. Dale wrote *Antique Gambling Chips*, available with price guide for $19.95.
Dale Seymour, Past Pleasures,
Box 50863,
Palo Alto, CA 94303

◆ **Unusual playing cards, poker chips, and gambling devices and memorabilia.** All early books and paper ephemera about cards or gambling are wanted but no coin operated machines. He asks that you photocopy the Joker and the Ace of spades, and indicate whether the box is present. "Bridge size cards with picture backs are usually worthless," to this 23 year veteran dealer who offers an attractively illustrated auction catalog of cards for sale.
Gene Hochman, Full House,
Box 4057,
Boynton Beach, FL 33424

◆ **Poker chips and other gambling markers** made of ivory or mother-of-pearl with scrim-shawed designs. Designs can be numbers, animals, birds, or other patterns and figures. Prices start at $10 and up. Especially desired are chips or markers enscribed with the words "Dealer," "Your Deal," or picturing an Indian or a deer. These are worth $300 up depending on size, condition, and design. Does not want chips made of plastic, paper, clay, metal, rubber, or any mass production process. Send a photocopy of the chips you have to sell. If the chips are in a rack, describe the rack and indicate whether any chips appear to be missing. Note any maker's name. Strongly warns: **Do not clean your chips!** Eggers is editor of the *Poker Chip Newsletter*. Write for sample copy if you're a collector.
Bryan Eggers,
Box 3491,
Westlake Village, CA 91359
(805) 373-1586

◆ **Anything concerning playing cards and card games.** Unusual playing cards including transformation cards, non-standard decks, and decks with a different picture on the face of each card. Also single cards in quantity with colorful backs and unusual jokers, Aces or court cards. Also books, magazines, and other items on the games of contract bridge, auction bridge, and whist. Will consider early or limited edition books on other card games as well as plates, figurines, and other artwork depicting card playing. Will pay $100 up for *Royal Bayreuth* "Devil and the Cards" patterned pieces. Photocopies almost essential. Include an SASE to get an answer.
Bill Sachen,
927 Grand Ave.,
Waukegan, IL 60085
(312) 662-7204

◆ **Gambling and cheating devices** and pre 1900 **playing cards.** Steamship cards will bring at least $25 a deck and ivory **poker chips** are worth $10-$35 each.
Charlie Smith,
1006 NE 4th St.,
Milton-Freewater, OR 97862

◆ **Scratch off type lottery tickets.** "I'll buy instant rub-off lottery tickets from 1970's and 80's."
Bill Pasquino,
1824 Lyndon Ave.,
Lancaster PA 17602

◆ **Scratch off type lottery tickets.** Wants a variety of state and local lottery tickets.
Karen Lea Rose,
4420 Wisconsin Ave.,
Tampa, FL 33616

9
Sports

Dr. Hyman's Prescription

The world of sports is another area where nearly everything is collectible. Almost all sports related items from before 1960 (and many later) will find ready buyers if in good condition.

Uniforms, balls, trophies, photos, programs, and other items are collected, with top prices usually going to relics from Hall of Fame baseball players.

There are hundreds of thousands of sport card collectors, with new ones joining the ranks each year. Because of the popularity of card collecting numerous bubble gum cards, some less than 20 years old, have substantial value.

Any of the early cigarette company ball player cards are also of great interest. Rare but unimportant players of 1900 are often worth less than star players of the 1960's and 70's, however.

Another very hot collectible of the 1990's will be fishing tackle and plugs. These brightly colored imitation baits have already brought as much as $10,000 for hand made rarities, and plugs by major makers from the 1930's can exceed $100. Don't ever sell fishing equipment without first making certain about what you have.

The importance of condition varies with the item. Collectors of sports gum cards are very fussy, while there are other sports collectors willing to pay $30 and up for broken major league bats. You describe the condition carefully and let the collector decide how important condition is.

tony hyman

All Sports

◆ **Sports memorabilia of all types, especially baseball**, but also football, boxing, hockey, and others. Buys programs, baseball bats, autographed balls, major league uniforms and shoes, gum cards, sports advertising, contracts, sheet music, buttons, books, scorecards, tickets, prints, films, photos, and more. Kenrich, one of the largest mail order sports dealers, has 23 years' experience.
  Bill Colby, Kenrich Co.,
  9418T Las Tunas Dr.,
  Temple City, CA 91780
    (818) 286-3888

◆ **Baseball, football, boxing, basketball, and Olympic memorabilia** nature is wanted:
  (1) Uniforms, trophies, and medals from
        famous athletes past and present;
  (2) Baseball gum cards pre 1920;
  (3) Cabinet size sports photographs;
  (4) Posters and advertising display pieces
        related to sports, pre 1930;
  (5) World Series (1903-11) and all star game
        programs, and press pins;
  (6) Black baseball bats;
  (7) Rare autograph material of now deceased
        important players;
  (8) Championship boxing belts and robes;
  (9) Song sheets, games, and toys related
        to sports pre 1920;
"Unique, unusual, and rare" sports equipment and other material, especially related to Hall of Fame players from the 1920's and 1930's. All items must be old, rare, and original.
  Joel Platt,
  Sports Immortals Museum,
  807 Liberty Ave.,
  Pittsburgh, PA 15222
    (412) 232-3008

◆ **Women in sports.** "I'll buy early photos, programs, calendars, posters, etc. of women in sports, either individuals or team sports. Please photocopy and price."
  C. Smith,
  84 Plummer Road,
  Gorham, ME 04038

◆ **Baseball, football, and boxing memorabilia** including gum cards, World Series programs, books pre 1920, display posters, baseball scorecards pre 1900, baseball equipment pre 1920, football equipment pre 1930, all uniforms pre 1960, baseball guides pre 1920, football guides pre 1930, and advertising display pieces. "Premium prices paid for 19th century baseball items." Sought after boxing items are those dealing with James J. Corbett, Jim Jeffries, and John L. Sullivan. This 30 year veteran collector offers $1,500 for an *Allen & Ginter* poster depicting 1890's baseball cards, but does not want *anything* after 1970.
  John Buonaguidi,
  2830 Rockridge Drive,
  Pleasant Hill, CA 94523
    (415) 372-9093

◆ **Early sports memorabilia.** "I'll buy sports ephemera 1860-1970, mainly early baseball items. I want cards, pins, postcards, silks, leathers, advertising, and autographs from boxing and football as well as baseball." Describe the condition and indicate the price you have in mind.
  Steve Applebaum,
  5210 N. Arsdell Pl.,
  Arcadia, CA 91006
    (818) 350-1041

◆ **Baseball memorabilia,** pre 1948: postcards, photos, games, programs, yearbooks, guides, advertising, fans, sheet music, etc. Buys autographs from early deceased hall-of-fame players. Pictures of major league baseball players on gum and tobacco cards, programs, silks, sheet music, photographs, and advertising before 1950 are wanted by this 25 year advanced collector-dealer, but he does not buy anything after 1960. Be as accurate as possible with descriptions and include your phone number with your letter. Photocopies are helpful.
  William Mastro,
  25 Brook Lane,
  Palos Park, IL 60464
    (312) 361-2117

◆ **Philadelphia Phillies memorabilia,** especially pre 1920 programs.
  Gary Gatanis,
  3283-B Cardiff Ct.,
  Toledo, OH 43606

◆ **Negro League memorabilia** including autographed balls, bats, gloves, and uniforms. Anything related to the old Negro Leagues will be considered as long as it's in good condition.
   Robert Faro,
   Box 11286,
   Boulder, CO 80301

◆ **Babe Ruth material.** Send photocopy to this major Eastern stamp and ephemera dealer.
   Harvey Dolin & Company,
   5 Beekman St. #406,
   New York, NY 10038
      (212) 267-0216

◆ **Baseball memorabilia from the Pacific Coast League** and selected other minor leagues. Most items wanted date from the 1940's and early 50's and include programs, selected team and League year books, *P.C.L. Baseball News*, postcards of ball parks, 1947 *Signal Oil* cards, and team photos. No cards from *Mothers Cookies, Union Oil, Remar*, or 1948 *Signal* gas. Also buys programs and other ephemera associated with **the non-baseball use of Gilmore field, Gilmore stadium, and the Pan Pacific auditorium.**
   Jerry Mezerow,
   442 Via Porto Ave.,
   Anaheim, CA 92806
      (714) 630-6198

◆ **Notre Dame football programs and other memorabilia** from pre 1960, especially Knute Rockne and George Gipp autographs and other items. Other Notre Dame sports considered.
   Michael Tiltges,
   2040 185th St.,
   Lansing, IL 60438
      (312) 895-3222

◆ **Balls** including pre 1950 footballs, baseballs, soccer balls, basketballs. Also wants old **wooden skis, lacrosse equipment, bamboo poles, snow shoes, trophies, and riding equipment.**
   Joan Brady,
   834 Central Ave.,
   Pawtucket, RI
      (401) 723-4693 or 725-5753

◆ **Canadian sports memorabilia.** "I'll buy all items associated with **Canadian hockey** teams and players before 1960, **Canadian lacrosse** teams and players, and **Canadian basketball** teams and players. I'm particularly looking for game schedules and calendars, programs, autographed photos, gum cards, etc. If practical, a clear photocopy is best. Small items can be sent on approval as I will always refund postage."
   Michael Rice,
   Box 286,
   Saanichton, BC V0S 1M0
   CANADA
      (604) 652-9047 eves

◆ **Boxing memorabilia of all types.** "I'm the world's largest dealer in boxing memorabilia. Large stocks on hand to buy, sell, or trade." Please photograph of photocopy.
   Jerome Shochet,
   6144 Oakland Mills Rd.,
   Sykesville, MD 21784
      (301) 795-5879

◆ **Strongmen, weightlifters, and bodybuilders.** "I'll buy magazines, photos, books, posters, sculpture, and equipment related to these fields."
   David Chapman,
   2377 Teviot St.,
   Los Angeles, CA 90039
      (213) 667-2430

◆ **Ephemera related to Frank Gotch**, a turn of the century wrestling champion. Wants posters, postcards, books, photographs, etc.
   Don Olson,
   Box 397,
   Humboldt, IA 50548

◆ **Ice skating memorabilia.** Wants early skates, skater's lanterns, Ice Show programs, and related books, magazines, postcards, photos, autographs, etc. Send details and prices.
   Keith Pendell,
   1230 N. Cypress,
   La Habra, CA 90631

◆ **College and pro football programs** pre 1950.
> Farley,
> Ridge Road,
> West Orange, NJ 07052

◆ **Roller skating memorabilia.**
> Frank Zottoli,
> Box 241,
> Holden, MA 01520

◆ **Recreational and competitive horseback riding.** Wants ephemera related to Morgan horses, Arabians, saddlebred horses, polo ponies, sidesaddles, and Lippizzaners. Buys books, catalogs, prints, and tack. She would especially like to find books by or illustrated by Paul Brown and George Ford Morris.
> Barbara Cole,
> October Farm,
> Rt. 2, Box 183-C,
> Raleigh, NC 27610

◆ **Pool tables** and other ephemera related to pool or billiards. Wants cased custom cues, catalogs, advertising, and other items.
> Time After Time,
> 9A Main St.,
> Danbury, CT 06810
> (203) 743-2801

◆ **Rugby and soccer memorabilia** wanted for resale. Can be either US or foreign. Wants prints, cigarette cards, stamps, postcards, and paper ephemera. Also buys large items like coin operated games and strength machines with soccer or rugby themes.
> Matt Godek,
> Box 565,
> Merrifield, VA 22116

Golf & Tennis

◆ **Golf memorabilia pre 1930,** especially:
(1) **Unusual wood shaft golf clubs;**
(2) **Golf books, magazines, and catalogs** pre 1930;
(3) **China and pottery** with a golf motif by Lenox, Doulton, other fine makers;
(4) **Old golf balls** and golf ball molds;
(5) **Quality miscellaneous items** related to "the knickers era."
This 35 year veteran collector does **not** want petty jewelry, reproductions, modern ashtrays, trinkets, common wood shaft clubs and common golf bags. Frank prefers you set the price you want, but will make offers on rare items.
> Frank Zadra,
> Rt. 3, Box 3318,
> Spooner, WI 54801

◆ **Old golf books, magazines, and ephemera.** No paperback reprints or post 1950 magazines.
> George Lewis,
> Golfiana,
> Box 291,
> Mamaroneck, NY 10543

◆ **Golf award medals from before WWII** and other pre 1930 golf ephemera. If it's early and in good condition, ship it insured for his offer.
> Rich Hartzog,
> Box 4143 BBL,
> Rockford, IL 61110
> (815) 226-0771

◆ **Tennis memorabilia** such as trophies, figurines, art, postcards, cartoons, tableware, trade cards, lighters, first day covers, and all sorts of other little tennis-related knicknacks from before 1940. He does *not* want to buy rackets, photos, newspaper clippings, books, autographs, or programs, but "I'll buy any quantity of other reasonably priced items if they send a photo or photocopy and price what they have."
> Sheldon Katz,
> 211 Roanoke Ave.,
> Riverhead, NY 11901
> (516) 369-1100

Auto Racing

◆ **Auto racing ephemera,** including books, programs, posters, and what have you.
   Walter Miller,
   6710 Brooklyn Pkwy,
   Syracuse, NY 13211
      (315) 432-8282

◆ **Auto racing memorabilia.** One piece or a complete collection of anything and everything associated with automobile racing: awards, arm bands, board games, dash plaques, entry forms, flags, goggles, magazines, movies, photographs, paintings, passes, postcards, posters, rule books, toys, trophies, uniforms, you name it. If you know any history of the item, let him know.
   George Koyt,
   8 Lenora Ave.,
   Morrisville, PA 19067

◆ **Indianapolis 500** pit badges pre 1952, race tickets pre 1950, racing programs pre 1941, and all rings or trophies. Jerry will pay $300 for a 1946 pit badge!
   Jerry Butak,
   242 W. Adams,
   Villa Park, IL 60181
      (312) 834-3729

Horse Racing

◆ **Thoroughbred racing memorabilia** including racing and breeding books, magazines, prints, games, photos, trade cards, trophies, postcards, etc., especially early Kentucky Derby programs and anything unusual. All thoroughbreds will be considered. No harness horses.
   Gary Medeiros,
   1319 Sayre St.,
   San Leandro, CA 94579

◆ **Trotters, pacers, and harness racing memorabilia,** 1800-1960, including racing newspapers, histories, yearbooks, sires & dams books, registers, pre 1900 veterinary books, horseshoeing books, posters and prints, and other ephemera.
   Fred Rinker,
   1168 Kaladar Dr.,
   London, Ontario N5V 2R5,
   CANADA
      (519) 455-5531

◆ **Dan Patch memorabilia,** especially a Dan Patch cigar box and mechanical postcard. Also wants pre 1930 **Kentucky Derby programs.**
   Gary Gatanis,
   3283-B Cardiff Ct.,
   Toledo, OH 43606

Gum Cards
Sports & non-sports

◆ **Baseball and all other sports and non-sports cards** from gum, tobacco, dairy, candy and other sources. This major sports card dealers especially wants baseball cards pre 1930. Also buys **wrappers** from pre 1970 gum packs, and lots of other sports memorabilia.
    Bill Colby,
    Kenrich Co.,
    Box 248T,
    Temple City, CA 91780

◆ **Baseball and other sports cards** from gum, cigarettes, or candy. Also buys all yearbooks, programs, press pins, ticket stubs, autographs. "To a lesser degree" he also buys **basketball, football, and hockey items,** especially cards 1930-1959. Give condition details.
    Robert Sevchuk,
    70 Jerusalem Ave.,
    Hicksville, NY 11801
        (516) 822-4089

◆ **Baseball and football cards** pre 1980. Singles, sets, or cases.
    Robert DeLong,
    Bob's Cards & Coins,
    Box 38,
    Black River Falls, WI 54615
        (715) 284-2135

◆ **Pre 1975 non-sports cards from candy, tobacco, and other sources.** Wants *Horrors of War, Dark Shadows, Hogans Heroes, Lost in Space, Mars Attack,* etc. Also seeks unopened boxes, wrappers, original artwork, and advertising, especially for test issues of *Hee Haw, The Waltons, Green Acres* etc. "I'll pay $1,000 for the set of *Horrors of War.*" Items must be in excellent to mint condition with no creases and fairly sharp corners.
    Roxanne Toser,
    4019 Green St.,
    Harrisburg, PA 17110
        (717) 238-1936

◆ **Baseball cards pre-1940,** from gum, tobacco, candy, and other products.
    William Mastro,
    25 Brook Lane,
    Palos Park, IL 60464

◆ **Non-sports gum cards from 1930-49.** Wants cards featuring pirates, World War II, Indians and cowboys, and comic strip characters only.
    Walter Koenig,
    Box 4395,
    North Hollywood, CA 91607

Bobbing head dolls

◆ **Bobbing head sports and non-sports dolls of all types,** especially composition/papier mache dolls from the 1960's. Wants all types of dolls from all sports, but especially miniature bobbing heads about 4" tall and real player dolls. When you write, give the color of the base.
Dale Jerkins,
1647 Elbur Ave.,
Lakewood, OH 44107
(216) 226-7349

◆ **Bobbing head sports and non-sports dolls,** Japanese ceramic or composition models only, no plastic dolls or dolls made in Taiwan or Korea. Indicate team or character portrayed. Also give the size, color, and shape of the base. Will pay $150 for any Blackface bobbing baseball doll in perfect condition and $600 for a perfect Roberto Clemente. Also wants **sports and non sports plastic statues by Hartland.** Will pay between $100 and $700 for excellent and complete statues, depending on the character.
Chip Norris,
Box 235,
Leonardtown, MD 20650
(301) 475-2951

◆ **Bobbing head and nodder dolls.** Prefer people or famous characters. Special wants include the *Pillsbury Doughboy, Elsie* the Borden's cow, Popeye, Presidents Eisenhower and Kennedy, Maynard, Minnie Mouse, Porky Pig, and Elmer Fudd. Also want double nodder salt and pepper shakers, ashtrays, and other unusual nodders.
Roxanne Toser,
4019 Green St.,
Harrisburg, PA 17110
(717) 238-1936

◆ **Bobbing head dolls.** "I'll buy sports teams and sports personalities as well as some non-sports nodders, especially comic characters and advertising personalities. Interested in all sizes, but I want only the old papier mache ones, not vinyl or made in Taiwan or Korea. Indicate the size, color, and shape of the base, what the figure is holding, and its condition in detail."
Keith Schneider,
6501 20th NE,
Seattle, WA 98115
(206) 524-1606

Decoys

◆ **Wooden decoys and calls** for ducks, geese, crow, and fish. Buys ice fishing decoys, wooden plugs, and early reels made by *Meek, Talbot, Milan*, or *KY Bluegrass* (for which he will pay $100 up). Joe quotes prices of $200+ paid for better duck calls. Also buys various hunting and fishing signs. He suggests you send photos, but may require you to send the item for inspection.
  Joe Tonelli,
  Box 459,
  Lake Andes, SD 57356
    (605) 337-2301 or (815) 664-4580

◆ **Wooden decoys, especially Canadian.** Buys ducks, geese, shore birds, crows, owls, and fish spearing decoys. Does not want new items or reproductions. A photograph should accompany your letter. Make certain to include your phone number and the best time to call. Valiant is an active dealer who sends out catalogs of decoys for sale.
  Hugh Valiant,
  7 Tuxedo Drive,
  Dauphin, Manitoba, R7N 0A2
  CANADA
    (204) 638-6710

◆ **Wooden decoys of all types** including duck, swan, goose, crow, owl, shorebirds, and fish. Only old wooden items with original paint and patina. You must include photos.
  Art Pietraszewski, Jr.,
  60 Grant St.,
  Depew, NY 14043
    (716) 681-2339

◆ **Early decoys of all types** are wanted by this well known auctioneer, noted for his record setting decoy sales. Many duck decoys have value in excess of $1,000 so you are encouraged to send a good photograph along with a tracing or sketch of any markings or signatures on the bottom. No decoys made after 1940 please.
  James D. Julia Auctions,
  Rt. 201, Skowhegan Rd.,
  Fairfield, ME 04937
    (207) 453-9725

◆ **Wooden fish decoys used for ice fishing and spearing,** both factory and handmade, as long as they are pre 1960. Principally interested in Michigan made fish decoys, but will consider all high quality wooden fish, especially those whose maker can be identified. Also duck decoys, spears, bait shop signs shaped like fish, and wooden carved wall plaques. Particularly interested in fish decoys by Oscar Peterson, Wm. Jesse Ramey, and Hans Jenner, Senior, especially in sizes over 10" which can be worth from $100 to $1,000 depending on the item, maker, size, and condition.
  Gary Miller,
  Nautic Antiques,
  Rt. 2, Box 852,
  Suttons Bay, MI 49682
    (616) 271-6747

◆ **Old duck, crow, and goose calls.** "I'll buy them in any quantity. I also buy **crow decoys** made of wood." Send a note or call with the description and the price you'd like.
  Jack Morris,
  821 Sandy Ridge,
  Doylestown, PA 18901
    (215) 348-9561

Hunting & Fishing

◆ **Hunting, fishing, and trapping licenses, buttons, and badges from any state** pre 1945, especially pre 1920 non-resident licenses which can be worth $25-$150. A 1927 NY deer tag will bring $150. All minnow and set line tags are worth from $2-$25. Although items from before the turn of the century are best, almost any tag from before 1930 is worth at least $5, so well worth your time.
   James Case,
   Box 168, Cane Rd.,
   Lindley, NY 14858

◆ **Antique fishing tackle** including bait and fly reels, bamboo fly and bait casting rods, willow creels, wooden nets, fishing lures (especially those with glass eyes), and early tackle boxes made of leather. Wants to find a brass *Snyder* bait casting reels from early 1800's. Also buys fishing equipment **catalogs and books**.   Not interested in anything made in the last 20 years.
   Robert Whitaker,
   2810 E. Desert Cove Ave.,
   Phoenix, AZ 85028
     (602) 992-7304

◆ **Fishing tackle from before 1945** including wooden lures (especially with glass eyes or made of hollow metal), high quality fresh or salt water reels, fine cased bamboo rods, and tackle boxes. "Most people can't tell good stuff from bad. I'll check it all for them," says this 6 year veteran collector. List all brand names and numbers and make photocopies of lures.
   Rick Edmisten,
   Box 686,
   North Hollywood, CA 91603
     (818) 763-9406

◆ **Odd fish scalers.**
   Thomas McKinnon,
   Box 86,
   Wagram, NC 28396

10
Americana

Dr. Hyman's Prescription

"Americana" is a catch-all word used to describe popular relics of American history, usually associated with politics, but including other facets of life that are uniquely American.

There are no special considerations when describing Americana. Follow the rules for describing glass, paper, books, photos, depending upon what it is you wish to sell.

Items in this chapter can be quite valuable. A 1920 campaign button featuring Roosevelt and Cox has sold in excess of $30,000. That's an extreme, of course, but many political items can be worth your attention.

Nearly everything having to do with the Old West, cowboys, Western lawmen, early cattle ranches, and the like will find ready market. Almost all pre 1900 items from west of the Mississippi will sell. You should check your paper goods, including old letters, carefully.

Indian rugs, blankets, carvings, baskets, masks, and, to a lesser extent, jewelry, are all worth getting expert advice prior to selling. Prices in excess of $5,000 are not unusual for pre 1900 items, and prices twenty times that are not unknown.

Surprisingly, Scouting items can be worth your time and attention. Most items are worth under $100, but a few are substantially higher. Pre 1925 items should be treated with particular care.

tony hyman

Indian artifacts

◆   **Anything pertaining to the American Indian and Eskimo**, including art, rugs, crafts, baskets, pottery, weapons, and clothing. Buys anything, but especially interested in old beaded buckskin moccasins, offering to pay up to $100, depending on condition and tribe. Does not buy modern Indian items. Prefers a color photo be sent with your inquiry. The Museum prefers that you price what you have to sell, but "our appraiser will suggest a value after examination."
Lynn Munger,
Potawatomi Museum,
Rt. 1 Box 147A,
Angola, IN 46703
     (219) 833-4700

◆   **Museum quality American Indian relics.** "I'll buy fine baskets, pre 1900 Plains beadwork, quillwork, weapons, etc., Southwestern pots, pre 1950 jewelry, Kachinas, Navajo blankets and rugs, Northwest Coast masks and carvings, Eskimo objects, old photos of Indians, and more. Some of these items can be worth $10,000 or more. Dan does not want anything modern, small pots, or fake / reproductions of early work.
Daniel Brown,
Box 149,
Davenport, CA 95017
     (408) 426-0134

◆   **Hopi and Southwest pottery**, new or old.
Dwight Huber,
3805 Torre,
Amarillo, TX 79109

◆   **Hopi and Zuni Pueblo Kachina dolls.** "I especially want those made between 1900 and 1940. Other Indian items, dance wands, costume parts, pottery, baskets, and jewelry from Southwest Indians are also of interest." Kachina dolls can range in value from $100 to $5,000 or more, but there are many fake Kachinas., "An expert can tell the difference." He'll need a photo and all background information.
John C. Hill,
6990 E. Main,
Scottsdale, AZ 85251
     (602) 946-2910

◆   **North and South American Indian rugs** and weavings are purchased by this major dealer in Oriental rugs.
Renate Halpern,
Halpern Galleries,
325 E. 79th Street,
New York, NY 10021

◆   **Indian baskets and other art** are wanted by this dealer in American arts and crafts.
Louis Picek,
Box 340,
West Branch, IA 52358

Cowboys

◆ **Cowboy relics, spurs, bits, chaps, cuffs, boots, hats, brand books, etc.** Offers $100 to $500 for silver mounted spurs and bits.
Charlie Smith,
Western Americana,
Rt. 3, Box 3,
Milton-Freewater, OR 97862

◆ **Buffalo Bill memorabilia** including his personal history, his Wild West Show, his associates and the Sioux Indians. Wants photographs, programs, business paper, souvenir items sold at the Wild West Show, advertising, pre 1918 newspaper clippings, tobacco cards, tickets, letters, and many other items. Seldom makes offers, preferring you to set the price.
Melvin Schulte,
211 4th Ave., SW,
Pocahontas, IA 50574
(712) 335-3904

◆ **Cowboy equipment and regalia** including:
(1) **Spurs** of all type except English and new military. Especially unusual spurs that are silver and maker marked;
(2) **Cuffs** made of leather, chaps, hats, scarves, and fancy boots;
(3) **Western saddles**, pre 1920, all types, if maker marked, including black military McClellan saddles;
(4) **Saddle bags** with maker's marks;
(5) **Rawhide** riatas, quirts, bridles, etc., that are marked, tooled, or carved;
(6) **Horse bits** more than 50 years old with silver mounts or inlay, although some plain and some foreign are sought, so inquire;
(7) **Prison made spurs**, horse bits, quirts, belts, and lead ropes;
(8) **Saddle maker's catalogs** pre 1936;
(9) **Photographs** of old cowboy scenes;
(10) **Advertising related to the frontier**, especially watch fobs;
(11) **Movie posters** of cowboy movies;
(12) **Books by Will James**.
Especially wants marked spurs authenticated as having been made for some well known personality. Does not want anything made in the last 25 years or made in the Far East. In your description, make certain to mention all marks. Give dimensions and mention all damage or repairs. He prefers if you set the price, but will make offers to assist amateur sellers. No guns! Will buy single items of collections for resale.
Lee Jacobs,
Box 3098,
Colorado Springs, CO 80934
(719) 473-7101

Politics, politicians & political symbols

◆ **Presidential campaign memorabilia made of paper or cloth,** from any campaign before 1976. *All* candidates are wanted including third party or those who lost in primaries, but Lincoln is a particular favorite. Small paper items from the 19th century are generally worth from $5-$15 and include pamphlets, posters, tickets, sample ballots, and cards of any kind. Cloth items such as bandanas, flags, ties, ribbons, and handkerchiefs are wanted, as long as they were used in a presidential campaign. He'll pay $75-$250 for bandanas picturing candidates. **He does not buy** buttons, bumper stickers, or daily newspapers, and prefers to buy piles of paper rather than single pieces, unless the items are early or unusual. When writing to him, indicate which candidate, the year (if you know), the size of your item, any slogans or message, and any pictures.

Charles Hatfield,
1411 South State St.,
Springfield, IL 62704

◆ **Election memorabilia of all types, 1780-1960,** for resale, especially higher quality items (not paper). Wants china, ribbons, plates, mirrors, clocks, boxes, glass, paintings, textiles, etc., that are political or patriotic in content. "I'll pay from $500-$5,000 for small historical medallions with pewter rims and lithographed portraits of military and political figures.

Rex Stark,
49 Wethersfield Rd.,
Bellingham, MA 02019
(508) 966-0994

◆ **Political buttons, tokens, and ribbons from any election before 1925.** From before 1910, he will buy glass, china, paper, ribbons, canes, figures, silks, etc. The only buttons after 1925 that he wants are those that catalog for more than $20 in Ted Hake's book on buttons.

Rich Hartzog, World Exonumia,
Box 4143 BBL,
Rockford, IL 61110
(815) 226-0771

◆ **Items personally used by U.S. Presidents or their families.** He'll buy White House china, glasses, canes, hats, cigarette boxes, and all sorts of other trivia associated with the White House and its occupants. Also presidential autographs. Crucial to any relic, however, you *must* be able to give an item's history. No fakes, repros, reprints, souvenirs, or common items.

Raleigh DeGeer Amyx,
Box 465,
Vienna, VA 22183
(703) 938-1956

◆ **Presidential memorabilia** including glass, china, campaign buttons and ribbons, posters, White House gift items, inauguration medals, invitations, Xmas cards, etc. Will pay $4,000 for a mint condition Theodore Roosevelt inaugural medal. This expert dealer is author of *Collectors Guide to Presidential Inaugural Medals and Memorabilia* available for $8.95.

H. Joseph Levine,
6550-I Little River Turnpike,
Alexandria, VA 22312
(703) 354-5454

◆ **Victoria Woodhull memorabilia.** Anything, in any condition, wanted about this spiritualist, feminist, and Presidential candidate, from the time prior to her leaving for England in 1877. Wants portraits, photos, programs, flyers, handbills, personal effects, and any publications by or about her that were written prior to 1900. Materials from **the 1872 Presidential campaign of the Equal Rights Party** are sought.

Ronald Lowden, Jr.,
314 Chestnut Ave.,
Narberth, PA 19072
(215) 667-0257 anytime

◆ **Calvin Coolidge ephemera** including postcards, commemoratives, campaign items, ephemera, and the like. List what you have and price it.

John Waterhouse,
76 Hillcrest,
Glastonbury, CT 06033

◆ **William Jennings Bryan memorabilia** including campaign items, letters, banners, autographs, newspapers, photographs, etc. Also books by or about Bryan, and personal items owned by him.
Francis Moul,
Wordsmith Stores,
Box O,
Syracuse, NE 68446

◆ **William Jennings Bryan and Tom Dewey memorabilia.**
Rich Hartzog,
World Exonumia,
Box 4143 BBL,
Rockford, IL 61110
(815) 226-0771

◆ **Personal and other memorabilia related to Harding, Coolidge, Hoover, FDR and Al Smith.** If offering personal items, documentation will be requested.
Michael Graham,
345 Cleveland Ave.,
Libertyville, IL 60048
(312) 362-4808 days

◆ **Illinois and Chicago politicians of the 1920's.** Wants posters, pamphlets, photographs, and buttons from Chicago politicians of the prohibition era such as Mayors William Thompson, William Dever, and Anton Cermak. Also Illinois Governor Len Small, US Senator Charles Deneen, and Cook County States Attorney Robert Crowe. Especially wants items related to prohibition and gangsters. If offering personal items, documentation will be requested.
Michael Graham,
345 Cleveland Ave.,
Libertyville, IL 60048
(312) 362-4808 days

◆ **John F. Kennedy ephemera.** "Top dollar paid," he says, for unusual items associated with Kennedy. No newspapers, *Life* magazine, or clipping books, please.
Robert Flemming,
14755 Ventura Blvd. #840,
Sherman Oaks, CA 91423
(818) 762-0001

◆ **Women's suffrage and political campaign** items, especially buttons, ribbons, posters, and pennants.
Ken Florey
153 Haverford,
Hamden, CT 06517
(203) 248-1233

◆ **Tennessee political campaigns.** "I'll buy buttons, posters, postcards, and other souvenirs of Tennessee political campaigns, especially for governor. I'll also pay $30-$100 newspapers that cover the assassination of Edward Ward Cermack." Photocopies and SASE, please.
Peggy Dillard,
Box 210904,
Nashville, TN 37221
(615) 646-1605

◆ **Canadian election memorabilia** especially pinback buttons and badges from political campaigns prior to 1965, especially John MacDonald and Wilfred Laurier material. Small items may be sent on approval. If Mike does not buy them, he will reimburse your postage.
Michael Rice,
Box 286,
Saanichton, BC V0S 1M0,
CANADA
(604) 652-9047 eves

◆ **White House memorabilia** including china, dinnerware, silverware, jewelry, pieces of the White House itself, and anything that authentically came from the White House.
Paul Hartunian,
127B East Bradford Ave.,
Cedar Grove, NJ 07009
(201) 857-7275

◆ **Statue of Liberty items.** What have you? Send a photocopy of what you have to this well known stamp dealer.
Harvey Dolin & Company,
5 Beekman St., #406,
New York, NY 10038
(212) 267-0216

Scouting

◆ **Boy and Girl Scout items from the early years** of the programs especially uniforms, badges, medals, dolls and games, postcards, posters, and official literature. Some later uncommon badges and pins are also needed such as the insignia of the Senior Scouting programs, Scout Jamborees, Order of the Arrow Honor Society, and important adult insignia. "I'm especially interested in the first dark blue Girl Scout uniform and will pay $500 for one." Also historical items related to founders of Scouting, including Baden-Powell, Juliette Low, Seton, Beard, West, Boyce, and Robinson. No fiction, or items less than 40 years old, except for rare patches. "A photocopy is worth 1,000 words."
> Cal Holden,
> 257 Church St.,
> Doylestown, OH 44230
>   (216) 658-2793

◆ **Boy Scout items of all sorts** including posters, toys, photos, badges, Order Of the Arrow items, magazines, Rockwell plates, etc. *Boy Scout Handbook* pre 1940, *Patrol Leader Handbook* pre 1945, and many other pre 1945 fiction and non-fiction Scouting books including *Every Boy's Library* with original dust jackets. Buys Cub, adult, and Air Scout uniforms pre 1940 and all pins and medals before 1960. Offers up to $750 for a 1924 World Jamboree patch. Also items from the founders of Scouting.
> Doug Bearce,
> Box 4742,
> Salem, OR 97302
> (503) 399-9872

◆ **Pre 1960 Boy Scout memorabilia.** "I will buy official and semi-official items, including toys, card games, pins, patches, uniforms, etc., especially National and International events. Handbooks before 1940 are wanted as are books by Baden-Powell, J.E. West, E.T. Seton, Dan Beard, and other Scouting authors." Sayers wrote *Value Guide to Scouting Collectables.* Sayers buys outright or resells on consignment.
> Rolland Sayers,
> 607 NW 7th St.,
> Andrews, TX 79714
>   (915) 523-2902

◆ **Boy Scout memorabilia and patches,** especially World Jamboree items pre 1951, National Jamboree patches pre 1940, Order of the Arrow items pre 1940 and anything "old and rare." Pays $1,000 each for 1924 World Jamboree patch or Lodge 219 Order of the Arrow pocket flap. Other World and National events can be worth $100 each.
> Ron Aldridge,
> 14908 Knollview,
> Dallas, TX 75248
>   (214) 239-3574

◆ **Girl Scout memorabilia.** Wants to buy pre 1960 catalogs, postcards, magazines, uniforms, handbooks 1912-1920, equipment, and other items. Send a list of what you have along with a photo or Xerox©. Do not send items without prior arrangement.
> Jerry King,
> 8429 Katy Freeway,
> Houston, TX 77024
>   (713) 465-2500

◆ **Camp Fire Girls memorabilia** including hat pins, pocket knives, first leaders pin, catalogs of Camp Fire items, pre 1940 membership cards, and more. Also pre 1940 Camp Fire magazines and manuals, and a long list of fictional "girl's series" books.
> Alice O'Rear,
> WO-HE-LO Museum,
> 113 N. 19th Ave.,
> Cornelius, OR 97113

◆ **Uniforms, diaries, historical ephemera from** *all* **Scouting organizations,** 1910-1930, including Air Scouts, Sea Scouts, Girl Scouts, Brownies, Lone Scouts, Pioneer Scouts, etc. No fiction, post 1925 magazines, or high priced items. NO OFFERS.
> Chester County Scout Museum,
> 1225 Dogwood Dr.,
> West Chester, PA 19380

Famous folks

◆ **Samuel Gompers memorabilia** including photographs, autographed documents, letters, books, speeches, newspaper clippings, magazine articles, political cartoons, pamphlets, etc., having to do with his activities *prior to* founding the AFL in 1886. A few later items also wanted so please inquire about any Gompers item. Gompers was associated with the cigar industry for 20 years and unionism for more than half a century. Even though a nationally important figure, Gompers hand wrote almost everything.
Tony Hyman,
Box 699,
Claremont, CA 91711
(714) 621-5952

◆ **Lillie Langtry memorabilia** including postcards, photographs, cigarette cards and silks, trade cards, letters, personal endorsements, theater programs, posters, performance tickets, costume or set sketches, and cosmetics issued under her name. Also wants a wine label or bottle produced on Langtry Farms, 1889-1906, which could be worth as much as $500. Langtry was also known as Langtree, the Jersey Lily, Lady Lillie de Bathe, Mr. Jersey, and Emilie Charlotte Le Breton. Also wants material on **Edward Langtry and Freddie Gebhard(t)**.
Orville Magoon,
Lillie Langtry Collection,
Box 279,
Middletown, CA 95461
(707) 987-2385 days

◆ **Carrie Nation memorabilia** including vinegar bottles in her caricature, souvenir hatchet pins, photos, tickets to lectures, *The Hatchet*, newspaper articles about her, *anything* else.
Steve Chyrchel,
Route #2 Box 362,
Eureka Springs, AR 72632
(501) 253-9244

◆ **John Chapman ("Johnny Appleseed")** **memorabilia** including books and personal items.
Frederic Janson,
Pomona Book Exchange,
Rockton PO,
Ontario L0R 1X0,
CANADA

◆ **John Philip Sousa ephemera**, especially items with a Marine Corps tie-in. Make a photocopy of paper goods.
Dick Weisler,
3-07 213th St.,
Bayside, NY 11364
(718) 428-9829 eves 626-7110 days

◆ **Commodore Matthew Perry material** including autographs, letters, and manuscripts, especially related to his expedition to Japan.
Jerrold Stanoff,
Rare Oriental Book Co.,
Box 1599,
Aptos, CA 95001-1599

◆ **Charles A. Lindbergh memorabilia** including autographs, checks, flight covers, letters, personal items, and items associated with his aircraft.
Lou Lufker,
184 Dorothy Rd.,
Islip, NY 11795
(516) 661-1422

◆ **Houdini memorabilia** of all types, including apparatus, posters, letters, books, and postcards.
Joe and Pamela Tanner, Escapes,
Box 349,
Great Falls, MT 59403
(406) 453-4961

◆ **Frank Lloyd Wright material** including drawings, furniture, letters, photographs, books, smaller publications, and other ephemera about Wright.
J.B. Muns,
Fine Arts Books,
1162 Shattuck Ave.,
Berkeley, CA 94707
(415) 525-2420

◆ **Personal effects from Al Capone and other prohibition era figures,** both good guys and bad guys, including gangsters, police chiefs, presidents, states attorneys, FBI men, Elliott Ness, etc. If they were connected with prohibition era Chicago, Mike wants to know about it. He is particularly interested in Capone and will pay from $50 to $1,000, depending on what you have, its condition, and its documentation. If offering personal items such as clothing, guns, jewelry, letters, etc., you must telephone him or provide a complete description, documentation, and your phone number.
   Michael Graham,
   345 Cleveland Ave.,
   Libertyville, IL 60048
      (312) 362-4808 days

◆ **Noel Coward memorabilia.** "Anything and everything."
   Marcia Perry,
   560 Pomeroy Ave.,
   Pittsfield, MA 01201

◆ **"Texas Jack" Omohundro memorabilia** including photographs of Jack alone or with other scouts. Also buys dime novels, posters, or "what have you?" Claims to pay "top prices."
   D.J. Greene,
   515 Palos Verdes Drive West,
   Palos Verdes, CA 90274

◆ **Richard Halliburton ephemera** including books, films, photographs, manuscripts, and personal possessions of this 1920's-30's author and adventurer. He wants first edition books, foreign editions, signed copies, and "some paperbacks." Also seeks anything associated with the 1933 Halliburton film *India Speaks*, including a much desired actual print of the film. Selected items from the 1949 re-release are also wanted. Also snapshots, news photos, news clippings, and magazine articles by or about Halliburton. Also personal items from his home in Laguna Beach or "anything related to" the US Navy ship *Richard Halliburton*. In addition to Halliburton material, Michael wants anything relating to his associate **Paul Mooney.**
   Michael Blankenship,
   5320 Spencer Drive SW,
   Roanoke, VA 24018
      (703) 989-0402 eves

◆ **Jack London memorabilia, books, and personal effects.**
   Russ Kingman,
   Jack London Bookstore,
   Box 337,
   Glen Ellen, CA 95442
      (707) 996-2888

Famous Foreigners

◆ **Sherlock Holmes** items, particularly the rare and unusual. Wants pre 1930 books, early magazines, games, pamphlets, non-books, and "curious items." If items are very rare, they may date after 1930 and still be of interest. John is a Baker Street Irregular, owns 12,000 Holmes items, and is well known as a Holmes authority.
John Bennett Shaw,
1917 Fort Union Dr.,
Santa Fe, NM 87501
(505) 982-2947

◆ **Sherlock Holmes.** Wants rarer editions, foreign editions of books and other ephemera, including movie posters, games, and the like.
Alla T. Ford,
114 South Palmway,
Lake Worth, FL 33460
(407) 585-1442

◆ **Sherlock Holmes.** Wants "anything related to Sherlock Holmes or Sir Arthur Conan Doyle" including figurines, drawings, autographs, posters, photos, etc. Wants first edition books only. Also wants ephemera from actors who have played Holmes including Basil Rathbone, Nigel Bruce, and William Gillette.
Robert Hess,
559 Potter Blvd.,
Brightwaters, NY 11718
(516) 665-8365

◆ **Paul Gauguin ephemera** and books, bought and sold.
Gene Snyder,
991 McLean,
Dunedin, FL 34698

◆ **Lafayette memorabilia.** Items associated with or portraying General Marquis de Lafayette such as ribbons, tokens, medals, books, prints, etc. Describe and price.
Andrew Golbert,
RR Box 1820,
North Ferrisburg, VT 05473

◆ **Queen Victoria.** Buys a wide range of items directly and indirectly associated with the monarch including 19th century advertising, Victorian letters, diaries, autographs, and rare books. Try her with anything distinctly Victorian with a Queenly tie-in.
Barbara Rusch,
36 Macauley Dr.,
Thornhill, Ontario, L3T 5S5
CANADA

◆ **Queen Victoria.** Buys a variety of items associated with the Monarch and her era. "Anything small (no furniture)."
J. Markowitz
139-12 84th Drive,
Briarwood, NY 11435

◆ **Sigmund Freud.** Wants any documents, photos, or letters signed by Freud. Please send a photocopy and your price.
M. David Zentman,
83 Stony Hollow Rd.,
Centerport, NY 11721

◆ **Stalin, Hitler, and Mussolini** especially during the 1920's and 1930's. Wants documented personal effects, autographs, letters, photos, and selected magazine and newspaper accounts.
Michael Graham,
345 Cleveland Ave.,
Libertyville, IL 60048
(312) 362-4808 days

11
Pets & Holidays

Dr. Hyman's Prescription

Holidays are times associated with all of life's good things, family, and music, sharing, tenderness... It's no wonder holiday items are such popular collectibles.

Christmas leads the popularity parade, with interest in pre-*Coke©* Santas, turn-of-the-century ornaments and early lighting. Christmas buyers want advertising, toys, games, cards, stickers, stamps, and die-cut figures. Fine German ornaments can bring $50+ and Santa on an early tin sign will bring well over $1,000.

There is less interest in other holidays (prices reflect this), but July 4th and Halloween have more fans every year. Mardi Gras is more an *event* than a holiday, so its buyers will be found on page 81 in Amusements.

◆ ◆ ◆ ◆

I'll Buy That! brings you twice as many buyers of items associated with dogs, cats, and other animals than any of our previous books. We've even got a buyer of worms!

Pet collectors subscribe to:

Canine Collector's Companion, a 20 page bimonthly. $20 a year from Box 2948, Portland, OR 97208.

Cat Talk, a 16 page bimonthly. $15 a year from 31311 Blair Drive, Warren, MI 48092.

The Owl's Nest, a 20 page bimonthly. $15 a year from PO Box 5491, Fresno, CA 93755.

tony hyman

Christmas

◆ **Christmas decorations from before 1920.**

[1] **Ornaments:** paper and tinsel die cuts, pressed cardboard animals, cotton batting ornaments, Christmas tree dolls of any material, glass ornaments... basically, anything figural;

[2] **Santa games:** board games with lithographed boxes depicting Santa;

[3] **Santa toys:** any toy based on St. Nick;

[4] **Santa ephemera:** all types of items are wanted, including advertising, banners, greeting cards, paintings, die-cuts, chromoliths, prints;

[5] **Die cut Children's books** 1880-1900 about Santa;

[6] **Litho on tin candle holders** (for Christmas trees);

[5] **Victorian toys:** jack-in-the-boxes, animals on rolling platforms, nine pins, and other traditional toys, especially those with nursery rhyme tie-ins;

He does not want anything made after 1920. There are many reproductions of Santa items, some of which are quite good and require an expert to authenticate. This 25 year veteran requests a photo or photocopy of what you'd like to sell.

Dolph Gotelli, Father Christmas,
Box 160164,
Sacramento, CA 95816
(916) 456-9734

◆ **German glass Christmas ornaments,** pre 1920, in the shape of animals, people, and cartoon characters. Also wants painted cotton ornaments, paper Dresdens, and **old candy containers,** especially Santas. Also buys pre 1930 **postcards and photos of Christmas** events.

Jim Bohenstengel,
Box 623,
Oak Park, IL 60303
(312) 524-8870 or 386-5319

◆ **Early handmade folk art Christmas decorations.**

Louis Picek,
Main Street Antiques,
Box 340,
West Branch, IA 52358

◆ *Matchless "Wonder Stars"* **Christmas lights.** "I'll buy all stars, working, dead, or broken. Boxed sets are particularly desirable, but even empty boxes have value, especially those with attractive decorations. I am particularly interested in the factory wholesale literature and price sheets, as well as store display stands."

He also buys other *Matchless* products plus lights by *Paramount, Sylvania, Alps, Royal, Peerless, Mazda, Majestic* and others. Especially interested in nice boxed light sets by *Propp* and *Clemco*. If you have any old light sets, especially those that twinkle, bubble, or whatever, drop him a line. He wants a good description and if you still have the box, the information on it. "I generally avoid plastic items, and Christmas lights later than the mid 1950's. I don't need any more common *NOMA* or *Royal* bubble lights." Although he buys dead bulbs (except *Sylvania* florescents), he requests return privilege if things aren't as described.

David Speck,
35 Franklin St.,
Auburn, NY 13021
(315) 253-8495 days

◆ **Christmas tree ornaments.** Buys a variety of antique ornaments including Kugel ornaments; glass birds with spun glass wings, tails, or crests; Czech beaded ornaments with satin glass rings; birds perched in satin glass rings; unusual strings of glass beads; spun glass and paper decorations; chandelier or fantasy ornaments (where two or three small bells, pine cones, or other items hang from a larger ornament); and other delicate and unusual figural ornaments. Also buys catalogs from ornament manufacturers in any language.

David Speck,
35 Franklin St.,
Auburn, NY 13021
(315) 252-8566 eves

◆ **Old Christmas stickers.** "I'll pay $1 each (sometimes as much as $5) for Christmas stickers stuck on postcards, envelopes, and letters. Loose OK too, but prefer used. I am not looking for Christmas Seals, Red Cross Seals, etc., only old glue-on decorative dime store package stickers with trees, Santas, etc."

E.L. Sikinger,
695 Greencrest St. NE,
Salem, OR 97301
(503) 585-9607

◆ **Hallmark ornaments** from 1973-1986. Excellent condition only. In original box preferred.

Sharon Vohs-Mohammed,
Box 822,
Auburn, IN 46706
(219) 925-5756

◆ **Select Christmas die-cut chromoliths and other prints.**

David Speck,
35 Franklin St.,
Auburn, NY 13021
(315) 252-8566 eves

4th of July

◆ **Anything with a fireworks company name on it** including:
(1) **Firecracker packs and labels;**
(2) **Fireworks catalogs** from before 1969 (many bring $100+);
(3) **Fireworks boxes** of any size or material from any American manufacturer;
(4) Anything about fireworks manufacturing;
(5) **Salesmen's display boards** and samples;
(6) Rockets, Roman candles, and **fireworks;**
(7) **Paper goods**: stock certificates, posters, banners, photos, letters, billheads, magazine articles about fireworks manufacturers, and all other paper about American fireworks companies.

Would like to hear from former employees of US fire works companies. Not interested in items which carry the DOT warning. Include your phone number when you write.

Barry Zecker,
Box 1022,
Mountainside, NJ 07092
(201) 232-6100 from 8 to 8

◆ **Firecracker labels.** "I'll buy pre-1940 labels with aviation, space, atom bomb, animals, and Americana themes. Also fireworks catalogs. Send photocopy. No modern labels.

Stuart Schneider,
Box 64,
Teaneck, NJ 07666
(201) 261-1983

◆ **Fourth of July fireworks, firecrackers, and firecracker labels.** Wants "anything prior to the early 1970's, especially packs of *Golliwog, Picnic, Tank, Oh Boy, Typewriter, Atlas, Evergreen, Lone Eagle, Spirit of 76, Minute Man, Columbia, Crab, Blue Dragon, Golden Bear, Green Jade, Boa, Santa Claus, Watermelon, Dwarf, Rochester Special, China Clipper, and many others.*" He wants most of these badly enough to pay $50 or more per pack! NOTE: if your package or label contains the letters "DOT" and/or "Contents do not exceed 60 mg," he's probably not interested. He eagerly buys catalogs of fireworks too, so send a Xerox© of the cover if you have one.

William Scales,
130 Fordham Circle,
Pueblo, CO 81005
(719) 561-0603

◆ **Fireworks related items,** especially American and Chinese made. "I'll buy boxes, labels, advertising, catalogs, salesman's samples, display boards, company letters, patents, and posters." Colorful labels are worth from $5-$50 each, but Hal does **not** want those marked "DOT."

Hal Kantrud,
Route 7,
Jamestown, ND 58401
(701) 252-5639 eves

Easter

◆ **Russian Easter eggs** made of solid glass, silvered hollow glass, porcelain, and other materials. They are characterized by the letters "XB" which stands for "Xhristos Voskrece" (Christ is risen) in paint, enamel, or other material. Value depends upon rarity, authenticity, and condition.

David Speck,
35 Franklin St.,
Auburn, NY 13021
(315) 253-8495 days   252-8566 eves

◆ **Papier mache or composition Easter rabbit candy containers** of rabbits wearing clothes.

Dolph Gotelli,
Box 160164,
Sacramento, CA 95816
(916) 456-9734

Valentine's Day

◆ **Fine Valentines,** including handmade valentines from before 1940, interesting mechanical valentines, and any unusual ones. Evalene especially likes lacy 8 x 10's and large fan shaped cards from the 1800's (particularly if they say "A token of love"). Pays $25-$50 for folding ships, planes, and better fans. She asks that you send a photocopy of what you wish to sell. She does not want children's penny valentines from any era. Evalene no longer has a shop, but runs an extensive mail auction of valentines. She is available for talks and displays of valentines.
   Evalene Pulati,
   Valentine Collector's Association,
   Box 1404,
   Santa Ana, CA 92702
      (714) 547-1355

◆ **Valentines.** Buys *only* German or English 3D type pullout valentines in good condition.
   Jack Matlack,
   Box 14067,
   Portland, OR 97214

◆ **Valentines.** Wants early die-cut and elaborate valentines made before 1910, but buys others "if reasonable."
   Madalaine Selfridge, Forgotten Magic,
   Box 413,
   Norco, CA 91760

◆ **Valentines, 1889-1920,** but only the three dimensional fold-out stand-up type.
   James Conley,
   2405 Brentwood Rd.NW,
   Canton, OH 44708
      (216) 477-7725

Halloween

◆ **Halloween.** "I'll buy older paper items, Dennison Boogie books, Halloween pins, jewelry, decorations, etc, **if before 1945.** Nothing new, please."
   Stuart Schneider,
   Box 64,
   Teaneck, NJ 07666

◆ **Halloween skeleton costumes.** She wants costumes for child or adult printed on black rayon from from the 30's through 50's. Good condition. Worth $10 to $20 each.
   Linda Campbell Franklin,
   Box 383 Murray Hill Station,
   New York, NY 10156

◆ **Candy containers in glass or plastic** especially scarce glass items and early 1950's figural headed plastic PEZ dispensers. Pays to $300 for pumpkin headed witches, goblins, or a pop-eyed Jack-0-Lantern. No paper or tin items.
   Ross Hartsough,
   Psych Department,
   University of Manitoba,
   Winnipeg, R3T 2N2
   CANADA

◆ **Halloween candy containers in glass, composition, or papier mache.**
   Dolph Gotelli,
   Box 160164,
   Sacramento, CA 95816
      (916) 456-9734

Dogs

◆ **Great Dane items** including prints, lithographs, bronzes, calendars, magazine covers, and porcelains (especially *Boehm*). Pre 1940 only, nothing newer.
Leon Reimert, Rockbridge,
9 Highland Dr.,
Coatesville, PA 19320
(215) 383-6969

◆ **Greyhounds and whippets.** "I'm interested in paper, porcelain, pewter, wood, and ceramics. But not in recent pottery, reproductions, or damaged items. Give the marks on your item."
June Mastrocola,
W137 N9332 Hwy 145,
Menomonee Falls, WI 53051
(414) 251-8347

◆ **Scottie dog items in any form**, especially decorated glassware of the 1940's, advertising pieces, lamps, playing cards, matchbook covers, greeting cards, and a *Black and White Scotch* advertising pieces featuring a jack-in-the-box. Also reference material of all sorts, including catalogs from manufacturers of scottie items. No damaged items. NO OFFERS. Donna is publisher of *Scottie Sampler*, a quarterly journal for collectors.
Donna Newton,
Country Scottie,
Box 1512,
Columbus, IN 47202

◆ **Borzoi, Russian wolfhound, and greyhound collectibles.** Will also buy some items from other breeds as well. Wants "everything from old postcards to bronzes, but antique porcelain figurines are a favorite, as are all *Morten Studio* and *Erphila* dogs." Give her the breed, the dimensions, the material and list any damage. Photo or photocopy is helpful. SASE gets her catalog of items available in your favorite breed.
Denise Hamilton,
2835 Carson Drive,
Elmira, NY 14903
(607) 562-8564

◆ **Pekingese, Japanese Spaniel, and pug dog collectibles** including Vienna bronze figures, doorstops, and books. Will also buy quality **paintings depicting small dogs**, and **dog show medals** with any breed of dog on them. Give condition and approximate age.
Elenore Chaya,
4003 S. Indian River Dr.,
Ft. Pierce, FL 34982
(407) 465-1789

◆ **Doberman pinscher collectibles** including plates, statuettes, and paper. No reprints.
Connie Terbrueggen,
5069 Beige St.,
Jacksonville, FL 32288
(904) 268-0238

◆ **Cocker spaniel memorabilia** of all types including calendars, greeting cards, playing cards, postcards, magazine articles and illustrations, etc. Describe and price.
Sharon Giese,
Box 75586,
Seattle, WA 98125

◆ **Scottish Terrier items**, especially linens, paper, jewelry, toys, and novelties. No figurines, bookends, or doorstops. Please photocopy or describe well. Prefers items priced.
Trent,
7501 Windswept,
Colleyville, TX 76034

◆ **Bull terrier dog material** including books, manuscripts, photos and relevant ephemera.
Frank Klein, Bookseller,
521 W. Exchange St.,
Akron, OH 44302
(216) 762-3101

◆ **Labrador retriever books, art, figurines, and cigarette cards.** He is not interested in repros, fakes, reprints, or common items, nor is he interested in any other breed of dog. Please provide a detailed description of what you have.
Bill Eberhardt,
682 Ranch Wood Trail,
Orange, CA 92669
(714) 639-0882

Pets and
Other critters

◆ **Pet photos** especially of dogs on real photo postcards, Carte d'visites, or cabinet photos before 1930. Buy them with or without people in the photo.
> B. Sherwood,
> 1535 Dakota,
> Lincoln, NE 68502

◆ **Dog and cat figurines** in porcelain or metal, as long as they're purebred. Will pay from $75 to $600 for *Boehm* dogs, especially a cocker spaniel. "I do not want Japanese porcelain animals nor cloisonne made in China. Give all markings, dimensions, pose, and damage. Photo is helpful.
> Jeffrey Jacobson,
> 6424 Jefferson Ave.,
> Hammond, IN 46324

◆ **Cat items of any sort** including porcelain, carvings, prints, Orientalia, needlework, pottery, jade, jewelry, cookie jars, calendars, art deco, advertising, steins, medals, doorstops, bronzes, crystal, postcards, playing cards, prints and fine art, ivory, etc. Also depictions of cartoon cats (Felix the Cat, Sylvester, Kliban cats) but no Garfield, chalk figures, or anything broken or damaged.
> Marilyn Dipboye, Cat Collectors,
> 31311 Blair Dr.,
> Warren, MI 48092
> (313) 264-0285

◆ **Musk oxen figurines, prints, book plates, and other small ephemera,** 1750-1930. Especially wants postcards, cigarette silks, trading cards, pottery, stamps and other small paper items. Will pay up to $100 each for plates (illustrations) from *History of Quadrupeds* (1781) or *Arctic Zoology* (1784) both by Thomas Pennant.
> Ross Hartsough,
> Psych Dept, U of Manitoba,
> Winnipeg, R3T 2N2
> CANADA

◆ **Horses.** Everything related to work or recreation horses including polo, horseback riding, carriage driving, sidesaddle, draft horses, **horseshoeing, veterinary,** etc. Wants posters, prints of riding and recognized horse breeds, books (1st editions in d/j only), magazines, stud books, and breed registers. "I don't buy common books still in print, book club editions, *Diseases of the Horse,* or books on horse betting. Everything must be in fine condition for resale."
> Barbara Cole, October Farm,
> Rt. 2, Box 183-C,
> Raleigh, NC 27610
> (919) 772-0482

◆ **Zebras in many different forms,** including porcelain, carvings, paintings, folk art, etc. To be of interest, an item must be of a zebra, not just zebra striped. No hides or parts of dead zebras.
> Dave Galt,
> 302 W. 78th Street,
> New York, NY 10024
> (212) 769-2514

◆ **Pigeon related items** including books, magazines, postcards, and prints, pre 1960.
> Stan and Monty Luden,
> 11908 Abingdon St.,
> Norwalk, CA 90650
> (213) 863-0123

◆ **Owls.** Donna buys owls, but only (1) owls made by American Indians, (2) owls on postcards, (3) *Sclarrafia* owls, (4) *Zsolnay* owls, (5) *Meissen* owls, or (6) owl decoys. She does not want anything current or produced for the mass market. You must include a detailed description of all damage, plus a photograph. "We will not respond to offers that do not indicate the price wanted." She publishes a bimonthly newsletter for owl collectors. Sample copy $3.
> Donna Howard,
> PO Box 5491,
> Fresno, CA 93755
> (209) 439-4845

◆ **Wild boar ephemera.** "I'll buy paintings, bronzes, ceramics, advertising, anything featuring the wild European boar or its American counterparts, the peccary or javelina." Describe condition.
Henry Winningham,
3205 S. Morgan St.,
Chicago, IL 60608

◆ **Elephants.** "I buy and sell all kinds of elephants" says Shirley, who seeks craftspeople who can make elephant items for her elephant catalog. Antique and expensive elephants are of less interest. Give dimensions, colors, and wholesale price. Shirley does not buy postcards.
Shirley Peterson,
Pachyderm Parade,
HC69 Box 114,
Atkinson, NE 68713
(402) 925-5882

◆ **Snakes and other reptiles made of wrought iron.** Wants wrought iron snakes and other reptiles created by blacksmiths as whimsies or useful items (such as pot or watch holders, for example). Can depict one snake or several, or other reptiles such as alligators and turtles. **Other figural animal and human whimsies made of iron** are also sought.
Linda Campbell Franklin,
Box 383 Murray Hill Station,
New York, NY 10156
(804) 973-3238

◆ **Worms and caterpillars.** "Not real ones," she hastens to add, "but just about any figural in any material. I prefer small ones that can fit on a shelf, but I'll buy cookie jars, bookends, figurines, books, toys, dolls, novelties...any worm or caterpillar I don't have. I'm especially looking for a *Lowly Worm* in a car figure based on the *Lowly Worm* books." Give size, material, and general description.
Nita Markham,
529 Wave St.,
Monterey, CA 93940

◆ **Oyster memorabilia.** Got anything related to oysters? Cans, figurines, what have you?
Sheldon Katz,
211 Roanoke Ave.,
Riverhead, NY 11901
(516) 369-1100

Pet licenses

◆ **Pet license tags, rabies tags, and all other metal tags related to animals.** Especially interested in Illinois tags. Especially wants tags pre 1900 for which he pays $12 and up.
Rich Hartzog,
Box 4143 BBL,
Rockford, IL 61110

◆ **Dog license tags** including: (1) tags from any state if they are shaped like the date of issue; (2) tags from anywhere in the world pre-1910; (3) all NY tags issued before 1918; and (4) NY Conservation Dept. tags, 1917-35, which are worth from $10-$40. Pre Civil War tags can bring up to $150, and pre 1900 tags start at $5.
James Case,
Box 168, Cane Rd.,
Lindley, NY 14858

◆ **Dog and cat license tags before 1950,** especially colored ones or those cut into shapes. Dog tags before 1910 and any quantity of cat tags are sought.
George Chartrand,
Box 334,
Winnipeg, Manitoba R3C 2H6,
CANADA

12
Miscellaneous

Dr. Hyman's Prescription

This chapter covers a surprising range of collectibles and should be read carefully.

Many of these buyers are serious historians of an industry or movement. The items they buy are often not worth much, perhaps only $1-$20, but there are many items with substantial value.

Take the time to go through your possessions, looking at letters and photos, as you may own things you have forgotten...little pieces of ephemera that can be helpful to a historian. Ephemera means "items intended to be thrown away" so each time you prevent destruction by selling pamphlets, tickets, programs, memos, and other trivia, you are helping to preserve our culture, and better tell the story of our past.

Photocopy paper goods and smaller three-dimensional items. Provide complete bibliographic information when selling books (see chapter 24 for info about how to describe books).

If you haven't read pages 2-11 about how to best sell what you have, it's a good idea for you to stop and do so. There are many tips that can help you have happy and profitable experiences.

tony hyman

Odd & Morbid

◆ **Anything odd, unusual, or morbid,** especially **two headed calves and other freak animals,** natural or man-made, alive or mounted and preserved. Also buys:
 (1) **Mummies;**
 (2) **Skeletons and human skulls;**
 (3) **Shrunken heads;**
 (4) **Headhunter and cannibal items;**
 (5) **Funeral equipment,** coffins and coffin plates, caskets, embalming kits, and tombstones;
 (6) **Torture and execution devices** and photos of executions;
 (7) **Mounted reptiles, trophy heads, and uncommon animals** (like kangaroos);
 (8) **Man-made mermaids** he'll pay to $300;
 (9) **Merchant Marine memorabilia** including photos, uniforms, medals;
 (10) **Medicine show photos and literature;**
 (11) **Tattoo equipment,** tattoo photos, and tattooed skin;
 (12) **Voodoo and black magic ephemera;**
 (13) **Flea Circus** props and photos;
 (14) **Reward posters** and crime photos;
 (15) **Human oddity photos and artifacts.**
For 50 years, this wheel chair bound vet has been buying unusual items for public exhibit in his traveling and stationary museums. He does not buy furniture, clothing, plates, or jewelry.

He asks for a photo, a description, a statement of condition, and your lowest price. If you're driving through, drop in and see The Palace of Wonders.
 Harvey Lee Boswell,
 The Palace of Wonders,
 Box 446,
 Elm City, NC 27822

◆ **Human skeletons and skulls.**
 Steve DeGenaro,
 Box 5662,
 Youngstown, OH 44504
 (216) 759-7151 eves

◆ **Tattoo memorabilia and information.** What do you have?
 Marvin Yagoda,
 28585 So. Harwich Dr.,
 Farmington Hills, MI 48018

◆ **Animal trophies and skulls.** Please give your phone number with your description.
 David Boone's Trading Company,
 562 Coyote Rd.,
 Brinnon, WA 98320
 (206)796-4330

◆ **Steer horns, cow skulls with big horns, mounted steer heads, and old buffalo horns.** "I want the real thing, and **do not want** horns wrapped with the wide, tooled, tapered leather center, nor those wrapped in vinyl and rope." Please give dimensions and send a photo or rough sketch.
 Alan Rogers,
 1012 Shady Dr.,
 Gladstone, MO 64118
 (816) 436-9008

◆ **Caskets.** "I'll buy wicker or wooden caskets. Wicker ones were used for display of bodies at wakes and funerals. The bodies were removed and buried in plain pine boxes. Wooden caskets are also wanted, especially those that are dove-tailed, made of odd woods, tapered, or with face plates." Describe as best as you can, giving dimensions. Also buys **photos of caskets with bodies.**
 Steve DeGenaro,
 PO Box 5662,
 Youngstown, OH 44504
 (216) 759-7151 eves

◆ **Human hair mourning pieces.** Human hair jewelry with black "beads" worked in, or human hair woven into wreathes, mounted in frames with photos worked in.
 Steve DeGenaro,
 PO Box 5662,
 Youngstown, OH 44504
 (216) 759-7151 eves

◆ **Leper colony tokens and other ephemera.**
 Rich Hartzog,
 Box 4143 BBL,
 Rockford, IL 61110
 (815) 226-0771

People & Movements

◆ **Immigration memorabilia.** "I'll buy documents, photos, passports, pre-1920 naturalization certificates, books, postcards, and other material related to immigrants, immigration, Immigrant Aid Societies, Immigrant Social and Political Clubs, Ellis Island, Castle Garden, and ethnic festivals before 1950." Also Immigration and Naturalization Service material prior to 1930. Photocopies requested.
K. Sheeran,
Box 520251,
Miami, FL 33152

◆ **Immigrant and ethnic stereotypes** of Jews, Orientals, Scandinavians, French, Poles, Russians, and other immigrants printed before 1920. Wants stereotypes on prints, photos, valentines, postcards, magazines, posters, sheet music, trade cards, and what have you. Wants Blacks only if shown with immigrant characters. Subject matter can include life in their country of origin, arrival, settlement, assimilation, etc. Not interested in reproductions, native costume, *Harper's Weekly* material, or general articles on immigration. Prefers photocopies of priced items. No unsolicited material, please.
John and Selma Appel,
219 Oakland Dr.,
East Lansing, MI 48823
(517) 337-1859

◆ **Everything about the homeless children who sold newspapers to survive** in 19th century NYC and elsewhere. "I buy photographs, paintings, statues, prints, badges, passes, magazine articles, and newspaper accounts which pertain to them, Printing House Square, Newspaper Row, or Father John C. Drumgoole, founder of Mount Loretto, the largest child care facility in the US at the time." Also material about Charles Loring Brace and the Children's Aid Society, especially about their orphan trains to the West.
Peter Eckel,
1335 Grant Ave.,
South Plainfield, NJ 07080
(201) 757-0748

◆ **Anything pertaining to statues of newsboys around the US** including photographs of the statues, souvenir figurines, advertising for the figurines, and photos of any statue of a newsboy. Replicas of the statues are generally worth $50 and up.
Gary Leveille, Newsboy Antiques,
Box 562,
Great Barrington, MA 01239

◆ **Chinese in America.** Anything about the Chinese immigration and life in America, especially as it relates to San Francisco.
George Sarris,
1177 Shotwell St.,
San Francisco, CA 94110

◆ **Socialism and Communism in the U.S. before 1940.** "I'll buy anything pre 1940: books, magazines, leaflets, brochures, buttons, postcards, pennants, etc., that were produced by radical groups such as the Communist Party, Socialist Party, I.W.W. (Industrial Workers of the World), Socialist Labor Party, etc. Would especially like to find the magazines *Masses, New Masses,* and *International Socialist Review.*" Mike will purchase items written in Yiddish, Italian, and other foreign languages, but "I'm really not too interested in material not written in the U.S.A." What does Mike consider important? "Condition Condition Condition!"
Michael Stephens,
2310 Valley St.,
Berkeley, CA 94702
(415) 843-2780

◆ **Labor union and Socialist material** "I'll buy just about everything relating to organized labor, unions, and working people" including dues buttons, pins, convention and parade ribbons and badges, photographs of workers or Unions, programs, contracts, dues books, labor trade cards, union magazines, books, and most any type of labor collectibles. "I'd like to find the old and unusual from groups like The Knights of Labor, I.W.W., Railroad Brotherhood, AFL, and CIO. Also items about labor leaders. I'll consider almost anything but most interested in items before 1960.
Scott Molloy,
Box 2650,
Providence, RI 02907
(401) 792-2239 or 782-3614

◆ **Cigar Maker's Union and Sam Gompers.** "I'll buy almost anything from the Cigar Maker's Union or any of its top officers, including stamps, pamphlets, regulations, photographs, and letterhead." Does anyone have a letter by Samuel Gompers on CMIU stationery or a copy of the papers that dissolved the Union? Please include photocopies and price or ask for offer.
   Tony Hyman,
   Box 699,
   Claremont, CA 91711

◆ **Ku Klux Klan** paper, documents, photos, and small items.
   Steve DeGenaro,
   Box 5662,
   Youngstown, OH 44504
      (216) 759-7151 eves

◆ **Items related to Ku Klux Klan activity in the U.S.** during the 1920's.
   Michael Graham, Roaring 20's,
   345 Cleveland Ave.,
   Libertyville, IL 60048

◆ **Ku Klux Klan items of all types.**
   Historical Collections,
   Box 42,
   Waynesboro, PA 17268

◆ **All items depicting Blacks:** dolls, folk art, sewing items, walking sticks, miniature bronzes, jewelry, paintings, valentines, playing cards, games, children's books, cookie jars, string holders, small advertising items, souvenir spoons, Golliwogs, linens, jigsaw puzzles, candy containers, Christmas ornaments, and items associated with the Our Gang Comedy's Farina. No postcards, sheet music, tradecards, photos, outhouse figures, ads, large signs, damaged items, or reproductions. NO OFFERS.
   Jan Thalberg,
   23 Mountain View Dr.,
   Weston, CT 06883
      (203) 227-8175

◆ **Black memorabilia** including cookie jars, plates, pads, lamps, clocks, salt and pepper shakers, stringholders, table cloths, towels, plaster or ceramic items, and other kitchen or household items depicting Blacks. "I also buy advertising pieces of all kinds that depict a Black person on the label or logo, including biscuit tins, candy packaging, coffee tins, peanut butter pails, peanut cans, stove cleaner, whiskey advertising, beer signs, Aunt Jemima items, *Cream of Wheat* packs, *Uncle Ben's Rice* memorabilia, etc." Also wants punchboards and other items featuring Blacks.
   Diane Cauwels,
   3947 Old South Road,
   Murfreesboro, TN 37129
      (615) 896-3614

◆ **Black memorabilia that is exaggerated, comical, insulting or derogatory** made between 1800-1960. Images of mammys, chefs, Uncle Tom, picaninnies, Aunt Jemima, butlers, Topsy, etc., are all wanted in almost any form:
   (1) **Folk art** and primitives including rag dolls, whirligigs, etc.;
   (2) **Figural kitchen items** including tea pots, pitchers, sugar bowls, cookie jars, string holders. Especially wants large faced items and Black cookie jars;
   (3) **Mammy and chef saltshakers** with matching stove grease jars and mammy tea pots with wire handles;
   (4) **Ceramic jugs** by *Weller*;
   (5) **Plastic cookie jars**, sugar bowls, syrup jugs, etc., from *F&F Die Works* or marked *Luzianne*, especially with green yellow, or blue skirts;
   (6) **Humidors and bisque figurines** from Europe or Japan;
   (7) **Papier mache**, composition and glass **figurals** such as candy containers and Xmas ornaments depicting Blacks;
   (8) **Advertising** on paper or tin, trade cards, die-cuts, packaging, and cereal boxes such *Cream of Wheat* and *Korn Kinks,* and all Aunt Jemima products and ads;
   (9) **Games of all types**, card and board, with Blacks even if pieces missing.
Needs a detailed description, colors, size, condition, place of origin or manufacturer's name. Clear close up photo or photocopy is strongly urged. Describe all damage, chips, stains, tears, faded spots, repairs, or missing pieces. Wants to know the color of skin and expression on face. Prefers black to brown. On pottery pieces, describe whether surface is shiny or matte (flat).
   Mary Anne Enriquez
   651 So. Clark,
   Chicago, IL 60605
      (312) 922-1173

◆ **Racism and the civil rights movement.** "I'll buy buttons, posters, and other ephemeral items having to do with Martin Luther King, but no newspapers, magazines, or damaged items."
Peggy Dillard,
Box 210904,
Nashville, TN 37221
(615) 646-1605

◆ **Atomic bombs, nuclear war, and the anti-nuclear movement** from the 1950's to mid 60's. Wants all information, official and anti-bomb, including stuff on CONELRAD, civil defence, government pamphlets on atomic survival, books, comic books, and anything else from that period on atomic boms and survival, including postcards of the bomb tests. Would love to find *How to Build an Atomic Bomb in Your Kitchen* by Bob Bale. Also "funky" atomic stuff from the 1950's and mid 60's.
Edy Chandler,
Box 20664,
Houston, TX 77225
(713) 531-9615 eves

◆ **Paper ephemera about the counter culture movements of the 1960's** and other earlier radical movements including the Wobblies.
Ivan Gilbert, Miran Arts & Books,
2824 Elm Ave.,
Columbus, OH 43209
(614) 236-0002

◆ **Peace movement pins and related memorabilia.** No reproductions.
Tom Guenin,
310 No. Hambden St.,
Chardon, OH 44024

◆ **British Royalty.** Buys souvenirs, tins, plates, mugs, medals, busts, postcards and programs from various ceremonies and events involving British royalty from Queen Victoria to Queen Elizabeth Reign. Also wants commemorative souvenirs from special events involving Prince Charles and Princess Diana. Wants pictorial items. Audrey is the author of *British Royal Commemoratives*. ($21.95).
Audrey Zeder,
6755 Coralite T,
Long Beach, CA 90808
(213) 421-0881

◆ **All fraternal order** materials that are small and flat, such as coins, tokens, medals, and badges. Especially interested in Masonic chapter pennies and hand engraved badges of precious metal. If what you have is pre 1930, simply ship it to him for an offer, but *do not* ship COD. Hartzog will send you a check for the lot. He claims to pay higher prices than anyone else.
Rich Hartzog, World Exonumia,
Box 4143 BBL,
Rockford, IL 61110

◆ **B.P.O.E. (Elks) memorabilia.** "I'll buy just about anything marked as B.P.O.E. whether it has a specific Lodge number or not: tokens, flasks, badges, cards, knives, silver, buttons, postcards, *Elks Magazine*, photographs, paintings, books, sheet music, and the like." Especially wants Grand Lodge Reunion medals and pin back buttons before 1930.
Dick Hale,
1541 Malabar Way,
Big Bear City, CA 92314
(714) 585-5625

◆ **Mafia or organized crime items** including books, magazines, photographs, autographs, videotapes, recordings, documents, government reports, and any other memorabilia or artifacts. "I'd love to find a cigar box from the Yale Cigar Co., of Chicago and a poster from the Italian American Civil Rights League meeting of June 28th, 1971. He does not want anything fictional.
Ron Ridenour,
Box 6818,
Santa Barbara, CA 93160

Cults & Religions

◆ **Russian religious icons,** especially those with silver covers. Also **enameled bronze crosses** (wall size), icon lamps (*lampadki*) especially with cut to clear glass, and other pre-revolutionary religious items. Prices depend upon rarity, authenticity, and condition. Wants a full description but a good clean color photo is probably necessary. Phone and discuss your piece; he'll probably request that you ship for inspection and will instruct you on how to best ship. What you know of the item's history could be important.
   David Speck,
   35 Franklin St.,
   Auburn, NY 13021
      (315) 252-8566 eves

◆ **Stained glass church windows and other religious artifacts.** Older items wanted. If you don't own any, but know of them for sale, please call and tell me.
   David Schmitt,
   Box 322,
   Cheektowaga, NY 14225
      (716) 896-6174

◆ **Holy water fonts.** Most periods. No plastic.
   Marilyn Swenson, Basswood Heights,
   RR #4,
   Rochester, MN 55904

◆ **Judaica and early Hebrew memorabilia.** Primary interest is in Jewish and Hebrew books, particularly illustrated material before 1920, Jewish scholarly books, and Jewish cookbooks. **Photos of Jews** and Jewish subjects are also wanted.
   Elliott Brill,
   249 W. 34th St.,
   New York, NY 10001
      (800) 562-9911

◆ **Stained or beveled glass windows.** Please include photos and your phone number.
   Carl Heck,
   Box 8416,
   Aspen, CO 81612
      (303) 925-8011

◆ **Watchtower Society publications and ephemera** including *Golden Age, Consolation,* and *Awake* magazines, Millenial Dawn books, Watchtower books before 1927, items related to Pastor Russell, and any pre-1940 Jehovah's Witness literature.
   Mike Castro,
   Box 2817,
   Providence, Rhode Island 02907

◆ **Paper ephemera about Mormons,** pre 1900, especially illustrated.
   Warren Anderson,
   Box 100,
   Cedar City, UT 84720
      (801) 586-9497

◆ **Ephemera from early American religions.** Especially interested in Mormonism, the Disciples of Christ, and Reverend Ethan Smith. Wants books, ephemera, and newspapers with articles about these groups.
   Kofford,
   280 Rector Place #3J,
   New York, NY 10280

◆ **Catholic art calendars, 1938-1969.** "Over $100 paid for certain issues. No *Messenger* Catholic calendars, please. Call for more information."
   J. Speciale,
   Box 1322,
   San Jose, CA 95109
      (408) 247-0819

◆ **Holy cards (religious cards).** Small decorated cards similar to trade cards but depicting various religious figures and events. Usually beautifully printed, often decorated with lace.
   Mary Jo O'Neil,
   618 Riversedge Ct.,
   Mishawaka, IN 46544
      (219) 259-0357

◆ **New Testaments** before 1820 in any language printed anywhere in the world. They may be in any condition. "You may ship for an offer and I will respond within three days."
Miles Eisele,
Thoreau Place,
1951 Sagewood Lane #7,
Reston, VA 22091

◆ **Bibles before 1900.**
Norval White,
Rt. 1, Box 85B,
Rosanky, TX 78953

◆ **Sacred books, including Bibles before 1800, Books of Common Prayer, The Koran,** and other unusual, beautiful, significant, or early sacred books.
Ron Lieberman,
Family Album,
RD #1, Box 42,
Glen Rock, PA 17327
(717) 235-2134

◆ **Crystal balls, tarot cards, and other mystical devices and ephemera,** especially early books, pamphlets, and literature on astrology, alchemy, spiritualism, pyramids, palmistry, Yoga, Atlantis, Tibet, numerology, Angels, psychic research, prophesy, herbology, Kabbala, or UFO's.
D.E. Whelan,
Box 729,
Newberry, FL 32669

◆ **Phrenology items** including heads showing trait lines, or numbered zones on the head, posters, and wall hangings. No books.
Donald Gorlick,
Box 24541,
Seattle, WA 98124
(206) 824-0508

Miscellany

◆ **Slave tags.** These small metal tags worn by slaves to indicate their status or occupation. Pays $200-600 for tags reading "servant, porter, mechanic, seamstress, fisherman, fruiterer," etc. Some rare types, dates, styles, or occupations can bring $1,500. If you have one for sale, call collect or ship insured for his offer. *Do not clean your tags.*
Rich Hartzog,
Box 4143 BBL,
Rockford, IL 61110
(815) 226-0771

◆ **American flags.** "I'll buy cloth hand held size (smaller than 3') American flags with 47 stars, 43 stars, and all others with less than 39 stars. I especially like those with unusual star patterns and any flags with advertising printed on them. Larger ones will be considered. Description should include the size, condition, and star pattern. No repros or pictures of flags.
Mark Sutton,
2035 St. Andrews Circle,
Carmel, IN 46032
(317) 844-5648

◆ **Rationing material from anywhere in the world** for addition to an important research collection. The Library buys only paper items, already owns most American items, and seeks a great many foreign items. No U.S. ration books wanted. He reminds sellers that State Governments are slow but certain payers.
Ronald Mahoney, Special Collections,
Madden Library, Calif. State University,
Fresno, CA 93740
(209) 294-2595

◆ **Ration tokens.** Pays 2¢ each for red tokens and 3¢ each for blue. Over 250, he pays 1¢ each. Pays more for those that are off-center, double struck, or have other errors. Simply ship for his check. Rich is one of world's largest buyers of medals and tokens.
Rich Hartzog, Exonumia,
Box 4143 BBL,
Rockford, IL 61110
(815) 226-0771

◆ **Cave or cavern memorabilia** from before 1950, including books, magazine articles, pamphlets, prints, postcards, etc. "Any items that would make a contribution to the history of a particular cave or area such as journal entries, deeds, wills, maps, tickets, and advertising, are of interest." Common souvenirs and chrome postcards are not desired.

> Jack Speece,
> 711 East Atlantic Ave.,
> Altoona, PA 16602
> (814) 946-3155 eves

◆ **Caves or cavern memorabilia of all sorts,** "essentially anything old or unusual pertaining to caves or caverns worldwide" including brochures, postcards, photos, souvenirs, silver spoons, plates, bottles depicting caves, etc. Does not want anything after 1940, prefers items pre 1900.

> Gordon Smith,
> Box 217,
> Marengo, IN 47119
> (812) 945-5721

◆ **Electrical apparatus** including old radios, tubes, test equipment, open frame motors, generators, switchboard meters, knife switches, **neon signs, fans,** Tesla coils, **quack medical devices** (Violet Ray, etc.), **unusual clocks,** etc., as well as books on radio and electrical theory and practice. Give info from the items ID plate, and include a sketch or photo.

> Hank Andreoni,
> 2650 Alessandro,
> Riverside, CA 92008
> (714) 849-7539

◆ **Propagating material (cuttings) of uncommon tree fruit varieties.** If you have an unusual fruit tree, Fred wants a cutting. Temperate climate fruits, especially apples, but also pears, plums, quinces and medlars are wanted by this veteran horticultural experimenter. Also buys **books on fruit propagation** before 1920.

> Fred Janson,
> Rockton PO,
> Ontario L0R 1X0,
> CANADA
> (519) 621-8897

◆ **Items made from macerated (ground up) currency** by the U.S. mint, including statues, plaques, plates, postcards, animals, shoes, hats, etc., and have a small tag affixed which reads "This item made of U.S. greenbacks redeemed and macerated by the U.S. Government."

> Donald Gorlick, Box 24541,
> Seattle, WA 98124
> (206) 824-0508

◆ **Credit cards.** "I have collected credit cards for over ten years an am seriously interested in buying both the older metal charge cards and modern plastic cards. Please ship any quantity of used or new cards. I pay $4 up for older metal charge cards and will pay *at least* $10 for any metal one I need for my own collection. Pre 1980 plastic cards bring $1 up, and those before 1970 average $2. More paid for local businesses, unusual types, etc. Post 1980 cards worth 25¢ each, a few bring more. I will also reimburse your postage."

> Rich Hartzog,
> Box 4143 BBL,
> Rockford, IL 61110
> (815) 226-0771

◆ **Social dance items** from the earliest days of American dance before 1840. Wants books, news articles, programs, diaries, pictures, and music.

> Gail Ticknor,
> 107 Indian Springs Road,
> Williamsburg, VA 23185

◆ **Snowmobiles.** Wants all ephemera from all brands, U.S. and Canadian, including owners' manuals, catalogs, toys, advertising, etc. Please describe thoroughly.

> Ideal,
> Box 1370,
> Fairbanks, AK 99707

◆ **Popcorn memorabilia** including boxes, cans, crates, brochures, catalogs, old machines, parts of machines, *Creator's* Steam Engines, and everything else related to popcorn.

> Jack Cory,
> 3395 W. Pinks Place,
> Las Vegas, NV 89102
> (702) 367-2676

◆ **Objects which depict hands.** Will consider sculpture, vases, carvings, jewelry, posters, as well as old books about hands or palmistry. Would love to find the brass or copper life-size hand from a Buddha statue. No praying hands, milk glass hands, or plastic hands are wanted by this long time hand analyst.

   Geraldine Swigart,
   12362 Kensington Rd.,
   Los Alamitos, CA 90720
     (213) 431-3705

◆ **Wooden hands that have fully articulated fingers** such as glove stretchers and sizers.
   Donald Gorlick,
   Box 24541,
   Seattle, WA 98124
     (206) 824-0508

◆ **Geiger counters** bought, sold, traded, and repaired.
   Bill Nash,
   1531 Avohill Dr.,
   Vista, CA 92083

◆ **Twentieth century plastic items.** "Don't donate your old plastic dishes to a thrift shop, I'll buy 'em" says this veteran collector and one of the few people we've found, who care about Bakelite and other kitchen plastic.

(1) **Dishes**, singles or sets, especially serving pieces, sugars, creamers, etc. Look for *Branchell, Color-Flyte, Arrowhead, Russel Wright* Ideal Ware, others;

(2) **Salt and peppers**, especially boxed sets of figurals or geometrics;

(3) **Character mugs** of people or animals, especially *Dennis the Menace* by *F&F;*

(4) Funny face and Big Pitcher, such as *Tony the Tiger;*

(5) *Soaky* **Bubble Bath,** other figural bottles;

(6) **Cookie jar** figurals in plastic.

Give dimensions, colors, and maker, as well as a piece count and statement of condition.
   Mary Anne Enriquez
   651 So. Clark,
   Chicago, IL 60605
     (312) 922-1173

EDITOR'S NOTE: If you ever have problems with a listee... make certain to tell us about it.

13
Transportation

Dr. Hyman's Prescription

Transportation is a collecting category with buyers for nearly everything, from timetables to parts of old vehicles and vessels.

Like many hobbies, old and obscure is best. Railroad collectors and auto buffs often share a passion for finding relics of the rare and short-lived.

Don't overlook paper items, especially catalogs and company brochures. Letters about experiences aboard early trains, planes, ships, and automobiles are also of interest. Many small tokens, pins, badges, and the like are worth your time to sell when you find them.

Your description should include:

    (1) What it is and what it is made from;

    (2) Size, shape, and color, especially of glass;

    (3) All markings and whether they are embossed (raised) or incised (stamped in);

    (4) Any patent dates or maker's information;

    (5) Weight, if something heavy.

License plate collectors want to know the number of chips and cracks on old porcelain plates. Set your photocopy machine to legal size, lay the plate gently down on the glass, and make a photocopy. Clean the license plate first so grit won't get on the glass.

Most transportation collectors do not want damaged items, those with questionable (possibly fake) markings, or things that have been altered or reproduced.

tony hyman

Railroads

◆ **Railroad items** including dining car china, silverware, lanterns and lamps, stock certificates, engine builder's plates, ticket dating machines, depot signs, advertising, postcards of depots, brochures and timetables pre 1940, historical documents, hat and cap badges, wax seals, Express Company signs, annual passes pre 1920, and books, manuals, and guides. Nothing newer than 1959, no letters, receipts, or minor paper. This 30 year veteran requests your phone number.
> Fred Arone, The Depot Attic,
> 377 Ashford Ave.,
> Dobbs Ferry, NY 10522
> (914) 693-1832

◆ **Almost anything related to American Railroads** especially dining car china, silverware, and glass. Also marked lanterns, and marked brass locks. Pays $20-85 for sugar tongs or spoons marked with railroad names. Make certain your description includes dimensions and all marks and logos. Rick does not want date nails, books, or model trains. This 25 year veteran says he'll be helpful and answer questions from amateurs, with or without things to sell.
> Richard Wright,
> West Coast Rick's,
> Box 8051,
> Rowland Heights, CA 91748
> (714) 681-4647

◆ **Railroad items from the states of New Jersey and Colorado** pre 1945. Wants dining car china, silverware, lanterns, globes, padlocks, keys, embossed brass padlocks, uniform buttons, etc. Also excellent condition pre 1920 paper ephemera such as passes. Especially would like dinnerware from CRR of NJ (*The Blue Comet*) and "would pay up to $500+ for some pieces." Seeks *Poor's Manual of Railroads*, pre 1940. Prefers seller to price but will make offers.
> Dan Allen,
> Box 917,
> Marlton, NJ 08053
> (609) 953-1387 eves

◆ **Railroad and Express Company memorabilia** including dining car china, silverware, ashtrays, playing cards, paperweights, brass lamps and lanterns (including unmarked ones), locks, badges, switch keys, builder plates, steam whistles, caps pre 1960, uniforms pre 1920, railroad pocket watches if in perfect condition, pre 1916 timetables, posters, and calendars. Also Cyclopedias or dictionaries or other reference books published by RY Gazette, Simmons-Boardman, Moody, or Poors pre 1950. No large tools, large oil cans, spikes, low value paper, junky or damaged items, or material other than US or Canadian. No "overly cleaned" or replated items. This 15 year veteran dealer carries an extensive list of items for sale so always needs new merchandise.
> Scott Arden,
> 20457 Highway 126,
> Noti, OR 97461
> (503) 935-1619 (9 to 9)

◆ **Canadian railroad memorabilia** pre 1950, especially *White Pass and Yukon Railway, Grand Trunk Railway, Canadian Pacific,* among others.
> Michael Rice,
> Box 286,
> Saanichton, BC V0S 1M0,
> CANADA
> (604) 652-9047 eves

◆ **Railroad dining car memorabilia** including china, silver, glassware, menus, and anything else. Items without markings as to the railroad are "worthless" to him.
> Charles Goodman,
> 636 W. Grant Ave.,
> Charleston, Il 61920
> (217) 345-6771

◆ **Railroad dining car china and silverware** are a particular interest, but "I'll consider any item marked with the initials of a railroad, including uniforms. I'll pay $200 or more for the 10 1/2" service plates used on dining cars." No model trains. Please include phone number.
> Les Winn,
> Box 80641,
> Chamblee, GA 30366
> (404) 458-6194

◆ **Memorabilia from Arkansas railways** including Eureka Springs Railway, St. Louis and North Arkansas Railroad, Missouri and Arkansas Railroad, and the Missouri and North Arkansas Railroad. "I'll buy advertising, passes, china and silver, photos, switch locks and keys, lanterns, tickets, bills of lading, stock certificates, etc."
Steve Chyrchel,
Route #2 Box 362,
Eureka Springs, AR 72632
(501) 253-9244

◆ **Railroad date nails and other small railroadiana items** such as lanterns, locks, and keys. Will buy almost any date nails (nails about 4" long with a date on the head). If you describe the shape of the head, the number, and whether it is incised or raised, he says he's glad to tell you what you have. Dick is a collector with limited storage so is interested only in small fine items.
Dick Gartin,
619 Adams,
Duncanville, TX 75137
(214) 296-8742 anytime

◆ **Date nails** used by railroads, telephone, telegraph, and power companies to record when their ties or poles were placed in service. Most, but not all, have either round or square heads and have numbers (or other symbols) either raised or indented on the head. Nails may be steel, copper, or aluminum. Although there are many common nails, there are also nails worth $50 up so describe what you have and Jerry will make an offer. Jerry is editor of *Nailer News* a brief bi-monthly newsletter for nail collectors.
Jerry Waits,
501 W. Horton,
Brenham, TX 77833
(409) 830-1495

◆ **All railroad, airline, and shipping timetables,** passes, brochures, and other paper.
Ken Prag, Prag's Paper Americana,
Box 531,
Burlingame, CA 94011
(415) 566-6400

```
Your Name
Your Address
```

**If you send an SASE
You get faster responses.**

Ships & the Sea

◆ **Marine art and antiques** are wanted by this nationally known dealer in fine maritime items **who buys nearly everything** related to the China trade, whaling, yachting, and the US Navy under sail. Lowe buys **paintings, prints, ship models, scrimshaw,** ships' logs, cannons and cannon models, **nautical instruments,** compasses, clocks, telescopes, lanterns, sextants, **China trade porcelain,** charts, flags, china with ship designations, and **folk art** including new and old **ship models.** He emphasizes interest only in quality items having to do with seagoing sail or steam vessels in fine condition and notes "We restrict our appraisals to museums but will discuss prices with someone who sends us an item that is for sale so we can inspect it."
　　Samuel Lowe Jr.,
　　80 Charles St.,
　　Boston, MA 02114
　　　(617) 742-0845

◆ **Steamship memorabilia** including china, silver, ashtrays, playing cards, brass whistles, locks, lanterns, paperweights, badges, signs, uniforms and caps, calendars, posters, route maps, and numerous similar items. **Does not want** paper ephemera after 1910, low value paper goods, fake or altered items, or big heavy tools. Nor does he buy items that are shabby or missing important parts. Scott is a major national dealer who issues regular catalogs.
　　Scott Arden,
　　20457 Highway 126,
　　Noti, OR 97461
　　　(503) 935-1619　(9 to 9)

◆ **Steamship memorabilia from all lines and companies** including deck plans, menus, souvenirs, pins, ribbons, models, and passenger lists from Cunard, French German, White Star, Italian, Canadian, Dutch, and all others. You are "invited to send items on approval."
　　Alan Taksler,
　　New Steamship Consultants,
　　Box 30088,
　　Mesa, AZ 85275

◆ **Ocean liner memorabilia** including deck plans, paintings, furniture, postcards, posters, and "anything relating to passenger ship travel" especially from "disaster ships" such as the *Titanic* or *Andrea Doria.* After 1945, only maiden voyage items are wanted. Ken produces a large illustrated catalog four times a year at $15/issue.
　　Ken Schultz,
　　Box M753,
　　Hoboken, NJ 07030
　　　(201) 656-0966

◆ **Canadian steamship memorabilia** including all pre 1950 ephemera such as calendars, stock certificates, bonds, fancy letterheads, original envelopes, deck plans, etc. Seeks Canadian Pacific Steamships, BC Coast steamships, and others.
　　Michael Rice,
　　Box 286,
　　Saanichton, B.C. V0S 1M0, CANADA

◆ **Great Lakes ships and shipping.** "I'll buy photos, documents, books, anything historic, having to do with Great Lakes shipping. I'll pay $250 for James Curwood's *The Great Lakes.*"
　　James Baumhofer,
　　Box 65493,
　　St. Paul, MN 55165
　　　(612) 698-7151

◆ **Riverboats.** *Anything* related to Ohio and Mississippi River steamboats, including advertising, waybills, bells, letters, photos, whistles, china, furniture, what have you.
　　Bert Fenn,
　　Box 157,
　　Tell City, IN 47586

◆ **Ephemera from paddlewheel river boats and similar boats in foreign countries,** 1810-1930, including paper ephemera, flyers, catalogs, menus, checks, tradecards, postcards, sheet music, tickets, posters, photos, maps, paintings, and books (only 1st editions with dust jackets). Nothing after 1950. NO OFFERS.
　　Bill Warren Mueller,
　　Rt. 1, Box 262,
　　Middlebourne, WV 26149
　　　(304) 386-443

◆ **Wooden motor boat memorabilia** especially items related to Gar Wood, the man and his boats, 1923-47. Also *Chris Craft, Hacker, Old Town*, and others. Buys sales literature, catalogs, art work for ads, magazines, etc. Give date and condition of articles.
   Tony Mollica,
   Box 6003,
   Syracuse, NY 13217
       (315) 433-2643 days

◆ **Nautical instruments by American and foreign makers** including brass sextants, wood octants, spyglasses, pocket sundials, and cased navigating devices for charts and globes, as well as map drawing tools. Must be pre 1890.
   Jonathan Thomas,
   Scientific Americana,
   74 Wright St.,
   Westport, CT 06880
       (203) 227-2622

◆ **Outboard motors.** "I'll buy outboard motors, boat and sales literature, and engine manuals from before 1940. Also boating magazines, nautical books, and other ephemera including information about marine engines, outboard motors, yachts, canoes, treasure hunting, Arctic voyages and exploration, and boat building." Nothing after 1940 please. Condition must be described carefully on paper goods. When describing outboard motors, give the serial number and indicate whether the engine is frozen or will still turn. Offers large wants list and catalogs of items for sale 5 times a year.
   Robert Glick,
   Columbia Trading Co.,
   2 Rocklyn Dr.,
   Suffern, NY 10901
       (914) 368-3078

◆ **Lighthouses, U.S. Coast Guard, and rescue services at sea.** All ephemera pre 1940.
   Robert Glick,
   Columbia Trading Co.,
   2 Rocklyn Dr.,
   Suffern, NY 10901
       (914) 368-3078

Airplanes

◆ **Antique airplane instruments, parts, and propellors.** Also early aviation memorabilia including helmets, goggles, and wings. Particular interest in Charles A. Lindbergh.
Lou Lufker,
184 Dorothy Rd.,
West Islip, NY 11795
(516) 661-1422

◆ **All early airplane memorabilia** including propellors, instruments, badges, flight awards, tools, manuals, emblems, accessories, checks, bonds, and virtually any good quality early item.
Joseph Russell,
455 Ollie St.,
Cottage Grove, WI 53527
(608) 839-4736 eves

◆ **Antique airplane memorabilia** including entire airplanes, parts, early flight equipment, books, magazines, photos, etc., are sought by the 6,000 members of The Antique Airplane Association. Write what you have for sale in the way of early air memorabilia, and President Taylor will forward your letter to a member who is looking for what you have to sell. The Association is the parent organization of the Airpower Museum and Bob is empowered to accept tax deductable donations of significant and interesting items from the history of air flight.
Bob Taylor
Antique Airplane Association,
Box 172,
Ottumwa, IA 52501
(515) 938-2773 days

◆ *Pan Am's China Clipper* and all Chinese **airlines, 1925-45,** including uniforms, medals, photos, diaries, caps, badges, posters, diaries, and what have you.
Gene Christian,
3849 Bailey Ave.,
Bronx, NY 10463
(212) 548-0243

◆ *Ford* tri-motor airplane memorabilia. Will pay $100 for Ford Airplane Co. employee's badge.
Tim O'Callaghan,
46878 Betty Hill,
Plymouth, MI 49170
(313) 459-4636

◆ **Commercial aviation memorabilia, American or foreign, 1919-50** including books, letters, magazines, photographs, and miscellaneous small artifacts. Especially interested in uncommon items. No books on how to fly, radio, or navigation. Book club editions or defective books are not wanted.
Ron Mahoney,
Air Age Book Co,
Box 40,
Tollhouse, CA 93667
(209) 855-8993

◆ **Commercial airline memorabilia** including pilot and stewardess wings and hat emblems, display models, anniversary pins, playing cards, postcards with airplanes, buttons, flight schedules, kiddie wings, and almost anything else old and unusual from the airlines. Especially seeking ephemera from *Northeast Airlines, Delta, Chicago and Southern,* and *Western Airlines.*
John Joiner,
245 Ashland Trail,
Tyrone, GA 30290
(404) 487-3732

◆ **Airline pilot and stewardess wings and hat badges** pre 1970. Also stewardess uniforms pre 1965 *if they are complete.* Looking for pilot and stewardess wings from the 1940's and 50's from airlines such as *Mohawk Airlines, Northeast Airlines, Inland Airlines, Pioneer Air Lines, Empire Airlines, Colonial Airlines, Chicago and Southern Airlines, Mid-Continent Airlines,* and others. Also **metal desk models of airliners** (travel agent type) from the 1940's, 50's, and 60's. No military items. Xerox© copies are very helpful.
Charles Quarles,
204 Reservation Dr.,
Spindale, NC 28160
(704) 245-7803 eves

◆ **Air sickness bags from foreign airlines,** especially small, old, or out of business companies. Prefers knowing when and where it was obtained and if you have the original tickets, boarding pass, etc., all the better. No current domestic air carrier bags are wanted.
Jack Forsbach,
8306 Wilshire Blvd., Suite 1232,
Beverly Hills, CA 90211
(213) 739-8475

◆ **Desk display models of aircraft and weapon products** from various manufacturers such as *Convair, General Dynamics, Vultee, Douglass, Lockheed,* and others. Models created by Topping are preferred but all are considered. All models should have their original stands.
Bob Keller, Starline Hobbies,
Box 38,
Stanton, CA 90680
(714) 826-5218 days

◆ **Zeppelin, blimp, and dirigible memorabilia** including virtually anything shaped like, or about, the giant gas bags such as photos, paper ephemera, postcards, china marked "LZ," stereocards, timetables, books, souvenirs, stamps and covers, training films, tokens and medals, toys, games, and Christmas ornaments. Especially wants pieces and parts of zeps. No repros, repainted or restored items, homemades, or fakes. "I am a historian not a dealer."
Zeppelin,
Box 86,
Riverton, NJ 08077
(609) 829-3959

◆ **Aviation magazines, pilot's handbooks, and overhaul manuals** before 1970.
Alan C. King,
PO Box 86,
Radnor, OH 43066

Automobiles

◆ **Classic American and foreign automobiles.** One of the nation's largest auctioneers of high quality foreign and old domestic automobiles. If you have anything fast, sleek, limited production, or unusual, give Cole a call and discuss putting it up for sale in California's lucrative automobile market. Also Corvettes, T-Birds, older convertibles, and selected other American cars of the 1950's and 1960's. Don't sell your old car for too little.
> Rick Cole Auctions,
> 10701 Riverside Dr.,
> No. Hollywood, CA 91602
>> (818) 506-6533

◆ **Automobiles made between 1940 and 1969.** Want any well maintained low mileage auto, especially a *Cadillac* convertible from the 1950's or 60's. "I'd keep it as long as I live!" Also buys automotive related **signs**: auto sales and service, gasoline, motor oil, etc. Also **auto toys**.
> Gus Garton,
> Garton's Auto,
> 5th & Vine,
> Millville, NJ 08332

◆ *Dan Patch* **automobile** or parts and other ephemera from that brand. Call collect if you have one of these cars for sale.
> Donald Sawyer,
> 40 Bachelor St.,
> West Newbury, MA 01985
>> (508) 363-2983

Automobile ephemera

◆ **Paper ephemera, advertising, and promotional items associated with automobiles,** trucks, buses, campers, taxis, auto racing, police cars, ambulances, and hearses. Jay operates a large mail order business selling **transportation memorabilia of all sorts** and always needs clean old items such as catalogs, promotional items, emblems, promotional models given away by car dealers, auto company service pins, owners manuals, and other small items associated with any form of vehicle. Will buy US and foreign items, and multiples of some things. "I will accept boxes sent to me on approval and will make immediate offers to buy." Requests that you include your phone number. Does **not** want shop manuals, parts lists, and magazine ads.
> Jay Ketelle,
> 3721 Farwell,
> Amarillo, TX 79109
>> (806) 355-3456

◆ **Automobile related memorabilia** including promotional giveaways, **owner's manuals**, repair manuals, radiator emblems and caps, dial type tire gauges, fancy gear shift knobs, car clocks, **spark plugs**, horns, dash panels, brass speedometers, **DAV keychains**, automobile magazines, plant employee badges, canceled checks from auto companies, **stocks and bonds**, porcelain or leather *license plates*, driving awards, and anything you can imagine having to do with automobiles except magazine ads.
> Joseph Russell,
> 455 Ollie St.,
> Cottage Grove, WI 53527
>> (608) 839-4736 eves

◆ **Books, magazines, and factory literature about cars, trucks, motorcycles, and bicycles.** Also buys newsletters and magazines produced by automobile clubs devoted to one particular make of vehicle or another. Documents related to vehicle history 1895-1990 also purchased.
> Ralph Dunwoodie,
> 5935 Calico Drive,
> Sun Valley, NV 89433
>> (702) 673-3811

◆ **Automobile sales catalogs, brochures, owner's manuals, and repair guides** printed by the auto company. Also **auto dealer promotional items,** including signs, salesmen's awards, etc. Wants material for all cars and trucks, American or foreign, especially before 1970. No magazines, clipped ads, *Motor's* or *Chilton's* manuals, and books not printed by the auto company. "Please send me a list of each item by year and make. If not practical to make a list, give me total count of brochures by decade, such as, so many from 1950 to 1959, so many from 1960 to 1969, etc., separating US cars, foreign cars, and trucks."
   Walter Miller,
   6710 Brooklyn Parkway,
   Syracuse, NY 13211
      (315) 432-8282

◆ *Ford* **Motor Company memorabilia** from before 1955, including books, coins, pins, badges, postcards, and literature.
   Tim O'Callaghan,
   46878 Betty Hill,
   Plymouth, MI 48170
   (313) 459-4636

◆ **Parts and sales literature for** *Gardner* **and other automobiles made in St. Louis** including parts, hubcaps, mascots, owners manuals, and the like. St. Louis cars include *Moon, Diana, Ruxton,* and *Windsor.* Pays $75 for brochure about front drive on a 1930 *Gardner.* Also wants entire *Gardner* automobiles, complete or not. Also sales literature for other autos, 1900-1940.
   Robert Owen,
   Box 204,
   Fairborn, OH 45324

◆ **Advertising literature for the** *Chevrolet Corvette*, 1953-85, including newspaper and magazine ads, sales brochures, direct mailings, race programs, sports programs, and auto show literature. Also "related Corvette memorabilia," including promotional giveaways. No reprints.
   David Facey, Auto-Ads,
   111 Carey Place,
   Lakeland, FL 33803
      (813) 688-1412

◆ **Paper ephemera about pre 1970** *Chevrolet*, including ads, showroom literature, pinback buttons, coins, tokens, and manuals, particularly obscure ads and information about the 1932 Chevy.
   Reed Fitzpatrick,
   Box 369,
   Vashon, WA 98070

◆ *Chrysler* **Town and Country.** "I want anything you have, 1946-1950."
   Mel Rosenthal, DC,
   507 S. Maryland Ave.,
   Wilmington, DE 19804
      (302) 322-8944

◆ *Buick* **promotional items.**
   Alvin Heckard,
   RD 1, Box 88,
   Lewistown, PA 17044
      (717) 248-7071

◆ *Studebaker* **printed ephemera** is his specialty, but Charles says "I'll buy anything printed pertaining to cars, including automobile books, literature, manuals, and magazines." He needs to know the date and condition, and, if an official company publication, its form number.
   Charles Conway,
   Box 102,
   Attleboro, MA 02703

◆ *Packard* **parts and literature.** Especially desirous of picking up new old stock of old *Packard* parts complete with *Packard* part numbers. Also wants dealer and promotional literature.
   Bob Cowan,
   818 Hill,
   Hoquiam, WA 98550

◆ *Mercedes* and *Rolls-Royce* radiator mascots and other parts, accessories, manuals, and literature made before 1960.
   Joseph Weber,
   604 Centre St.,
   Ashland, PA 17921
      (717) 875-4401 3-5 pm

◆ *Rolls Royce* advertising, pamphlets, cards, toys, and other information. Has particular interest in all models from the years 1957 through 1962, Princess through Silver Cloud.
Richard Melcher,
1206 Okanogan St.,
Wenatchee, WA 98807
(509) 662-0386

◆ *Cunningham* Auto Company ephemera. "I want anything regarding this 1920's Rochester, NY, auto maker. Priced approvals are requested. Your postage will be reimbursed."
David Lamb,
48 Woodside Dr.,
Rochester, NY 14624

◆ Trucking literature, books, and advertising, 1906-1986.
P.C. Manwiller,
773 Spruce St.,
Emmaus, PA 18049
(215) 965-4953

◆ Odd looking spark plugs. "I'll buy as many as you have, the odder looking the better." He especially wants those with priming cups. No *AC* or *Champion* plugs.
Joseph Weber,
604 Centre St.,
Ashland, PA 17921
(717) 875-4401 3-5 pm

◆ Factory original automobile AM radios 1926-1962. Only AM-FM from 1963-77. Wants brand and model number. Also auto wheelcovers (*not hubcaps*), 1950 to the present. Tell him the make, model, condition, and quantity. Include your price, phone number and hours to reach you.
John Sheldon,
2718 Koper Dr.,
Sterling Heights, MI 48310
(313) 977-7979 days

Tire companies

◆ *Firestone* Tire Company promotional items especially those shaped like tires including tire ashtrays, clocks, penholders, cigarette cases. Also radios shaped like batteries, and other "figural selling aids." List everything printed on the tire and on the insert. Does not want domestic ash-trays made after 1950. Pays $20-$35 for most items.
Wayne Ray,
10325 Willeo Creek Trace,
Roswell, GA 30075
(404) 998-5325

◆ Tire company promotional items especially tire ashtrays, tire clocks, penholders, radios, globes, *Tires* magazines, tire catalogs, and other literature and promotional items. "Will pay $50 for any original *Michelin* or *Overman* rubber tire ashtray." Also want foreign tires, tires with commemorative inserts, and other unusual promotional tires. Long priced wants list available.
Jeff Mc Vey,
Box 201,
Moffett Field, CA 94035
(408) 739-8530

License plates

◆ **Pre 1920 license plates,** especially undated plates made of leather, brass, or porcelain. Will buy old collections or accumulations. Describe condition carefully, including damage, chips, and crazing. He offers to answer questions about license plates and says "If I don't want your plates, perhaps I can find someone who does." Gary is secretary of the Automobile License Plate Collector's Association and a valuable source of information.

Gary Brent Kincade,
Box 712,
Weston, WV 26452
(304) 842-3773 eves

◆ **Extraordinary license plates, especially undated** or those made of porcelain, leather, or wood. Also all license plates issued on or for Indian reservations. Also U.S. pre 1915; all motorcycle pre 1950; all foreign pre 1950; all Southern and Southwestern plates pre 1935; New Mexico, Alaska, and Hawaii pre 1950 in good condition and pre 1920 in any condition; and personalized plates "with cute names or phrases." Also any pictorial plates. Will buy any good condition pre 1935 plate plus collections or accumulations of plates. "Plates from populated states like NY, OH, and PA are worth little even if they date as far back as 1915 whereas Alaskan, Hawaiian, and Puerto Rican plates are desirable even in poor shape." George also buys miniature plates from DAV, *Goodrich*, *Wheaties*, or *Post* cereals. Also car club emblems such as AAA, especially foreign ones or those before 1925. Also all **pre 1940 chauffeur's badges** in good original condition. Will make offer on **any item if** two unglued stamps are sent.

George Chartrand,
Box 334,
Winnipeg, MB R3C 2H6,
CANADA

◆ **License plates from Southern states pre 1958.** Other states pre 1935. Wants *only* automobile plates except from Mississippi, a state from which he will buy all types and classes of plates. 1912 and 1913 Mississippi plates are worth up to $1,000 each. Wants first year of issue plates from all 50 states, as well as any undated or handmade plates.

Eugene Gardner,
Route 1, Box 166,
Palmetto, GA 30268
(404) 463-4264

◆ **License plates from Missouri, Kansas, and Colorado.** Also other states from the years 1936, 1976, and 1989. Also miniature license plates produced by DAV or cereal companies. Provide a list of the items you have and the price you'd like.

George Van Trump Jr.,
Box 260170,
Lakewood, CO 80226
(303) 985-3508

◆ **All types of old license plates.** "I buy license plates from anywhere issued to any type of motor vehicle at any time. My number one find would be a 1905 VT porcelain plate, for which I'd pay $1,500 if in good condition." Describe all chips, bends, repainting, rust, etc.

Andy Bernstein,
154 Murray Drive,
Oceanside, NY 11572
(516) 764-0273

◆ **Porcelain license plates** from U.S. and Canadian cars, trucks, and motorcycles before 1923. Also wants early **photos and photo postcards of vehicles clearly showing readable plates.** Pays especially well for plates from Southern and unpopulated Western states. Does not buy painted metal plates. Photocopies suggested.

Rodney Brunsell,
55 Spring St.,
Hanson, MA 02341

◆ **License plates and license plate related items,** chauffeurs badges, hack (taxi) badges, Disabled Veterans key chain tags, B.F. Goodrich key chain tags, dashboard discs, registration windshield stickers, inspection windshield stickers, early drivers licenses and auto registrations.

Dr. Edward Miles,
888 8th Ave.,
New York, NY 10019
(212) 765-2660

Space Program

◆ **Memorabilia of all early rocket research** including "newsletters, journals, books, magazines, reports, studies, correspondence, blueprints, drawings, photographs, films, and any other documentation from France, Germany, UK, USSR, USA, or any other nation regarding speculation, research and development, experimentation and implementation conducted by any amateur, military, or civilian group or any individual pertaining to the history and development of rockets and missiles and eventual space travel from the period of 1900-1960." He especially wants "any material from WWII pertaining to the work done at Peenemunde, Germany, which was carried out by Wernher Von Braun and led to the development and implementation of the V-2 and other rocket weapons. Also any material having to do with Robert H. Goddard and the experiments he conducted in Worcester, Massachusetts, and Roswell, New Mexico, during the 1920's thru 1940's." He is not interested in science fiction or pop culture figures like Buck Rogers but does want speculative articles that are scholarly or serious in intent.
 Randy Liebermann,
 305 East 40th Street,
 New York, NY 10016-2189
  (212) 972-2061

◆ **Space shot memorabilia** including souvenirs such as commemorative magazines, buttons, autographs, etc. Especially wants "internal" souvenirs such as special coins, medallions, mission patches, models, etc., produced for people directly involved with some aspect of a space "event" such as a launching or completion of construction. Also internal documents such as manuals, flight plans, charts, and so on. Also hardware, pieces of spacecraft, and other items discarded as part of mission preparation or completion. Also video tapes of launchings or reports from space. Does not want recent items which NASA still sells such as slide sets, T-shirts, etc.
 Mike Smithwick,
 25215 La Loma Drive,
 Los Altos Hills, CA 94022
  (408) 244-8987 eves

◆ **NASA and space program items**, including anything produced or distributed by NASA, authentic patches, manuals, medallions, space shuttle tile samples, pieces of spacecraft or spacecraft construction materials, and items owned or carried into space by astronauts.
 Paul Hartunian,
 127B East Bradford Ave.,
 Cedar Grove, NJ 07009
  (201) 857-7275

◆ **Space age memorabilia** including souvenirs issued to commemorate various launchings, US or Soviet. Buys glasses, coasters, ashtrays, cards, plates, paperweights, jewelry, and other trinkets as well as books, coloring books, magazines, and albums of newspaper clippings. He requests that you price what you have. NO OFFERS.
 Barry Burros,
 160 East 48th St.,
 New York, NY 10017
  (212) 688-1581

◆ **Apollo XI moon landing souvenirs.** No magazines or newspapers. NO OFFERS.
 Bernard Passion,
 3517 1/2 Kinney St.,
 Los Angeles, CA 90065
  (213) 256-8291

```
┌────────────────────────────┐
│                        ███ │
│                            │
│   Your Name                │
│   Your Address             │
│                            │
└────────────────────────────┘
```

When you send an SASE use a long (#10) envelope.

Public Transportation

◆ **Horsedrawn streetcars and pre 1920 electric railways.** "I'll buy bells marked with the name of a streetcar line, car gongs, car maker's plates, fare registers both wall mounted and hand held, car signs reading "Have fare ready," "Pay at Rear," etc., hat badges, motorman's and conductor's certificates, and photos of early cars.

Jonathan Thomas,
Scientific Americana,
74 Wright St.,
Westport, CT 06880
(203) 227-2622

◆ **Memorabilia from buses, taxi cabs, hearses, ambulances, and any other public conveyance** before 1960 including emblems, badges, licenses, license plates, advertising, promotional giveaway trinkets, operator's manuals, sales literature, etc. May be foreign or US as long as they are old, genuine, and small. Will accept items sent on approval.

Jay Ketelle,
3721 Farwell,
Amarillo, TX 79109
(806) 355-3456

◆ **Bus, trolley, and streetcar memorabilia** pre 1940 including photos, artifacts, driver's badges, caps, bus emblems, route maps, and advertising. Has particular interest in Florida companies but says "I will consider any items."

Sam LaRoue,
5980 SW 35th Street,
Miami, FL 33155

◆ **Greyhound bus memorabilia.** Wants wide range of items, toys, awards, ticket punches, photos, and the like. Prefers a picture or photocopy. No magazine ads, timetables, or posters.

Eugene Farha,
Box 633,
Cedar Grove, WV 25039
(304) 340-3201

◆ **Taxi cabs.** "If it pictures an American taxi cab, I'll buy it," says Henry, who seeks a wide variety of taxi related items. If it has do do with taxis, give him a call.

Henry Winningham,
3205 S. Morgan St.,
Chicago, IL 60608
(312) 847-1672

◆ **China from bus terminals** marked with names of a bus line.

Les Winn,
Box 80641,
Chamblee, GA 30366
(404) 458-6194

◆ **Transportation tokens.** Will buy in any quantity from any years. Prices vary widely depending on value. "Most modern pieces with cut-out letters are very common. We sell a nice mixed collection of 2,500 tokens for $99, so you can see modern tokens aren't worth a great deal." There are a few common old tokens, but some can be worth $750 each if they picture a ship, trolley, horse car, ferry, or stagecoach. Look for the words "Depotel, Hotel, Baggage, Omnibus, Drayage, Depot to hotel," etc. Simply ship your tokens if you want this well known dealer to make an offer.

Rich Hartzog,
Box 4143 BBL,
Rockford, IL 61110
(815) 226-0771

◆ **Transportation or toll tokens** for bridges, toll roads, ferries, horsecars, depot hacks, and early streetcars. Tokens *must* be made of metal or plastic. Cardboard tokens are wanted *only* if round, *not* square or rectangular. "Hotel to depot" or "transfer line" tokens are worth $25-$100, more if pictorial. A token reading "I Gibbs Belleville & New York USM stage//Good for one ride to the bearer" would be worth $1,500 in nice condition.

Rev. John Coffee,
Box 1204,
Boston, MA 02104
(617) 277-8111

Bicycles

◆ **Balloon tire bicycles** made between 1934-1960 in new or mint condition only, especially *Schwinn, Shelby, Monarch, Columbia,* or *Elgin* (Sears Roebuck). Please include a photo.
Gus Garton,
Garton's Auto,
5th & Vine,
Millville, NJ 08332

◆ **Bicycle memorabilia,** generally before 1900 although some items are wanted to 1930. Wants all material about high wheelers and velocipedes ("bone shakers") including posters, advertising, trophies, photos, prints, medals, watches, toys, and all other representations or depictions, especially ephemera created by the Pope Manufacturing Company. He *does not want* anything related to balloon tire bicycles.
Pryor Dodge,
Box 71 Prince St. Station,
New York, NY 10012
(212) 966-1026

◆ **League of American Wheelmen (LAW) memorabilia** and other pre 1910 bicycling artifacts including medals, pins, awards, ribbons, photos, and figurines made of glass, porcelain, silver, etc. Small items or large. Especially interested in high wheeler items.
Charlie Stewart,
900 Grandview Ave.,
Reno, NV 89503
(702) 747-1439 mornings

◆ **Bicycle memorabilia** including paper ephemera, sales literature, catalogs, advertising, and small objects such as pins, medals, and give-away trinkets. Jay specializes in mail order sales of transportation memorabilia of all types and always needs good fresh new stock. He accepts boxes of good clean items sent on approval and "makes immediate offers."
Jay Ketelle,
3721 Farwell,
Amarillo, TX 79109
(806) 355-3456

◆ **All early quality items associated with bicycles** including badges, awards, sales and promotional items, emblems, accessories, stock certificates, etc.
Joseph Russell,
455 Ollie St.,
Cottage Grove, WI 53527
(608) 839-4736 eves

◆ **Pre 1930 bicycle license tags,** often called "sidepath licenses," from any state. Depending on their age and place of issue, they are worth from $5-$40.
James Case,
Box 168, Cane Rd.,
Lindley, NY 14858

Motorcycles

◆ **Motorcycle memorabilia** including pins, awards, clothing, signs, postcards, trade cards, racing trophies and memorabilia, motorcycle toys, and any unusual items. Also buys American motorcycles and racing motorcycles from before 1950.
   Chris Savino,
   Box 419,
   Breesport, NY 14816
      (607) 739-3106

◆ **Motorcycles and bicycle ephemera.** "I pay top prices for just about anything related to motorcycles and bicycles including sales brochures, photos, tour awards, advertising, parts catalogs, pins, watch fobs, books, badges, clothing, magazines, trophies, nameplates, etc. I'm especially interested in early **motorcycle toys** in any material." NO OFFERS.
   Chris Kusto,
   Antique Cycle Supply,
   Route 1,
   Cedar Springs, MI 49319
      (616) 636-8200

◆ **Motorcycle memorabilia** including owner and shop manuals, badges, promotional toys, emblems, license plates, instruments, lights, spark plugs, stock certificates, and "virtually any quality item." No magazine ads.
   Joseph Russell,
   455 Ollie St.,
   Cottage Grove, WI 53527
      (608) 839-4736 eves

◆ **Motorcycle memorabilia** including advertising, giveaway trinkets, watch fobs, and other items. Both foreign and domestic, pre 1960. "I will accept boxes sent to me on approval and will make immediate offer to buy." Will reimburse postage if offer not accepted.
   Jay Ketelle,
   3721 Farwell,
   Amarillo, TX 79109
      (806) 355-3456

◆ **American made motorcycles and motorcycle parts.** "I'm in the parts business and will travel to pick up large lots. Describe what you have, giving markings and numbers when appropriate."
   Robert Fay,
   Star Route Box AF,
   Whitmore, CA 96096
      (916) 472-3132

◆ *Cushman* motorscooters and related ephemera, especially signs and sales literature. Also **pre 1965 motorcycle** photos, postcards, manuals, sales literature, and magazines.
   Don Olson,
   Box 397,
   Humboldt, IA 50548

14
Business & Trades

Dr. Hyman's Prescription

Since the first colonists landed, America has been a land of builders and inventors, commerce and farming, trade and manufacture. A land of doers....

Unfortunately for historians, few of those doers took the time to sit down and record what they did and how they did it.

Serious collectors who want to learn about the manufacture and marketing of the items which interest them today often find it difficult to obtain information about what went on 20 years ago. You can imagine how hard it is to obtain info from before the turn-of-the-century!

Collectors gladly buy products, advertising, business records, letters, bills, posters, store displays, and the like. Difficult to find does not necessarily make them valuable, although large illustrated company catalogs from the turn of the century usually sell for more than $100 and signs made of tin often bring $500+.

Collectors also buy tools, instruments, signs, badges, emblems, uniforms, and other three-dimensional items.

There are some industries whose histories and artifacts are being preserved by fewer than a half dozen people. In some cases, *I'll Buy That!* will put you in touch with the *only* person in the country who cares about what you have!

tony hyman

Business

◆ **All sorts of things related to banking and business.** Larry buys safes, money bags, cash registers, nail bins, tools, and other items that might be found in the office of doctors, dentists, undertakers, blacksmiths, watchmakers, gunsmiths, locksmiths, opticians, jewelers, and the like.   He buys items from

◆ **State Farm Insurance Company memorabilia,** 1922-52. He wants all items marked with their 3 oval emblem depicting a car, fire helmet, and cornucopia. Also selected items marked with the home office or an old Buick. He buys signs, ashtrays, pocket knives, pencils, tape measures, stationery, and everything else **except** bumper plates that are not made of brass. He **does not want** anything marked with the three ovals and the words *auto, life,* and *fire*.
Ken Jones,
100 Manor Dr.,
Columbia, MO 65203

"Your readers should not expect to get rich from decorator items.
It is expensive for dealers to buy, transport, restore, and then try to
find a buyer for items. I prefer to buy collections or estates, but
I will make some sort of offer on anything offered to me.
If I can resell their item quickly, the offer will be more
than if I am going to have to warehouse the item."
Larry Franklin

---

saloons, hotels, brothels, police stations, firehouses, asylums, mines, prisons, roadhouses, arcades, breweries, factories, boat wright, etc., including furnishings, signs, tools, and the like. He especially likes to find glass counters and countertop displays. "I will respond to any honest inquiry for help to identify an item for sale." He requests a complete description indicating all wear or broken parts. If you know the item's history, it is helpful. Photos of larger items, and photocopies of smaller ones, are recommended.
Larry Franklin,
3238 Hutchison Ave.,
Los Angeles, CA 90034
   (213) 559-4461

◆ **Fire service and fire insurance items** such as badges, histories of insurance companies, pre 1900 fire insurance policies, firemarks, signs, plaques, advertising, postcards, stamps, and envelopes with pictorial return addresses. Doesn't want anything except fire related items, and nothing modern. Please quote fire related books.
Glenn Hartley,
2859 Marlin Dr.,
Chamblee, GA 30341
   (404) 451-2651

◆ **Anything relating to fire insurance companies** before 1940. Wants fire marks, illustrated policies, advertising, signs, and giveaways.
Ralph Jennings,
301 Fort Washington Ave.,
Fort Washington, PA 19034
   (215) 646-7178

◆ **Bookbinding tools and equipment.**
Frank Klein,
The Bookseller,
521 W. Exchange St.,
Akron, OH 44302
   (216) 762-3101 days

◆ **Fur company items** from before 1945, including posters, calendars, catalogs, and scent shipping containers. Nothing damaged or cut.
Ron Willoughby,
Route 171,
Woodstock, CT 06281
   (203) 974-1226

◆ **Pre 1900 electrical devices** manufactured by Stanley Electric, Edison General Electric, Thomson Houston, Weston, Westinghouse, Crocker Wheeler and Sprague. "I want small open frame bipolar motors and generators, switchboard voltmeters and ammeters, carbon arc lamps, electric fans with brass blades, and watt-hour meters. I also want catalogs, photographs and paper related to these companies printed before 1905." Provide all nameplate data including patent dates and numbers. Prefers the seller to set the price, but will make offers.
William F. Edwards,
State Road,
Richmond, MA 01254
(413) 698-3458

◆ **Cigar Stores. Everything associated with the manufacture and sale of cigars** before 1920 including cigar maker's mechanical tools, catalogs, advertising, cigar boxes, cigar labels, signs, company records, and related items having to do with cigar taxation. This includes items related to the Cigar Makers' International Union and its leaders, Strasser, Perkins and Gompers.
Tony Hyman,
Box 699,
Claremont, CA 91711
(714) 621-5952

◆ **Coal company scrip, stocks and bonds, and cap lamps worn underground.**
"Tip" Tippy,
102 1/2 Meadow Rd.,
Oak Ridge, TN 37830
(615) 483-1017

◆ **Mining company memorabilia**, primarily Pennsylvania and the Western U.S. Buys books, stocks and bonds, sheet music, photographs, and selected artifacts.
Jeffrey Viola,
475-B Eltone Rd.,
Jackson, NJ 08527
(201) 928-0666

◆ **Mining memorabilia from Colorado 1859-1915** including photos, paper ephemera, stocks, maps, stereoviews, advertising, and small souvenirs. Especially from towns of Cripple Creek, Victor, Altman, Goldfield, Leadville, Breckenridge, Idaho Springs, Telluride, others. No photos of mountains unless a mine is featured. Also books about Colorado mining and any city directories pre 1915. No interest in "flatland cities" like Denver, Colorado Springs, and Boulder, nor in Colorado tourist attractions and parks. No postcards or bottles.
George Foott,
6683 S. Yukon Way,
Littleton, CO 80123
(303) 979-8688

◆ **Mining ephemera, especially paper goods from Arizona and Colorado mines.** Interested in buying stock certificates and other paper pertaining to mining other than coal. Buys books on mining and gems, catalogs of mining equipment, photographs, etc.
Russell Filer, Mining,
Box 487,
Yucaipa, CA 92399
(714) 797-1650

◆ **Sawmills, coal mining, and logging in Arkansas.** Wants correspondence, invoices, photographs, postcards, trade publications, and anything else about these three industries in Arkansas.
Bill Pollard,
32 Fairoaks,
Conway, AR 72032

◆ **Tin can manufacturing ephemera and artifacts.** Also want ephemera related to commercial stone lithography (label printing and box making) before 1925, especially the printing of packages, labels, tin cans, and advertising.
Tony Hyman,
Box 699,
Claremont, CA 91711
(714) 621-5952

Business Machines

◆ **Check writers and check protectors,** pre 1910 in working condition. May be home, office, or hand held models. No machines by *Todd, F & E Lightning, Hedman, Paymaster,* or *Safeguard.*

William Feigin,
45 W. 34th Street, #405,
New York, NY 10001
(212) 736-3360

◆ **Calculating devices before 1915** and associated ephemera including catalogs and advertising. Wants mechanical calculators such as arithmometers, generally in wooden cases. Brand names to look for include *Autarith, Baldwin, Calculmeter, Grant, Madas, Rapid, Spalding, Thomas,* but interested in anything odd. Also rotary machine, heavy devices operated by a crank, and other types of calculators including **slide rules,** but *only* slide rules that don't have patent numbers. Comptometers with wooden cases are also desired as are **planimeters,** devices for measuring area on maps. Give a photo or sketch of what you have plus a description of all markings, serial numbers, etc. Weight and dimensions are helpful as are photocopies of paper goods.

Robert Otnes,
2160 Middlefield Road,
Palo Alto, CA 94301

◆ **Calculators and adding machines.** "I am very eager to purchase unusual and scarce calculators and adding machines, and I am prepared to pay well for information leading to location of these. I am prepared to travel anywhere in the world in search of these machines, and will pay in cash immediately without fuss or bother for the right items. I am happy to buy single items or entire collections. I also buy **typewriters.**"

Peter Frei,
Box 500,
Brimfield, MA 01010
(800) 942-8968
(413)245-4660 in MA

◆ **Typewriters** pre 1910, especially those with fancy or strange mechanisms, such as the *Sholes & Glidden* from 1870's which strikes from below so the typist can't see her work. "I'm always willing to give an opinion about a machine by mail if you send a picture or good description." This 13 year veteran promises, "I will never try to buy your machine for less than it's worth."

Joseph Weber,
604 Centre St.,
Ashland, PA 17921
(717) 875-4401 3-5 pm

◆ **Pre 1925 American typewriters and ephemera** including ribbon tins, ribbon, accessories, tools, oilers, advertising, catalogs, instruction manuals, shipping cases if they are imprinted with the name of a typewriter, catalogs for business schools if they picture early typewriters, cardboard or metal signs, paperweights, blotters, clocks, rulers, or any other item imprinted with the name or illustration of a typewriter. "If in doubt, write or call anyway." Also early typewriter tables with fancy cast iron frames or legs (they usually have two drop leaves and a center drawer). Also typewriting instruction books pre 1910. **Some small very early hand held adders and calculators** are of interest. "If the machine is not one that I want, buy may be wanted by another collector of early typewriters, I will help you find a buyer. I am not a dealer and do not buy typewriters for stock. I'll happily answer any inquiry rather than risk missing something I would like to hear about," but common brands are not of interest to anyone. Name, model, type of lid and base, and condition. Photocopy accessories. "Never ship a typewriter until a deal is made. I have to provide shipping and packing instructions first."

Paul Lippman,
1216 Garden St.,
Hoboken, NJ 07030
(201) 656-5278 eves

◆ **Unusual antique typewriters.**
Carter Bays,
135 Springlake Rd.,
Columbia, SC 29206
(800) 332-2297

◆ **Unusual antique typewriters.** Want items dating between 1870-1920. Look for typewriters with odd designs, curved keyboards, no keyboards, pointers, or more or less than the standard four rows of keys. The most desired machine is a *Sholes & Glidden,* worth as much as $5,000 in outstanding condition. Give the make and model number if shown on the machine, the serial number, and "an in-focus photo." Rehr will provide you with a checklist to help you describe your machine to him. Send an SASE.
Darryl Rehr,
11433 Rochester Ave. #303,
Los Angeles, CA 90025
(213) 559-2368

◆ **Cash registers made of brass or wood,** especially early wooden registers with inlaid cabinets, dial registers, or multiple drawers. Also registers that ring only to $1. He also buys "amount purchased" signs that were found on top of registers and literature about registers. Machines can be in any condition since he uses damaged machines for parts. Give both the brand name and model number of your machine and include the serial number. Provide your phone number so Ken can make arrangements to pick up your machine. Nothing after 1917.
Ken Konet,
849 Oak Hill Rd.,
Barrington, IL 60010
(312) 382-7799

◆ **Display cases and lighting fixtures,** especially from old drugstores. Wants early countertop display cases with original glass, especially revolving cases, bow-front cases, and double tower cases. Also **lighting fixtures** of early

◆ **Stock market tickers, books, and other memorabilia** having to do with speculation, panics, commodities, cycles, and other activities pre 1940. Also turn of the century prints depicting the stock market, and **stock market magazines** pre 1935.
R.G. Klein,
Box 24A06,
Los Angeles, CA 90024

◆ **Stock market tickers.** "I'll pay $2,000 for Edison glass domed tickers and $1,500 for those made for Western Union.
Frank Guarino,
Box 89,
DeBary, FL 32713

◆ **Mimeograph memorabilia.** Catalogs, instructions, advertising, brochures, you name it, if it's old and about mimeos, he may be interested.
Francis,
Box 6941,
Syracuse, NY 13217

◆ **Microcomputer literature and computers** including just about anything, machines, literature, catalogs, you name it, if it's from the pre-*Apple* pre-*Radio Shack* days (before 1977). Names to look for include *Mark-8, Sphere, Scelbi, Intel* and other machines originally created for hobbyists and do-it-yourselfers.
Harold Layer,
SF State University-AV,
1600 Holloway Ave.,
San Francisco, CA 94132

EDITOR'S NOTE: If you recognize the brand name on your typewriter, collectors probably don't want it. Remington, Underwood, Smith-Corona & Oliver are common.

---

wrought iron or tin, especially from commercial buildings. List all damage. Nothing after 1900. Give all numbers or data on maker's plates.
Jerry Phelps,
6013 Innes Trace Rd.,
Louisville, KY 40222
(502) 425-4765

◆ **Time clocks.**
Steve Chyrchel,
Route #2 Box 362,
Eureka Springs, AR 72632
(501) 253-9244

Business paper

◆ **Business cards of all type.** "We buy business cards of all types with particular interest in cards 1700-1960. We even buy cards that are damaged or written upon. We also buy other paper items such as **photos, letters, and bill heads related to business cards.** We will pay postage both ways on items sent to us on approval." Few business cards have much monetary value, but Jack will pay well for Mathew Brady and Benjamin Franklin. Jack emphasizes that chromolith cards were stock items issued in large quantities. Photocopies are the best description. Jack edits *The Business Card Journal.*
    Jack Gurner,
    116 Dupuy St.,
    Water Valley, MS 38965
        (601) 473-1154

◆ **Business cards.** "I'll buy business cards that are (1) more than 75 years old, (2) from the years 1930-1959, (3) from celebrities in any field of endeavor, or (4) unusual in shape, color, message or material. I only want mint cards that tell what the business is, where it is located and who belongs to the card. I don't want cards that have been written on or are damaged. I don't want trade cards." Photocopy, please. Darrell is President of The American Business Card Club.
    Darrell Christopher,
    31759 Stricker,
    Warren, MI 48093
        (313) 293-2865

◆ **Trade catalogs and piles of business letters,** pre-1920, from manufacturers, wholesalers, and retailers. "The earlier the better," says Jim. Most common catalogs bring $5-$10, but "we have paid as high as $400 for some." Please check that all pages are present as you list the company, type of products, size and number of pages, and the type and number of illustrations (photocopies helpful). Mention *I'll Buy That!* for a free copy of Jim's catalog of catalogs.
    Jim Presgraves,
    Bookworm & Silverfish
    Box 639,
    Wytheville, VA 24382

◆ **Business letterheads and bills with pre 1920 illustrations** of products, plant operations, outdoor scenes, people, and unusual trade marks. He no longer buys buildings or letterheads that are all type, no matter how decorative. Nor does he want heads that have been cut off correspondence or that have been punched for filing. Please photocopy.
    E. Scott Pattison,
    2382 Mangrum Dr.,
    Dunedin, FL 34698

◆ **Envelopes with color advertising for products,** pre 1940.
    Gordon McHenry,
    Box 117,
    Osprey, FL 33559

◆ **Trade cards** for patent medicines, political candidates, ships or shipping lines, railroads, and farm machinery. Also wants mechanical or metamorphic cards (cards with moving parts or that fold over to change the picture). Photocopies or approvals.
    A. Walker Bingham,
    19 E. 72nd St.,
    New York, NY 10021

◆ **Illustrated trade cards, bill heads, and handbills,** pre 1900. Also wants **all trade cards of musicians, bands, and orchestras.**
    Alfred Malpa,
    9 Waterville Road,
    Farmington, CT 06032

◆ **Trade catalogs** for consumer products. "These are exciting peeks into their time, giving the unvarnished truth about their era. Prices vary from two figures (most) to over $10,000.
    Ivan Gilbert,
    2824 Elm Ave.,
    Columbus, OH 43209

◆ **Employee photo ID passes.** All photo ID badges are wanted, especially the celluloid buttons with a pin back. Pays $1 each except for older ones. Ship for check.
    Rich Hartzog,
    Box 4143 BBL,
    Rockford, IL 61110

Telephones

◆ **Old telephones, parts of phones, and select phone company memorabilia** especially signs and pre 1900 magazines with telephone ads. No modern or electronic phones. They offer the *History and Identification of Old Telephones* with 6,000 pictures of old phones for $58.
　Ron and Mary Knappen,
　Phoneco,
　RR #2, Box 590,
　Galesville, WI 54630
　　(608) 582-4124

◆ **Telephones made before 1930,** especially unusual or early pay phones. Ask for his wants list and parts catalog since its handy numbered illustrations will help you describe what you want to sell. Also buys **telephone books** pre 1950, the earlier the better. A *History of Old Telephones* with price guide is available for $6. Correspondence in Spanish or French welcome.
　Gerry Billard,
　Old Telephones,
　21710 Regnart Rd.,
　Cupertino, CA 95014
　　(408) 252-2104

◆ **Telephone stamps and franks of any American telephone company** and tokens of any phone company worldwide. Also any international reply coupons.
　Daniel K.E. Ching,
　Box 75423 Sanford Station,
　Los Angeles, CA 90075-0423

◆ **Rare glass insulators** especially in rare colors. Wants you to describe the color, dimensions, embossing, whether or not it has threads, and its condition. He prefers you describe your insulators using the standard numbering found in Milholland's *Most About Glass Insulators*, available from Linscott with the latest price guide for $39. No damaged insulators.
　Len Linscott,
　3557 Nicklaus Drive,
　Titusville, FL 32780
　　(407) 267-9170

Telegraph

◆ **Telegraph instruments and related ephemera pre 1900** including keys (worth $50-$100), sounders, relays, signs, catalogs, and stationery. Especially instruments marked with initials of a railroad. Names to look for include *L.G. Tillotson, Partrick and Carter, Greeley, Chester, Clark, Davis, Redding, Jones, Williams, Pope,* and about 100 others. Wants registers (clockwork driven devices that inscribe dots and dashes on a paper tape) and will pay to $800-1,000 for them. Also seeking "linemen's sets" of very small portable keys in a hard rubber case. Items do not need to be in perfect condition. No *Boy Scout, Western Electric, Signal,* or *Menominee* equipment or post 1900 paper or telegrams, but loves to find signs advertising pre-1890 telegraph companies. Photo or even a crude sketch is most appreciated.
　Roger Reinke,
　Brasspounder,
　5301 Neville Ct.,
　Alexandria, VA 22310
　　(703) 971-4095

◆ **Telegraph instruments** if old, complete, and professional quality, especially from railroads.
　Scott Arden,
　20457 Highway 126,
　Noti, OR 97461
　　(503) 9935-1619 (9 to 9)

◆ **Western Union and Postal Telegraph** instruments, books, and anything else. List every marking found on items you wish to sell. No cracked or damaged pieces.
　Charles Goodman,
　636 W. Grant Ave.,
　Charleston, Il 61920
　　(217) 345-6771

Architecture & Building Trades

◆ **Items related to building and architecture pre 1930** including books on architecture, building, carpentry, and surveying. Also manuals and catalogs of cast iron, steel, plumbing, hardware, paint, and other building materials. Also **blueprints, architects renderings,** drafting instruments made of brass, early drafting or drawing machines, slide rules, and watercolor boxes.
> Robert Des Marais,
> 618 West Foster Ave.,
> State College, PA 16801
> (814) 237-7141

◆ **Blueprints for buildings or machines.**
Jim Presgraves,
Bookworm & Silverfish,
Box 639,
Wytheville, VA 24382

◆ **Slide rules and related literature.** Also wants unusually fine mechanical drawing sets and devices and associated literature. Also combination or compendium tools (pre "calculator"). Ed would like to correspond with other collectors.
> Ed Straker,
> Box 8970,
> La Jolla, CA 92038
> (619) 741-5220

◆ **Antique surveying instruments,** including compasses, transits, levels, wire link-type measuring chains, circumferentors, semi-circumferentors, railroad compasses, and solar compasses. Tools may be wood, brass, or wood and brass. "Also have interest in **mathematical and philosophical instruments** of the past." Give all names and numbers found on the body or lens.
> Michael Manier,
> Box 100,
> Houston, MO 65483
> (417) 967-2777 24 hours

◆ **Old tools of the trades and crafts** especially those used by woodworkers: wooden and metallic planes, folding rulers, chisels, levels, saws, plumb bobs, scribes, spokeshaves, hammers, squares, axes, trammel points, measuring devices, drills, bid braces, making gauges, wrenches, fancy tool boxes, hand and foot powered machinery. Also wants advertising items and hardware store displays, catalogs, and documents. "I'll pay $200+ for *Stanley* Tool catalogs from before 1900. I also especially want tools made in Ohio, although they're not worth as much as tools from New England." Does **not** want levels made in Akron, or any machinists or mechanics tools, electric tools, agricultural and farm tools, or any that have been "reconditioned." Give all markings. Keep your eyes open for a **catalog for John Henry Belter furniture company.** "I'll pay $5,000 for one!"
> John Walter,
> The Tool Merchant,
> Box 6471,
> Akron, OH 44312
> (800) 542-1993

◆ **Joiner's planes and other tools.** "I'll buy planes or any pre 1900 paper ephemera about them."
> Richard Wood,
> Alaska Heritage Books,
> Box 22165,
> Juneau, AK 99802
> (907) 586-6748

◆ *Stanley* **tools and catalogs.**
Robert Kaune,
511 W. 11th,
Port Angeles, WA 98362

◆ **Antique woodworking tools.** Also catalogs and books related to woodworking pre 1900.[88
> Vernon Ward,
> Iron Horse Antiques,
> Rt. 2,
> Poultney, VT 05764

Builder's Supplies

◆ **Sidewalk or paving bricks** which are marked with the name and or address of a maker. "They're hard to mail, but fun to collect." No fire bricks.
Ken Jones,
100 Manor Dr.,
Columbia, MO 65203

◆ **Ornate doorknobs and other builder's hardware** including knockers, hinges, escutcheon plates, doorbells, push plates, bin pulls and any other fancy Victorian hardware. I'll pay up to $200 for some knobs. No plain porcelain or common octagonal glass knobs are wanted. Sets of knobs routinely bring $20-$30, but get my offer before you sell. Send SASE for my illustrated wants list. Photocopies expedite offers."
Charles Wardell,
Box 195,
Trinity, NC 27370
(919) 434-1145

◆ **Pieces of famous buildings, structures, monuments, aircraft, etc.**, such as the Statue of Liberty, Independence Hall, The Eiffel Tower, etc. "These must be legally acquired pieces and **not vandalized items**. They must be well documented."
Paul Hartunian,
127B East Bradford Ave.,
Cedar Grove, NJ 07009
(201) 857-7275

◆ **Parts from buildings** including cornices, gargoyles, arches, fireplaces, mantels, anything unusual. Nothing after 1930. No material not related to building.
Robert Des Marais,
618 West Foster Ave.,
State College, PA 16801
(814) 237-7141

Barbershop

◆ **Decorated shaving mugs depicting the owner's occupation, trade, or hobby** above or below his name. Also hand painted personal occupational barber bottles. Since each was custom made, they must be evaluated individually. Also **salesman's sample barber chairs** made in porcelain or wood. No Japanese reproductions or "Sportsman's Series" mugs from the 1950's.
Burton Handelsman,
18 Hotel Drive,
White Plains, NY 10605
(914) 761-8880

◆ **Shaving mugs depicting occupations**. Must have both a picture and a man's name. "I'll buy those with photo portraits for $500 and up and will pay $500-$1,500 for athletes (especially a high jumper), $400-$1,200 for automobile related professions, $500-$750 for an undertaker, $500-$1,000 for a tugboat worker. Will also buy some mugs with emblems of fraternal organizations. Please give any maker's name on the bottom of the mug and indicate any damage, hairline cracks, or chips no matter how small.
Robert Fortin, Barber Shop,
459 S. Main St.,
North Syracuse, NY 13212
(315) 458-7465

◆ **Barbershop memorabilia of all types** including any good quality item associated with barber shops such as decorated shaving mugs, barber bowls, bottles, waste jars, catalogs, silver or pearl handled straight, razors with scenes engraved on the blades, strops, tokens, tools, curling irons, barber's emblem pins, barbershop trade or business cards, salesmen's samples of barber chairs, and much more. Powell both collects and deals so buys a wide range of fine items or accepts them on consignment. Names to look for include Koken, Kochs, Kern, Archer, Buerger, and others. Include a tracing or close up photo. New shaving mugs are not wanted.
Robert Powell,
Box 833,
Hurst, TX 76053
(817) 284-8145

Food & Lodging

◆ *McDonalds* **memorabilia** including:
  (1) **Uniforms,** employees, with the M logo;
  (2) **Paper goods** including boxes, place mats, napkins, flyers;
  (3) **Displays** such as signs, decals, posters;
  (4) **Premiums and promotions;**
  (5) **Anything in foreign languages;**
  (6) **Not for public items** such as ID cards, newsletters, worksheets;
  (7) **Fixtures, signs, and lights;**
No items currently available in all restaurants.
  Matt Welch,
  Box 30444,
  Tucson, AZ 85751
    (602) 886-0505

◆ **Fast food premiums** from *McDonalds, Kentucky Fried Chicken, Bob's Big Boy*, others.
  William Hamburg,
  Box 1305,
  Woodland Hills, CA 91365
    (818) 346-9884

◆ *Bob's Big Boy* **items**, especially lamps and nodders. No plastic banks.
  Steve Soelberg,
  29126 Laro Dr.,
  Agoura Hills, CA 91301

◆ **Fast food character drinking glasses.** "I'll buy those give-away glasses that have cartoon characters or sports figures on them given away by *Pepsi, Coca-Cola, McDonalds's, Arby's*, etc. When you write, give the size of the glasses, all writing, and the name of the character."
  Ken Clee,
  PO Box 11412,
  Philadelphia, PA 19111
    (215) 722-1979

◆ *Coon Chicken Inn* **memorabilia** including plates, holders, and what have you.
  Jack Matlack,
  Box 14067,
  Portland, OR 97214

◆ *Coon Chicken Inn* **memorabilia** of all kinds that features Blacks.
  Diane Cauwels,
  3947 Old South Road,
  Murfreesboro, TN 37129

◆ **Items taken from or associated with famous Chicago hotels** and their shops. Wants furniture, menus, stationery, light fixtures, signs, etc., from places like the *Lexington, Metropole, Hawthorne Inn, Hawthorne Smoke Shop*, and *Scholfields Flower shop*.
  Michael Graham,
  345 Cleveland Ave.,
  Libertyville, IL 60048
    (312) 362-8531 eves

◆ **Swiss hotels paper ephemera** if it shows a picture of the hotel before 1930. Will buy illustrated bills, letterheads, wine lists, rate cards, envelopes, and anything else pictorial.
  Ronald Lowden, Jr.,
  314 Chestnut Ave.,
  Narberth, PA 19072
    (215) 667-0257 anytime

◆ **Pre 1920 hotel register books** with signatures of guests. All books must be at least 10 pages long. Will consider registers after 1920 "if the city or the hotel is unique." Wants to know where you got the register. Describe, and she will ask to see those which interest her. Hotels in Colorado and Texas are sought, but will buy registers from any "interesting little place." Does not have to be fancy or have famous guests. "Plain vanilla registers are fine."
  Ginger Carver Daily,
  Box 33862,
  San Antonio, TX 78265
    (512) 657-3242

◆ **Tourist courts, tourist camps, and motel ephemera.** Wants *Tourist Court Journal* magazine and other pre 1950 ephemera related to motor travel lodging.
  Kevin Regn,
  2127 15th St., NW,
  Washington, DC 20009

Oil Companies

◆ *Gulf Oil* memorabilia including signs, cans, maps, advertising mailouts, magazine ads, blotters, postcards, ash trays, key chains, and anything else marked *Gulf*. Especially older correspondence, paper items, and signs. This retired petroleum geologist also wants postcards which depict oil fields and wells. Prefers items to be sent on approval after first contacting him.
Charles Roach,
3212 Tudor,
Oklahoma City, OK 73122
(405) 942-4520

◆ *Mobil Oil* memorabilia including "*anything* picturing the red horse." Also collecting service pins given to Mobil employees. Also buys porcelain signs from *Gargoyle, White Eagle*, and *Magnolia* gas and oil. No repros...and Billie says she has enough globes. She insists that the seller set the price wanted as **she and Bob do not make offers** for additions to their herd.
Bob and Billie Butler,
1236 Helen St.,
Augusta, KS 67010
(316) 775-6193

◆ **Gasoline pump globes,** preferably one piece glass globes that have the oil company name etched into the glass or baked (glazed) onto the surface. The more colorful the better. Globes with glass inserts within metal frames are also acceptable. Plastic globes and inserts are less desirable, although Scott does buy a few colorful examples. You *must* make a sketch or take a photo of the globe as each company had numerous variations. Will pay $2,500 for *Benzol* globe with a fox. No reproductions.
Scott Benjamin,
7250 Franklin Ave. #216,
Los Angeles, CA 90046

◆ **Oil cans in all sizes, all types, and all materials,** including brass, aluminum, glass, tin, granite-wear, or plastic. Wants everything from "sewing machine" size up to and including railroad oil cans, advertising cans, novelty cans. Not all desirable cans have names on them. Pays $10-25 for a graniteware can especially with the name "White" on it, $10-15 for most others, more for railroad cans. Make a sketch. If it is a pump can, tell whether the pump works.
Robert Larson,
Box 1556,
Pinecrest, CA 95364
(209) 965-4103

◆ **Oil company memorabilia 1859-1939.** Wants "virtually anything" that can be connected to specific companies, wells, or famous oil pioneers including pre 1900 books about oil and oil exploration, oil stocks especially early with engraved views of oil fields, sheet music (from the 1860's), newspapers from early Pennsylvania oil towns, clippings, photos, deeds, and engravings.
Jeffrey Viola,
475-B Eltone Rd.,
Jackson, NJ 08527
(201) 928-0666 eves

◆ **Oil company memorabilia** including including pump globes, signs, and oil cans and bottles. Especially interested in items from the following companies: *Phillips 66, Manhattan Oil Company, Independent Oil and Gas Co., Wasatch Oil*, and *Paraland*.
Randy Morris,
3100 Camelot,
Bartlesville, OK 74006
(918) 333-5807

Farms & Horses

◆ **Antique farm equipment**, horse drawn vehicles, and "tools of all type."
Harvey Lee Boswell,
The Palace of Wonders,
Box 446,
Elm City, NC 27822

◆ **Wagons, carriages, and commercial horse drawn vehicles, in whole or in part.** Buys carriage lamps, dashboard clocks, wagon tools, nameplates, wheel making machines, coachman's and groom's clothing, jacks, tack room fixtures, whip racks, wagon odometers, hitching post statuary, rein clips, wagon seats, wagon poles, veterinary tools, lap robes, life size harness makers horses, zinc animal heads, and anything else related to carriages and wagons. Offers up to $500-$2,500 for lamps marked *Studebaker, Brewster,* or *Healey.* **Also buys goat carts and dog carts.** If your item is old, genuine, and in good condition you may ship on approval. No harnesses. Don sends a large illustrated wants list for an SASE with four stamps.
Don Sawyer,
West Newbury Wagon Works,
40 Bachelor St.,
West Newbury, MA 01985
(508) 346-4724 days (508) 363-2983

◆ **Everything related to work or recreation with horses** including polo, horseback riding, carriage driving, sidesaddle, draft horses, **horse-shoeing, veterinary,** etc. Wants horse farm catalogs, brochures, posters, prints of riding and recognized horse breeds, books (1st editions in d/j only), magazines, postcards (if horse is named), stud books, and breed registers. "I don't buy common books still in print, book club editions, *Diseases of the Horse,* books on horse betting, or books with highlighting or underlining in the text. Everything must be in fine condition for resale.
Barbara Cole, October Farm,
Rt 2, Box 183-C,
Raleigh, NC 27610
(919) 772-0482

◆ **Tractor memorabilia** including all sorts of paper ephemera and small trinkets given away as advertising promotion, such as watch fobs, pens, cigarette lighters, etc. You may ship what you have on approval if it's old, original, and clean.
Jay Ketelle,
3721 Farwell,
Amarillo, TX 79109
(806) 355-3456

◆ **Tractor, farm machinery, and gasoline engine paper ephemera** including pre 1970 manuals, catalogs, parts books, in-house publications, and sales literature. Also buys farm magazines such as *Implement Record, Farm Machinery & Hardware,* and *Farm Mechanics.* Also buys "giveaways" such as signs, ashtrays, buttons, etc. associated with any farm machinery. No textbooks or reprints. Please indicate the color of the item and the price you'd like.
Alan C. King,
PO Box 86,
Radnor, OH 43066

◆ *J.I. Case* **Tractor Company memorabilia** including tractors and implements, toy tractors, advertising signs, catalogs, books, and anything else marked "JI Case". Where is item located?
Ed and Carla Schuth,
RR 2 Box 6,
Wabasha, MN 55981
(612) 565-4251

◆ **Horse bits.** "I'll buy old iron, fancy, or strange horse bits. Also want foreign military, and medical bits. I also buy reference material about horse bits, including catalogs. I'd like to find Civil War bits and cowboy bits decorated with buffaloes. Make me a drawing of what you have."
Jean Gay, Three Horses,
7403 Blaine Rd.,
Aberdeen, WA 98520
(206) 533-3490

Dairy

◆ **Harness maker and saddler's tools,** catalogs, and advertising. Especially wants items by Dodd, Osborne, Huber, English, Sauerbier, etc. Also wants harness maker's shop signs and ads.

    X. Boston,
    1547 Hunting Ave.,
    McLean, VA 22102
        (703) 448-8252

◆ **Books, magazines, and paper ephemera about poultry raising,** pre 1930.

    W.L. Bill Zeigler,
    10 Lincolnway West,
    New Oxford, PA 17350
        (717) 624-2347

◆ **Everything about fruit raising and varieties before 1900,** including illustrated books, magazine articles, ceramic tiles depicting fruit, postcards, prints, folders, and greeting cards depicting apples. Especially books and paper with color plates or descriptions of fruit varieties. May be in any language. No tropical fruit, or anything later than 1940.

    Fred Janson,
    Pomona Book Exchange,
    Rockton PO,
    Ontario L0R 1X0,
    CANADA

> Your Name
> Your Address

If you want an answer include an SASE

◆ **Milk or dairy industry items marked with the name and address of a dairy** including old and unusual bottles, advertising, toys and signs. Especially from institutional bottlers such as prisons, colleges, railroads, hotels, and the like. Bottles with cartoon characters are always desirable (bringing $50-$100 each) as are those with WWII slogans. Unusually shaped bottles or those made of colored glass are always wanted, as are creamer size bottles marked with name of dairy, hotel, or restaurant. Bottles with tin or glass lids can go as high as $150. Anything related to *Borden's* or their Elsie the Cow trademark is wanted, especially their ruby red bottles which can bring from $600-$1,000. WWII milk posters or bottles. Large items like cream separators, churns, milk cans, and the like are not wanted. Ralph will take postcards, trade cards and other small advertising on approval if it is priced individually and by lot.

    Ralph Riovo,
    686 Franklin St.,
    Alburtis, PA 18011-9578
        (215) 966-2536

◆ **Round milk bottles with dairy names** embossed or printed on them. Square bottles OK if amber or from Western states. Nothing worn, cracked, or chipped.

    Leigh Giarde,
    The Time Travelers,
    Box 366,
    Bryn Mawr, CA 92318
        (714) 792-8681

◆ **Dairy creamers** made of glass with the names of dairies embossed or printed on. Do not want ceramic creamers or those without names. Also **milk bottles** with cop tops, baby tops, or war slogans, in excellent condition only.

    Ken Clee,
    PO Box 11412,
    Philadelphia, PA 19111
        (215) 722-1979

15
Advertising

Dr. Hyman's Prescription

Do you own a sign, counter display, tip tray, package, box, neon clock, flyer, broadside, advertising figure, or any other advertising or promotional item?

If so, there's a buyer for it. Advertising has become a form of "pop culture" or "pop art" and is being bought and sold by specialty dealers across the U.S. and Canada.

Items made of wood, cardboard, tin, porcelain on metal, cast iron, neon, plastic, celluloid, and paper can find a buyer. Rare bottles, tin signs, and store figures tend to bring the highest prices.

When describing, make certain to explain:

    (1) What it is;
    (2) What product or service is advertised;
    (3) What is pictured, in what colors;
    (4) What is its condition.

Like so many other folks, advertising collectors are fussy folks. Signs with damage or serious scratches may be worth as little as 10% of fine condition items.

Although this chapter lists many important people in the world of advertising collecting and dealing, you should look throughout *I'll Buy That!* for buyers, since collectors of almost everything are also interested in advertising for the products they collect.

Sketches are acceptable, but to sell brilliantly colored items, a color print or slide is to be preferred.

tony hyman

Advertising

◆ **Colorful tin signs and trays** advertising beer, whiskey, soda pop, medicines, tobacco, and food such as peanuts, peanut butter, tea, coffee, and the like. Especially likes rare one-pound coffee cans from New York companies. Nothing rusty or damaged. Describe colors. Photocopy please.
    Burton Spiller,
    49 Palmerston Road,
    Rochester, NY 14618
        (716) 244-2229 eves

◆ **Pre 1920 advertising** including tin, porcelain, and cardboard signs and posters, tin cans and trays, calendars, syrup dispensers, and other advertising for candy, gum, groceries, soft drinks, ammunition, tobacco, beer, and the like. No magazine or newspaper ads. "We pay the highest prices but **do not make offers**. Let us know what you have and your price."
    Don Stuart, House of Stuart,
    Box 327,
    Centerport, NY 11721
        (516) 549-8222

◆ **Pocket tobacco tins**, but only rare ones. No *Prince Albert, Dial, Kentucky Club, Velvet, Edgeworth,* or other common tins. Selected tin signs advertising smoking or chewing tobacco.
    Ken Jones, 100
    Manor Dr.,
    Columbia, MO 65203

◆ **Canadian or British lithographed tin containers** and other advertising of all types "with interesting graphics in excellent condition." Especially British figural biscuit tins for which he will pay $100 up if mint. Also Canadian cabinets, trade figures, posters, and signs.
    Glen Paruk,
    05-2004 Fullerton Ave.,
    No. Vancouver, B.C. V7P 3G8, CANADA
        (604) 684-1181 eves

◆ **Coffee tins.** "I'll buy mint or near mint condition coffee tins that are old and colorful, particularly those with pictures of birds, buildings, children, animals, people, etc. No vacuum (key) cans. No paper label cans. Tin signs which feature coffee may also be of interest."
    Tim Schweighart,
    1123 Santa Luisa,
    Solana Beach, CA 92075
        (619) 481-8315

◆ **Cigar boxes, labels, tins, and other advertising from the cigar industry** in fine condition, pre 1920, especially boxes featuring nudes, sports, gambling, comic characters, transportation, and other colorful scenes. Also **gambling devices, trade figures, or signs related to cigars.** Also tin **tobacco cans** and boxes. Photocopy the inside lid of boxes you'd like to sell. Long SASE will bring you a priced wants list. No items covered with cigar bands, please, except as donations. Nothing in poor condition. Will pay $200 each for *Asthma Cure, Cheez It,* or any xxx rated box. Hyman wrote *Handbook of American Cigar Boxes,* an illustrated signed and numbered limited edition for $29.95 with price guide.
    Tony Hyman,
    Box 699,
    Claremont, CA 91711
        (714) 621-5952

◆ **Fruit crate labels.** "I'll buy fruit and sweet potato crate labels and can labels before 1960 if they are in good to mint condition and are colorful and pictorial. I'll buy 1 or 10,000."
    Dick Maule,
    4207 Calle Juno,
    San Clemente, CA 92672

◆ **Southern labels, packaging, signs, and posters.** Wants decorative advertising in any form for any product or company that was in the South before 1950. Photocopies helpful. Publishers of *The Southern Label Collector's Newsletter*.
    David & Marcia King,
    Box 24811,
    Tampa, FL 33623
        (813) 888-8234

◆ **Florida citrus labels.** Also ads and other paper related to pre-1940 Florida citrus industry.
Jerry Chicone,
Box 547636,
Orlando, FL 32854
(407) 298-5550

◆ **Old salmon can labels.** "Singles or collections. Only pre 1960 items are wanted. You may send approvals."
W.E. Nickell,
102 People's Wharf,
Juneau, AK 99801
(907) 586-1733

◆ **Cotton produce sacks with pretty pictures or dolls to be cut out,** including flour, sugar, salt, etc. No damaged or plastic sacks or sacks with words only. Pays "about $250" for sacks from *Sleepy Eye* Flour Mills. Do not wash sacks.
Dr. Ross Hartsough,
Psychology Dept, Univ of Manitoba,
Winnipeg R3T 4N1, CANADA

◆ **Sales literature from makers of hammered aluminum.** Wants literature, catalogues, from all companies from the 1930's through the 50's.
Baumann,
Box 415,
Hammond, IN 46325

◆ *Pillsbury* **Doughboy ephemera** and advertising, especially tin signs.
Linda Woodward,
6720 Crest Ave.,
Riverside, CA 92503
(714) 687-0868

◆ **Elsie the Cow and other** *Borden's* **ephemera** including games, toys, cookbooks, comic books, cups, glasses, Xmas cards, employee magazines, neon signs, milk bottles, and trade cards. Would especially like an Elsie string puppet and a *Borden's* "Good Food Line" train. No Elsie postcards or charms. Also buys milk bottles and advertising from Du Page County in Illinois.
Ronald Selcke,
Box 237,
Bloomingdale, IL 60108
(312) 543-4848 eves

◆ *Morton's* **Salt advertising,** 1848 to date, especially items which picture the *Morton's* little girl in the rain.
Linda Woodward,
6720 Crest Ave.,
Riverside, CA 92503
(714) 687-0868

◆ *Campbells* **Soup twins** depicted on anything, especially tin signs.
Linda Woodward,
6720 Crest Ave.,
Riverside, CA 92503
(714) 687-0868

◆ **Bottles and other memorabilia from all West Virginia food companies,** including Flaccus, Hunter, Exwaco, and Mc Mechen. Pays to $200 for stoneware Flaccus & Elliot water cooler.
Tom & Deena Caniff,
1223 Oak Grove Ave.,
Steubenville, OH 43952
(614) 282-8918

◆ **Items associated with the** *Larkin Soap Company.* "We're primarily interest in catalogs and other historically interesting paper ephemera pre 1920." Larkin is also known as Larkin Mfg., Larkin, Inc., Larkin Co., and People' Mfg. Co. Ayars and his wife wrote and published *Larkin Oak* ($16) about the Company's venture into furniture retailing. Working on book on *Larkin* china and pottery. "Readers who have questions about Larkin are welcome; there is no charge for our research. Include title, year, issue number, or a photocopy of the cover.
Walter Ayars III,
PO Box 279,
Summerdale, PA 17093
(717) 732-9886

◆ **Everything associated with the** *Larkin Soap Company.*
Thomas Knopke,
1430 E. Brookdale Pl.,
Fullerton, CA 92631
(714) 526-1749

◆ Fairbank's *Fairy Soap* advertising pamphlets, ads, signs, calendars, boxes, bars of soap, trade cards, and other miscellany.
Robert Williams,
Box 117,
Damascus, MD 20872

◆ *Speedy Alka Seltzer* dolls, toys, and ephemera wanted.
Jim Frugoli,
960 N. Northwest Hwy.,
Park Ridge, IL 60068

◆ **Gun and ammunition related advertising.** "I buy posters, calendars, envelopes with ads, cardboard shotshell boxes, gunpowder cans, pinback buttons, glass target balls, catalogs, etc. Ron buys only items produced by a gun or ammunition maker (not secondary vendors) before 1940.
Ron Willoughby,
Route 171,
Woodstock, CT 06281
(203) 974-1226

◆ **Shotgun shell boxes** illustrated with pictures of birds, dogs, or other animals. Wants to buy any old cardboard boxes in fine to mint condition only. Send photocopy and price.
Mike Eckles,
2102 Rocky View Rd.,
Diamond Bar, CA 91795

◆ *Dixie* **ice cream cup picture lids** and other memorabilia 1930-54 including premium pictures and offers, albums, scrapbook covers, ads, and company literature. Also buys some non-*Dixie* pictorial ice cream cup lids such as Tarzan or American Historical Shrines series.
Stephen Leone,
94 Pond St.,
Salem, NH 03079
(603) 898-4900

◆ **Advertising paperweights** made of glass.
S. Kurtzman,
Box 275,
Cambria, CA 93428
(805) 927-4177

◆ **Neon advertising clocks and signs**, 1920-50. Buys those entirely of neon as well as those with "reverse painting on glass" that are lit by neon. Prefers smaller sizes that can be safely shipped via UPS. His favorite clocks have 6"-10" dials and sit on a countertop, not a wall, although he buys both kinds. Also buys **signs that bubble, create optical illusions, or are animated**. Value is based on "visual appeal" so a photograph is essential. Does not want new neon beer signs, plastic signs of any sort, or signs lit by flourescent tubes. Does not want signs or clocks with broken neon tubing or with paint flaking off the glass.
Roark Vane,
6839 Havenside Dr.,
Sacramento, CA 95831
(916) 392-3864

◆ **Advertising pocket mirrors with colorful pictures** of women, children, nudes, or pictures of the product. "Please send a photo copy of what you have. Your postage returned." John will pay from $100-$200 for mirrors depicting nudes along with advertising. Send a photocopy of your mirror, along with notations as to color and any imperfections.
John Andreae,
51122 Mill Run,
Granger, IN 46530
(219) 272-2337

◆ **Advertising mirrors of all types**, both pocket and paperweight. Higher prices paid for anything from Illinois, Florida, or Michigan. Better prices paid for those with a product or female or both. Condition of the advertising side is very important; the mirror (unless missing or broken) is not. Spots, rips, brown areas, foxing, etc., in the celluloid will lower the value substantially. Please ship or send photocopy for offer. Particularly wanted are any mirrors with words "Good for 10¢ in trade" or similar variation for which he pays from $35-2,000. "I consider paperweight mirrors to be less desirable than pocket mirrors, and rarely pay over $20 except for exceptional mirrors."
Rich Hartzog,
Box 4143 BBL,
Rockford, IL 61110
(815) 226-0771

◆ **Salesmen's sample stoves.** Wants small cast iron, later tin and iron, miniature stoves used by 19th century salesmen as samples, premiums, and giveaways. Especially seeking a *Monarch*. Would like to correspond with other collectors or owners of mini-stoves.
    Marilyn Wren,
    9073 Weidkamp Rd.,
    Lynden, WA 98264

◆ **Salesmen's sample and toy stoves.** Wants salesmen's sample stoves, particularly made by *Majestic, Home Comfort, Quick Meal,* and *Engman-Matthews*. Also wants *Dolly's Favorite* and all models of *Buck's Jr.* and larger sizes of stove made by *Classic*.
    Ed Hullet,
    5200 No. Lorraine,
    Hutchinson, KS 67502
        (316) 662-9381

◆ **Trade stimulators** are games of chance intended to stimulate you to buy a particular product. Charlie buys them.
    Charlie Smith,
    1006 NE 4th St.,
    Milton-Freewater, OR 97862

◆ **Damaged, bent, or rusty tin cans or signs** which are difficult to sell. They aren't worth much but Ron's the only person we know who buys them at all.
    Ron Knappen,
    RR #2, Box 590,
    Galesville, WI 54630

EDITOR'S NOTE: If you have advertising to sell, make certain to check the chapter relevant to that product or service.

Soda Fountain

◆ **Ice cream and soda fountain memorabilia:**
  (1) **Salesmen's samples** or patent models of soda fountain apparatus;
  (2) **Postcards** depicting ice cream or soda fountains (any year);
  (3) **Photographs** of soda fountain interiors;
  (4) Plaster ice cream concoction **displays**;
  (5) Letterheads, envelopes, fans, and all other **paper** with ice cream images;
  (6) Soda Fountain and ice cream trade **magazines** pre 1925;
  (7) **Trade cards** picturing ice cream, freezers, or soda fountains;
  (8) **Catalogs** pre 1930;
  (9) **Advertising** give-aways, fobs, buttons, tape measures, etc.

Mr. Ice Cream would love to find a stereoview of Tuft's soda fountain display at the 1876 Centennial, and a cover from a mid 1920's issue of *American Druggist Magazine* which depicts a plum lady at a soda fountain counter while the clerk/druggist adds a cherry to her dish. Allan's interests are wide ranging, but nothing damaged or made after 1945. He prefers not to make offers, and requests you price what you have.
  Allan "Mr. Ice Cream" Mellis,
  1115 West Montana,
  Chicago, IL 60614
    (312) 327-9123

◆ Pre 1945 *Coca-Cola* memorabilia including fancier *Coke* items with pretty girls and lots of color especially cardboard cut out signs and back bar decorations. These active dealers of 18 years experience will pay up to $5,000 for pre 1900 calendars. Pays well for metal tins, trays, and signs. Magazine ads from before 1932 only. No commemorative bottles, please.
  Randy Schaeffer,
  C-C Trayders,
  611 N. 5th St.,
  Reading, PA 19601
    (215) 373-3333

◆ *Coca-Cola* advertising in any format from before 1940. Pays $1,000 for 1922 pocket mirror depicting a girl on beach with umbrella. Pays $2,000 for cardboard standup sign of child running with pack of *Coca-Cola* gum. Premium prices paid for early cardboard cutouts and calendars. An advanced collector of more than 20 years experience, Thom does not want common items.
  Thom Thompson,
  123 Shaw Ave.,
  Versailles, KY 40383
    (606) 873-8787 eves

◆ *Coca-Cola* ephemera pre 1960 including signs, clocks, calendars, toys, ads, bottles, machines, coupons, bottle carriers, dispensers, uniforms, trucks, photos, etc., especially *Coca-Cola* chewing gum items. "I'll consider *anything*," he says, except items that read "enjoy" *Coca-Cola* as they are too new. Older items read to "drink" *Coca-Cola*. Include your phone number.
  Marion Lathan,
  Rt. 1 Box 430,
  Chester, SC 29706
    (803) 377-8225

◆ *Coca-Cola, Pepsi-Cola* and *Chero-Cola* advertising. Wants smaller pieces such as trays, tip trays, smaller signs, door pushes, match strikers, etc., especially porcelain on tin. No paper.
  Dick Shay,
  514 Stevenson Ave.,
  Worthington, OH 43085

◆ *7-Up* memorabilia. "I'll buy almost any American made item advertising 7-Up, especially items from the 1930's-50's. I also want historical items, company memos, photos of store displays and the like. The older the better. Watch for ads or **items from Howdy Company's "Bid-Lable Lithiated Lemon-Lime Soda"** which later became 7-Up. Your description should include the shape of the 7-Up logo (round, oval, square, or rectangular). Not interested in foreign items or most stuff after 1960. I'm a collector not a dealer and will try to help you find a buyer.
  Don Fiebiger,
  1970 Las Lomitas Dr.,
  Hacienda Heights, CA 91745
    (213) 693-6484

◆ **Root Beer advertising** including bottles, mugs, signs, caps, cans, syrup dispensers, and paper items. It *must* have the words "root beer" on the item. "If you don't recognize the brand name, or if it was sold only in a limited area, I'll probably be interested. For many of the 400 makers of root beer, only bottle caps survive. Love to find a *Dr. Swett's* root beer mug in majolica with a false bottom half way up the mug and will pay $200 for a perfect one. I pay $3 each for bottle caps I don't have." Doesn't want anything from brands sold on the market today or any *A&W* mugs except those that say 5¢. No picture needed if you give complete info.
   Tom Morrison, 2930
   Squaw Valley Dr.,
   Colorado Springs, CO 80918
      (719) 598-1754

◆ *Hires Root Beer* memorabilia pre 1930 in fine to mint condition. Wants trays, dispensers, and signs. No syrup extract bottles or reproductions.
   Steve Sourapas,
   1413 NW 198th St.,
   Seattle, WA 98177
      (206) 542-1791

◆ **Root beer mugs** from *A&W*, *Hires*, *Frostee*, etc., in excellent condition, with no chips.
   Ken Clee,
   PO Box 11412,
   Philadelphia, PA 19111
      (215) 722-1979

◆ **Soft drink advertising.** "I'll buy pre 1960 calendars, trays, signs, sales aids, syrup bottles, cans, shipping crates, clocks, thermometers, menu boards, ashtrays, cartons, playing cards, lighters, blotters, knives, matchbook covers, and just about anything else with a *Coca-Cola*, *Pepsi-Cola*, *RC Cola*, *Hires Root Beers*, *7-Up*, *Lemon Crush*, *Nu Grape*, or other soft drink logo." Loves to find salesman's sample coolers and dispensers. Does not want repro trays, bottles of any sort including commemorative, or magazine ads. Describe condition carefully.
   Terry Buchheit,
   Rte. 7 Box 62,
   Perryville, MO 63775

◆ *Moxie* **memorabilia.** Wants signs, fans, toys, advertising posters, metal trays, and other pre 1940 items associated with this old time soft drink. Will buy *Moxie* bottles only if the name of a town is part of the inscription. Bowers is the author of *The Moxie Encyclopedia*, a 760 page illustrated history of the company available for $19.95.
   Q. David Bowers,
   Box 1224,
   Wolfeboro, NH 03894
      (603) 569-5095

◆ **Soda pop cans pre 1965,** especially local brands. Will buy quantities of rare cans, but no rusty cans are wanted by this ten year veteran collector-dealer, but "some light spotting and aging is natural. I do require cans be sent before a final purchase offer is made because condition so greatly affects the value and I need to examine cans closely."
   Tony Steffens,
   615 Chester,
   Elgin, IL 60120
      (800) 443-8712

◆ **Soda pop bottles with painted labels** (sometimes called applied color labels "ACL") from minor bottlers anywhere in North America. Would be interested in hearing from people with foreign soda pop bottles. "I like to think that I have West Virginia well covered, but I'm buying bottles from anywhere." Other ephemera related to local and regional bottlers including photos and advertising. Would like to find a three colored *Uncle Tom's Root Beer* from California. Please describe all wording and colors on the bottle.
   Gary Brent Kincade,
   Box 712,
   Weston, WV 26452
      (304) 842-3773 eves

◆ **Soda pop bottles with painted labels from New England.** If offering for sale, pay particular attention to describing all colors and wording.
   Steve Daniels,
   Box 1362,
   Dedham, MA 0202

Bottles

◆ **Antique American bottles**, both glass and pottery, especially old beer and medicinals from the Buffalo, NY, area. Also wants mineral waters, poisons, barber shop bottles. Buys trade cards, advertising, billheads, and other items associated with makers or users of glass bottles in Western New York. Sven publishes the newsletter of the Western NY Bottle Collectors Association.
Sven Stau,
Box 1135,
Buffalo, NY 14211
(716) 825-5448

◆ **All types of bottles and ephemera from bottle companies** including calendars, signs, brochures, and promotional giveaways. Gayner Glass Company is of interest, as are Salem squats, a type of soda bottle made in Salem, NJ. "Any way I can help anybody out, I will be glad to."
Charles Mc Donald,
Old Bottle Museum,
4 Friendship Dr.,
Salem, NJ 08079
(609) 935-5631

◆ **Early American bottles and historical flasks.** Wants hand blown figural bottles or those with embossed figures and portraits. Will pay $3,000 for *"The American System"* bottle depicting a paddlewheeler. Also wants **figural bitters bottles** and hand-blown, pontil marked, **colored ink** and **medicine bottles.** Burt also buys **rare fruit (canning) jars** complete with lids, round and **colored milk bottles,** and mineral water bottles. No cracks, chips, or bad stains are acceptable. Burt advises reading McKearin's *American Glass* to see bottles capable of attracting top dollar. He does not want machine made bottles or reproductions.
Burton Spiller,
49 Palmerston Rd.,
Rochester, NY 14618
(716) 244-2229 eves

◆ **Bottles from California and the Old West.** "I'll buy whiskey, medicine, food and other bottles from the days of miners, loggers, and cowboys in the West. I especially like bottles with the names of California towns and companies on them. He especially wants **whiskey bottles with pictures** embedded in the glass, which can bring from $100 to as much as $2,500 for a *California Club* bottle." If your bottle says "Federal Law forbids the resale..." it isn't old enough to be of interest. Bottles without names or designs embossed in the glass are generally valueless to collectors as are most cracked or chipped ones. Tell him what it says on your bottle, what color it is, and what condition it is in.
John Goetz,
Box 1570,
Cedar Ridge, CA 95924
(916) 272-4644

◆ **Patent medicine bottles.** "I'll buy pontilled, embossed bottles, especially colored and labeled ones, and will pay from $500 to $6,000 for fine ones. Also patent medicine advertising.
Jerry Phelps,
6013 Innes Trace Rd.,
Louisville, KY 40222
(502) 425-4765

◆ **Early bottles and jars with colorful food labels,** pre 1910. Has special interest in food jars, bottles, and crocks from Flaccus, Hunter, EXWACO, and McMechen of Wheeling, WV, but will buy **any jars marked as being made or used in Wheeling or Wellsburg, WV.** There's $200 waiting for a Flaccus stoneware water cooler. Give the color of the glass or stoneware and its size. Report *exactly* what is written or embossed on the jar or crock, and note any cracks, chips, dings, or unwashable stains.
Tom & Deena Caniff,
1223 Oak Grove Ave.,
Steubenville, OH 43952
(614) 282-8918

◆ **Older fruit (canning) jars with unusual closures or in unusual colors** other than aqua or clear. Colors wanted include amber, brown, deep green, and shades of cobalt blue. Is willing to pay to $400 for a pint size jar embossed *Cadiz Jar* with a glass screw top. Also want pre 1960 **advertising**, promotional brochures, letterheads, signs, paperweights, etc., from jar and bottle manufacturers, including **wooden canning jar boxes** or box ends, which generally bring $10-30. Give the size, color, and report *exactly* on what is embossed on the jar. Note all cracks, chips, dings, or unwashable stains.

    Tom & Deena Caniff,
    1223 Oak Grove Ave.,
    Steubenville, OH 43952
       (614) 282-8918

◆ **Early American bottles.** Buys a wide range of glass bottles, including campaign bottles, bitters, figurals, whiskey flasks, **and glass jugs with handles.** Wants glass bottles with agricultural symbols, flags, sunbursts, portraits of national heroes, and the like, or bottles in the shape of log cabins, cannons, lighthouses, pigs, etc. Many of these items are worth in excess of $1,000. ◆ **Pottery pig bottles** are also wanted, as is **advertising for medicine and whiskey companies.** No *Jim Beam* type whiskey bottles.

    Robert Daly,
    10341 Jewell Lake Ct.,
    Fenton, MI 48430
       (313) 629-4934

◆ **Bottles of all types from Washington state or Alaska,** including beer, whiskey, food, soda, medicine, etc. He wants embossed and / or early paper label bottles.

    Reed Fitzpatrick,
    Box 369,
    Vashon, WA 98070

◆ *Schafer & Vater* German figural bottles. "I'll buy monks, dancers, animals, etc., in singles or advanced collections." Describe the bottle carefully, indicating all chips and marks. Include the color of clothing and the base.

    Marylou Smith,
    1252 W. Negrove,
    Lancaster, CA 93534
       (805) 948-3412

◆ **Antique bottle or jar collections.** "I'll travel to buy good collections."

    Jack Stecher,
    230 Eileen Drive,
    Rochester, NY 14616
       (716) 621-4701

16
Gov't Service & Professions

Dr. Hyman's Prescription

Collectors of professions and government services are similar to business collectors in that their interests are wide ranging. It's the collectibles that differ the most.

Since there is less advertising associated with these collectibles, the focus is more an small realia like badges, emblems, and the tools of the various occupations.

It is probably worth your time to familiarize yourself with the collectibles in this chapter, since they range from embalming tools to school report cards.

Follow standard practice for describing items

    (1) What it is and what it is made from;

    (2) Size, shape, and color;

    (3) All markings and whether they are embossed (raised) or incised (stamped in);

    (4) Any patent dates or maker's information;

    (5) Weight, if something heavy.

Photocopy paper goods and small items like badges, you'd like to sell.

tony hyman

Law enforcement

◆ **Law enforcement memorabilia** such as badges, patches, nightsticks, handcuffs, and restraints from all types of law enforcement officers including fish and game, railroad security, sheriffs, marshals, constables, Indian police, city police, and other. Also likes studio portraits of law enforcement officers. Make a photocopy of the front and rear of your badge and give its history if you can. No security company, college police, or "gun show" brass badges.
Gene Matzke,
Gene's Badges,
2345 So. 28th St.,
Milwaukee, WI 53215
(414) 383-8995

◆ **Law enforcement memorabilia from prohibition era Chicago** including photos, police bulletins, warrants for arrests, court transcripts, police uniforms (1920's only), badges, and personal items from police chiefs Garrity, Fitzmorris, Collins, Hughs, and Russell. Only well documented personal effects, please, with value in part dependent upon the authenticity and "story" accompanying the item. If offering personal effects, tell how you obtained it and provide your phone number.
Michael Graham,
Roaring 20's,
345 Cleveland Ave.,
Libertyville, IL 60048
(312) 362-4808 days or 362-8531 eves

◆ **Any pre 1950 items connected with the Northwest Mounted Police,** Royal Northwest Mounted Police, the Royal Canadian Mounted Police, the BC Provincial Police, or the Alberta Provincial Police. Especially awards and medals, cap badges, collar badges, uniforms, and law enforcement items marked with the initials of one of these agencies.
Michael Rice,
Box 286,
Saanichton, BC V0S 1M0,
CANADA
(604) 652-9047 eves

◆ **Old handcuffs, leg irons, and other police or prison restraint devices.** Also police department badges, photographs, and histories especially from Ohio. Make certain to mention whether your items work and have a key.
Stan Willis,
6211 Stewart Rd.,
Cincinnati, OH 45227
(513) 271-0454 days

◆ **Police and prison memorabilia, particularly handcuffs and other restraints.** Wants ball and chains, manacles, leg irons, thumb screws, nippers, iron claws, and comealongs as well as badges and uniforms. Has particular interest in handcuffs and locks
Larry Franklin,
3238 Hutchison Ave.,
Los Angeles, CA 90034
(213) 559-4461

◆ **Handcuffs, leg irons, torture and execution devices, and electric chairs,** both authentic or reproduction. Also photos of these devices in use.
Harvey Lee Boswell,
Palace of Wonders,
Box 446,
Elm City, NC 27822

◆ **All items related to imprisonment, restraint, and locking** including handcuffs, shackles, ball & chains, leather restraints, straight jackets, prison uniforms, and **antique or unusual padlocks.** Also wants magician's escape locks, lock picks, and books about lock picking. These well known dealers in magic and escape devices offer a catalog for $2.
Joe and Pam Tanner,
Tanner Escapes,
Box 349,
Great Falls, MT 59403
(406) 453-4961

Fire Fighting

◆ **Prison, jail, or penal colony related memorabilia** including items from juvenile detention centers and reform schools. Items include coins, tokens, uniforms, weapons, badges, letters about prison life, restraint devices, photos of prisons, items made by prisoners, postcards, and "just about anything at all." His prime interest is in **scrip,** the privately printed paper money used in institutions as a medium of exchange. If you have genuine prison material you may send it for his offer.
   "Jailhouse Jerry" Zara,
   2414 Mark Place,
   Point Pleasant, NJ 08742

◆ **Fingerprinting equipment.** "I'll buy old police fingerprinting equipment including Bertillon equipment, fingerprint cameras, microscopes and especially books and magazines concerning fingerprinting." Also buys "Wanted" posters and police mug shots.
   Michael Carrick,
   1230 Hoyt St. SE,
   Salem, OR 97302
      (800) 852-0300

◆ **Legal memorabilia** such as wigs, gowns, and documents pre 1850.
   Byron Gregerson,
   Box 951,
   Modesto, CA 95353
      (209) 523-3300

◆ **Fire fighting and fire insurance ephemera** including, but not limited to, fire grenades, awards, helmets, buckets, axes, badges, **toys,** fire marks, fire insurance signs, advertising items, nozzles, apparatus parts, alarm equipment, photos, lanterns, **extinguishers,** postcards, books, salesmen's samples, models, etc., especially pre 1900. Nothing after 1940.
   Ralph Jennings, Jr.,
   301 Ft Washington Ave.,
   Fort Washington, PA 19034
      (215) 646-7178 eves

◆ **Fire department items which are pre 1920** including actual **fire engines** that are steam, horse, or hand operated. Also helmets, horns, fire house gongs, fire marks, fire insurance tin signs, and early catalogs. Also **children's books or toys** with fire department themes, fire department histories, early fire magazines, and postcards or photos depicting fire departments, firemen, and their equipment. No nozzles, convention badges, or large soda acid extinguishers.
   Matt Grimley,
   Box 224,
   Oakland, NJ 07436

◆ **Wood cased fire station gongs.** "I'll buy any wood cased fire station gong, working condition or not, made by *Gamewell Fire Alarm Telegraph Co., Star Co., Moses Crane Co.,* or other manufacturer. Gongs have wooden cases, glass doors, and key wind movements." Also wants literature describing gongs or photos of fire station watch desks showing a wall gong."
   Gary Carino,
   805 W. 3rd St.,
   Duluth, MN 55806
      (218) 722-0964

◆ **Fire and casualty insurance company memorabilia.** "I'll buy pre 1890 policies, reverse glass signs, automobile insurance tags, and pre 1900 stock certificates. No life insurance.
   Byron Gregerson,
   Box 951,
   Modesto, CA 95353

Schools

◆ **School, teacher, and student memorabilia** especially pre 1920 postcards, photographs, diaries, documents, records, and books having to do with teaching or operating schools. No schoolbooks except early teachers' editions.
Tedd Levy,
Box 2217,
Norwalk, CT 06850

◆ **School report cards** from before 1850.
Alfred Malpa,
9 Waterville Road,
Farmington, CT 06032
(203) 677-4708

◆ **Rewards of Merit** given to school children 1700-1890. Wants illustrated rewards given as school awards for conduct or scholarship only. The best ones are hand made, with watercolor illustrations. These can be worth from $25 to $1,000 to him.
Alfred Malpa,
9 Waterville Road,
Farmington, CT 06032
(203) 677-4708

Other gov't services

◆ **Civilian Conservation Corps (CCC)** memorabilia from the 1930's.
Ken Kipp,
Box 116,
Allenwood, PA 17810
(717) 538-1440

◆ **Immigration Service and Border Patrol memorabilia.** Wants either USIS or INS insignia, uniforms, badges, flags, and related items. Asks that you price what you have.
Mattice,
1600 So. Eads St. #521N,
Arlington, VA 22202

◆ **Forest Service items** such as badges, locks, dishes, signs, and tools marked USFS.
William Lehman,
4310 Cascade St., RR 1,
Enid, OK 73703

◆ **Obsolete U.S. Post Office memorabilia** including steel postmarking devices, locks and keys, uniform badges and buttons, scales, marked handguns, and postcards depicting post offices. Many other items are also wanted, but not postage stamps. His large illustrated wants list can be had for 45¢ postage on a large envelope. If you have a postmarking device, make an imprint.
Frank Scheer,
18 E. Rosemont Ave.,
Alexandria, VA 22301
(703) 549-4095 eves

Health & Medicine

◆ **Everything medical!** "I'll buy medicines, in the broadest sense. New and old, patent and fold, scientific and crackpot, plebeian and colorful, sincere, absurd, and ridiculous."
(1) **Bottles and other containers**, whether full of pills and powders, or empty;
(2) **Bottling and filling materials**;
(3) **Ads, flyers, signs, trade cards, and other advertising**;
(4) **Medical catalogs**;
(5) **Health devices**, real or quack, such as vaporizers, electric gadgets, etc.;
(6) **Any item that makes a health claim** such as tobacco, water, etc.;
(7) **Books and booklets** of all types, from serious to humorous;
(8) **Medical teaching devices**.
"I'd like as complete a description as possible, including the item's age, condition, price, and its unique characteristics."
August Maymudes,
10564 Cheviot Dr.,
Los Angeles, CA 90064
(213) 839-4426 eves

◆ **Pre 1900 medical and apothecary (drug store) equipment** including **doctor's instruments**, bleeding bowls, leech jars, apothecary tools, colored and pontil marked **patent medicine** bottles, patent medicine tax stamps 1860-80, and all patent medicine advertising in *any* form especially signs, clocks, tins, and 3-dimensional papier mache figures. A 26 year veteran collector dealer. He'll pay from $150 to $3,000 for leech jars and to $1,500 for figures.
Jerry Phelps,
6013 Innes Trace Rd.,
Louisville, KY 40222
(502) 425-4765

◆ **Stethoscopes.** "I'll buy antique and unusual physician's stethoscopes, both monaural and binaural." Give any markings, patents, maker's marks, etc.
Chris Papadopoulos,
1107 Chatterleigh Circle,
Baltimore, MD 21204
(301) 825-9157 eves

◆ **Medical instruments such as monaural stethoscopes, ear trumpets and conversation tubes**, anesthesia masks from the drop ether days made of brass, bleeders of all types especially mechanical, and old dental instruments made from wood or ivory.
Lucille Malitz,
Lucid Antiques,
Box KH,
Scarsdale, NY 10583
(914) 636-3367

◆ **Microscopes and other medical or scientific instruments.** "I'll buy pre-1900 microscopes by the following makers: Zentmayer, Grunow, Bullock, McAllister, Gundlock, Tolles, Queen, Pike and Charles Spencer." Give the maker's name and serial number. Describe overall condition of the instrument, case, and accessories. "Don't clean or polish anything," he warns.
Dr. Allan Wissner,
Box 102,
Ardsley, NY 10502
(914) 693-4628

◆ **Embalming tools and bottles.** Embalming kits and tools are often in black bags and can be recognized by long aspiration needles. Many tools and bottles are marked with skulls and crossbones. Look for *Dioxin* brand, and others. "I have enough embalming tables unless they're priced at $20 or less."
Steve DeGenaro,
Box 5662,
Youngstown, OH 44504
(216) 759-7151 eves

◆ **Enema and douche equipment.** Wants a variety of rubber fountain syringes, sinus fountain syringes, bulb syringes, etc, especially in different colors. Especially interested in the *Buckingham* and *Boots* enema syringes, both of which come in a metal box. Also buys books and catalogs related to the subject, from any maker. "No new type fountain syringes with white plastic hoses." Items must be made of rubber, not plastic, and have black not white fittings. Do you have the original box?
Helen Roman,
115 Baldwin St.,
Bloomfield, NJ 07003

◆ **Electric and pre-electric vibrators and hand held massagers.** "I especially like those with metal casings rather than plastic, those with hand-cranks, and vibrators with wooden handles or parts. Not interested in battery operated devices. You won't make a fortune selling to me, but your item could reside in the world's only vibrator museum and will be happier than in your attic." No *Oster* vibrators which are worn on the back of the hand. Describe, give numbers, and indicate whether the box and any attachments are present. Will buy items which do not work but are not physically broken.

Joani Blank, Good Vibrations,
3492 22nd St.,
San Francisco, CA 94110
(415) 342-2536

◆ **Pre 1960 Chiropractic equipment and books** especially electronic diagnostic gear or items from the Palmer College/School.

Mel Rosenthal,
507 S. Maryland Ave.,
Wilmington, DE 19804
(302) 322-8944

◆ **Dental cabinets, instruments, and catalogs.**

Peter Chu, DDS,
5470 Folkestone Dr.,
Dayton, OH 45459
(513) 435-6849

◆ **Dental trade cards.** "I'll buy trade cards from dentists, dentifrices, pain medications, dental parlors, breath fresheners, and the like." Will consider any dental related paper.

Ted Croll, DDS,
East Street and North Main St.,
Doylestown, PA 18901

◆ **Ephemera and information about twins, multiple births, and freak parasitic twin births.** This dedicated nurse, historian, and archivist wants photos, newspaper clips, souvenirs, personal information, and *anything* statistical, scholarly, or informative. If there was ever a twin in your family, or you are one of a multiple birth, this is the lady who will preserve the experience. She always wants first hand information from multiples about their life. *She does not want* undated clippings or items that have been damaged by pinning, pasting, or taping. When describing scrapbooks, make certain to note whether the clippings are dated. "My collection is not a hobby but a full time job in research, internationally recognized for its accuracy and extent, a source of factual information for physicians, researchers, and news media of all types." She has been at it since 1939, but *Miss Helen always appreciates help*, especially people sending clippings from local papers and obscure magazines about twins (as long as you tell where it came from and the date). Especially wants photos and **Dionne quints** memorabilia.

"Miss Helen" Kirk,
Multiple Birth Museum,
Box 254,
Galveston, TX 77553
(409) 762-4792

◆ **All human glass eyes** in any size or color, rights or lefts.

Donald Gorlick,
Box 24541,
Seattle, WA 98124
(206) 824-0508

◆ **Veterinary medicine ephemera**, pre 1900.

Barbara Cole,
October Farm,
Rt 2, Box 183-C,
Raleigh, NC 27610

Drugs & Quacks

◆ **Drug store memorabilia** including apothecary bottles with glass labels and stoppers, show globes, all **related advertising, and catalogs.** No scales or mortar and pestle sets.
Mart James,
8269 Scarlet Oaks Cr.,
Cordova, TN 38018
(901) 757-0214

◆ **Patent medicine advertising.** "I'll buy 19th century advertising, trade cards, almanacs, booklets, postcards, posters, sheet music, tokens, and giveaway items related to *Hadacol* and other patent medicines. I'll take *Hadacol* items to 1950. I am looking for "private" trade cards, made for one manufacturer, not stock cards with overprints. Please send Xerox© or send the item on approval.
A.Walker Bingham,
19 E. 72nd St.,
New York, NY 10021
(212) 628-5358

◆ *Warner Safe Cure* or *Remedy Co.* products. "I'll pay top prices for advertising, posters, packaged products, *Throatine*, asthma cure or remedy, powder, plasters, yeast, and any *Warner* or *Craig* boxed or labeled bottles. Any materials relevant to company history are wanted. I'll travel to buy good a good collection of patent medicine advertising.
Jack Stecher,
230 Eileen Drive,
Rochester, NY 14616
(716) 621-4701

◆ **Patent medicine bottles,** especially from G.W. Merchant of Lockport, NY.
Sven Stau,
Box 1135,
Buffalo, NY 14211
(716) 825-5448

◆ **Old quack medical devices** which shock, spark, buzz, vibrate, or do nothing at all. Most devices were built into fancy boxes with dials, wires, hand electrodes, plated terminals, coils, and levers. Other devices consisted of therapeutic gloves, brushes, charms, and the like. There is an extensive list of brand names he seeks but he does not want common massage vibrators, violet rays, and *Electreat* devices. He also buys books, catalogs, pamphlets, and other paper ephemera promoting quack electrical devices or other therapeutic gimmicks. Keller prefers you price what you have but will make offers.
Leland Keller,
1205 Imperial Dr.,
Pittsburg, KS 66762

◆ **Almanacs published by patent medicine companies, between 1840-1920.** Many of these pay $20-$30. If you have many of them to sell it is advisable to have his detailed wants list. No Almanacs by *Swamp Root, Nostetters,* or *Ayers.* No foreign language editions. No post 1920. No medical booklets, pamphlets, cookbooks, etc.
Rodney Brunsell,
55 Spring St.,
Hanson, MA 02341

Your Name
Your Address

**For faster response
include an SASE.**

17
Guns & War

Dr. Hyman's Prescription

The relics and souvenirs of the various wars in America's past are all of interest to collectors.

Not too many items turn up from earlier wars, but choice items can be found from the Civil War, probably the most popular war with collectors. Note how many items from 20th century wars are being sought. Among the most valuable later items are Japanese swords, some of which are worth $10,000 or more.

Only recently, collectors have started acquiring items from the Korean and Viet Nam Wars. There is also interest from home front items, and from the peace movement associated with the Viet Nam era.

When offering guns for sale, make certain to include all the information found on the barrel or breech. Pay particular attention to serial numbers. If they do not match from one part to another, make certain to note that fact. When describing the condition, note all changes, modifications, and repairs.

Knives and swords should be measured. Include a tracing or photocopy of any designs on the blade. Many military insignia and other small military items are easily photocopied.

Important publications for gun buyers and sellers are:

Shotgun News, 250+ page tabloid published 36 times a year for $15. Box 669, Hastings, NE 68901.

Gun List, 150+ page tabloid published monthly for $16.95 a year. 700 E. State St., Iola, WI 54990.

tony hyman

Guns

◆ **Many different rifles.** "I'll buy a wide range of items, from Civil War carbines, Indian wars guns, trap doors, rolling blocks, cap and ball, etc., on to early *Winchester, Marlin, Savage,* and *Remington.*" This 25 year veteran dealer also buys some *Colt* handguns. If your gun or rifle is before 1964 and all wood and metal surfaces are original and unrestored, it might be worth a call.

Rudy Dotzenrod,
Rt #2 Box 26,
Wyndmere, ND 58081
(701) 439-2646

◆ **Guns and gun collections of all types.** Always searching for **Gattling guns**.

Ed Kukowski, Ed's Gun House,
Route 1,
Minnesota City, MN 55959
(507) 689-2925

◆ **High grade shotguns, fine sporting rifles, and English double rifles.** "I'll pay up to $5,000 for pre 1964 *Winchester* Model 70 rifles, and up to $250,000 for *Parker* shotguns, and $100,000 for English double rifles and shotguns. I do not want old, worn, guns showing little or no original finish." Give the make, serial number, caliber/gauge, and condition if you'd like an offer.

Alan Phillips,
Box 7852,
Laguna Niguel, CA 92677
(714) 499-4196

◆ **Old double barrel shotguns** are wanted in any condition. Will buy any kind, wall hangers, hammerless, etc., that is worth $300 or less and made before 1940. "I especially want *L.C.Smith*, old side plate *Lefevers*, and most English or Belgian guns. Describe the condition, amount of bluing, missing parts, rust, engraving, butt plates, etc.

Charles Black,
The Gun Doctor,
Rt. 6 Box 237D,
Athens, AL 35611
(205) 729-1640

◆ **American percussion and early cartridge firearms, both long guns and revolvers.** These date from 1840-1920. Want guns by any makers but especially *Colt, Winchester, Remington, Smith & Wesson, Marlin, Manhattan, Sharps, Stevens,* and *Bacon.* He would especially like to buy derringers of all types, especially those that are particularly small or short barreled, those that are very large caliber (.41 cal. up) or those which take metallic cartridges. Any pocket size pistols made by *Colt, Remington, Bacon, Marston, Moore, National, Reid, Star, Terry, Warner,* and *Williamson.* Pays $300 to $3,000 for these guns. Wants photos or photocopies of both sides of the weapon and *all* markings and numbers found anywhere on the gun.

Steve Howard
Past Tyme Pleasures
101 First St., #404
Los Altos, CA 94022
(415) 484-4488 eves

◆ *Newton Arms Co.* guns and memorabilia. "I'll buy rifles, catalogs, loading tools, letters, stock, cartridges, and any other paper or memorabilia from the *Newton Arms Co.* or the *Chas. Newton Rifle Corp.* I will pay $5,000 for a .22 *Newton* rifle or a rifle in .276, .280, .33 or .40 (.400) calibers if in mint condition. Also want these cartridges. I will also pay a finder's fee for these five rifles and for the first model *Newton* with the set triggers opposed. I'll take anything signed by Chas. Newton. I don't want anything marked *Buffalo Newton Rifle Co.* Items must be original condition. Describe thoroughly."

Bruce Jennings,
70 Metz Road,
Sheridan, WY 82801
(307) 674-6921

◆ **Black powder muzzle loading guns made** by *Miller, Ellis & Plimton* and other New York State makers. Any information about or memorabilia of NY gun makers is of interest. Antique guns only. Black powder tins also wanted.

Alan Stone,
Box 500
Honeoye, NY 14471
(716) 229-2700

◆ *Colt* **Patent Firearms Manufacturing Company ephemera** including:
   (1) All correspondence on factory letterhead;
   (2) Pamphlets and brochures by *Colt*;
   (3) Empty black and maroon boxes that *Colt* guns were packed in;
   (4) Instruction sheets and manuals, and "anything else pertaining to *Colt* firearms or other products."
John especially wants *Colt* factory catalogs, 1888-1910, for which he pays from $40-$500. Later, 1910-1940, catalogs bring $20-$75. **Also plastic and electrical items marked *Coltrock*.** John buys *The Book of Colt Firearms* by Sutherland and Wilson, 1971, for which he'll pay over $100.
   John Fischer,
   7831 Peachtree Ave.,
   Panorama City, CA 91402

◆ **Marlin Firearms Company items** including rifles from 1881, and all other advertising, catalogs, posters, and whatever dating between 1881-1957.
   R. Runge,
   RD #1 Box 192,
   Frenchtown, NJ 08825
      (201) 996-4190

◆ **Junk guns and gun parts** in any condition. "I'm in the parts business, and will travel to pick up large lots." Nothing wanted having to do with current guns. Describe, including all markings and numbers. Robert does appraisals of fire damaged gun collections.
   Robert Fay,
   Star Route Box AF,
   Whitmore, CA 96096
      (916) 472-3132

Other weapons

◆ **Japanese swords, daggers, armor, and Samurai items,** especially fine swords and daggers, and sword and dagger parts. No other guns, bayonets, or non Japanese items. Ron will send you a checklist to help you describe a sword for sale. Ron has been treasurer of the Japanese Sword Society and editor of its newsletter for ten years. Ron appeals, "Many of these items have been brought back to America after WWII and now rust away in basements and attics. It is important that these items be preserved by placement into a collection."
   Ron Hartmann,
   5907 Deerwood Drive,
   St. Louis, MO 63123

◆ **Bowie knives and dirks,** especially Western.
   Charlie Smith,
   1006 NE 4th St.,
   Milton-Freewater, OR 97862

◆ **Primitive weapons** from around the world. Also **trade beads** in various cultures.
   David Boone's Trading Company,
   562 Coyote Rd.,
   Brinnon, WA 98320
      (206) 796-4330

EDITOR'S NOTE: Buyers of guns and swords will help you with the regulations covering the transportation of weapons.

War & Military

◆ **French and Indian War, the Revolutionary War, or the War of 1812 in northern New York** especially the Lake Champlain, Lake George, or Ft. Ticonderoga. All ephemera about the campaigns or the men involved, especially Benedict Arnold and Rogers' Rangers.
Breck Turner,
With Pipe and Book,
91 Main St.,
Lake Placid, NY 12946

◆ **Confederate Civil War letters,** envelopes, paper money, posters, pardons, passes, and other ephemera. Also Lincoln photos and manuscripts.
Gordon McHenry,
Box 117,
Osprey, FL 33559
(813) 966-5563

◆ **Handwritten Civil War documents, letters, and diaries**, 1861-65. Smith is a Civil War historian and researcher who purchases documents, studies them, and then he says "I give nearly all to the proper State or National library where they will be available for study by other scholars and kept in the proper humidity and conditions so necessary for this material."
Stephen B. Smith,
Grandpa's Wastebasket,
Box 50391,
Ft. Myers, FL 33905

◆ **Civil War, especially Southern Unit histories,** battle accounts, biographies,and personal memoirs. He can provide a detailed wants list to those who regularly deal in Civil War material. No books published by *Grosset & Dunlap*.
James Baumhofer,
Box 65493,
St. Paul, MN 55165
(612) 698-7151

◆ **Civil War regimental histories and first person narratives.**
Jim Presgraves,
Bookworm & Silverfish,
Box 639,
Wytheville, VA 24382

◆ **Civil War Veteran's materials, 1866-1949,** including all Reunion, badges, ribbons, flags, pictures, letters, invitations, and souvenirs. Also all Grand Army of the Republic (GAR) badges, ribbons, flags, diaries, glassware, uniforms, hats, canes, canteens, etc. Also similar memorabilia from other Civil War veteran's groups including UVL, ULU, UCV, S of U, WRC, L of GAR, D of V, Kansas Brotherhood, and various state groups whose names begin "Army of..." Nothing in poor condition, please. You *must* set the price. NO OFFERS.
Roger Heiple, Sr.,
Box 16,
South Lyon, MI 48178

◆ **G.A.R. china, mugs, and spoons.** Any pieces marked G.A.R. (Grand Army of the Republic).
Don McMahon,
385 Thorpe Ave.,
Meriden, CT 06450

◆ **French or British military forces overseas,** British Indian Native States forces, Spanish or French Foreign Legion, Abraham Lincoln Brigade, Camel Corps, Free French & Vichy forces, French forces in China, Devils Island, White Russian forces, Chinese Customs Service, Chinese bandits or pirates, China Navigation Company, international settlements in China, Chinese airlines, and similar topics. **Wants badges, banners, medals, photos, certificates, headdresses, souvenirs,** etc. Material about American volunteers or famous soldiers of fortune of any nationality is particularly welcome. No souvenir items produced by the Foreign Legion Veteran's Home or repros of Devil's Island folk art.
Gene Christian,
3849 Bailey Ave.,
Bronx, NY 10463
(212) 548-0243

◆ **Non fiction books and manuscripts about** *combat* in the Civil War, Spanish-American War, or World War One, printed before 1940 only. No fiction, recent books, book club editions, or items with poor bindings. "We *never* consider anything not priced by the sender."
G. Thomas Brasser,
Brasser's Used Books,
8701 Seminole Blvd.,
Seminole, FL 34642

◆ **Trench art brass vases and lamps made from WWI shell casings.** "I am only interested if they are engraved or embossed." Also **carved bone objects** made by POWs during WWI. No plain shell casings. Make a sketch or take a photo and include dimensions.
Al Lanzetta,
Box 340220 Ryder Station,
Brooklyn NY 11234

◆ **Half tracks, armored cars, tanks, Gattling guns, howitzers, and cannons,** especially a FT-17 Renault (M1917) tank in any condition (worth $10,000 minimum). Larry will make all arrangements for transporting what you have. Also wants
(1) **U.S. women's uniforms** and accessories from WWI or WWII;
(2) **military diving equipment** and related items including sales catalogs;
(3) **Mercedes Benz 500K or 540K autos** from between 1930-40 (will pay to $150,000);
(4) German military **Staff cars;**
(5) **Military aircraft** pre 1940.
Provide all information on the machine's data plates. A photograph is recommended. Only uniforms in fine condition, please.
Larry Pitman,
Zanzibar War Museum,
5424 Bryan Station Rd.,
Paris, KY 40361
(606) 299-5022

◆ **Painted steel WWI helmets.** Make sketch or photo of illustration.
Al Lanzetta,
Box 340220 Ryder Station,
Brooklyn NY 11234

◆ **WWI aviation relics and memorabilia from all nations,** especially log books, diaries, awards, certificates and medals, aircraft insignia and manufacturer's plates, trench art made from aircraft parts, medals, and anything belonging to famous WWI aces. He asks for a detailed description, sketch or photo, its history, and your lowest acceptable price. Will also buy pulp magazines from the 1930's about WWI air combat. Does not want photos, books, or other magazines.
Kenneth Smith,
345 Park Ave. 42nd Floor,
New York, NY 10154

◆ **Army Air Force A2 flight jackets,** AAF pocket insignia, military **aviation wings** in sterling or bullion, and WWI **enlisted man's round collar discs.** Nothing later than the Korean War.
Jerry Keohane,
16 St. Margarets Court,
Buffalo, NY 14216

◆ **WWII aviation leather or cloth flight jackets** with squadron patch and or painted artwork on the back. "I'm interested in jackets from any branch of the service Army, Navy, or Marine and any branch of aviation fighter, bomber, transport, etc. I am also interested in any squadron patches, escape flags, **squadron history books,** and photos or any airplane "nose art." I don't want any currently made flight jackets with antiqued paintings or patches. If the seller did not acquire the jacket from the veteran or his family, it is probably not old. I need any label information in the jacket, a statement of condition of both the jacket and its patches or art," plus details about the art. Photos are extremely helpful. I also buy documented **Flying Tiger memorabilia.**
Gary Hullfish,
16 Gordon Ave.,
Lawranceville, NJ 08648
(609) 896-0224

◆ **Flying Tigers and CBI WWII aviation memorabilia.**
Christiano,
RD #2 Box 49,
Walla Walla, WA 99362

◆ **Photos and bits and pieces of WWII aircraft.** It doesn't matter whether allied and axis, crashed or operational, Ken wants single snaps, albums, or negatives of photos of any aircraft used in WWII. Also wants instruments, gauges, fabric, fittings, data plates, unit or group insignia, and miscellaneous bits and pieces of the combat aircraft of any nation.
Ken Francella,
Box 127,
Amawalk, NY 10501
(914) 245-8230

◆ **Home Front and anti-fascist collectibles from World War II** especially those related to important events or phenomena including the holocaust, resistance, women during war, chaplaincy, soldier benevolent funds, etc. "All items, from paper to pottery, considered if made during the period 1939-1946. Must be related to allied war effort or to **anti-Semitism.**" Items directly related to **military occupation of Germany or Japan** through 1955 considered. Interested in the rare or unusual. He **does not want** military uniforms, weapons, medals, or insignia nor does he want souvenirs from Germany or Japan other than those related to anti-Semitism. No magazines, newspapers, or damaged items. Requires some items be sent on approval. Will reimburse.
Richard Harrow,
85-23 210th Street,
Hollis Hills, NY 11427
(718) 740-1088

◆ **Nazi notables especially Heinrich Himmler,** commander of the SS and Gestapo. Wants items given by or to Hitler, Hess, Ribbentrop, Goering, Goebbels, etc., including promotion and award documents, letters, silver or porcelain trophies, uniforms, medals. "I would particularly like to hear from veterans who brought back collections of material and are interested in selling the lot. I am generally not interested in any item you or a member of your family did not personally bring back from overseas." He prefers you to call him while you have the item in hand. Otherwise write, describe what you have, or make a photocopy of it, and include your phone number in your letter. Tom will pay $10,000 cash for some Nazi documents.
Thomas Pooler,
Box 1861,
Grass Valley, CA 95945
(916) 268-1338

◆ **German and Japanese military daggers.** "I'll buy daggers, dagger parts, medals, badges, spike helmets, and swords. I only appraise items for sale. You may write, giving me your phone number, or send insured for cash offer."
Dick Pankowski,
Box 04421,
Milwaukee, WI 53204
(414) 281-8611

◆ **British and American military knives of WWI and WWII** especially British Commando daggers, Wilkinson Sword fighting knives (marked "F-S Fighting Knife"), and American special unit fighting knives. Value ranges from $50 to $1,500 depending on rarity, condition, and its scabbard. It is very important for you to copy *every* word and symbol on the blade, handle, guard, and scabbard. John does *not* want bayonets that attach to the end of a rifle.
John Fischer,
7831 Peachtree Ave.,
Panorama City, CA 91402

◆ **Brass military shell casings.** "I want to buy the casings for shells and projectiles in 37mm and larger sizes. All weapons, all nations."
Charles Eberhart,
3616 Seward,
Topeka, KS 66616
(913) 253-1016

◆ **Military newsreel and training films from WW II** on any military, naval, or aviation subject will be considered. May be British, American, Canadian, German, or Russian, but must be 16mm sound films shot during 1939-45. Films may be training, propaganda, or documentary. "I'll buy military aviation related films from 1903-1985, especially World War One, the Korean Conflict, and Vietnam. Give the complete title, producer, running time, and a list of defects. If you don't know the running time, measure the diameter of the reel and the diameter of the film on it. If you can, give a brief summary of contents." Nothing damaged. Also buys **military magazines.**
Edward Topor,
4313 South Marshfield Ave.,
Chicago, IL 60609
(312) 847-6392

◆ **Korean and Viet Nam War military unit histories** from any branch of the service. Will buy other eras, particularly fighter and bomber groups of WWII. "I also collect unit photos, military postcards, holiday menus, distinctive unit insignia, shoulder patches, medals, guidons, **scrapbooks**, berets and **toy soldiers**. I'm not interested in reprints or later editions. If someone has an item for sale and wants an offer, they must allow me to examine it."
Lt. Col. Wilfred Baumann,
RD #1 Box 188,
Esperance, NY 12066
(518) 875-6753

◆ **Canadian military medals and cap badges.** "I'll buy all cap badges with the initials C-E-F on them, or badges with a number and the words 'overseas battalion' and 'Canada' or 'Canadian' on them. Any war or period. Look for the name rank and military unit on the rim of medals as some can be worth $1,000 or more. Will answer all inquiries."
Michael Rice,
Box 286,
Saanichton, BC V0S 1M0,
CANADA
(604) 652-9047 eves

◆ **Airplane identification models,** 1940-1970. Also promotional models, travel agency models, and squadron and bomb group unit histories. When writing, copy all info printed on the plane.
John Pochobradsky,
1991 E. Schodack Rd.,
Castleton, NY 12033
(518) 477-9488

◆ **Military regimental unit flags,** colors, or standards from all nations and periods. "I'll also buy **associated items** such as pole tops, cords and tassels, official issue cover bags, color sergeant insignia, carrying harnesses, battle streamers, and photographs showing the flags. Ben wants original **hand embroidered flags only**. No national flags or reenactment group unit flags. Please make a sketch of the flag, noting its dimensions and type of material. Ben volunteers to provide information about unit flags if you send an SASE with your inquiry.
Ben Weed,
Box 4643,
Stockton, CA 95204

◆ **Anything related to the U.S. Navy ship** *Richard Halliburton.*
Michael Blankenship,
5320 Spencer Drive SW,
Roanoke, VA 24018
(703) 989-0402 eves

◆ **Photos or photo albums taken or collected by soldiers during WWI or WWII.** Please set the price you'd like.
Ted Fonseca,
785 So. Bryant,
Denver, CO 80219

◆ **Military items of Great Britain or Common wealth nations**. This well known military author says "I'll buy hat, collar or shoulder badges, head-dresses, uniforms, field equipment (belts, packs, pouches, etc.), edged weapons, and other items too numerous to mention," particularly Scottish items such as bagpiper's headdress and badges, kilts and sporrans (leather kilt purses), dirks, and knives. This 40 year veteran collector will consider 1910-1945 items, especially cloth patches, from other countries. No fakes or repros. Describe what material the item is made from, colors, etc. Note if anything seems to be missing, and all chips, dents, nicks, cracks, mothholes, stitch marks, corrosion, fading, stains, polish wear, etc. Please Xerox.
Charles Edwards, Pass in Review
PO Box 622
Grayslake, IL 60030
(708) 223-2332

◆ **Small U.S. military relics and photographs** including ribbons, awards, paperwork, letters, buttons, canteens, knives, insignia, flags, etc. Rex operates one of the largest mail auctions of Americana in the country and is always looking for new stock, especially 19th century items.
Rex Stark,
49 Wethersfield Road,
Bellingham, MA 02019
(508) 966-0994

◆ **Propaganda and surrender leaflets** from Viet Nam and other conflicts. Make photocopy.
Al Zaika,
Box 65,
Bellmawr, NJ 08031

◆ Manchukuo memorabilia from the Japanese occupation of Manchuria, 1930-45, including Japan Manchukuo yearbooks 1939-42, Shanghai business directories 1938-42, artifacts from the Fourth Marines of Shanghai, and occupation money. Also wants **Vietnam war memorabilia** including postcards, servicemen's club tokens, chits, propaganda leaflets, communist money, etc.

Daniel K.E. Ching,
Box 75423 Sanford Sta.,
Los Angeles, CA 90075-0423

◆ **Medals, Decorations, and Orders,** especially military gallantry awards from US and England, but will consider all governmental awards from any Western nation. No Asian awards, please.

Alan Harrow,
2292 Chelan Dr.,
Los Angeles, CA 90068

◆ **U.S. Marine Corps everything.** Anything used and or worn by Marines from 1776 to 1946, including uniforms, medals, helmets, and weapons. Also wants documents, unit history books, documents, and recruiting posters. Wants photographs of Marines at war, work, or play, especially photos taken by amateur photographers. Also wants trench art created by Marines and souvenirs of war brought home by Marines. When you write, tell what you know of the item's history. Make certain to describe the condition.

Bruce Updegrove,
RD5 Box 546,
Boyertown, PA 19512
(215) 369-1798 eves

◆ **U.S. Marine Corps memorabilia of all types** including recruiting posters and materials, books, photos, sheet music, belt buckles, cigarette lighters, steins, mugs, documents, autographs, art work, postcards, trench art, bronzes, novelties, and **John Phillip Sousa** ephemera. Also buys toy soldiers, trucks, and planes with Marine markings. Describe or photocopy.

Dick Weisler,
53-07 213th St.,
Bayside, NY 11364
(718) 428-9829 eves 626-7110 days

◆ **U.S. Navy memorabilia** including postcards, ship or station postmarks, documents, and what have you. Describe. Pricing appreciated.

Frank Hoak III,
Box 668,
New Canaan, CT 06840

◆ **All military related paper goods, medals, and cloth insignia.** All wars. All eras.

Hank McGonagle,
26 Broad St.,
Newburyport, MA 01950

```
                              ▨

        Your Name
        Your Address

```

Put an SASE in your letter.

Dr. Hyman's Prescription

If you wish to read, or advertise in, antiques and collectibles periodicals, there are hundreds of specialty publications from which to chose. Among the more popular which offer general coverage are:

The Antique Trader Weekly. 100 page weekly tabloid of classified ads for every collectible imaginable. National. $22 a year from Box 1050, Dubuque, IA 52001.

Maine Antique Digest. 300+ page monthly tabloid paper covering art, folk art, furniture, and other better antiques. Most scholarly and interesting of antiques publications. Many New England dealer and auction ads. $29 a year from 71 Main Street, Waldoboro, ME 04572.

Antique Gazette. 75+ page monthly tabloid covering the South. $14 per year from 6949 Charlotte Pike, #106, Nashville, TN 37209

NY-PA Collector. 90+ page monthly tabloid covering shows and auctions of that area. $15 per year from Drawer C, Fishers, NY 14453

Antiques and the Arts Weekly. 150+ weekly tabloid of dealer and auction ads in New England. $32 per year from 5 Church Hill Rd., Newtown, CT 06470.

Paper and Advertising Collector. 34 p. monthly tabloid. Excellent place to advertise for paper things you want. $10 per year from Box 500, Mount Joy, PA 17552.

Paper Collectors' Marketplace. 64 page monthly magazine. $12 per year from Box 127, Scandinavia, WI 54977.

Samples are available for $3 from these publications.

tony hyman

18
Money, Medals, & Tokens

Dr. Hyman's Prescription

Coins and currency are among the easiest collectibles upon which to place a value because annual price guides are issued. "The red book" or "the blue book" of coins can be purchased at many newsstands or through any bookstore, or can be borrowed from most libraries.

The **condition of coins is critical** in determining value. Amateur sellers have a problem grading coins accurately, but so do many dealers.

You can assume that items with values listed as only a few cents will find few if any takers. Dealers will tend to pay from 30%-50% of prices listed. If you own anything that catalogs over $100, you have a good item and should be extra careful about its dispersal.

There are far too many dishonest people in the world of coins. ***Never sell your coins* or jewelry to someone operating out of a motel room.** More times than not, you will get less than you would be paid elsewhere.

So many tokens and medals exist, that 400 books are currently in print on the topic! Most tokens sell for 25¢ to $3, but it's important to have an expert evaluate your tokens because a few can be worth $500 or more. They photocopy beautifully. Set your copier for lighter copies.

Medals are issued by governments, civic and athletic organizations, charities, police departments, schools, and dozens of other groups. Military valor awards bring the most money, especially those with original paperwork. Many other medals sell for bargain prices (under $20). Buyers of medals and tokens will be found throughout *I'll Buy That!* in many different topics. See especially sports, business, government service, and miscellaneous.

tony hyman

Money

◆ **Better quality ancient Greek and Roman coins.** He also buys related books and auction catalogs, especially the book *Greek Coins* by Kraay and Hirmer, for which he'll pay $150. In business for eighteen years, McKenna issues monthly sales catalogs and holds quarterly auctions of coins and numismatic literature.
Thomas McKenna,
Box 1356,
Fort Collins, CO 80522

◆ **Ancient coins, especially Biblical, Greek, and Roman.** Also other ancient artifacts including Egyptian, Greek, Roman, and Biblical. This well known expert is author of *Guide to Ancient Jewish Coins* and other books. This twenty year veteran collector/dealer issues periodic catalogs.
David Henderson,
Amphora,
Box 805,
Nyack, NY 10960

◆ **Ancient and modern Chinese coins.** Also Japanese military occupation currency of WWII. Although not particularly valuable, counterfeit coins of China are also of interest.
Daniel K.E. Ching,
Box 75423 Sanford Station,
Los Angeles, CA 90075-0423

◆ **Spanish pieces of eight.** Wants *reales* minted in Spanish or South American mints. Looking for those with globe and pillars known as "pillar dollars," "pieces of eight," or "pirate dollars."
Sven Stau,
Box 1135,
Buffalo, NY 14211
(716) 825-5448

◆ **Coin collections of all types, "from pennies to gold."** Also individual gold coins, medals, and artifacts. Also pre 1930 U.S. banknotes and commemorative coins. No pennies after 1955, nickels after 1939, dimes, quarters, and halves after 1964, or silver dollars after 1936.
Ron Aldridge,
14908 Knollview,
Dallas, TX 75248
(214) 239-3574 eves

◆ **Silver and gold coins from any country** but especially wants perfect proof US silver dollars. "No junk coins."
Robert Hiett,
Maple City Coin,
Drawer 80,
Monmouth, IL 61462

◆ **Paper money.** "I'll buy all U.S. paper money issued before 1929, all Confederate paper money, all Southern states money from 1861-65, and all broken bank notes from any state. I especially want to find **novelty items made of ground up paper money** before 1930, and will pay 60% of retail for them. I recommend making photocopies of bills you'd like to sell."
William Skelton,
Highland Coin,
Box 55448,
Birmingham, AL 35255
(205) 939-3166 ex#3

◆ **All foreign paper money.** "I'll buy collections, accumulations, dealer's stock, hoards, rarities, notgeld, specimens, printer's proofs, banknote presentations, sample books, and numismatic libraries. Will travel. Have been buying since 1964."
AMCASE,
Box 5376,
Akron, OH 44313
(216) 867-6724

EDITOR'S NOTE: The periodical of the coin world is: *Coin World.* 100+ page weekly tabloid. $40 per year from Box 150, Sidney OH 45365

> **EDITOR'S NOTE: Use Registered Mail for shipping coins,
> currency, stocks, tokens, or medals with values over $100.**

◆ **Printed or manuscript items relating to
coins, currency, medals, tokens, or counterfeiting**. Especially scholarly books on coins
from any period or language. Also scholarly
numismatic periodicals and catalogs of coin
auctions pre 1940 in any language. A Chapman
Brothers Auction catalog between 1870-1920
will bring $50-$2,000. Also **counterfeit
detectors and bank note reporters** issued in
the U.S. from 1820 to 1900. No modern works,
or general surveys of numismatics. Will make
offers on better items.
George Frederick Kolbe,
Drawer 3100,
Crestline, CA 92325
(714) 338-6527

◆ **Any machine or device used to detect
counterfeit coins or currency** including coin
scales, coin detectors, scanners, grids, reporters,
magnifiers, Detectographs, Laban Heath
Detectors, and any other device to check weight,
thickness and diameter of coins. Also any scale
with markings in amounts, such as "20 dol."
Donald Gorlick,
Box 24541,
Seattle, WA 98124
(206) 824-0508

◆ **Elongated coins pre 1960.** Also **machines
to make them.**
C. Meccarello,
Elongated Coin Museum,
228 Vassar Rd.,
Poughkeepsie, NY 12603

◆ **Elongated coins.** If what you have is pre
1930, ship it to him for an offer, but *do not* ship
COD. Hartzog will send you a check for the lot.
Pays $1-5 and up for elongates before 1940.
Rich Hartzog,
World Exonumia,
Box 4143 BBL,
Rockford, IL 61110
(815) 226-0771

◆ **Mis-strike and error coins created by the
U.S. Mint.** Under most circumstances, it is best
to send a good clear pencil rubbing or photocopy
for his inspection and evaluation if you wish an
offer. **Also** paper money of 1929 issued by
banks. Send photocopy with your inquiry.
Don't forget your Self-Addressed Stamped
Envelope (SASE) if you want an appraisal of
your coin.
Neil Osina,
Best Variety Coin Center,
24 W. Valley Blvd.,
Alhambra, CA 91801
NOTE: In Summer of 1990,
Neil plans to relocate to the
town of Glendora

◆ **Coin scales.**
Rich Hartzog,
Box 4143 BBL,
Rockford, IL 61110
(815) 226-0771

◆ **Error coins.**
George VanTrump, Jr,
Box 260170,
Lakewood, CO 80226

Stocks, Bonds & Financial Paper

◆ **Stocks and bonds from any industry** but especially mining, railroads, automobile companies, expositions, and aviation. Also all other stocks if they are well illustrated and pre 1900. Stocks signed by famous people can be worth as much as $1,000. Please include your phone number. Ken also buys photos, stereoviews, and photo postcards from western states.
  Ken Prag, Prag's Paper Americana,
  Box 531,
  Burlingame, CA 94011
    (415) 566-6400

◆ **Stocks and bonds** pre 1910, especially mining, railroads, or unusual companies. *Must* be signed and have a company seal.
  Phyllis Barrella, Buttonwood Galleries,
  Box 1006, Throggs Neck Station,
  New York, NY 10465

◆ **U.S. and Canadian stocks and bonds,** especially railroads, mining, oil, shipping, automotive, aviation, expositions, and others. Also documents with a printed revenue stamp. Also stocks or bonds signed or owned by someone famous. This past president of the Bond & Share Society also wants all pre 1800 certificates from any company.
  Bob Kluge,
  American Vignettes,
  Box 155,
  Roselle Park, NJ 07204-0155

EDITOR'S NOTE: Financial paper includes all documents having to do with money, including stocks, bonds, checks, mortgages, IOU's, scrip, revenue stamps, business permits, and the like.

Collectors buy fiscal paper for a variety of reasons, usually for elaborate engravings (called vignettes) found on most late 19th century financial documents. Financial paper is also sought if signed by famous people, or if it is quite old (pre 1830).

To sell financial paper, a photocopy is almost essential. The value range is enormous, from a dollar or less to elaborate documents worth $500 or more.

◆ **Fiscal paper** including rare currency (US and foreign), checks, stocks and bonds, certificates of deposit, books on books, other items. He is particularly expert in California currency, national currency, Mexican currency, etc. Doesn't want items after 1935 or any kind of reproduction. A photocopy will often do, but "I'll usually request to see the item in person."
  Lowell Horwedel,
  Box 2395,
  West Lafayette, IN 47906
    (317) 583-2784

◆ **Bank ephemera from Nevada,** including pre 1950 bank documents, letterheads and bank bags. Also stocks, bonds, checks, scrip, and anything else financial, such as photos of banks.
  Douglas McDonald,
  Box 20443,
  Reno, NV 89515

◆ **Pre 1930 stocks, bonds, checks**, drafts, and warrants from Western states.
   Warren Anderson,
   American West Archives,
   Box 100,
   Cedar City, UT 84720
      (801) 586-9497

◆ **Stocks, bonds, wooden nickels and merchant's trade tokens** from ID, MT, or WA.
   Mike Fritz,
   1550 Stevens St.,
   Rathdrum, ID 83858
      (208) 687-0159

◆ **All paper items printed with fancy engraved illustrations by security printers**, including railroad passes, semi-postals (advertising stamps), souvenir cards, and annual reports. Security Printers include the Bureau of Printing & Engraving, USPS, American Bank Note Co., Canadian Bank Note Co., and Homer Lee Bank Note Co. Wants to find *Annual Reports* of American Bank Note Co. & other security printers and engravers.
   Robin M. Ellis,
   Box 8468,
   San Antonio, TX 78208

◆ **Fiscal paper from South Carolina** pre 1910, especially Charleston.
   Bob Karrer,
   Box 6094,
   Alexandria, VA 22306

◆ **Checks with interesting vignettes**, 1782-1914. Also all other ephemera related to checks, sight drafts, notes, traveler's checks, etc.
   Neil Sowards,
   548 Home Ave.,
   Fort Wayne, IN 46807
      (219) 745-3658 eves

◆ **Elaborately illustrated stocks and bonds**, checks, Railroad passes, letterheads and billheads, preferably before 1900. Especially want western items and autographs of important people in financial history. Also buys books on the history of mining, telegraph, and railroads.
   David Beach,
   Box 431,
   Hibbing, MN 55746

```
┌─────────────────────────────┐
│                        ▓▓▓   │
│                              │
│                              │
│     Your Name                │
│     Your Address             │
│                              │
└─────────────────────────────┘
```

A REMINDER:
Use photocopies and SASE

Dr. Hyman's Prescription

Stamps are the most popular collectible worldwide.

Like coins, stamps are well documented, and have new prices guides issued annually. If you own only a few stamps you can look them up at your local public library, almost all of which will have copies of Scott's Catalogs to Stamps. If you have many stamps, you are facing many hours of tedious work...work unlikely to be rewarding.

Only a few 20th century U.S. stamps have substantial value, but **you should watch for stamps on envelopes or folded letters before 1900.** Those dating before the Civil War can have surprising value. Value is affected by the condition, the stamp, the cancellation, the carriers, and where it was mailed from and to. The contents of the letter can also determine value.

Look for commercial correspondence giving prices or information about local areas. Personal tales of travel, Indians, mining, war, colorful people, famous events, disasters, and other activities are also desirable.

Buyers for early letters are often interested in the postmarks, so those too should be examined, looking for historic places, vanished cities, and the like.

The basic periodical among stamp aficionados is:

Linn's Stamp News. 70+ page weekly tabloid of articles, dealer ads, and classifieds. $28 per year from Box 29, Sidney, OH 45365.

tony hyman

Stamps

◆ **Stamps from any country in any quantity.** "We will buy everything you have," says Harvey, who has been dealing through the mail since 1934! He wants collections of singles, plate blocks, sheets, covers, and rarities. If you have a large or valuable collection, Harvey Dolin & Company will come to your home. Smaller collections may be shipped to them for their cash offer. "Your satisfaction is always guaranteed," say their ads. Dolin buys stampless (pre-Post Office) letters, **Confederate stamps and envelopes, Wells Fargo envelopes, and Duck Hunting stamps.**
>Harvey Dolin & Company,
>5 Beekman St. #406,
>New York, NY 10038
>>(212) 267-0216

◆ **U.S. or foreign stamp collections**, pre 1960.
>Ron Aldridge,
>14908 Knollview,
>Dallas, TX 75248
>>(214) 239-3574

◆ **Federal and state revenue and special tax stamps** including document stamps and all stamps used to show that taxes had been paid on a product. Special tax stamps are large and "appear more like licenses to engage in various occupations," such as liquor dealer, cigar salesman, wine maker, etc. Photocopies are strongly urged by this 30 year veteran buyer.
>Hermann Ivester,
>5 Leslie Circle,
>Little Rock, AR 72205
>>(501) 225-8565 eves

◆ **Various stamps and envelopes.** McHenry has been in business for 30 years and provides a long list of covers (envelopes) he wants, including Presidential free franks, letters mailed without stamps, color advertising on envelopes, expositions, pioneer flights, and more. You should request his list if you have early or unusual envelopes for sale. In addition to covers, he buys **revenue stamps, Confederate stamps and letters, precancels, and stamps from U.S. Possessions.**
>Gordon McHenry,
>Box 117,
>Osprey, FL 34231
>>(813) 966-5563

◆ **U.S. envelopes mailed to overseas destinations before 1870.** Claims to pay top prices. Photocopy and mail for his offer.
>Tim Kepler,
>24291 Pinecrest,
>Novi, MI 48050

◆ **U.S. Internal Revenue special tax stamps,** licenses and permits for making and selling beer, liquor, wine, tobacco, cigars, margarine, firearms, opium and marijuana. Also for businesses as brokers, pawnbrokers, dentists, lawyers, etc., No stamps from between 1873 and 1885 with punched holes are wanted. Also want state stamps and licenses for any business, activity, or product including hunting and fishing. **USDA export stamps** and certificates for meat and meat products are also sought. **Ration coupons** for gasoline, fuel oil, sugar etc., are wanted, but no war books (1,2,3, or 4) or any red/blue tokens. "Photocopies are very helpful."
>Bill Smiley,
>Box 361,
>Portage, WI 53901
>>(608) 742-3714 eves

Medals & Tokens

◆ **All types and quantities of tokens, medals, ribbons, badges, and related items.** He buys trade tokens, medals of all sort, hard times tokens, Civil War tokens, transit tokens especially with pictures on them ($10-$750), amusement tokens, telephone tokens, sales tax tokens, **any token or medal that is made from another item,** medals related to medicine or the arts and humanities, **love tokens, Worlds Fair medals** and elongated coins, **GAR badges** and tokens, **Indian peace medals** ($1,500 up), slave tags, all **Canadian** tokens and medals, counterstamped coins, and just about everything similar to the above including advertising mirrors and **Franklin Mint token sets.** There are literally millions of varieties, and condition plays an important role in value. If what you have is pre 1930, simply ship it to him for an offer, but *do not* ship COD. Hartzog will send you a check for the lot. "We cannot make individual offers on a long list of material. Our offers are for the entire lot as we want to purchase everything. We are not interested in pricing your material for you to sell to others, sorry!" He claims to pay higher prices than anyone else. **If your collection is very early, very large, or very valuable,** phone collect and Hartzog will make arrangements to see what you have. Hartzog can also auction your materials for you if you prefer. A sample of his auction catalog is available for $3. Hartzog's lengthy wants list shows prices paid and is highly recommended.

Rich Hartzog,
World Exonumia,
Box 4143 BBL,
Rockford, IL 61110
(815) 226-0771

◆ **Medals and tokens of all sorts** are wanted by this 22 year veteran dealer. Identify what the token or medal is made from, and provide a photocopy or a good rubbing. Buys them all.

William Williges,
Box 1245,
Wheatland, CA 95692
(916) 633-2732

◆ **Tokens and medals of all kinds and countries** including transportation tokens, advertising tokens, gambling tokens, merchants' "good for" tokens, and the like. All old coin-like items are purchased as well as related items such as elongated or encased coins, engraved coins, pre-1900 dog tags, advertising pocket mirrors, political buttons, and stage or movie money. **Also wants "Hobo nickels"** which are buffalo nickels with the Indian head re-engraved into another face. Steve will pay $10 to $35 each for these. Commemorative and award medals from Fairs are also wanted. Photocopies are usually the best way to describe what you have to sell. No large modern fantasy tokens are wanted. No Franklin Mint medals. No modern arcade tokens. Steve runs mail auctions of tokens and medals and has written books on amusement tokens and souvenir coins, both of which are available from the author at reasonable prices.

Stephen P. Alpert,
Box 66331,
Los Angeles, CA 90066
(213) 478-7405 from California
(800) 478-7405 outside Calif.

◆ **Medals and medallions from Canada, Britain, and other English speaking countries** issued for coronations, jubilees, town celebrations, victories, fraternal groups, achievement, and athletic competition. Especially military valor medals awarded to Canadians. Also **love tokens** engraved with names, initials, dates, pledges, and the like from around the world especially pre 1900. Also **merchant's "good for" trade tokens from Canada,** Britain, and English speaking countries. Also **Canadian money,** singles or collections, but only pre 1937.

Michael Rice,
Box 286,
Saanichton, BC V0S 1M0,
CANADA
(604) 652-9047 eves

◆ **Medals, Decorations, and Orders,** especially military gallantry awards from U.S. and England, but will consider all governmental awards from any Western nation. No Asian awards, please.

Alan Harrow,
2292 Chelan Dr.,
Los Angeles, CA 90068

◆ **Military awards, orders, and decorations,** especially for valor. If what you have is pre 1930, simply ship it to him for an offer, but *do not ship COD*. He will send you a check for all you have.
  Rich Hartzog, World Exonumia,
  Box 4143 BBL,
  Rockford, IL 61110
    (815) 226-0771

◆ **Official presidential inaugural medals.** Levine, who has been a dealer for twenty-three years, will pay $4,000 for the Theodore Roosevelt inaugural medal.
  H. Joseph Levine,
  6550-I Little River Turnpike,
  Alexandria, VA 22312

◆ **Medals commemorating or depicting Black Americans.** "I'll buy medals, medallions, badges, or tokens relating to, or depicting, Afro-Americans or including the words "Negro," "colored," or "Black-American." Articles may be positive or negative in tone. I'll pay $1,200 for the Franklin Mint set of 70 American Negro Commemorative Society tokens." Tell him the material (silver, bronze, or aluminum), the size in millimeters, and the inscriptions on both sides.
  Elijah Singley,
  2301 Noble Ave.,
  Springfield, IL 62704
    (217) 546-5143 eves

◆ **Medals or tokens related to the behavioral sciences, including psychology, psychiatry, mental health, and medicine.** No French Mint or Franklin Mint items.
  Dr. BCC,
  210 Deer Park Ave.,
  Babylon, NY 11702

◆ Medals and badges related to **animal rescue, heroism, school attendance, or truant officers.**
  Gene Christian,
  3849 Bailey Ave.,
  Bronx, NY 10463

◆ **Gold and silver medals given for school attendance or scholarship** before 1900.
  Alfred Malpa,
  9 Waterville Road,
  Farmington, CT 06032
    (203) 677-8746 days

◆ **Medals, especially foreign, related to medicine,** photography, printing, cycling, railroads, aviation, Judaica, ships, Olympic Games, Africa, Australia, West Indies, Far East, Monaco, or New Zealand. No badly worn items.
  Hedley Betts,
  Box 8122,
  San Jose, CA 95155
    (408) 266-9255

◆ **US, British, and Soviet valor decorations** and war medals. Foreign awards given to Americans are of great interest, especially Soviet World War II orders and decorations. All items *must* have supporting documentation of the award to U.S. personnel. Hlinka also buys all paper letters, certificates, or documents pertaining to valor awards. Will pay $2,000-$2,500 for U.S. Medal Of Honor awarded 1917-1970. He encourages you to photocopy both sides of medals and supporting paperwork. Hlinka has been dealing in medals for 40 years and has been an officer in various collectors societies.
  Peter Hlinka,
  PO Box 310,
  New York, NY 10028
    (212) 409-6407

◆ **Tokens, medals, and exonumia (non money coinage) from Georgia** including "good for" tokens issued by merchants, saloons and lumber companies, encased and elongated coins, advertising and commemorative medals and tokens, including those issued for the 1895 Atlanta Cotton States Exposition, and any agriculture awards and medals from Georgia state fairs. "Top prices paid for collections or single items."
  R.W. Colbert,
  4156 Livsey Rd.,
  Tucker, GA 30084

◆ **Tokens and medals from Washington, Idaho, and Montana.** Buys others, but is particularly interested in Territorial and other pre 1900 items from those three states. Pays $3-$100+ but buys nothing made after 1930.
　Mike Fritz,
　1550 Stevens St.,
　Rathdrum, ID 83858
　　(208) 687-0159

◆ **Tokens and medals issued by magicians,** magic shops, hypnotists, and ventriloquists especially advertising. Watch for actual coinage which has been stamped with advertising by performers. Some coins are worth more than $100. No trick or double headed coins unless unusual.
　F. William Kuethe, MagiCoin Shop,
　PO Box 218,
　Glen Burnie, MD 21061
　　(301) 761-6603

◆ **Medals given to Masonic "Past Grand Masters."** Must be handcrafted and inscribed.
　George Walsh,
　RFD #2 Box 145,
　Epsom, NH 03234
　　(603) 798-5200

◆ **Masonic chapter pennies** all varieties and countries, but especially from Maine. Indicate the chapter name, number, and location. Storck will pay from $3-$40 each. No modern coins counterstamped with Masonic emblems.
　Maurice Storck, Sr.,
　Box 644,
　Portland, ME 04104

◆ **Franklin and other private mint issues.** "I will purchase all bronze, silver and gold singles, sets and other items such as plates, bronzes, etc., in any quantity. Virtually all bronze tokens and medals are worth less than issue price. Many silver or gold pieces are worth substantially above issue price. I pay a reasonable price for all modern mint items; however, as I do not specialize in these, please write FIRST with price wanted, or for an offer. We do not pay return postage on modern mint medals in the unlikely event our offer is unsatisfactory." For common bronze, he pays 25¢ each for those half dollar size, less for smaller ones.
　Rich Hartzog,
　World Exonumia,
　Box 4143 BBL,
　Rockford, IL 61110
　　(815) 226-0771

◆ **Chinese-American tokens, telephone tokens** (worldwide), any **tokens from Shanghai,** tokens with incised initials "ETR", and **military club tokens from Vietnam.**
　Daniel K.E. Ching,
　Box 75423 Sanford Station,
　Los Angeles, CA 90075-0423

◆ **Tokens, scrip, stocks and bonds from coal or lumber** companies and their stores. Photocopy.
　"Tip" Tippy,
　102 1/2 Meadow Rd.,
　Oak Ridge, TN 37830

Haviland is identified, and often dated, by a backstamp on each piece. Below, the left column shows samples of manufacturer's stamps, and the column on the right shows decorator's stamps. It is not unusual for the china to be marked with both stamps, but it is a rare, and probably very old, piece of Haviland that is not marked with either.

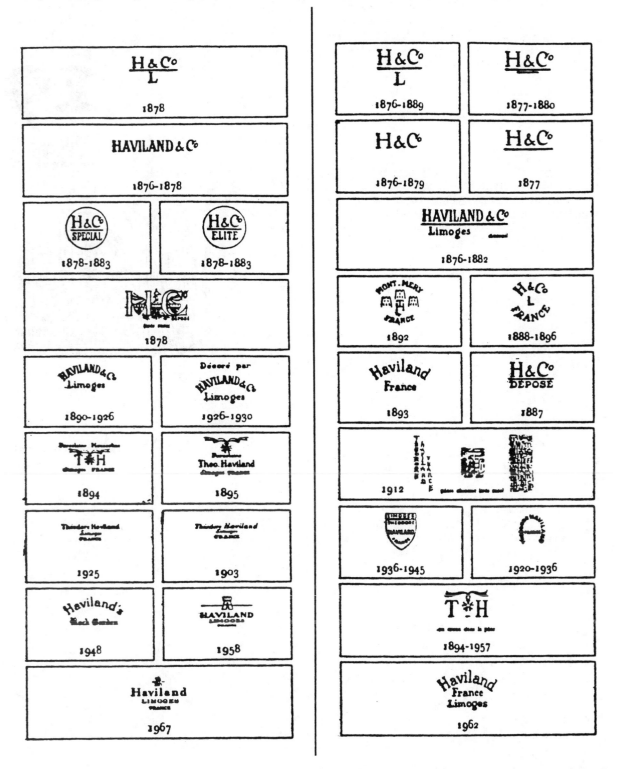

Courtesy of Eleanor Thomas. See page 40.

19
Art

Dr. Hyman's Prescription

Most paintings and prints have little value, but some can be worth $10,000 and more.

If you are not an art critic and do not know which are which, expert advice is essential. Paintings and prints that look sloppy or amateurish to an untrained eye can be snapped up knowledgeable buyers for big dollars.

If you own an original painting which has been passed down in your family for a generation or two, it is advisable to check the current value of that artist's work. Many painters whose work could be purchased for $100 or less at the turn of the century are worth 100 times that today.

Prints that are signed and numbered in pencil are most likely to have value, but some "penny prints" like Currier & Ives, Sarony and Knapp, and a few others have developed cult status and some dollar value. Be particularly careful about signed prints from the 1930's, as prints of that period are "hot" right now.

To sell paintings, a sharp 35mm photo is essential. You must also give the dimensions of the painting or art. Selling prints requires the dimensions of the image and of the border. Photocopy prints if possible. List all signatures and dates on paintings and prints.

Folk art is another area where amateurs should not make judgments about value. Take good quality 35mm slides or prints of any handmade items on pages 230-31.

When selling figurines, you must tell the buyer about the marks on the bottom, including their color. A photo is essential, although smaller items may be photocopied.

tony hyman

Paintings & Prints

◆ **Paintings by listed artists of all types and periods**, including 20th century. This first rate auction house regularly handles works of art from $100 to $100,000 and may be the perfect outlet for your better quality paintings. Send a photo and note any signature.
James D. Julia Auctions,
Route 201, Skowhegan Rd.,
Fairfield, ME 04937
(207) 453-9493

◆ **Paintings, prints, and photographs made by artists** in *Who Was Who in American Art.* Primarily interested in American Impressionism, Peter will consider a wide range of works from 1800-1950, as long as the artist is listed. Among special interests are:
(1) Prints and paintings about the sport of **competitive rowing** ($500-$1,500);
(2) **Color woodblock prints**, particularly the *White Line* prints of the Provincetown, MA, printmaker group ($500-$2,000);
(3) **Paintings and prints by American women artists** ($500 -$10,000+);
(4) Vintage **photos of Abraham Lincoln** ($500-$10,000).
No wood engravings from *Harper's, Leslie's,* etc. Send photograph and the dimensions.
Peter Falk,
206 Boston Post Rd.,
Midison, CT 06443
(203) 245-2246

◆ **Oil paintings of military or sporting scenes.**
Roger Wolf,
5559 North Elston Ave.,
Chicago, IL 60630
(312) 775-2005

◆ **Paintings.** Give the size and condition. Include photograph.
Ivan Gilbert, Miran Arts,
2824 Elm Ave.,
Columbus, OH 43209
(614) 236-0002 eves

◆ **Paintings of 18th and 19th century American political figures** or historic events. Please send a photo along with a description of the painter's signature if there is one.
Rex Stark,
49 Wethersfield Road,
Bellingham, MA 02019
(508) 966-0994

◆ **Paintings featuring the industrial-machine age.** Wants paintings and signed prints depicting workers in industrial settings. **WPA paintings and prints** are sought. Send photo.
David Zdyb,
Box 511,
Buffalo, NY 14225
(716) 892-7993

◆ **Marine artwork depicting boats, ships, and the life of men at sea.** Will buy paintings, watercolors, etchings, prints, **folk art, scrimshaw, ship models, or illustrated logs and diaries** on the subjects of whaling, yachting, the sailing Navy, river boats, and other marine activities. No reproductions or modern prints or other art created by living painters. "We restrict our appraisals to museums, but will discuss prices with someone who sends us the item that is for sale beforehand" writes this well known nautical dealer. He encourages you to telephone "so we can ask the important questions."
Samuel L. Lowe, Jr. Antiques,
80 Charles St.,
Boston, MA 02114
(617) 742-0845

◆ **Paintings and prints depicting smoking.** Buys a wide range of prints, paintings, and other items with a tobacco theme. All sizes, all media, all nationality, all tobacco topics considered but prefer smaller paintings. Buys pre 1930 magazine illustrations, prints, advertising, signs, posters, photographs, and other items. Especially interested in cigars, but anything related to tobacco consumption will be considered. Buying for resale and for personal collection.
Tony Hyman,
Box 699,
Claremont, CA 91711
(714) 621-5952

◆ **Illustrations by well known 20th century illustrators** such as Maxfield Parrish, the Leyendecker brothers, Norman Rockwell, Rolf Armstrong, Vargas, Petty, Rose O'Neill, Mucha, Erte', Grace Drayton, Will Bradley, or Coles Phillips. Wants original art, prints, posters, advertising, calendars, magazines, and books 1895-1930. Especially Maxfield Parrish calendars for *Mazda* and pin up calendars 1920-1960. Dennis is the author of price guides for Parrish, Rockwell, Petty/Vargas, and others, and edits *The Illustrator Collector's News*.

Dennis Jackson,
Box 1958,
Sequim, WA 98382
(206) 683-2559

◆ **Paintings of the American West.** Wants oils or watercolors of California, the Pacific Coast, Alaska, or British Columbia. Send a color photo. Describe signature.

Jay Friedman,
1225D Coast Village Road,
Montecito, CA 93108
(805) 969-1739

◆ **Paintings of the Hudson River or Catskill Mountains.** No modern works.

Edward Sheppard,
221 Water St.,
Catskill, NY 12414
(518) 943-2169

◆ **Paintings and prints depicting children ages 4-10** especially Prang chromoliths.

Marguerite Cantine,
Box 798,
Huntington, NY 11743

◆ **Pre 1900 prints, engravings, and woodcuts** on many topics including city scenes of the U.S. and Canada, natural history (birds, bugs, fish, and animals), military uniforms, fashion, the old West, children, Expositions and Fairs, disasters, mining, Indians, and Oriental life in America. Also buys bound volumes of illustrated 19th century newspapers like *Harpers, Leslie's,* etc.

John Rosenhoover,
100 Mandalay Road,
Chicopee, MA 01020
(413) 536-5542

◆ **Engraved portraits and photographs of famous people** in all walks of life. Will consider items loose or in books. Photocopies make the best descriptions.

Kenneth Rendell,
154 Wells Ave.,
Newton, MA 02159
(800) 447-1007

◆ **Prints, American and European.** Buys a wide range of prints. Generally prefers topical prints rather than scenics.

Kenneth, Harry, and Robert Newman,
The Old Print Shop,
150 Lexington Avenue at 30th Street,
New York, NY 10016
(212) 683-3950

◆ **Black and White steel engravings** of birds, animals, all nature subjects, romance, and fantasy. Interested in just about everything except cities and violence.

Mr. Mills,
Box 2073,
Hollywood, CA 90078

◆ **Damaged art of all kinds** is wanted. "If people send a good sharp photo I will make an offer on paintings, sculpture, and Currier & Ives prints that have been damaged but can be restored."

Alan Voorhees, Art Restoration,
492 Breesport Rd.,
Horseheads, NY 14845

◆ **Art Deco color prints,** posters, calendars, from the 1920's and 30's.

R. Bright,
Box 449,
Noel, MO 64854
(417) 475-6367

◆ **Egyptian, Greek, Roman, and Biblical art, artifacts, coins, pottery, glass, and other relics.** This well known expert is author of *Guide to Ancient Jewish Coins* and other books. This twenty year veteran collector/dealer issues periodic catalogs.

David Hendin, Amphora,
Box 805,
Nyack, NY 10960

◆ **W.P.A. Artwork.** Wants to buy paintings, sculpture, ceramics, paper, textiles, and toys. Top prices paid if you send photos, a copy of the signature, and condition and an SASE.
D. Morris,
305 E. 61st. #209,
New York, NY 10021

◆ **Original paintings by American illustrators for magazine covers**, magazine story illustrations, or advertising, 1910-1980, including artists such as Norman Rockwell and all his contemporaries. Also original art for magazine or calendar pin ups, especially by Vargas or Petty, but others as well.
Charles Martignette,
455 Paradise Isle #306,
Hallandale, FL 33007

◆ **Polish paintings.** Paintings by 19th and 20th Century Polish artists are wanted.
Alicja Czeck,
1839 Ditmars Blvd.,
Astoria, NY 11105
(718) 956-4177

◆ **California paintings.** Wants to purchase the work of Edgar Payne, William Wendt, Maurice Braun, Franz Bischoff, Hanson Puthuff, Elmer Wachtel, Ben C. Brown, and Clarence Hinkle.
Robert Lewis,
2940 Westwood Blvd #2,
Los Angeles, CA 90064
(213) 475-8531

◆ **Paintings by Cincinnati artists** and others. Buying work of Blum, Twachtman, Hurley, Sawier, Weis, Vogt, Wessel, Selden, Casinelli, Duveneck, Sharp, Farney, Nourse, Potthast, Volkert, and other American and European artists. Please send a good clear photo of items for sale. If in doubt, telephone. Have your work in hand when you do.
Cincinnati Art Galleries,
635 Main St.,
Cincinnati, OH 45202
(513) 381-2128

◆ **Paintings by New Orleans and Gulf Coast artists.** "I want to buy oil paintings from artists of New Orleans and the surrounding area, especially from the 1920's and 30's such as A.J. Drysdale, Clarence Millet, and G.L. Viavont among others."
Sanchez Galleries,
4730 Magazine St.,
New Orleans, LA 70115
(504) 524-0281

◆ **Sketches, drawings, and paintings by Philip Boileau and Robert Robinson**, American 20th century illustrators. Boileau is known for his 1900-1917 paintings of attractive women done for private customers and for magazine covers, and numerous other commercial purposes. Robinson worked commercially from 1907-1952 also on magazine covers and other commercial work. Please provide Bowers with a good close up color photograph and as much information about the work as you can. The value of paintings varies greatly, and Bowers will work with you to determine value.
Q. David Bowers,
Box 1224,
Wolfeboro, NH 03894
(603) 569-5095

◆ **Wallace Nutting pictures, books, furniture, and other memorabilia.** Collections are preferred, but single pieces will be considered. No size is too large. Mike says he'll travel anywhere to view collections of considerable size and diversity. Among Nutting pictures, Mike particularly wants interiors, scenes with people, animals, and houses. He does not want single pictures of common exteriors of apple blossoms, country lanes, trees, lakes, and ponds, although he will take these as part of a large collection. When describing pictures, give the title, frame size, and condition. When describing books give title, edition, color of the cover. Mike is author of a price guide to Nutting and accepts items on consignment for Nutting auctions.
Michael Ivankovich,
PO Box 2458,
Doylestown, PA 18901
(215) 345-6094

◆ **Italian paintings and watercolors** from the 19th and 20th centuries. Promises immediate payment for works by Delleani, Chierici, Campriani, D'Ancona, DeNittis, Induno, Gigante, Inganni, Lega, Michetti, and others.
C. Giovannelli,
853 7th Ave.,
New York, NY 10019
(212) 765-3055

◆ **R. Atkinson Fox prints wanted.** "I'm interested in prints, calendars, postcards, or anything else with artwork by R. Atkinson Fox." Please telephone or send a photocopy.
Pat Gibson,
38280 Guava Drive,
Newark, CA 94560
(415) 792-0586

◆ **Paintings and prints by R. Atkinson Fox, Maxfield Parrish, and Icart.** Claims she'll pay "top cash."
Christine Daniels, La Petite,
135 E. Shiloh Road,
Santa Rosa, CA 95403
(707) 838-6083

◆ **Commercial printed art and prints by F. Earl Christy** who specialized in beautiful society women. Wants covers from movie and women's magazines, advertising, fans, blotters, calendars, postcards, and anything else illustrated by Christy.
Audrey Buffington,
2 Old Farm Road,
Wayland, MA 01778

◆ **Original art by George Petty,** 1926-1960, and rare mint examples of his *Rit* dye and other store and counter display advertising pieces. Also prints of both Vargas and Petty girls from *Esquire* and *True* magazines. Also covers from 1938-39 *Saturday Home Magazine.* No *Old Gold* or *Jantzen* prints are wanted, but he'd love the original art for those campaigns. Reid has written on Petty and Vargas, and has been buying their work for 40 years. SASE required.
Reid Austin,
2110 Harbourside Drive,
Long Boat Key, FL 34228
(813) 383-4455

◆ **Inexpensive prints, magazine covers, and other art by Norman Rockwell.** Wants all magazines, advertising, and other Rockwell work *except* expensive signed prints or rare limited editions. Slight edge tears are acceptable, but no large tears or creases, water marks, writing, etc. You may ship your magazines containing Rockwell work flat, well protected, and insured, and they will make an offer. A list of magazines containing Rockwell work is available.
Harold Simmons,
2950 Northbrook Drive,
Atlanta, GA 30340
(404) 496-0175

◆ **Commercial printed art by J.G. Scott** who specialized in cute round faced children. Most of his work is signed "JG Scott" and can be found in women's magazine covers, advertising, blotters and calendars, postcards, and other places.
Robert Stauffer,
3235 Mudlick Road SW,
Roanoke, VA 24018
(703) 774-4319

◆ **Maxfield Parrish printed art.** "I'll buy prints, books, calendars, cards, posters, etc., especially Edison *Mazda* calendars. If you phone, have the piece in front of you!"
Michelle Ferretta,
888 Lasuen Dr.,
San Leandro, CA 94577
(415) 522-1823

◆ **Currier & Ives prints with Victorian themes.** Wants folio size prints rather than the smaller ones. Also buys **Victorian steel engravings** of any subject that appeals to her.
Ginger Carver Daily,
Box 33862,
San Antonio, TX 78265
(512) 657-3242

◆ **Currier & Ives prints,** and **chromos published by Prang.** No modern reproductions.
Edward Sheppard,
221 Water St.,
Catskill, NY 12414
(518) 943-2169

Folk Art

◆ **High quality folk art, especially with a maritime theme,** including wood carvings, weather-vanes, figural signs, ship models, ivory scrimshaw, and Eskimo carvings. This 25 year veteran maritime specialist says "we restrict our appraisals to museums, but will discuss prices with someone who sends us the item that is for sale beforehand." He recommends you phone first so "we can ask the important questions." Lowe does not buy reproductions or art by living painters.
Samuel L. Lowe, Jr., Antiques,
80 Charles St.,
Boston, MA 02114
(617) 742-0845

◆ **Ivory items of all sort,** including Eskimo and Oriental carvings, scrimshaw, ivory tusks, dresser sets, poker chips, dice, and billiard balls. Dave does not want bone or synthetic objects. David advises that bone has fine brown specks, and plastic imitations will sometimes have air bubbles or pits, whereas real ivory has grain, somewhat like fine wood. If you are selling tusks, give the length around the outside curve, and the diameter at the large end. He asks you to use a flashlight to carefully inspect for cracks in the hollow end. Follow standard description form. A sample of their lovely illustrated catalog is $1. Please list your phone number and best time of day to call.
David Boone's Trading Company,
562 Coyote Rd.,
Brinnon, WA 98320
(206)796-4330

◆ **Figures and native carvings made of ivory.** Ivory can be elephant, walrus, whale, hippo, wart hog, or narwhale, but he wants ivory art, not small items like pins, combs, spoons, brooches, toothpicks, and other utilitarian objects. Picture is a necessity, and he prefers you to set a price. Terry also buys **Primitive and pre-Columbian artifacts.**
Terry Cronin,
207 Silver Palm Ave.,
Melbourne, FL 30901

◆ **American folk art** such as **carvings, weathervanes,** whirligigs, **duck decoys,** pre 1900 **quilts,** figural 19th century **pottery, fishing decoys,** windmill weights shaped like animals, figural **architectural pieces such as cherubs or gargoyles,** small hand painted boxes, **game boards, handmade dolls,** Indian rugs, baskets, Indian pottery, **folk paintings of children** and animals, and **hooked rugs** with pictorials rather than patterns. No damaged or repaired pieces.
Louis Picek,
Main Street Antiques,
Box 340,
West Branch, IA 52358
(319) 643-2065

◆ **American folk art before 1900.** "I'll buy unusual tramp art items, **wood carvings** of people or animals, circus or carnival related objects, **unusual canes, inlaid furniture or boxes, paintings of children** before 1860, paintings of farms and towns before 1900, paintings of Indians, stoneware with unusual decoration, **samplers with American scenes** or city names, and American Indian items. Excellent original condition is a must. Does not want items with restoration or repairs. Provide any details you might know about the history of your item.
Larry Wallerstein,
10917 W. Pico Blvd.,
Los Angeles, CA 90064
(213) 475-4757

◆ **Mourning pictures in watercolor or embroidery.** In either medium, these are characterized by willow trees, tombstones, birth and death dates, weeping women, etc. These are often for famous people, presidents, generals, etc. Those honoring "no-bodies" are more rare and desirable. Will pay at least $100 and as much as $300-400 for better ones.
Steve DeGenaro,
Box 5662,
Youngstown, OH 44504
216-759-7151 eves

◆ **Folk art from Michigan,** including fish decoys, duck decoys, wood carvings, paintings, sculpture, quilts, coverlets, hooked rugs, samplers, etc.
   Gary Miller,
   Nautic Antiques,
   Rt. 2, Box 852,
   Suttons Bay, MI 49682
      (616) 271-6747

◆ **Folk art including primitives, whirligigs, weathervanes, and the like.**
   Vernon Ward,
   Iron Horse Antiques,
   Rt. 2,
   Poultney, VT 05764

◆ **Wax carved portraits, paper cuttings, and pinpricked pictures** of scenery or people groups. Also **Lithopanes** of all types, including steins, lamps, cups, and fairy lights. DOES NOT MAKE OFFERS.
   Laurel Blair,
   Box 4557,
   Toledo, OH 43620
      (419) 243-4115

◆ **Prisoner of war straw figures** woven or plaited by French prisoners during the early 1800's. Other prisoner art from the 19th century, including **ivory carvings** are sought.
   Lucille Malitz, Lucid Antiques,
   Box KH,
   Scarsdale, NY 10583
      (914) 636-3367

◆ **Folk art in any medium** including painting, sculpture, weaving, wood, etc. Condition critical. Send photo. Appraisals are for a fee. Contact Ivan only if your item is for *sale*.
   Ivan Gilbert, Miran Arts,
   2824 Elm Ave.,
   Columbus, OH 43209
      (614) 236-0002

◆ **Folk art weavings worldwide,** including rugs, saddle blankets, tapestries, ponchos, and other old, fine, and rare pieces. Will consider Oriental, Middle Eastern, European, Indian, and South American fine quality rugs and other weavings. Also **Eskimo and American Indian carvings** and crafts. Also **Victorian needlepoint and hooked rugs,** especially figurals. Nothing after 1920 or that is machine made.
   Renate Halpern Galleries,
   325 E. 79th Street,
   New York, NY 10021
      (212) 988-9316

◆ **Micronesian, Polynesian, and New Guinea masks, ceremonial bowls, and the like.** Some interest in scrimshaw, but none in items from New Zealand and the Maori.
   David Lilburne,
   Antipodean Books,
   Box 189,
   Cold Spring, NY 10516
      (914) 424-3867

◆ **African or South Pacific tribal art** including masks, weapons, musical instruments, jewelry, household objects, bowls, furniture, feather work, textiles, and "almost anything else that was made for tribal use and not for the tourist trade." Especially old collections including artifacts with elaborate decoration and animal, human, or spirit figures. Collections of **pre-Columbian pottery from Mexico or Peru** are sought, but *only* if documented and authenticated. High quality tribal art can bring as much as $100,000 so is worth inquiry. **Does not want** items made after 1970, ebony carvings, tourist items, or figures holding spears. A photo is essential and Jones would like to know where the item was collected.
   Charles Jones African Art,
   6716 Barren Inlet Road,
   Wilmington, NC 28405
      (919) 686-0717

Figurines

◆ **Bathing beauties and "naughties" figurines.** Small porcelain figurines, 1900-1940, which are nude, in bathing suits, in their underwear, stockings, or dressed in lace. They are finely modeled and in coy poses. Some were hollow, intended to be filled with water so they peed or squirted out of their breasts. Others had actual mohair wigs. "I am especially interested in finding Black naughties or bathers with a wig, but I am interested in *all* fine examples of bathing beauties and naughties. I am also looking for old catalogs, advertisements, and other information about them. A good wigged naughty is worth from $250-450, depending upon the pose and execution." **No Japanese figures** or reproductions. Generally does not want damaged pieces, but will consider extraordinary figures with minor damage. Size and pose is important so accurate measurements and a sketch, copy, or photograph is almost essential. Include your phone number. Will buy only if you grant right of refusal after inspection. If you collect these, please call. She'd love to meet you.
Sharon Hope Weintraub,
2924 Helena,
Houston, TX 77006
(713) 520-1262

◆ **Female figurines, especially nudes in bronze or porcelain** especially Art Deco and Art Nouveau, 1880-1930. Wants *Dresden, Meissen, Capo di Monte, Royal Dux, Amphora, Teplitz*, and other fine makers. Nothing that has been broken or repaired. No figurines of children or popular limited edition collectibles.
Madeleine France,
Past Pleasures for 20th Century Woman,
Box 15555,
Plantation, FL 33316
(305) 584-0009

◆ *Heubach* porcelain or bisque figurines and other items including children's tea sets, religious items, trays, and anything else. Porcelain portraits of the Three Fates, singly or as a group, would be a treat to her and worth hundreds of dollars. Draw a picture of the mark, and give all colors. Frances is cataloging every *Heubach* product made and she'd like to hear from anyone with anything unusual by Gebruder Heubach, even if it is not for sale.
Frances Sanda,
5624 Plymouth Rd.,
Baltimore, MD 21214

◆ *Hummel* collections. "We want to buy any size collection from 1 to 1,000, of any age, with any markings, including current. Top prices paid. We always try to offer the best possible prices. Will pick up if collection warrants. Call or write for more information."
The Limited, Ltd.,
2508 68th Ave.,
Zeeland, MI 49464
(616) 772-9640

◆ Pre 1971 *Hummel* figurines, especially figurines with the Triangle, Crown, or Full Bee marks. **Also wants** *Goebel* vases, figurines, half dolls, wall plaques, etc., especially "early red" *Goebels*. Also *Hummel* calendars from 1950-75. **Also** *Precious Moments* **figurines** with the triangle mark or with no mark, but not those with the hourglass or fish marks. All *Hummels* must be marked. Please give all marks and numbers and note whether you have the original box. Please don't offer *Hummel* plates, bells, or anything chipped or cracked.
Sharon Vohs-Mohammed,
Box 822,
Auburn, IN 46706
(219) 925-5756

1871   1890   1900   1914-1920   1923   1937

◆ *Lilliput Lane* cottages. "I'll buy them all, and will pay top dollar." Special wants include Old Mine, Drapers, Dale House, Dale Farm, Coopers, Miners, Tuck Shop, Old Post Office, Coach House, Warwick Hall, Cliburn School, Old Schoolhouse, Bermuda Cottage, Packhorse Bridge, Crendon Manor, Adobe Village, Adobe Church, Log Cabin, Grist Mill, Forge Barn, Cape Cod, San Francisco House, Wallace Station, Midwest Barn, General Store, Country Church, Lighthouse, and Covered Bridge.

Dr. Handley,
45245 Romeo Plank Rd.,
Mt. Clemens, MI 48044
(313) 263-1300

◆ **Human and animal figures made by** *Noritake.*

Tom Burns,
109 E. Steuben St.,
Bath, NY 14810
(607) 776-7942

◆ **Figurines depicting card playing**, such as "The Devil in the Cards" from the *Royal Bayreuth* series.

Bill Sachen,
927 Grand Ave.,
Waukegan, IL 60085
(312) 662-7204

◆ **Porcelain or bronze figurines, paintings and other art depicting chess players.**

David Hafler,
11 Merion Road,
Merion Station, PA 19066
(215) 839-7171

◆ **Miniature Viking figures** from 1" to 16" high, in mint condition. Send color photo.

W.R. Anderson,
Box 301,
Chicago, IL 60690
(312) 761-1888

◆ *Goebel* **figurines of cats.** "I don't want cats other than those made by *Goebel*. I don't want *Goebels* other than cats." Include marks and numbers on the bottom of the figurine.

Linda Nothnagel,
Rt. 3,
Shelbina, MO 63468
(314) 588-4958

◆ **Broken or damaged** *Hummel* **and** *Lladro* **figurines.** State the mark, the mold number, the extent of the damage, and the price you'd like.

Y. DiSalvo,
228 Washington Ave.,
Elmwood Park, NJ 07407

◆ **Collector's plates.** The Ernst family is one of the nation's larger dealers in collector's plates. If you have a collection of plates to sell, they will help you in one of two ways. If your plates are items they have requests for and can sell promptly and easily, they will purchase some or all of them outright. In the more likely event that you have some plates in less demand, they will sell them for you on consignment. They will price them according to the current market, catalog them, and notify their extensive mailing list that your plates are available. The price they ask is dependent upon how quickly you wish to sell them. They charge 20% of the item's selling price for this valuable service. When you call or write, they will send you complete information plus specific instructions on how to pack and ship your plates safely. The company has been in business for 21 years and is listed in Dun & Bradstreet.

Ross, Ruth, and Ruth Ann Ernst
Collectors Plates
7308 Izard
Omaha, NE 68114
(402) 391-3469

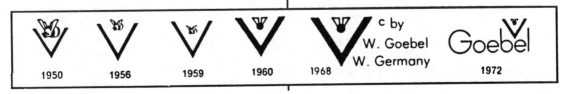

1950   1956   1959   1960   1968   c by W. Goebel W. Germany   Goebel 1972

20
Paper
Miscellany

Dr. Hyman's Prescription

Buyers abound for nearly every interesting paper item, especially those printed before 1900. You will find buyers of paper in nearly every chapter of *I'll Buy That!*

Billions of tons of paper have been printed upon, most of it ephemera, intended to be discarded. These paper items are collected because of who printed it, when it was printed, where it was printed, what it was used for, how or by whom it is illustrated, or what message is printed on it.

Buyers of paper items want to know about creases, tears, discoloration, fading, foxing (little brown spots), trimming, silverfish, or other damage. The amount of damage acceptable varies from collector to collector, topic to topic, but no one buys junk or brittle items.

Watch for sales literature, catalogs, instructions, and other paper about business or manufacturing. Historians of various professions and industries eagerly seek these. See the Index for help in identifying a buyer.

Autograph collectors agree that sellers must do two things. First, include a photocopy with your inquiry. Second, be prepared to ship your autographed item for inspection. Autographed items are often one of a kind, so every piece must be individually evaluated as to importance and condition. Only after viewing the actual document will most dealers be willing to pay your requested price or make you an offer. Too, there are many fake autographs, particularly of politicians and movie stars.

tony hyman

Miscellaneous paper

◆ **Rare documents in all fields**, from autographs to stock certificates, from song sheets to pardons and passes, including handwritten documents, land grants, maps, and "most any other unusual paper items." Gordon buys lots of all sizes, from single items to entire estates.
   Gordon McHenry,
   Box 117,
   Osprey, FL 34229
      (813) 966-5563 FAX 813-966-5563

◆ **Paper goods of all sorts if in good condition** are sought by one of the West's better known ephemerists. Kenrich Company buys postcards, sports cards, photographs, stamps and covers, philatelic items, posters, stereoviews, timetables, slave documents, brochures, calendars, original artwork, bumper stickers, blotters, book marks, playing cards, pin-back buttons, comic books, cookbooks, insurance policies, scorecards, match book covers, menus, napkins, coasters, seed packets, guide books, reward cards, panoramic photos, letterheads, movie lobby cards, scrapbooks, diaries, letters, logs, signs, autographs, medals, souvenirs, games, trade cards, paper dolls, fans, almanacs, directories, and more. If it's paper, collectible, and in fine condition, Bill will probably buy it. Closed Sunday and Monday.
   Bill Colby,
   Kenrich Company,
   9418T Las Tunas Drive
   Box 248,
   Temple City, CA 91780
      (818) 286-3888

◆ **Small items fringed in silk.** Buys Victorian greeting cards from any holiday or event and made in any style from single sheet to little booklets, as long as they have silk fringe. Also wants sachets, menus, advertising, and similar trinkets, as long as they are silk fringed, 1875-1925,
   Ronald Lowden, Jr.,
   314 Chestnut Ave.,
   Narberth, PA 19072
      (215) 667-0257 anytime

◆ **Invitations to pre 1900 dinners, social events, or festivities** especially ornately engraved, illustrated, or for important events. Presidential invitations of particular interest.
   Alfred Malpa,
   9 Waterville Road,
   Farmington, CT 06032
      (203) 677-4708

◆ **Birth certificates.** Seeking the older elaborate color certificates popular around the turn of the century. Wants ones that are 8" x 10" or larger and have a place for you to mount a photo of the infant. Will buy good condition certificates whether they have been used or not.
   Mark Sutton,
   2035 St. Andrews Circle,
   Carmel, IN 46032

◆ **Rebus puzzles.** Rebus puzzles are combinations of pictures, syllables, and letters which create a message when decoded. Linda wants hand drawn rebus puzzles in letters or post cards. She only wants noncommercial hand drawn puzzles, not printed ones, but they can be from any period, if they're interesting. Preferably wants pencil or pen and ink rather than paintings, with less sophisticated drawings the most interesting to her. She doesn't care how difficult the puzzle is. Doesn't want trade cards, greeting cards, or puzzles printed in books.
   Linda Campbell Franklin,
   Box 383 Murray Hill Station
   New York, NY 10156
      (804) 973-3238

◆ **Prints, calendars, trade cards, advertising, and magazine covers** featuring the work of name artists such as Frances Brundage, Ida Waugh, Jessie Wilcox Smith, Maud Humphrey, Torres Bevins, Mable Lucie Attwell, Henry Clive, Harrison Fisher, Coles Phillips, Fern Bissel Peat, Rose O'Niell, Grace Drayton, Charlotte Becker, Maxfield Parrish, and others.
   Madalaine Selfridge,
   Forgotten Magic,
   Box 413,
   Norco, CA 91760
      (714) 735-6242

◆ **Passports** and some other travel documents, pre 1940 American or any foreign. Documents must be complete, nothing missing, removed, or torn. Photocopy the page giving the owner's description and inside pages that have been used. No overpriced passports belonging to "celebrities."
> Dan Jacobson,
> Box 277101,
> Sacramento, CA 95827

◆ **Consular and foreign service stamps on documents** of any type, 1906-1955. Send photocopy.
> H. Ritter,
> 68 Heatherwood,
> Norristown, PA 19403

◆ **Folded road maps of all types.** Dave buys road maps of any age, issued by any producer, by any publisher of "Official" road maps of the USA and Canada. Wants original maps in good to mint condition. Please tell where the map is from and give the date and describe condition.
> David Compas,
> 5615 Bramblewood Rd.,
> La Canada, CA 91011
>   (818) 790-5332 eves

◆ **Admission tickets of all types.** "I buy sports, political, theatrical, social. No stubs or foreign. Please price what you have and ship it on approval."
> David Lamb,
> 48 Woodside Drive,
> Rochester, NY 14624

◆ **Catalogs for musical instruments** published by the manufacturers before 1950. All sales literature for instruments is wanted, except that for pianos, organs and drums.
> John McCardle,
> 1655 N. Goodlet Ave.,
> Indianapolis, IN 46222

Scrapbooks

◆ **Scrapbooks compiled by children or adults before 1895.** Books can be any size and a variety of contents may be of interest *except* those consisting primarily of newspaper clippings or postcards. You must write detailed descriptions of contents, noting materials that are damaged or trimmed. Your alternative is to photocopy pages from the book. He promises to return your materials promptly and unmarked if he invites you to ship it for inspection. Condition is an important factor in value for this 40 year vet.
> Ronald Lowden, Jr.,
> 314 Chestnut Ave.,
> Narberth, PA 19072
>   (215) 667-0257 anytime

◆ **Scrapbooks and collections of loose die-cut, embossed Victorian paper.**
> Madalaine Selfridge,
> Forgotten Magic,
> Box 413,
> Norco, CA 91760
>   (714) 735-6242

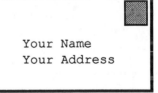

Selling paper? Photocopy!
Don't forget your SASE.

Autographs

◆ "The list of autographs I'd buy is almost endless," says Paul. He wants presidents and their wives, statesmen, scientists, inventors, entertainers, characters from the old West, and famous people in all walks of life. Especially wants handwritten letters of any president, particularly modern presidents. "Autographs of most politicians are worth little unless they became president or rose to great prominence. Most TV and movie stars since 1960 are worth little, except for a few exceptions such as Marilyn Monroe." Purchase offers are free. Appraisals are for a fee. His sample catalog of autographs for sale is available for a long SASE.
　　Paul Hartunian, Autographs,
　　127B East Bradford Ave.,
　　Cedar Grove, NJ 07009
　　　　(201) 857-7275

◆ Autographed letters and documents from ancient times to modern days in all fields. Significant medieval documents and manuscripts are always of interest. This 28 year veteran dealer **does not want** autographs obtained by writing celebrities, modern politicians, or movie stars. A photocopy is suggested.
　　Kenneth Rendell,
　　154 Wells Ave.,
　　Newton, MA 02159
　　　　(800) 447-1007

◆ Letters, signed photographs and signatures of famous people in any category: Presidents, Hollywood, NASA, sports, Civil War, art, music, literary, scientific, historical, rock and roll, theater, aviation, old west. Also interested in old handwritten diaries, collections of letters from the not-so-famous, handwritten recipe books, and anything written while traveling across America. Wants California and New Orleans letters from 1800-1870. Offers $1,000 for signed Buddy Holly photo. Please photocopy what you have. **Does not want** autopen or printed signatures.
　　Michael Reese II,
　　715-9 One Appian Way,
　　S. San Francisco, CA 94080
　　　　(415) 588-7608

◆ Autographs, signed books, and rare documents in all fields. Particularly wants U.S. Presidents and first ladies and "investment quality items." Handwritten letters of Presidents while in office, particularly of William Henry Harrison and James A. Garfield, whose letters could be worth as much as $50,000! No facsimile or secretary signatures. "It is usually necessary to see the actual item, particularly in order to make a firm offer." They publish a free monthly catalog of autographs for sale.
　　Michael Minor and Larry Vrzalik,
　　Lone Star Autographs,
　　PO Drawer 500,
　　Terrell, TX 75160
　　　　(214) 563-2115 days (214) 932-6050 eves

◆ Historical documents signed by U.S. Presidents. "I'll buy land grants, military and civil commissions, ship's papers, passports, appointments of judges, postmasters, ambassadors, etc. I search for clean documents with no holes, stains, tape, or trims. I concentrate on quality. I'd love to find a George Washington land survey (to $10,000) or a Supreme Court appointment. Every mark, every fade, every crease or wrinkle *must* be described accurately.
　　Richard Lechaux,
　　HC-60 Box 3712,
　　Fort Valley, VA 22652
　　　　(703) 933-6305

◆ Handwritten documents and letters of famous Americans. "We specialize in Presidents, and are particularly interested in Washington, Adams, Jefferson, Franklin, Hancock, and Lincoln's assassination." Include mention of all imperfections in your letter.
　　Steve and Linda Alsberg,
　　9850 Kedvale Ave.,
　　Skokie, IL 60076
　　　　(312) 676-9850

◆ Autographed non-fiction books. Will consider any, but is particularly interested in the Soviet Union, Eastern Europe, Asia, Communism, Socialism, and conservative authors.
　　Edward Conroy,
　　SUMAC Books,
　　RD#1 Box 197,
　　Troy, NY 12180
　　　　(518) 279-9638 eves

◆ **Signatures of the famous on documents, books, or photos** including fields of history, music, literature, science, fine arts, aviation, psychoanalysis, revolution, exploration, and other human endeavor. No sports, Hollywood, Nazi, or "loose" signatures on cards or cut off documents. Would like to know how you came to own the item.

David Lowenherz,
Lion Heart Autographs,
12 W. 37th St. # 1212,
New York, NY 10018
(212) 695-1310

◆ **Autographs of Presidents, literary figures, and early movie stars** on documents, letters, and signed photos. Also wants "vintage rock and roll," Beatles, and Marilyn Monroe. No contemporary movie folks. Photocopy.

William Linehan,
7 Summer St.,
Concord, NH 03301
(800) 346-9827

◆ **American and foreign autographs in all fields throughout Western history,** including politicians, Presidents, signers of the Declaration of Independence, music and the arts, literature, the military, and scientists. Will buy one or collections. This 20+ year veteran is not interested in unsigned documents of any sort.

Robert Batchelder,
1 West Butler Ave.,
Ambler, PA 19002
(215) 643-1430

◆ **Famous people's signatures on manuscript documents, land grants, maps, photographs,** and other early paper. Has particular interest in Southern and Civil War figures and in letters signed by James McHenry, Washington's Secretary of War.

Gordon McHenry,
Box 117,
Osprey, FL 33559
(813) 966-5563

◆ **Historic early American autographed documents,** letters, and ephemera in all fields. Also buys autographed books, maps, prints, stock certificates, and bonds.

Earl Moore,
Box 243,
Wynnewood, PA 19096
(215) 649-1549 anytime

◆ **Composers, musicians, and singers of classical music** including signed photographs, letters, musical notations, and manuscripts. No appraisals.

J.B. Muns,
Books & Fine Art,
1162 Shattuck Ave.,
Berkeley, CA 94707
(415) 525-2420

◆ **Composers, musicians, opera singers, and movie stars** from the late 1800's to the 1950's. Prefers to buy signed photos, letters with important content, or musical quotes. Among the many people they would like to find are Kathleen Ferrier, Conchita Supervia, Maria Galvany, Celestina Boninsegna, Fernando De Lucia, Guilio Grisi, and Marietti Alboni. "We are not interested in the autographs of current performers, but will pay very well for first class older items. Condition is very important. We request Xerox© copies and prefer to see the item in person, especially when large collections are involved." Will make offers for amateurs. Dealers price your goods.

Bill Safka & Arbe Bareis,
Box 886,
Forest Hills, NY 11375
(718) 897-7275

Posters

◆ **Old posters of all types.** This 30 year veteran dealer says "I'll pay top prices for any printed poster done before 1950, especially WWI and WWII, film, travel, theater, circus, and transportation (ocean liner, railroad, and air). Immediate answer if you include your phone number.
> George Theofiles,
> Miscellaneous Man,
> Box 1776,
> New Freedom, PA 17349
> > (717) 235-4766 day

◆ **Original posters 1890-1960** including, but not necessarily limited to, posters for airlines, air shows, automobiles, bars, books, cycles, circus, drinks, fashion, films, food, entertainers, medical subjects, restaurants, soap, sports, motorcycles, opera, theater, and travel. No reproductions. Provide photo, dimensions, and details of damage. NO OFFERS.
> John Campbell Fine Art,
> Box 22974,
> Nashville, TN 37202
> > (615) 242-6773

EDITOR'S NOTE: Poster people want to know the subject of your poster and its country of origin. Tell them what is pictured or make a sketch or photo. Give the dimensions and indicate the predominate colors.

Condition is critical (as with all paper goods) so indicate all trimming, holes, edge damage, soil, water stains, tears, fading, or anything and everything else wrong with your poster. If the poster is signed, tell the potential buyer.

◆ **Vintage posters 1880-1950, all countries and subjects,** especially U.S. posters from WWI and II and 1890-1910 American advertising. Army recruiting posters by Christy and Flagg from WWI bring $500-$1,500. No reproduction posters. Poster Master offers an illustrated $3 catalog of 800 posters for sale.
> George Dembo,
> The Poster Master,
> 9 Passaic Ave.,
> Chatham, NJ 07928
> > (201) 655-6505

◆ **Broadsides and posters prior to 1900.**
> Alfred Malpa,
> 9 Waterville Road,
> Farmington, CT 06032
> > (203) 677-4708

◆ **American posters of World War One.** No foreign, repros, or damaged. Give the main slogan on the poster, the size, the artist if known, and the condition.
> Ken Khuans,
> 155 Harbor #4812,
> Chicago, IL 60601
> > (312) 642-0554

◆ **Pre 1940 posters which advertise magazines.** Condition must be excellent.
> Leon Williams,
> 467 Portland Ave.,
> St. Paul, MN 55102
> > (612) 291-1639

Paper dolls

◆ **All types of paper dolls, cut or uncut, one or a collection as long as they're pre 1960.** Will buy commercial, magazine, or newspaper dolls, and especially likes to find Dionne Quintuplet, Jane Arden, and other celebrity paper dolls. She does purchase dolls with bruises, if they are scarce, but value is reduced. Does not want reproductions or dolls made after 1960. Sellers should list paper dolls by name, if possible, and indicate whether they are cut or not. Photocopies are helpful. Fran (a collector for 17 years) is available for slide shows about paper dolls.
   Fran Van Vynckt,
   433 Split Rail Court,
   Valparaiso, IN 46383
      (219) 462-7131

◆ **Paper dolls of all types.** Wants to buy antique dolls, 1910-1960 books, greeting card dolls, magazine dolls from adult or children's publications, newspaper comic strip dolls from the 1930's and 40's such as *Flash Gordon* and *Brenda Starr*. Celebrity or not. If neatly done, will buy cut dolls. When describing your doll, give the name, if possible, and include any writing on the front or back of the doll, the box, or the book.
   Madalaine Selfridge,
   Forgotten Magic,
   Box 413,
   Norco, CA 91760

◆ **Paper dolls and paper toys** of all kinds, cut or uncut, from boxed or book sets, newspapers, magazines, cereal boxes, etc. Especially wanted are paper dolls of real people.   For 23 years, Loraine has published *Celebrity Doll Journal*, a quarterly, available for $6.25/year. If you really want to sell your dolls, indicate names, dates, and quantity, and whether cut or not. Also indicate condition, mentioning bends, tears, missing parts, and tape. **ADVICE:** do not mend anything with tape. No need to photograph or photocopy any more than the doll (not the whole set). Will buy rare sets even when damaged, and buys some current items, but no Betsy McCall sheets.
   Loraine Burdick,
   Quest-Eridon Books,
   5 Court Place,
   Puyallup, WA 98372

◆ **All toys, figures, and buildings made of paper**, especially toys and models by Builtrite, but interested in any paper dolls and soldiers in good condition. In business for more than a decade, The Paper Soldier publishes a large and informative catalog for $4.
   Jonathan Newman,
   Paper Soldier,
   8 McIntosh Lane,
   Clifton Park, NY 12065
      (518) 371-5130

◆ **Dolly Dingle paper dolls.**
   Linda Woodward,
   6720 Crest Ave.,
   Riverside, CA 92503
      (714) 687-0868

**EDITOR'S NOTE: Make a photocopy of your dolls.
With few exceptions, collectors seldom want paper dolls
with bent arms and legs or with taped joints, although
dolls may be cut out and still be desirable.
Numbers on boxes or dolls are useful info savvy collectors.**

21
Places Around the World

Dr. Hyman's Prescription

Many people collect memorabilia from various towns, states, regions, or countries.

Check all paper ephemera, china, glass, souvenirs, advertising, photographs, letterheads, stock certificates, maps, postcards, prints, catalogs, etc. There is a good chance that someone is collecting the area from which they came.

People who collect souvenir china, and some other related collectibles, tend to read (and advertise in):

Antique Souvenir Collectors News. 16 page bimonthly magazine of ads and articles. It costs $11 per year from Box 562, Great Barrington, MA 01230.

If you are interested in selling things related to the history of the region in which you live, you might consider visiting the local historical society. Although local societies almost never purchase things for display, there are often tax advantages to donating your items.

If you prefer to sell, and you can't find a buyer in *I'll Buy That!,* you might pay a visit to local antique shops and see if there is a regional antiques paper covering your area. Small papers are found in all regions which may be of help in locating a buyer. These papers can often be obtained free at local antique shops.

tony hyman

The Northeast

◆ **Peaks Island, Maine.** Wants souvenirs, paper, china, spoons, other marked collectibles.
MacDermott's,
Island Ave.,
Peaks Island, ME, 04108

◆ **New Hampshire ephemera** from before 1900. Please price and photocopy.
Alf Jacobson,
Box 188,
New London, NH 03257

◆ **Hartford, Connecticut, material** including maps, photos, printed material, and books. Has a particular interest in the dedication of the Hartford Bridge in 1905.
J. Sullivan,
117 Olney Rd.,
Wethersfield, CT 06109

◆ **Great Barrington, Massachusetts, and Berkshire County souvenirs** including pictorial china, plates, pins, shakers, spoons, cups, postcards, photos., etc., especially souvenir china, 1905-1916. Names to look for: Housatonic, Van Deusenville, Risingdale, Egremont, North Egremont, Stockbridge, and Sheffield.
Gary Leveille,
Box 562,
Great Barrington, MA 01230

◆ **Cape Cod and vicinity.** Wants real photo postcards, better quality printed postcards, books and other paper ephemera. Pays your postage on returned items. Send for his wants list.
Art Ross,
Box 95,
Dennis, MA 02638
(508) 385-5480

◆ **Pennsylvania Turnpike memorabilia of all kinds.** What have you?
J.C. Keyser,
12 Springcreek,
Westerville, OH 43081

◆ **New Castle, Delaware.** Items of historic value, including books, photos, postcards, etc.
Mel Rosenthal,
507 S. Maryland Ave.,
Wilmington, DE 19804
(302) 322-8944

◆ **Delaware antiques, silver, and quality paper.** Describe and price.
John Reid,
Box 114CC,
Bear, DE 19701

◆ **Ocean Grove, New Jersey, memorabilia** including souvenirs, maps, photos, postcards, books, glass, porcelain, and anything else from this camp meeting seaside resort located south of Asbury Park. "Want everything including beach, hotels, auditorium, etc."
Norman Buckman,
Box 608,
Ocean Grove, NJ 07756
(800) 524-0632

◆ **Hoboken, New Jersey, memorabilia** including paper ephemera, books, photographs, postcards, prints, maps, articles, letterheads, labels, and any manufactured item with the word "Hoboken" molded or printed on the item. "We buy almost everything, no matter how trivial," including **personal reminiscences of early Hoboken residents** for inclusion in various local histories which they are writing. You have the Hans' permission to ship any pre 1949 Hoboken item on approval. They'll pay postage both ways.
Jim and Beverly Hans,
Box M-1220,
Hoboken, NJ 07030
(201) 653-7392

◆ **New Jersey's Morris Canal items.** All paper including stock certificates, postcards, bank notes, letterheads, specifications, plans, photographs, etc.
Roy Daniels,
333 Forest Hill Way,
Mountainside, NJ 07092

New York

◆ **Adirondack Mountains, New York, memorabilia** including all books, paper ephemera, photos, stereoviews, hotel brochures and registers, transportation timetables, manuscripts, maps, guide-books, diaries, postcards, sheet music and prints related to any mountain towns and lakes of New York. Lake George, Lake Placid, Old Forge, Keene Valley, Plattsburgh, Lake Luzerne, and the counties of Clinton, Essex, Herkimer, Lewis, Warren, St. Lawrence, Franklin, and Saratoga are among the many places which interest him.
    Breck Turner,
    With Pipe and Book,
    91 Main St.,
    Lake Placid, NY 12946
      (518) 523-9096

◆ **Manhattan, Brooklyn, Coney Island, Ellis Island.** Wants paper, photos, souvenirs of hotels, buildings, restaurants, etc.
    X. Shapiro,
    Box 525,
    Brooklyn, NY 11229

◆ **Manhattan (New York City).** Wants wide range of pre 1950 items including anything related to taxis, subways, elevated trains, buses, bridges, skyscrapers, hotels, department stores, restaurants, theaters, night clubs, ethnic neighborhoods, pushcarts, waterfronts, tugs, police, fire, utility workers. Buys original photos, posters, books, pamphlets, menus, billheads, signs, and other ephemera **except** postcards. Describe or photocopy.
    C. Meunier,
    498 Lakeview Ave.,
    Clifton, NJ 07011

◆ **Coney Island souvenirs** including Dreamland, Luna Park, or Steeplechase.
    John Belinsky,
    84 Day St.,
    Seymour, CT 06483
      (203) 888-2225

◆ **West Point memorabilia.** "I'll buy almost anything made of china or metal, but also want postcards featuring West Point. Send for my list of items I'm especially seeking."
    Pat Klein,
    5 Pasco Hill Road,
    Cromwell, CT 06416

◆ **Souvenir china and glass from Western New York state,** especially Rochester, LeRoy, and Batavia, but other cities as well.
    Burton Spiller,
    49 Palmerston Rd.,
    Rochester, NY 14618
      (716) 244-2229

◆ **Junction Canal between Elmira, NY, and Athens, PA (1856-1872).** Wants photos and all ephemera of any type about this canal. Also any branch extensions such as that along the Susquehanna River in Pennsylvania.
    F.C. Petrillo,
    95 Miner St.,
    Wilkes-Barre, PA 18702

```
Your Name
Your Address
```

**Plates, pamphlets, souvenirs...
Sell them all with an SASE**

The South

◆ **Tennessee.** Bookstore owner Snell says "I'll buy Tennessee history, authors, pamphlets, and maps. Also books and documents **by or about presidents Andrew Jackson, James K. Polk, and Andrew Johnson** and books by Tennessee authors such as Alfred Crabb, H.H. Kroll, and Samuel Cole Williams." Especially wants *Charles Egbert Craddock* by Edd Parks. No library discards.
William Snell,
3765 Hillsdale Drive NE,
Cleveland, TN 37312
(615) 472-8408

◆ **Richmond, Virginia.** Buyer wants any advertising in any medium that is related to Richmond. Wants signs, lithographs, trays, etc. Seeking better quality items.
R.W. Clifton,
Rt. #1 Box 296,
Mechanicsville, VA 23111
(804) 779-2702

◆ **Charleston, South Carolina memorabilia** including letters and envelopes, tokens and medals, maps, books, pamphlets, postcards, stock certificates and other fiscal paper. Also any South Carolina item having to do with the Confederacy.
Bob Karrer,
Box 6094,
Alexandria, VA 22306
(703) 360-5105 eves

◆ **Georgia, South Carolina, and Florida paper pre 1870** that is related to slavery, the Civil War, indentures, Kings's grants, state grants, wills, or historically interesting topics. Georgia is of particular interest and documents can bring from $100-$500 depending upon contents.
John Parks,
203 Tanglewood Rd.,
Savannah, GA 31419
(912) 925-6075

◆ **Augusta, Georgia.** Wants "interesting old items from and about Augusta."
Nesmith,
955 Clearwater Rd.,
No. Augusta, SC 29841

◆ **Great Smoky Mountains National Park** in NC and TN. "I'll buy guidebooks, maps, photos, brochures, pamphlets, and similar paper ephemera. Also souvenirs, especially plates and glassware associated with the Park. Also interested in similar items for the towns of **Gatlinburg and Townsend, TN, and Knoxville and Asheville, NC** which advertise the city's proximity to the Park. Not interested in accordion style color postcards, but do want real photo cards of the park. Pre 1970 items only." Photocopies appreciated.
Doug Redding,
9129 Turtle Dove Lane,
Gaithersburg, MD 20879
(301) 926-6158

◆ **Tennessee anything.**
Joe Copeland,
Box 221,
Oak Ridge, TN 37831

◆ **Eureka Springs, Arkansas, souvenirs** including plates, cups, spoons, etc. Also colorful or informative paper ephemera from the "resort capital of the Ozarks." If before 1930 and in fine condition, you may send what you have on approval.
Janis Watson, Bank of Eureka Springs,
Box 309,
Eureka Springs, AR 72632
(501) 253-8241

◆ **Eureka Springs, Arkansas, before 1920.** "Anything wanted from souvenirs to advertising, photographs to books, but I'll especially buy any information, maps, lawsuits, newspaper reports, etc., on the early land disputes in Eureka Springs. Also the Eureka Springs railroad. Also have strong interest in **Dr. Norman Baker's Cancer Hospital** in the Springs in the 1930's and will buy all ephemera related to it."
Steve Chyrchel,
Route #2 Box 362,
Eureka Springs, AR 72632
(501) 253-9244

◆ **New Orleans, Louisiana, and the Gulf Coast.** "I want to buy anything pre 1940 from New Orleans. I especially want *Newcomb* pottery, old **oil paintings** by local artists of the 20's and 30's like AJ Drysdale, Clarence Millet, and G.L. Viavont among others, **Mardi Gras** favors of all sorts, **prints and photos** of the people and events of New Orleans and surrounding areas, across the Lake, and the Gulf Coast."
Sanchez Galleries,
4730 Magazine St.,
New Orleans, LA 70115
(504) 524-0281

◆ **Florida historical paper and memorabilia,** especially items from Fort Jefferson, Florida.
Gordon McHenry,
Box 117,
Osprey, FL 34229
(813) 966-5563
FAX 813-966-5563

◆ **Orlando, Florida, memorabilia.**
Jerry Chicone,
Box 547636,
Orlando, FL 32854
(407) 298-5550

◆ **Paper ephemera about Florida** pre 1940. Items must be in good resalable condition. No fiction. Items *must* be priced by the seller.
G. Thomas Brasser,
Brasser's Used Books,
8701 Seminole Blvd.,
Seminole, FL 34642

◆ **Coral Gables, Florida, souvenirs and advertising,** especially related to land sales.
Sam LaRoue,
5980 SW 35th Street,
Miami, FL 33155

The Midwest

◆ **Put-In-Bay, Ohio, souvenirs** including glass, china, books, promotional material, spoons, etc., from before 1945. "Please price what you have to sell.
Jim Herbster,
5379 Harvest St.,
Dublin, OH 43107

◆ **Ohio memorabilia,** especially books, manuscripts, maps, and photographs, pre 1900. Particularly interested in local history prior to the Civil War, especially in the Akron area.
Frank Klein, The Bookseller,
521 West Exchange St.,
Akron, OH 44302
(216) 762-3101

◆ **Chicago souvenir china, glass, and pottery** from 1833-1933.
John Panek
1790 Hickory Knoll,
Deerfield, IL 60015

◆ **Small town Wisconsin memorabilia.** "I'll buy photos, brewery and other advertising, postcards, and other ephemera from Wisconsin towns other than Milwaukee. Buys pre 1950 items for resale. Likes **banks** made of iron, pot metal, or tin with small town names.
Robert DeLong,
Box 38,
Black River Falls, WI 54615
(715) 284-2135

◆ **Wisconsin china, glass, or *Red Wing* souvenir items,** especially from the towns of La Crosse, Fountain City, Waupaca, Reedsburg, and Kilbourn.
Dana Zimmerman,
1411 Briarcliff Drive,
Appleton, WI 54915

◆ **Michigan and the Great Lakes** ephemera and historically interesting paper goods of all types from that region.
   Jay Platt, West Side Book Shop,
   113 W. Liberty,
   Ann Arbor, MI 48103
      (313) 995-1891

◆ **Iowa souvenirs.** "All good items from all Iowa towns, especially Colfax, Clayton and Elkader."
   Abbie Bush,
   Elkader, IA 52043
      (319) 245-2128

◆ **Iowa souvenirs.** "Always interested in all Iowa souvenirs, especially china. Towns of Colfax, Ackley, and Sibley are particularly wanted."
   Mary Yohe,
   428 E. Howard,
   Colfax, IA 50554
      (515) 674-3138

◆ **Humboldt or Rutland, Iowa,** pictorial postcards and advertising from those two towns.
   Don Olson,
   Box 397,
   Humboldt, IA 50548

◆ **Rockford, Illinois, tokens, medals,** buttons, badges, ribbons, and other small flat collectibles. Also banks, early signs, coffee tins, bottles, etc. Loves to find larger items marked as being from Rockford. No paper or cardboard items.
   Rich Hartzog,
   Box 4143 BBL,
   Rockford, IL 61110
      (815) 226-0771

◆ **Waukesha, Wisconsin, memorabilia.** Waukesha was noted for its spring waters and a number of food products, so keep your eyes open for all sorts of things marked as being from Waukesha.
   W.E. Schwanz,
   45 W22339 Quinn Rd.,
   Waukesha, WI 53186

◆ **Dakota Territory, South Dakota, and the upper Midwest material** including all paper ephemera, advertising, postcards, letters, books, photographs, bottles, and small objects marked "DT," "Dakota Territory," "DAK" or "South Dakota." You may send approvals or a photocopy.
   Robert Kolbe,
   301 S. Duluth,
   Sioux Falls, SD 57105
      (605) 332-9662

◆ **North and South Dakota souvenirs,** especially glass, silver spoons, and postcards.
   Lyn Sheldon,
   312 Arizona Ave.,
   Watertown, SD 57201

The West

◆ **Paper ephemera about the Western U.S.** especially related to the military, early forts, ghost towns, Mormons, railroads, mining, banking, cowboys, Indians, lawmen, cattle, courts, and financial matters. Buys autographs of famous westerners, letters about the West, and almost all illustrated pre 1910 Western documents.
   Warren Anderson,
   American West Archives,
   Box 100,
   Cedar City, UT 84720
      (801) 373-6790

◆ **Dallas ephemera** pre 1915, including pamphlets, letters, documents, postcards, photos, and items related to **the Texas State Fair.** *The Artwork of Dallas* folio will bring $300 or more.
   Ron Pearson,
   10620 Creekmere Dr.,
   Dallas, TX 75218
      (214) 321-9717

◆ **Texas souvenirs,** especially china, spoons, postcards, stereoviews, and embossed bottles. Wants Austin, Fredericksburg, Llano, Comfort, New Braunfels, and Georgetown in particular.
   Dorothy Bauer,
   2730 South Congress,
   Austin, TX 78704

◆ **Texas maps and prints.**
   Shirley Sorenson,
   270 Sherri Dr.,
   Universal City, TX 78148
      (512) 658-2548

◆ **Yellowstone National Park souvenirs,** memorabilia, photographs, brochures, etc. Photocopy.
   Yellowstone Trading Post,
   27632 Saffron,
   Saugus, CA 91350

◆ **Montana and Yellowstone Park.** Wants photos, advertising, postcards, tokens, books, tack, brewery, and anything else Montana.
   Oxford Hotel,
   2411 Montana Ave.,
   Billings, MT 59101

◆ **Colorado mining district memorabilia,** 1859-1915, especially Cripple Creek and all other mining towns and camps and the railroads that served them. Wants photos, stereoviews, advertising, letterheads, billheads, brochures, pamphlets, mining papers, stock certificates, maps, souvenirs, and other small items marked with the name of one of these towns. Photos should be of mining, railroad, or downtown activities, not of people or scenery. Albums with numerous photos eagerly sought, as are City and Mining Directories and books on Colorado mining. No postcards or bottles. Does not want *anything* from the flatland Colorado towns like Denver, Colorado Springs, or Boulder, nor anything from state or national parks. Give info on back of photos.
   George Foott,
   6683 S. Yukon Way,
   Littleton, CO 80123
      (303) 979-8688

◆ **Colorado souvenirs** from before 1930 including real photo postcards, tokens, advertising, and the like. Interested in silks, ribbons, and awards from **fairs and rodeos** anywhere in Colorado.
   Edward Marriott,
   9191 East Oxford Dr.,
   Denver, CO 80237

◆ **Nevada ephemera** including mounted photos, pre 1930 postcards, law badges, bottles, railroad ephemera, fire department ephemera, cowboy relics, maps, stocks, Indian artifacts, posters, advertising, mining, military.... if it's marked "Nev." Ron is interested.
   Ron Bommarito,
   Box 114,
   Genoa, NV 89411
      (702) 782-3893

◆ **Las Vegas, Nevada, souvenirs and memorabilia** including postcards, books, maps, magazines, papers, chips, checks, tokens, playing cards, brochures, plates, and souvenirs.
 D. Durnin,
 Box 29381,
 Brooklyn Center, MN 55429
  (612) 537-1527

◆ **Las Vegas, Nevada souvenirs and memorabilia** from before 1960. Buys gambling tokens and chips, casino playing cards, match covers, postcards, business directories, showroom programs, magazines with stories about Las Vegas history, and photos of interiors of casinos, banks, hotels, motels, and restaurants.
 Marc Weiser,
 8615 Aura Ave.,
 Northridge, CA 91324
  (818) 885-7125

◆ **Nevada and Death Valley ephemera** including books, newspapers, magazines, diaries, letters, maps, promotional brochures, "and anything else printed or written on paper." Also stereoviews, merchant tokens, dog tags, hunting licenses, photographs, postcards, stock certificates, documents and what have you. He requests prices but will make offers.
 Gil Schmidtmann,
 Route 1, Box 371,
 Mentone, CA 92359
  (714) 794-1211

◆ **All Nevada memorabilia from before 1950** is wanted but especially that relating to banks and finance including bank bags, letterheads, documents, stocks, checks, scrip. Also photos, maps, postcards, stationery, tokens, and other ephemera from or about Nevada, including items related to prostitution.
 Douglas McDonald,
 Box 20443,
 Reno, NV 89515

◆ **Indian Territory.** Wants china, glass, or metal marked "IT."
 Claudine Lynch,
 4512 Grandad Drive,
 Yorba Linda, CA 92686

◆ **Idaho, Montana, and Washington items** including trade tokens, postcards, small town postmarks, letterheads, calendars, buttons, ribbons, wooden nickels, stocks, match holders, calendar plates, and other advertising china. Paying $1-$3 each for postcards with postmarks from discontinued post offices. Pays $2-10 for cards of small town scenes he can use. Nothing after 1930.
 Mike Fritz,
 1550 Stevens St.,
 Rathdrum, ID 83858
  (208) 687-0159

◆ **Yakima, Washington, memorabilia.** "Mainly, I want real photo postcards of Yakima and North Yakima, but I also buy photographs and other ephemera including newspapers, phone books, directories, souvenirs, and promotional booklets that are before 1950. I like Yakima H.S. items from the 1930's and photo postcards taken by Frank Lanternman.
 Ron Ott,
 10 N. 45th Ave.,
 Yakima, WA 98908
  (509) 965-3385

◆ **Washington Territory and Vashon/Maury Island material.**
 Reed Fitzpatrick, The Paper Scout,
 Box 369,
 Vashon, WA 98070
  (206) 463-3900

◆ **San Francisco Bay area historical ephemera** pre 1910, especially related to the 1906 quake. Photos, diaries, letters, family mementos, and the like are wanted with emphasis on the unusual. Ron has particular interest in items associated with schools and education in S.F. prior to 1906. Also meal tickets and other items related to life in relief camps immediately after the disaster. **No newspapers or postcards.** Although these items are for his personal collection, Ron is Chairman of the San Francisco History Association and can also accept tax deductible gifts related to San Francisco from any time period.
 Ron Ross,
 620 Church St.,
 San Francisco, CA 94114
  (415) 626-3666 eves

◆ **San Bernardino, California, items** from buildings, fairs, and resorts. Wants ceramic souvenirs including cups, plates, sterling silver spoons, badges, ribbons, pins, etc. Particularly interested in items associated with the 1903 Street Fair, 1908 Festival of the Arrowhead, 1910 Centennial, and the National Orange Show, from 1911 to 1920.
   Gary Crabtree,
   Box 3843,
   San Bernardino, CA 92413
      (714) 862-8534

◆ **Santa Catalina Island and Avalon** souvenirs, postcards, advertising items. Please price.
   Sandra Putnam,
   Box 705,
   Avalon, CA 90704

◆ **San Gabriel Valley, CA, items**. Wants older, pre 1930 items from any San Gabriel Valley town, Arcadia, Temple City, El Monte, San Gabriel, Baldwin Park, Rosemead, Pasadena, Covina, San Marino, Monrovia, Duarte, Azusa, etc. Also wants anything related to **Emperor Norton** and **Lucky Baldwin**. Suggests you ship your items to him via UPS (650 W. Duarte, #309) for offer.
   SC Coin & Stamp Co.,
   Drawer 3069,
   Arcadia, CA 91006
      (800) 367-0779

◆ **San Diego, California, memorabilia** including postcards, pamphlets, and photos.
   Ralph Bowman,
   5349 Wheaton Street,
   La Mesa, CA 92042
      (619) 462-6268

◆ **Alaskan memorabilia** including postcards, trade cards, early postal cancellations, saloon and other tokens of metal or cardboard, advertising, trade beads, labels, letterheads, and photographs. Especially items from pre 1875 Sitka or New Archangel. Buys for resale. Nothing damaged or after 1950. Approvals welcome.
   W.E. Nickell,
   102 People's Wharf,
   Juneau, AK 99801
      (907) 586-1733

◆ **Alaskan memorabilia.** "I'll buy nearly anything old about Alaska, the Yukon, or the Polar Region including books, maps, photographs, letters, souvenirs, china, spoons, and miscellaneous ephemera. One of my specialties is Alaskan postcards around 1910. I don't buy items newer than 1945, and buy for resale, so have no use for creased, dirty, or damaged items."
   Richard Wood, Alaska Heritage Books,
   Box 22165,
   Juneau, AK 99802
      (907) 586-6748

◆ **Hawaiian and South Seas ephemera.** Wants books, printed items, paintings, prints, photos, postcards, and other memorabilia from Hawaii, as long as it's pre 1920. Send insured.
   Bernie Berman,
   755 Isenberg St., #305,
   Honolulu, HI 96826

◆ **Virgin Islands (Danish West Indies) ephemera.** Items from U.S. or British Virgin Islands are wanted including maps, prints, postcards, and anything else.
   Harlan Hutchins,
   Box 4156,
   Christianasted, St. Croix,
   U.S. Virgin Islands

◆ **Puerto Rico.** Wants pre 1930 books, postcards, and other memorabilia of Puerto Rico. Please price and describe in your first letter.
   Frank Garcia,
   8963 SW 34th St.,
   Miami, FL 33165

◆ **Puerto Rico ephemera.** Wants maps, prints, postcards, and other small ephemera.
   Harlan Hutchins,
   Box 4156,
   Christianasted, St. Croix,
   U.S. Virgin Islands

Foreign Places

◆ **Canadian items:** calendars, stock certificates, bank notes, old letters in original envelopes, fancy letterheads, anything to do with Canadian railways, merchants' tokens from Western Canada, Canadian military or law enforcement, and postcards of BC, Yukon, NWT, Alberta, Saskatchewan, and Newfoundland. Nothing after 1950, please. No road maps, tourist brochures, and postcards of tourist attractions or scenery. Prefers that items be sent on approval or photocopied.
Michael Rice,
Box 286,
Saanichton, BC V0S 1M0,
CANADA
    (604) 652-9047 eves

◆ **Canada, the Arctic, and the Klondike.** All information wanted including maps, paper ephemera, prints, government documents, and photographs about Canadian immigration, travel, history, fur trade, mountaineering, Indians and Eskimos. NO OFFERS
Tom Williams,
Box 4126, Station C,
Calgary, Alberta T2T 5M9,
CANADA
    (403) 264-0184

◆ **Canadian postcards, stereoviews, and other ephemera** especially from Province of Ontario. Mainly interested in small town views, events, railroad stations, and transportation. No scenics or items after 1950. "A photocopy of the item is almost essential" to accompany your complete description. Also wants **Canadian made woodworking planes.**
Peter Cox,
Box 1655,
Espanola, Ontario P0P 1C0
    (705) 869-2441 winter
    (705) 859-2410 summer

◆ **Canadian pictorial souvenir china and glassware.** Street scenes are his favorite. Also buys postcards and political buttons from Canada.
Phil Groves,
RR #2,
Winchester, Ontario K0C 2K0
CANADA

◆ **Panama Canal Zone and the Isthmus of Panama memorabilia** including postcards, letters, stamped envelopes, scrapbooks, tokens, medals, maps, coins, stamps, and everything else including souvenirs. Especially likes pre 1915 picture postcards with cancellations from obscure Panama post offices. "I really will look at, and probably offer to buy, anything Isthmus." Bob has been editor of the journal for Isthmus collectors since 1976.
Bob Karrer,
Box 6094,
Alexandria, VA 22306
    (703) 360-5105

◆ **Pre 1960 Cuban memorabilia** including coins, stamps, money, historical documents, postcards, souvenir spoons, maps, stocks and bonds, lottery tickets, cigar bands, military decorations and insignia, "or any other collectible item including those related to the Spanish domination of the Island." He'll pay from $80-$400 for the 10, 20 and 50 peso bank notes of 1869. There is a 1916 coin and a 1944 banknote each worth more than $50,000, so it could pay you to look.
Manuel Alvarez,
1735 SW 8th St.,
Miami, FL 33135
    (305) 649-1176

◆ **Brazil.** Books, photos, and paper ephemera from the colonial period through 1945. Especially interested in travel and exploration books with early information about Rio de Janeiro and/or the Amazon. Also wants letters and diaries of military personnel who served in Brazil during WWII or in the Joint Brazil-US Military Commission. Material may be in any language. Please include your telephone number.

Lee Harrer,
1908 Seagull Drive,
Clearwater, FL 34624
(813) 536-4029 evenings

◆ **Philippine Islands.** "I'll buy postcards, photos, books, magazines, maps, and other paper items, especially real photo postcards from Manila or elsewhere in the Philippines. I don't want coins, stamps, paper money, or books on the Spanish American War. The postcard publisher's name is very helpful."

Michael Price,
Box 7071,
Ann Arbor, MI 48107

◆ **Australia and Antarctica items from before 1920,** including prints, maps, photographs, ship's logs, scholarly ethnographic studies, novels, travel books, children's books, postcards and paper ephemera. No interest in items from New Zealand or the Maori.

David Lilburne,
Antipodean Books, Box 189,
Cold Spring, NY 10516
(914) 424-3867

◆ **Antarctic and Arctic ephemera** especially books but also diaries, posters, photographs, letters, pamphlets, and *Aurora Austrailis*, the Antarctic newspaper 1907-09.

Jay Platt,
West Side Book Shop,
113 W. Liberty,
Ann Arbor, MI 48103
(313) 995-1891 days

◆ **Greenland, Pitcairn Island, and Hudson's Bay ephemera** especially tokens, but other small items, especially before 1930 are likely to be of interest.

Rich Hartzog, World Exonumia,
Box 4143 BBL,
Rockford, IL 61110
(815) 226-0771

◆ **Micronesia, Polynesia, and New Guinea ethnographic materials,** masks, ceremonial bowls, and the like. Also maps, mariner's charts, voyage books, and ship's logs from vessels traveling in that region, in any language. Some interest in scrimshaw. No items from New Zealand or the Maori.

David Lilburne, Antipodean Books,
Box 189,
Cold Spring, NY 10516
(914) 424-3867

◆ **Russian and Slovakian memorabilia** such as art, sculpture, icons, books, photographs, maps, and letters. Has particular interest in "Cossackiana," including Cossack swords and military insignia. **Does not want Soviet items,** only "Old Russia" before 1917. Buys only items in good condition. Xerox© is appreciated.

Igor G. Kozak,
Box 8867,
Washington, DC 20003
(301) 236-5966

◆ **Imperial Russian ephemera** whether civil, religious, or military. "Send photo or Xerox© copy along with the price you want, please."

Art Co.,
Box 417882,
Sacramento, CA 95841
(916) 386-8147

22
Postcards & Photographs

Dr. Hyman's Prescription

Collecting postcards is an immensely popular hobby. Millions of different cards exist, and values of most are very low. Although a few European artist-signed cards sell in excess of $100, most cards sell from 2¢ to $3.

Cards with real photos, rather than printed images, are the most sought after, selling for $3 to $15, depending upon the image. If you have real photo cards, you will almost certainly find a buyer in *I'll Buy That!*

Grading standards for postcards are:

Mint: A perfect card, unused and unmarked;

Excellent: No bends, creases, or rounded corners. May be used, but must be written and postmarked only on the address side. Picture must be unmarked.

Very good: Cards with very slightly rounded corners or with an almost undetectable crease or bend that does not detract from the appearance of the picture side. Must have writing or postal marking only on the address side.

Average: Cards with noticeably blunt or rounded corners or with slight but visible bends or creases.

Poor: Cards that show soil, creases, or stains. Any card with cancellation or writing on the picture side. Only *very* rare cards are bought or sold in this condition.

Dealers don't want cards in poor or average condition. If you have a collection of cards to sell, buyers will insist on inspecting the cards prior to purchase, since condition is so important in determining value.

Single topical cards can be sold easily by sending photocopies.

tony hyman

Postcards

◆ **Postcard collections, pre 1930,** especially American street views, disasters, railroad stations, fire departments, and diners. He also buys cards depicting foreign royalty, expositions, snowmen, full length Santas, and pre-jet commercial aircraft. Does not want foreign views, scenery, parks, woods, mountains, lakes, and flowers. Does not want damaged cards or those which have been pasted in albums. "If your cards are not for sale, or if my offer is not accepted, **I will appraise your cards at a cost of only one postcard of my choice for each 100 cards I appraise.**" Cards must be shipped for inspection for purchase or appraisal. John runs auctions, postcard shows, and heads the Postcard History Society. He can supply you with many interesting free or low cost items regarding postcard collecting. For more information send a Self Addressed Stamped Envelope for his "Postcard Opportunity" sheet.
John McClintock,
Box 1765,
Manassas, VA 22110
(703) 368-2757 eves

◆ **Pre 1950 postcards** are sought by this West Coast dealer.
Mike Rasmussen,
Box 726,
Marina, CA 93933
(408) 475-9148

◆ **Postcard albums and collections,** the older the better, in *very good condition only.* Interested in all topics, but does not want damaged cards. Joan conducts mail auctions and sells on approval.
Wants to know the number of cards, condition, types of subjects. Collector for nearly 50 years!
Jo Ann Van Scotter,
208 E. Lincoln St.,
Mt. Morris, IL 61054
(815) 734-6971

◆ **Pre 1950 postcards worldwide,** used or unused, from any country, but especially from the U.S. and Canada. Wants street scenes, buildings, occupationals, sports, transportation, and people. **Doesn't want** water, forests, mountains, deserts, trees, etc. Also buys some pictorial "greetings." Pays 25¢ to $5.00 for most postcards, but a few European cards drawn or painted by famous illustrators can bring $100 up. No quantity too large. Prompt payment if you send approvals, and unwanted cards are returned. All payment is in the currency of the seller.
Neil Hayne,
Box 220,
Bath, Ontario K0H 1G0,
CANADA
(613) 352-7456

◆ **All pre 1950 postcards, American and foreign,** all subjects, used or unused. "I'll pay competitive prices for better single cards or will buy collections, box lots, accumulations, estates, etc."
Sheldon Dobres,
4 Calypso Court,
Baltimore, MD 21209
(301) 486-6569

◆ **Various postcards from the 1920-1950 era.**
(1) Picturing **art deco or art moderne buildings** typical of those times, such as diners and gas stations;
(2) **New York World's Fair;**
(3) **Texas Centennial** of 1936;
(4) Houston, Texas;
(5) **Advertising products, services, and merchandise.**
Primarily wants "linen" cards with a slightly textured surface. Please photocopy.
Edy Chandler,
Box 20664,
Houston, TX 77225
(713) 531-9615 eves

◆ **Postcards made of macerated (ground up) U.S. currency.**
Donald Gorlick,
Box 24541,
Seattle, WA 98124

EDITOR'S NOTE: TYPES OF POSTCARDS

Early cards: Begin in mid 1870's, but not pictorial until 1893. Between 1898-1901 they are called SOUVENIR CARDS.

Postcards: Private printers allowed to use "POSTCARD." Real photo cards begin. Writing not allowed on address side. 1901-07.

Divided back cards: Message written on the left side and address on the right. Real photo, greetings, and ads. 1907-14.

White border cards: White border around picture. 1915-30.

Linen cards: Linen grained surface, with bright inks. 1930-45.

Chrome cards: Brightly colored, slick surface cards. After 1940.

◆ Cards showing automobiles, especially convertibles, trucks, used car lots, dealer show rooms, and any card showing a truck or car with clearly readable advertising on the side of it, any era, from anywhere in the world. Also "better grade" **commercial airline cards** showing propellor-driven planes. Only cards issued as advertising by the airlines are wanted. Most cards are purchased for resale, although many are for Jay's private collection. Jay recently released *The American Automobile Dealership,* illustrated with 340 postcards ($25 from the author).
Jay Ketelle,
3721 Farwell,
Amarillo, TX 79109
(806) 355-3456

◆ **Christmas, Easter, and Halloween hold-to-light cards.**
David Speck,
35 Franklin Street,
Auburn, NY 13021
(315) 253-8495 days   252-8566 eves

◆ Cards depicting or related to any war, 1885-1985. Also **small town mainstreets** which are identified.
Robert DeLong,
Box 38,
Black River Falls, WI 54615
(715) 284-2135

◆ Cards advertising any product or service. "I'll buy milk, medicine, automobiles, boats, shoes, musical instruments, tourist attractions, bands and singing groups, farm products, home items, clothing, entertainment, trains, auto dealerships, restaurants, highways, sporting events, races; the list is endless. I'll buy one card or a box full."
Jay Ketelle,
3721 Farwell,
Amarillo, TX 79109
(806) 355-3456

◆ Cards depicting trolley cars or depots. He doesn't care whether they're used or not, just as long as they are from before 1940 and identify the trolley. No NYC cards are wanted, but lots of other trolley and electric railway cards are, especially small towns.
William Reed Gordon,
232 Beresford Rd.,
Rochester, NY 14610

◆ Postcards illustrated with original drawings by the sender. Wants pen and ink or pencil sketches more than more elaborate paintings.
Linda Franklin,
Box 383 Murray Hill Station,
New York, NY 10156
(804) 973-3238

Dr. Hyman's Prescription

There is a big demand for photographs.

Besides people who collect photos, they are also sought by folks who collect items from a particular geographic area. Photos are also sought by historians who want to learn more about an industry or era.

Photos should be photocopied. Describe the condition of the photo and its mat. Note banged corners, stains, and the like. If the photo is faded, make certain you indicate that fact.

When reading entries in this chapter you will run across reference to various types of photographs. The glossary on page 261 will help you understand them and to describe photographs of your own.

If you find round photos with square mounts, you may have found pictures taken by one of the first *Kodaks*. For that reason, they are an interesting curiosity as they do not exist in great numbers.

Stereoviews are growing in popularity every year. Of particular interest are earlier, larger, cards with pictures of famous events, disasters, important people, and industrial processes, especially related to mining, oil, or transportation. Early stereo cards have colored mounts and were originally flat. After years of being stored with later curved cards, they too are often curved. Don't try to flatten them with pressure as you may crack the photographic emulsion.

tony hyman

Photographs

Pre 1915 photographs including tintypes, Daguerreotypes, ambrotypes, cartes d'visite, cabinet photos, albumen prints, stereocards, silver prints, platinum prints, cyanotypes, and photo albums. Fine subjects and condition only. **No ordinary portraits,** photo equipment, or 20th century books on photography. Wants to see a photocopy of both sides of your photo.
Richard Rosenthal,
4718 Springfield Ave.,
Philadelphia, PA 19143
(215) 726-5493

◆ **Rare old photographs,** especially those by important photographers. Also pre 1910 photo ephemera including manuals and books.
Ivan Gilbert,
Miran Arts & Books,
2824 Elm Ave.,
Columbus, OH 43209
(614) 236-0002

◆ **Autographed photos of important people** from any period. "I am especially interested in less common individuals, of whom there are many, so don't hesitate to phone me or send a Xerox©."
Barry Hoffman,
745 Boylston St.,
Boston, MA 02116
(617) 267-9000

◆ **Rare old photographs by American or European "name" photographers,** featuring famous people, historic events, the military, theatrical subjects, Indians, or early travel. Especially stereoviews, Daguerreotypes, and **19th century photo illustrated books.** This important photo gallery owner would appreciate your mentioning the color of any photos and matts.
Janet Lehr,
Box 617 Gracie Square Station,
New York, NY 10028
(212) 288-6234

EDITOR'S NOTE: If you have photos of events, business, industry, sports, or fraternal organizations, specialists in that subject are your best buyers. You are likely to get more for a photo of a cigar factory, for example, from an expert on cigars.

It is impossible to index every possible photo buyer. It could be worth $$$ in your pocket to read the chapter dealing with the subject matter of your photo.

◆ **Photos, and photographic literature.** Wants to buy Daguerreotypes, ambrotypes, tintypes, stereoscopic views, and interesting photos from any era in any process. Would love to find photos of photographers at work. Buys complete unpicked photo albums, specializing in Pittsburgh and Allegheny County, Pennsylvania. Wants **early cameras** and photographic accessories and **literature**.
Nicholas Graver,
276 Brooklawn Drive,
Rochester, NY 14618
(716) 244-4818

◆ **Original photos of Lincoln.** "I'll buy photos of Lincoln taken from life and printed before 1866, but will also purchase the Ayers photos of Lincoln printed in the 1880's and 1890's. I'll also buy photos of Lincoln look-alikes. I don't want photos of prints, statues, or Abe's house. Send a photocopy of what you have. Serious sellers only, please."
Stuart Schneider,
Box 64,
Teaneck, NJ 07666
(201) 261-1983

◆ **Stereoview cards,** particularly older Western scenes, transportation, mining, Mt. Lowe, fires, high wheel bicycles, famous people, Civil War, and early California. "However, I buy most common stereos, too," presumably for a lot less. He particularly wants **stereos of Lincoln** published while Lincoln was alive. If you want to sell your cards, Chuck wants to know the subject of the card quite specifically, an accurate description of condition, the publisher. If you have a price you want, say so. He does not want *printed* cards, in color or black and white.

> Chuck Reincke,
> 2141 Sweet Briar Rd.,
> Tustin, CA 92680
> (714) 832-8563 eves

◆ **Bathing beauties and nudie photos,** pre WWI.

> Steve DeGenaro,
> Box 5662,
> Youngstown, OH 44504
> (216) 759-7151 eves

◆ **Photographs and engravings of famous people** in all walks of life. Will consider items loose or in books. Please photocopy.

> Kenneth Rendell,
> 154 Wells Ave.,
> Newton, MA 02159
> (800) 447-1007

◆ **Stereoviews showing the development of the early west, 1860-1900** including expeditions, **railroad construction**, freighting through the Sierras, maritime scenes, **Indian portraits** and culture, **mining, logging,** and **early small town scenes** as well as cosmopolitan **San Francisco.** Particular interest in Custer, Teddy Roosevelt, Mark Twain, Bret Harte, John Sutter, artist Albert Bierstadt, and all early photographers and their equipment. The latter will bring "hundreds of dollars" in excellent condition. Also wants paper ephemeral advertising from early western photographers. Not interested in faded views or those with damaged mounts. No lithographed views, only real photos in excellent condition.

> Jim Crain,
> 131 Bennington St.,
> San Francisco, CA 94110
> (415) 648-1092 eves

◆ **Pre 1875 stereoviews, American or foreign.** Wants only flat cards with square corners but is "not interested in views on curved mounts." Particularly interested in views of Paris from the 1850's and studio made genre scenes from France and England from the 1850's and 60's. Also wants views of big city life and the Western US before 1880. All views "must be pristine, or of such unusual interest to warrant less than pristine condition." This 20 year veteran asks you to specify the color of the mount and give all information printed or written on the face or back.

> Fred Pajerski,
> 225 W 25th Street, #4K,
> New York, NY 10001
> (212) 255-6501

◆ **Glass or tissue stereoviews.** Also buys older and more interesting card views.

> T.K. Treadwell, Tower House,
> 4201 Nagle Rd.,
> Bryan, TX 77801
> (409) 846-0209

◆ **Stereoviews.** Buys most U.S. black and white views as well as other interesting pre 1920 photos. Very large, well-known sports paper dealer who buys for resale.

> Bill Colby,
> Kenrich Co.,
> Box 248 T,
> Temple City, CA 91780
> (818) 286-3888

◆ **Bizarre photos,** such as freaks, dwarfs, lynchings, slaves, public punishment, and what have you? Especially interested in photos of **death, especially post-mortem photos, but also mourning photos, executions, lynchings, embalming and medical photos with doctors and cadavers.** Wants all types of photos from Daguerreotypes to 1940. Will take later photos if someone famous. Likes to find old prints of the family gathered around the deceased. Worth from $5 to as much as $75-$100 for the very early and unusual.

> Steve DeGenaro,
> Box 5662,
> Youngstown, OH 44504
> (216) 759-7151 eves

◆ **Photos of very old people.** If you can provide the name of the person at birth as well as the date and place of birth, your photo of great grandma may have a buyer. You must set price.
Ms. Dormire,
PO Box 2145,
Carlsbad, CA 92008

◆ **Houses, people in front of houses, houses under construction.** Men posed with tools, from steam shovels to saws.
Linda Campbell Franklin,
Box 383 Murray Hill Station,
New York, NY 10156

◆ **Photos in memorial matts** These are ordinary portraits mounted in lithographed memorial matts after the person died. Memorial matts are characterized by printed and/or embossed angels, doves, Gates of Heaven, etc., and mottoes like "Free at last."
Steve DeGenaro,
Box 5662,
Youngstown, OH 44504
(216) 759-7151 eves

EDITOR'S NOTE: A PHOTO GLOSSARY

Daguerreotypes: **Earliest photo process, 1839-1854, recognizable by its silvery image on glass. Often the leather and early thermoplastic cases are worth far more than the photo. Outdoor and city views are rare. Large "Dags" can be very valuable. Do not try to clean them.**

Ambrotypes: **Photos on a glass negative backed with dark paper to make a positive image.**

Albumen photograph: **Paper prints using egg albumen in preparation of the image surface. Most pre 1890 paper photos.**

Tintypes: **Cheap popular portraits, 1858-1910, printed on sheets of blackened tin. Also called ferrotypes.**

Stereoviews: **Card containing two shots of the same subject to give a 3-D effect when seen through a viewer. Older views are larger, flat, and have colored mounts. Later views have curved grey mounts. Newest, and almost worthless, are colored printed stereoviews.**

Carte de visites: **Photos on card stock measuring 2.5" x 4" popular between 1860-1890. Watch for revenue stamps on the back of Civil War era cards. A few valuable ones exist.**

Cabinet cards: **Photos on 4" x 7" cards, usually with the photographer's name at the bottom.**

23
Magazines &
Newspapers

Dr. Hyman's Prescription

People buy old magazines for many reasons.

Some buy covers or illustrations by Norman Rockwell, the Leyendecker brothers, Rockwell Kent, and other famous illustrators. A few buy woodcuts and engravings by lesser known artists but with interesting subjects.

Historians and researchers seek industry trade magazines and others with early articles about their specialty. The trade magazines of nearly every profession can find a market, as can automobile magazines. Advertising from popular magazines is also salable, but the price per ad is usually so low that it doesn't pay the average person to sell them individually. Leave that to the paper dealers.

Science fiction, mystery, and other genre magazines have their fans.

Give the name and date of the magazines and note *all* creases, tears, writing, mailing stickers, or anything else which affects the cover or contents. If you have many issues, list them, counting only those with covers intact and no pictures removed. Give a general statement of condition.

If you are offering the magazines to someone because of an article contained in it, give the name and date of the magazine, name of the article, the author, and the number of illustrations.

Ship magazines by "Special 4th Class Book Rate," by far the cheapest way to ship books and magazines.

tony hyman

Magazines

◆ **Volume 1, Number 1, first issue magazines,** newspapers, comic books, or miscellaneous publications including news-letters, catalogs, fan publications, etc. Also buys pre-publication issues, proofs, dummies, and premier issues. "I buy only for my own collection but will buy desirable duplicates, and when I don't buy, I will try to help the seller find someone else who might." No national publications after 1970, although small regional or special interest magazines may be of interest.
Stan Gold,
7042 Dartbrook,
Dallas, TX 75240
(214) 239-8621

◆ **First issue and dummy issue magazines.** Seeking well known titles from before 1930. All should be in fine condition with especially clean covers and contents intact.
Leon Williams,
467 Portland Ave.,
St. Paul, MN 55102
(612) 291-1639

◆ **Most pre-1950 magazines in quantity.** "We will travel if you have a truckload." Also most newer fashion, movie, and quality photography magazines. Give quantity per title and a description, and "we will contact you immediately." **Does not want** *National Geographic* after 1910, *Reader's Digest* after 1930, *Life* after 1936, *Arizona Highways* after 1940, or *American Heritage* hardcover editions. One of the country's largest dealers in magazines.
The Antiquarian Bookstore,
1070 Lafayette Rd.,
Portsmouth, NH 03801
(603) 436-7250

◆ **Illustrated magazines, 1895-1950** including women's, children's, movie, pulps, theater, farm, motorcycle, and many more. Titles such as *Colliers, Esquire, Vogue, Saturday Evening Post, Vanity Fair, American* and others are wanted. "I am willing to consider any pre 1960 magazines you have for sale. Write!" Dennis is author of inexpensive price guides to magazines.
Dennis C. Jackson,
Box 1958,
Sequim, WA 98382

◆ **Old magazines with beautiful covers and illustrations.** "I'm primarily interested in the period from 1910 to 1930, but will buy a few earlier or later. The quality and condition of the artistic illustrations are the key. Mucha is a favorite, but the work of many other illustrators is sought. Titles that are the most interest are *Collier's* (1900-1910), *Delineator* (1910-1924), *Harper's Bazaar* (1900-1960), *Hearst's* (1912-1930), *Inland Printer* (1890-1910), *Ladies Home Journal* (1900-1930), *Ladies World* (1912-1918), *Metropolitan* (1912-1924), *Vanity Fair* (1913-1936), *Vogue* (1900-1960), *Pictorial Review* (1910-1924), and movie magazines 1900-1945). I don't buy much after 1940, and nothing less than excellent condition. I always prefer to buy whole stacks, not single issues."
Leon Williams,
467 Portland Ave.,
St. Paul, MN 55102
(612) 291-1639

◆ **20th century women's fashion magazines,** including *Harpers Bazaar* 1915-40, *Vogue* 1900-1940, *Vanity Fair* pre 1940, **and** *The Theater* 1900-30.
Larry Coleman,
26 W. 10th Street, #307,
St. Paul, MN 55102
(612) 291-0656

◆ **Fashion magazines** including *Harpers Bazaar, Delineator,* and others from 1890-1910 only. Also buys pictures, postcards, and catalogs showing women's fashions of that period.
Cheryl Abel,
103 Jacqueline Ave.,
Delran, NJ 08075

◆ **Magazines about fashion, costume, textiles**, sewing, beading, and the like. Especially wants pre 1870 fashion magazines like *Godey's Lady's* and others. NO OFFERS.
  Lois Mueller, Wooden Porch,
  Rte 1, Box 262,
  Middlebourne, WV, 26149

◆ **Women's fashion magazines before 1900** including *Delineator, Godey's, Peterson's, Grahams, Lady's Friend*, and others. Please price what you offer.
  Annie Nalewak, Shop 4,
  5515 So. Loop, East Crestmont,
  Houston, TX 77033

◆ **Women's magazines.** "I'll buy women's magazines such as *Good Housekeeping, McCalls, Better Homes & Gardens*, and *Ladies Home Journal*. I especially want issues from the 1930's and 40's but will consider issues from 1900-1950."
  Susan Cox,
  800 Murray Dr.,
  El Cajon, CA 92020

◆ **Men's adventure magazines.** Buys *Male, Stag, Safari, Climax, Exotic Adventures* and most others from 1940's through 1965 in any quantity as long as they are in nice condition. Digest size magazines are also bought. Price or describe condition in detail for offer.
  Stanley Slupczynski,
  31700 Concord #G,
  Madison Heights, MI 48071

◆ **Men's outdoor magazines** including *Field & Stream, Outdoor Life* pre 1920, and *Sports Afield* before 1932.
  Thomas McKinnon,
  Box 86,
  Wagram, NC 28396

◆ **Detective and mystery pulp magazines** such as *Black Mask, Dime Detective*, and others. West can be contacted by modem as all stock is computerized.
  Richard West,
  Box 406,
  Elm Grove, WI 53122
  (414) 786-8420

◆ **Pulp magazines of the 1930's** such as *Spider, G-8, Operator 5, The Shadow, Doc Savage, Black Mask*, and the like.
  Claude Held,
  Box 515,
  Buffalo, NY 14225

◆ **Pulp magazines**, pre 1950, such as *The Shadow, Doc Savage, The Spider, G-8*, in genres of aviation, science fiction, spicy, horror, etc.
  Ken Mitchell,
  710 Concacher Dr.,
  Willowdale, Ontario M2M 3N6,
  CANADA

◆ *Esquire* **magazines and calendars** from the 1930's and 40's.
  Leonard D. Dick,
  Box 3711,
  Bartlesville, OK 74006

◆ **American humor magazines and newspapers**, 1765 to date. Comic material and ephemera (but *not* comic books). Humorous periodicals included satire, cartoons, or comic sketches in a variety of formats, mostly to a popular audience. Does not want recent national titles such as *MAD* and *National Lampoon*.
  David Sloane,
  4 Edgehill Terrace,
  Hamden, CT 06517
  (203) 624-4206

◆ **Pipe, tobacco, and smoking magazines of all sorts.** Pays from $1 to $5 per issue. Particularly wants pipe magazines from 1930's and 40's and tobacco magazines 1860-1900. Pays all post and shipping.
  Tony Hyman,
  Box 699,
  Claremont, CA 91711
  (714) 621-5952

◆ **Magazines about diving and underwater activities.** "I'll buy hundreds of foreign and domestic magazines, many of which were very short run, but no hard cover books." Give complete description, noting all damage.
  Thomas Szymanski,
  5 Stoneybrook Lane,
  Exeter, NH 03833

◆ **Sports magazines, from before 1970,** especially baseball.
> Bill Colby, Kenrich Co.,
> Box 248T,
> Temple City, CA 91780
> (818) 286-3888

◆ **Magazines about boats, boat racing, yachting, marine engineering, and similar topics.** Buys for resale, but has strong personal interest in small boats, outboards, and canoes.
> Robert Glick, Columbia Trading Co.,
> 2 Rocklyn Dr.,
> Suffern, NY 10901
> (914) 368-3078

◆ **Scandal and exploitation magazines** from 1952-1973 including, but not limited to, *Anything Goes, Behind the Scenes, Blast, Bunk!, Celebrity, Confidential, Cuckoo, Confidential Love Secrets, Dare, Dynamite, Exclusive, Exposed, Front Page Confidential, Hollywood Tattler, Hush-Hush, Inside, Inside Story, The Lowdown, Naked Truth, Off the Record Secrets, Private Affairs, Private Lives, Private Story, Rave, Revealed, Secret Life, Sensation, Sh-H-H-H, Side Street, Suppressed, Top Secret, TV Scandals, Uncensored, Untold Secrets, Untold Story,* and *Whisper.* "I'm also interested in complete copies of *The Police Gazette* in good condition from any year, especially bound. I'll pay $35 each for clean complete issues of *Inside Stuff* from the 1930's. I'm not interested in anything current, nor in soiled or poor condition material with pages clipped or water or sun damage." Give the title, date, and volume number.
> Gordon Hasse,
> Box 1543 GCStation,
> New York, NY 10163-1543
> (212) 996-3825 eves

◆ *Billboard* **magazine** in good complete condition from any date before 1960, especially wants quantity purchases of bound volumes. Fine condition only. Give dates and volume numbers.
> Gordon Hasse,
> Box 1543 GCStation,
> New York, NY 10163-1543
> (212) 996-3825 eves

◆ **Lurid gangster magazines of the 1920's and 30's.**
> Michael Graham,
> 345 Cleveland Avenue,
> Libertyville, IL 60048

◆ **Military magazines published by U.S., British, or Canadian forces** between 1939-45. "I'll buy *Field Artillery Journal, Air Force, Infantry Journal, Sea Power, The Aeroplane, Coast Artillery Journal, Flight, Ordnance, Impact,* and the *Army-Navy Recognition Journal.* No other titles and no damaged, incomplete, or badly soiled magazines."
> Edward Topor,
> 4313 South Marshfield Ave.,
> Chicago, IL 60609
> (312) 847-6392

◆ **Movie magazines.** "I prefer larger quantities, not single issues, of magazines from 1925-1950. I also want **trade magazines sent to theater managers** with advertising selling films to theaters rather than the public: *MGM Lions Roar, Motion Picture Herald,* and *Boxoffice.*"
> Buddy McDaniel,
> 2802 West 18th St.,
> Wichita, KS 67203
> (316) 942-3561

◆ **Music and song magazines 1920-60** including *Downbeat, Billboard, Disc, Metronome, Bandleader,* and song magazines that print words to songs such as *Song Hits, Hit Parader, 400 Songs, Songs That Will Live Forever,* etc. He will consider those with damage or minor cut outs. "Just ship them for my offer." Also **Movie magazines,** 1920-49. He asks that you double check to make certain *nothing* has been clipped out of the magazine. Indicate whether there is a mailing label pasted on the cover.
> Ken Mitchell,
> 710 Concacher Dr.,
> Willowdale, Ontario M2M 3N6, CANADA

◆ *Downbeat, Metronome, Billboard* **and movie magazines.**
> Beverly Hamer,
> Box 75,
> E. Derry, NH 03041

◆ *Cash Box, Coin Machine Journal* and other publications which covered the coin operated amusement business. Particularly interested in issues featuring pinball. Fine condition only.
Gordon Hasse,
Box 1543 GCStation,
New York, NY 10163-1543

◆ **Tropical fish magazines** in any language, pre 1960 only, but the "older the better." Issues of *The Aquarium Journal*, a New York publication, and *The Aquarium Magazine* from Cincinnati or Brooklyn if pre 1900 are worth $200 each.
Ross Socolof,
Box 1987,
Bradenton, FL 34206

◆ **TV Guide**, 1948-70, including early local editions. Selected issues from 1971 to 1989 are also purchased. Issues of NY City's *Television Guide* from 1948 are worth $25-$50 each. Jeff wants to know if address labels are on the cover.
Jeffrey Kadet,
TV Guide Specialists,
Box 20,
Macomb, IL 61455
(309) 833-1809

◆ Brewers, saloon, coin-op, and "Police" magazines pre 1920 including *Brewers Gazette, Champion of Fair Play, Coin Machine Journal, Automatic Age, Automatic World, Spinning Reels, Pacific Coin Machine Review, The Billboard* (1894-1932 only), and *The National Police Gazette.* "I'm willing to pay $1,000 for each year of *Police Gazette* (1896-98).
Richard Bueschel,
414 N. Prospect Manor Ave.,
Mt. Prospect, IL 60056

◆ **Architects and builder's magazines, 1870-1950.** Typical titles include: *Northwestern Builder & Decorator; Builder, Architect & Decorator; Real Estate Review; Brick Builder; Building Budget; Inland Architect; Improvement Bulletin; Minneapolis;* and the like.
Charles Test,
2710 2nd Ave.,
South Minneapolis, MN 55408

◆ **Magazines about airplanes, boats, motorcycles, automobiles, and other vehicles.** Prefers to buy longer runs, rather than single issues. Pre 1960 only. Telephone or write first. If interested, he will request items be sent for inspection. Magazines must be in excellent condition for resale.
Jay Ketelle,
3721 Farwell,
Amarillo, TX 79109
(806) 355-3456

◆ *British Journal Photographic Almanacs* any year, and **other photo magazines** pre 1930.
Jim McKeown,
Centennial Photo,
Box 3605,
Grantsburg, WI 54840

◆ *Bicycling World* and other bicycling magazines. Want 1880's and 1890's only.
George Manzur,
3327 Portland Ave.,
Minneapolis, MN 55407
(612) 827-6691

◆ **Magazines with Norman Rockwell covers or illustrations** including *Saturday Evening Post.* Simmons deals in moderately priced Norman Rockwell items so they are always needed for additional stock. Harold can send you a list of those which contain Rockwell advertising. Please, no magazines with torn covers, creases, drink stains, and the like.
Harold Simmons,
2950 Northbrook Drive,
Atlanta, GA 30340
(404) 496-0175

◆ **Gaming magazines** including *The General, The Wargamer, Fire & Movement, Games & Puzzles, The Dragon,* and similar magazines in fine condition, any year.
H.M. Levy,
Box 197CC,
East Meadow, NY 11554
(516) 485-0877

Dr. Hyman's Prescription

Old newspapers, even those covering historical events more than 150 years ago, seldom sell for a lot of money.

A whole year of the *London Gazette* from 1800 is only worth about $300. Fascinating newspapers and magazines with first hand stories of Daniel Boone and Andrew Jackson can be bought from some dealers listed in *I'll Buy That!* for less than $20. One of our dealers recently sold a Baltimore paper describing the burning of Washington by the British in the War of 1812 for only $15.

To describe a paper, give the name, city, date, number and size of pages, and an indication of any significant stories. If bound, indicate the type and condition of the binding (leather or boards, loose, split, leather crumbling, etc.). If it is a small town 18th or 19th century paper with a fancy masthead, a photocopy is suggested.

The newspapers that bring the most are the illustrated weeklies like *Harper's* and *Leslie's* from 1855-1900. When selling 19th century illustrated newspapers, make certain they are complete as the value drops significantly when important pictures are missing. You should not foxing (brown spots), tears, rips, stains, and cut outs.

If the paper is dry, brown, or brittle, it is seldom of value unless pre 1750 or the only known copy of an obscure paper.

Both newspapers and magazines can be shipped "Special Fourth Class Book Rate," which is very inexpensive. Ask for the latest rates at your post office.

tony hyman

Newspapers

◆ **Newspapers covering any important event before 1945.** Also all half year bound runs of pre 1870 papers, especially from Southern US, Confederate States, Early West, or anywhere in the US pre 1800. Wants specialty papers covering the women's movement, labor, railroads, abolitionism, temperance, or the Civil war. Also **illustrated newspapers** like *Harper's, Leslie's, New York Illustrated News, Ballou's Pictorial, Southern Illustrated News, Canadian Illustrated News, London Illustrated News*, etc. Also bound volumes of British newspapers and magazines pre 1700 (although he will buy later issues if historically significant). Also bound runs or single issues of any American magazine published before 1800. Pays $100 an issue for newspapers before 1730 but notes that many reprints exist so they need be authenticated. *No 20th century items* except mint condition reports of important events. *No severely defective papers.* For $5 per year (free to buyers) Phil issues an interesting catalog of historic papers available reasonably. Send $3 for a sample.
> Phil Barber,
> Box 8694,
> Boston, MA 02114

◆ **Newspapers of historical significance** especially relative to Lincoln's speeches or death, George Washington, the Revolution, the Civil War, colonial America, early Illinois and the Chicago fire. Buys individual issues of historical significance or bound volumes.
> Steve and Linda Alsberg,
> 9850 Kedvale Ave.,
> Skokie, IL 60076
> (312) 676-9850

◆ **Bound volumes or single issues of illustrated pre 1890 newspapers** including *Harper's, Gleason's, Ballou's, Leslie's, Illustrated London News, Vanity Fair, NY Illustrated News, Aldine, Puck*, and the *NY Daily Graphic*.
> Shirley Sorenson,
> 270 Sherri Dr.,
> Universal City, TX 78148
> (512) 658-2548

◆ **Illustrated weekly newspapers** including bound volumes of *Harper's, Leslie's, Puck, London Illustrated News, Judge, Vim, Wasp, Gleason's, Ballou's, Verdict, Inland Printer, Aldine, Daily Graphic,* and others, but before 1890 only.
> John Rosenhoover,
> 100 Mandalay Rd.,
> Chicopee, MA 01020
> (413) 536-5542

◆ **Foreign language newspapers published in New York City** during the 19th century. Not interested in any papers published elsewhere or published after 1900.
> Peter Eckel,
> 1335 Grant Ave.,
> So. Plainfield, NJ 07080

◆ **Chicago newspapers which cover gangster activities, 1920-33.** He has more than 60 particular events he wants the papers for and will provide a list upon request.
> Michael Graham,
> Roaring 20's,
> 345 Cleveland Avenue,
> Libertyville, IL 60048
> (312) 362-4808 days

◆ *New York Times* **in bound runs.** Call or write with your price wanted.
> Michael Rivkin,
> 60 Halley Drive,
> Pomona, NY 10970
> (718) 859-1081

◆ **Modern spicy scandal sheet type newspapers** like *Top Secret, Inside Story*, and *Whisper*.
> Warren Nussbaum,
> 29-10 137th Street,
> Flushing, NY 11354

24
Books

Dr. Hyman's Prescription

All through *I'll Buy That!* you'll find book buyers, usually people seeking books on a specific topic. Book buyers also look for the work of specific authors, books published by certain publishers, books illustrated in a particular manner, books from a particular period or country, and books of a specific type, such as leather-bound, miniature, first edition, autographed, etc.

The recent interest in paperback books focuses on 25¢ mysteries, science fiction, and first editions of important authors, but many others will find a buyer as well. Make certain to list the publisher's number and the cover price. Pay particular attention to the condition of the binding and tightness of the pages. If there are owner's names, newsstand stamps, or writing in the books, mention them.

Give "Standard Bibliographic Information" on all books for sale, remembering that photocopies can save you lots of time. Don't waste your time offering books that are damaged, torn, recent, or not what people say they buy.

A dealer's price for books depends upon his customers, his present stock, the rarity of your offering, the current market, and his mood and cash flow at the moment. If you want an appraisal of your books, hire an appraiser and pay the fee. Understand before you do, however, that most family book collections, except large collections on a single topic, are not worth the expense.

Books may be shipped Special 4th Class Book Rate, which permits two pounds for less than a dollar. Remember, that books are fragile, and can be damaged in transit. If it's good enough to sell, it's good enough to protect with proper padding.

tony hyman

Fine Books

◆ **Large collections of good books,** especially subject collections of Americana, Civil War non-fiction, Michigan history, theology, golf, chess, etc. Also wants books with color plates, leather bound books, and autographed books by famous authors. Catalogs are issued periodically. If you want to sell, give standard bibliographic information. One of the nation's largest used and rare booksellers, John does not buy *Reader's Digest* books, *National Geographics,* book club editions, textbooks of any kind, encyclopedia sets, or anything that is in poor condition.
    John K. King,
    Books,
    901 W. Lafayette Blvd.,
    Detroit, MI 48226
        (313) 961-0622

◆ **Any book, pamphlet, or tract printed in English speaking America before 1800.** "Books need not be complete nor necessarily in good condition. We will purchase damaged books or even fragments." If you own a book without a title page that you believe to be very old you may send them the book for identification. It's always best to write first, though, and if possible send them a photocopy. The Haydn Foundation for the Cultural Arts is a non profit public institution.
    Michael Zinman,
    Haydn Foundation,
    495 Ashford Avenue,
    Ardsley, NY 10502

◆ **Books printed before 1710 on any subject in any language.**
    Edwin Glaser,
    Rare Books,
    Box 1765,
    Sausalito, CA 94966
        (415) 332-1194

◆ **Various fine and early books,** including:
    (1) **Books with fore edge paintings;**
        "Though we especially seek American views, please let us hear about all fore edge paintings, no matter the era;"
    (2) **Incunabula,** printed before 1501;
    (3) **European books** before 1800;
    (4) **English books** and manuscripts from before 1780;
    (5) **American books before 1810;**
    (6) **Dictionaries** of all languages, if early and important;
    (7) Books in **sets of fine bindings,** standard or limited editions;
    (8) **Negro history;**
    (9) **Books published in Pennsylvania** before 1850, in English or German. Especially seek items printed by Benjamin Franklin in Philadelphia, the Brotherhod in Ephrata, or the Saurs (Sower) in Germanatown;
    (10) **Bibles before 1800,** Books of Common Prayer, The Koran, and other unusual, beautiful, or **early sacred books**.
Please make a Xerox© of the title page. In business for nearly 20 years, Ron offers a series of fine catalogs. He is a member of numerous historical and professional organizations.
    Ron Lieberman,
    Family Album,
    RD #1 Box 42,
    Glen Rock, PA 17327
        (717) 235-2134

EDITOR'S NOTE: Books worth $100+ turn up regularly. Especially good are first editions of classic 1930's and 40's mystery writers. They must have their dust jackets to bring anything approaching top price.

Standard Bibliographic Information

Title, author, publisher, place and date(s) of publication,
number of pages, illustrator, and approximate number of illustrations.

Give the condition of (1) the binding, (2) the spine, (3) the pages, and
(4) the dust jacket. Note bookplates, writing, and other damage.
A photocopy of the title page will save lots of writing.

◆ **Any type of book from art and archery to Zen and zoology.** This important Florida dealer prefers rare books but is interested in a wide variety of topics and subject matter, especially limited edition books by fine presses such as Derrydale, Kelmscott Press, Black Sun Press, Grolier Club, Grabhorne Press and the like. He does not buy school books, encyclopedia, medical texts, book of the Month Club editions, or reprints of famous novels. He feels only tentative evaluations are possible without actually seeing your book, but provide him with complete Standard Bibliographic Information.
> Steven Eisenstein,
> Book-A-Brack,
> 6760 Collins Ave.,
> Miami, FL 33141
> (305) 865-0092

◆ **Collections or accumulations of rare books, illustrated books or photography books.**
> The Antiquarian Bookstore,
> 1070 Lafayette Rd.,
> Portsmouth, NH 03801
> (603) 436-7250

◆ **Autographed non-fiction books.** Will consider all, but has particular interest in the Soviet Union, Eastern Europe, Asia, Communism, Socialism, and conservative authors.
> Edward Conroy, SUMAC Books,
> RD#1 Box 197,
> Troy, NY 12180
> (518) 279-9638 eves

◆ **Book collections and libraries of fine items.**
> James D. Julia Auctions,
> Rt. 201, Skowhegan Rd.,
> Fairfield, ME 04937
> (207) 453-9725

◆ **Leather bound novels** in fine condition regardless of age.
> Leonard D. Dick,
> Box 3711,
> Bartlesville, OK 74006
> (918) 335-2179

◆ **Books illustrated by Japanese woodblocks.**
> Jerrold Stanoff,
> Box 1599,
> Aptos, CA 95001-1599

◆ **Books illustrated with photographs tipped (glued) in,** U.S. or foreign. Also books illustrated by important photographers.
> Janet Lehr,
> Box 617 Gracie Square Station,
> New York, NY 10028

Books by various authors

◆ **First editions and non-fiction titles by Gene Stratton Porter or Zane Grey.** Also all fishing books by Zane Grey. No Grosset & Dunlap books. Wants list available.
James Baumhofer,
Box 65493,
St. Paul, MN 55165

◆ **Books by Harlan Ellison,** U.S. or foreign, hardbacks with dust jacket or mint condition paperbacks, especially 1st editions, numbered editions, and autographed copies. Especially wants copies of *Sex Gang*, written under the pseudonym Paul Merchant.
Edy Chandler,
Box 20664,
Houston, TX 77225
(713) 531-9615 eves

◆ **Books by Jack London,** especially 1st editions. Pays $300-$800 for 1st editions in dust jackets, $100 to $500 without. No paperbacks, unless rare titles or unusual copies. Also all memorabilia including photos and handwritten manuscripts.
Russ Kingman, Jack London Bookstore,
Box 337,
Glen Ellen, CA 95442

◆ **Books by Joseph Conrad,** *only* if 1st editions or in nicely bound sets. Also books and ephemera about Conrad. Also **books by George Macdonald** in any edition and condition.
Chip Greenberg, Booksearch,
Box 123 Planetarium Sta.,
New York, NY 10024
(212) 362-9336

◆ **Thornton W. Burgess and Harrison Cady books and ephemera.** Does not want any of their books published by Grosset & Dunlop.
Mrs. Kruskall,
Box 418,
Dover, MA 02030

◆ **Books by or about Victoria Woodhull,** American spiritualist, feminist, and Presidential candidate.
Ronald Lowden, Jr.,
314 Chestnut Ave.,
Narberth, PA 19072

◆ **Books by or about Thomas Paine, Isaac Newton, Galileo, Archimedes, James C. Maxwell, Nikola Tesla, Nicholas Copernicus, Arthur Eddington, Michael Faraday, and the Wright Brothers.**
Merlin Schwegman,
Merlin's Bookshop,
6543 Pardall Rd.,
Isla Vista, CA 93117

◆ **Books by Richard Halliburton,** especially signed copies, 1st editions with dust jackets, and all foreign editions. Also paper ephemera.
Michael Blankenship,
5320 Spencer Drive SW,
Roanoke, VA 24018-4709

◆ **Books by Samuel Beckett or Franz Kafka.** Wants only English or German 1st editions of Kafka. Will pay $1,000 up for 1st edition or signed works by Beckett.
Breon Mitchell,
Peartree Books,
Box 1072,
Bloomington, IN 47402
(812) 876-4827

◆ **First edition books by Southern Appalachian authors,** including Harriett Arnow, Wilma Dykeman, Davis Grubb, and works by ministers and travelers in this area. Also Virginia, West Virginia, South Carolina, Kentucky, Tennessee, Louisiana, Texas, Delaware, and Washington DC, history, bibliography, natural history, and outdoor recreation, if published pre 1900.
Jim Presgraves,
Box 639,
Wytheville, VA 24382

Books by
Various Publishers

◆ **Peter Pauper Press books.** First published in 29, still going strong today, PPP is usually associated with 4.5"x7" illustrated books, but it has done larger ones too. Especially wants fine condition books from the 1930's, 40's, and early 50's. Include the name of the illustrator with the standard bibliographic information. It's important to include the *color of the cover* since these were offered in various colors and she buys variants. Small ones are usually under $5 and large ones under $20 "except something fabulous and unusual."
Mary Mac Franklin,
2716 Northfield Rd.,
Charlottesville, VA 22901
(804) 973-3238 before 9pm

◆ **Books published by Arlington House Publishers.**
Edward Conroy,
SUMAC Books,
RD #1 Box 197,
Troy, NY 12180
(518) 279-9638 eves

◆ **Rare editions of works published by the Elzevirs.**
Albert J. Phiebig, Inc.,
Box 352,
White Plains, NY 10602
(914) 948-0138

◆ **Books published by the Limited Editions Club.** "I'll buy all years, all titles, as long as they are in fine condition in a fine box. I'll also buy Club ephemera including monthly letters, prospectus, etc. Only *Lysistrata* and *Ulysses* are acceptable without original box.
Lee & Mike Temares,
50 Heights Rd.,
Plandome, NY 11030
(516) 627-8688

◆ **Books published by:**
(1) **Neale** in either NY or Washington, DC;
(2) **Henkel** of New Market, VA;
(3) Pennsylvania German **Folklore Society**;
(4) **Any Southern publisher** prior to 1865.
Write or phone, giving Standard Bibliographic information.
Jim Presgraves,
Bookworm & Silverfish,
Box 639,
Wytheville, VA 24382
(703) 686-5813

◆ **Books published in Pennsylvania before 1810, in English or German.** Especially seeks items printed by Benjamin Franklin in Philadelphia, the Brotherhood in Ephrata, or the Saurs (Sower) in Germantown.
Ron Lieberman,
RD #1 Box 42,
Glen Rock, PA 17327
(717) 235-2134

◆ **Books published by Roycroft.**
Thomas Knopke,
House of Roycroft,
1430 E. Brookdale Place,
Fullerton, CA 92631

Standard Bibliographic Information

Title, author, publisher, place and date(s) of publication,
number of pages, illustrator, and approximate number of illustrations.

Give the condition of (1) the binding, (2) the spine, (3) the pages, and
(4) the dust jacket. Note bookplates, writing, and other damage.
A photocopy of the title page will save lots of writing.

Children's books

◆ **Dime novels and serial story papers.** These were issued between 1860-1919, reprinted through 1933, and star such heroes as Frank Merriwell, Nick Carter, Buffalo Bill, Deadwood Dick, and many others. There are many he seeks, but especially Merriwell sports stories marked "Merriwell Football Stories" or "Merriwell Baseball Stories."
> Edward LeBlanc,
> 87 School Street,
> Fall River, MA 02720

◆ **Boys and Girls Series books in extremely fine condition** including *Tom Swift, Rover Boys, Radio Boys, Adventure Girls, Beverly Gray, Nancy Drew, Don Sturdy, Boy Scouts, Dana Girls,* etc. Especially want cloth bound Merriwell stories published by Street and Smith. He does *not* want Disney, juvenile fiction, classic children's literary works like *Tom Sawyer*, or anything that is crumbly and brittle. Ed is the editor of *Dime Novel Round Up*, <u>the</u> publication for those interested in dime novels and boys' and girls' series books ($10 for six bi-monthly issues). He is also publisher of various bibliographies of dime novels.
> Edward LeBlanc,
> 87 School Street,
> Fall River, MA 02720
> (617) 672-2082

◆ **First editions of children's books** in very good condition. Wants books illustrated by Mabel Lucie Atwell, Jessie Wilcox Smith, Charles Robinson, Maxfield Parrish, Charles Folkard, and Maurice Sendak, Edward Gorey, Ralph Steadman, among others. Also illustrated editions of *Alice In Wonderland* dating from before 1880. Especially interested in editions illustrated by Harry Furniss, in English or in Hebrew. Also wants any *Alice* presentation copies, fore-edge illustrated editions, or pop ups. No editions published by Whitman. Has wants list of books.
> Joel Birenbaum,
> 2486 Brunswick Circle #A1,
> Woodridge, IL 60517
> (312) 968-0664

◆ **1st editions of the *Bobsey Twins* series** published by Mershon or Chatterton-Peck. No Grosset & Dunlop editions. Also wants **Frank Merriwell items**, especially the Tip Top League badge and *Frank Merriwell's Book of Athletic Development*.
> Audrey Buffington,
> 2 Old Farm Rd.,
> Wayland, MA 01778

◆ **Children's series books.** Must be in dust jacket if originally issued that way. Especially seeking the last 3 or 4 titles in series. Describe condition of dust jacket.
> Lee & Mike Temares,
> 50 Heights Rd.,
> Plandome, NY 11030
> (516) 627-8688

◆ **Editions of *Alice In Wonderland*** illustrated by just about anyone other than Tenniel. All foreign editions are wanted.
> Alice Berkey,
> 127 Alleyne Dr.,
> Pittsburgh, PA 15215

◆ **Fine quality 19th century children's books** illustrated with children. German, French, English, or U.S. editions are sought.
> Marguerite Cantine,
> Box 798,
> Huntington, NY 11743

◆ **Children's books,** American or English, from the 1400's to 1925, including educational books such as McGuffey's readers.
> Ron Graham,
> 8167 Park Ave.,
> Forestville, CA 95436
> (707) 887-2856

◆ Old and rare colorfully illustrated children's books.
Ivan Gilbert,
2824 Elm Ave.,
Columbus, OH 43209

◆ Oz books by L. Frank Baum. Also OZ memorabilia.
Dennis Books,
Box 99142,
Seattle, WA 98199

◆ Oz books and ephemera by Baum, Neill, etc. Want *Oz* related games, posters, other ephemera.
Alla T. Ford,
114 South Palmway,
Lake Worth, FL 33460
(407) 585-1442

◆ Dr. Seuss ephemera wanted by collector.
Kent Melton,
1801 W. Kenneth Rd.,
Glendale, CA 91201
(818) 545-1139

◆ Children's coloring books, from the 1930's and 40's if all uncolored. Movie star coloring books may be from any year up to 1960.
Fran Van Vynckt,
6931 Monroe Ave.,
Hammond, IN 46324

EDITOR'S NOTE: If your children's books involve cartoon characters, movie tars, or TV personalities, be certain to check "Pop Culture" in Chapter 5.

Standard Bibliographic Information

Title, author, publisher, place and date(s) of publication, number of pages, illustrator, and approximate number of illustrations.

Give the condition of (1) the binding, (2) the spine, (3) the pages, and (4) the dust jacket. Note bookplates, writing, and other damage. A photocopy of the title page will save lots of writing.

Books on various topics

◆ **Art, architecture, music, dance, and photography.** Wants 19th and 20th century scholarly or out-of-print books. Also photographic albums of quality photographs. Buys for resale. Muns issues periodic catalogs in these fields.
J.B. Muns,
Fine Arts Books,
1162 Shattuck Ave.,
Berkeley, CA 94707

◆ **Mining, minerals, and gems** especially in Arizona and Colorado. Russ buys old, scarce, or out of print books and paper ephemera. Wants *System of Mineralogy* by James Dana in the first through sixth editions, 1837-1892.
Russell Filer,
Geoscience Books,
Box 487
Yucaipa, CA 92399
(714) 797-1650

◆ **Stock market.** There have been more than 4,000 titles written, and Klein has about half of them. He wants books on speculation, the various panics, the commodities markets, market cycles, and biographies of speculators. Will buy U.S. and British editions, especially pre Civil War. Will also buy old stock market mail order courses. He is most interested in pre 1940 titles.
R.G. Klein,
Box 24A06,
Los Angeles, CA 90024

◆ **Photography, photographers, photographs,** and selected how-to books. Only pre 1938 items. Also books with tipped in (glued in) photos.
Alan Voorhees,
Cameras & Such,
492 Breesport Rd.,
Horseheads, NY 14845

◆ **Newspaper editorials and comic strip art.** From how-to's to collections of the work of famous cartoonists, Bill is interested in all cartoon art books, American and foreign, in any language. Can be composites an a theme, work of one artist, collections from a single source or year, etc.
Bill the Booky,
PO Box 6228,
Long Island City, NY 11106
(718) 728-4791

◆ **Checkers or draughts.**
Don Deweber,
Checker Book World,
3520 Hillcrest #4,
Dubuque, IA 52001
(319) 556-1944 let ring

◆ **Coins of ancient Greece and Rome,** especially *Greek Coins* by Kraay and Hirmer for which he'll pay $150. No old editions of handbooks by Sear, Seaby, or others which are still in print.
Thomas Mc Kenna,
Box 1356,
Fort Collins, CO 80522

◆ **Electric organ owner's manuals.**
C. Ray Erler,
Box 140 Miles Run Road,
Spring Creek, PA 16436
(814) 563-7287

◆ **Sports books and paper ephemera,** pre 1960, especially baseball, football, golf, and tennis. Does not make offers.
G. Thomas Brasser,
8701 Seminole Blvd.,
Seminole, FL 34642

◆ **Marine history, whaling, sailing, yachting, steam, naval, engineering, and model building.** Out-of-print items only, please.
Samuel Lowe, Jr.,
80 Charles St.,
Boston, MA 02114

Standard Bibliographic Information

Title, author, publisher, place and date(s) of publication,
number of pages, illustrator, and approximate number of illustrations.

Give the condition of (1) the binding, (2) the spine, (3) the pages, and
(4) the dust jacket. Note bookplates, writing, and other damage.
A photocopy of the title page will save lots of writing.

◆ **Ships logs, manuscripts and letters about the sea** or ship building. Also maritime charts. Out-of-print items only, please.
> Samuel Lowe Jr.,
> 80 Charles St.,
> Boston, MA 02114

◆ **Travel and voyages,** pre 1920.
> David Lilburne,
> Antipodean Books,
> Box 189,
> Cold Springs, NY 10516

◆ **Adirondack mountain, New York, communities, people, events, or history** including French and Indian War, Revolutionary War, War of 1812, hunting and outdoor recreation, personalities. Offers $75 each for the **Birch Bark Books,** a series of 19 small volumes bound in simulated birch bark and given by Henry Abbott between 1914 and 1932 as Christmas gifts. Breck publishes both a catalog and wants list of Adirondack materials, available upon request.
> Breck Turner,
> With Pipe and Book,
> 91 Main St.,
> Lake Placid, NY 12946

◆ **Tennessee or Alabama history,** with some interest in all Southern materials. No textbooks, religious titles, library discards, or items in poor condition.
> William Snell,
> The Book Shelf,
> 3765 Hillsdale Drive NE,
> Cleveland, TN 37311

◆ **Nebraska history and books related to the Western movement and Western Americana.** Interested almost exclusively in hardback first editions, especially autographed books with dust jackets.
> Francis Moul,
> Wordsmith Stores,
> Box O,
> Syracuse, NE 68446

◆ **Canadian topics** including travel, history, politics, exploration, fur trade, Indians, immigration, or mountaineering.
> Tom Williams, Books,
> Box 4126, Station C,
> Calgary, Alberta T2T 5M9,
> CANADA

◆ **African exploration and development.** Also **Arabic studies** including all materials relating the spheres of Moslem influence, both ancient and modern. Buys books in Arabic and related languages.
> Ron Lieberman,
> RD #1 Box 42,
> Glen Rock, PA 17327
> (717) 235-2134

◆ **Japan, China, Tibet, Mongolia, Himalaya, and Central Asia.** "I'll buy pre 1960 books in any language about art, history, and natural history, Far Eastern bibliography, books of maps, and **books illustrated with Japanese woodblocks.** Also books about Asians in the US, Buddhism, Lafcadio Hearn, and Asian travel.
> Jerrold Stanoff,
> Oriental Books,
> Box 1599,
> Aptos, CA 95001
> (408) 724-4911   FAX (408) 761-1350.

◆ **Russia, Soviet Union, China, Afghanistan, Mongolia, Tibet, or Eastern Europe** before 1940.
  Edward Conroy,
  SUMAC Books,
  RD #1 Box 197,
  Troy, NY 12180
     (518) 279-9638 eves

◆ **Communism, socialism, Marxism** and books by or about **Russian Royalty.**
  Edward Conroy,
  RD #1 Box 197,
  Troy, NY 12180
     (518) 279-9638 eves

◆ **Utopian fantasy books.** No book club editions.
  Walter Robinson,
  Book Farm,
  Box 515,
  Henniker, NH 03242
     (603) 428-3429

◆ **Urban studies** including material about cities everywhere and in all eras, including architectural, social, and historical aspects. Also **city view books** showing buildings and streets of cities worldwide. Make certain to include count of pages and photos in your description.
  Ron Lieberman,
  The Family Album,
  RD #1, Box 42,
  Glen Rock, PA 17327-9707

◆ **Violin making, identification, and repair** in any language from any period. Illustrated works are of particular interest.
  David N. Jones
  Jones Violin Shop,
  3411 Ray St.,
  San Diego, CA 92104
     (619) 584-1505

◆ **Books about books.** No book club editions.
  Walter Robinson,
  Book Farm,
  Box 515,
  Henniker, NH 03242
     (603) 428-3429

◆ **Antique Pewter.**
  Albert J. Phiebig, Inc.,
  Box 352,
  White Plains, NY 10602
     914) 948-0138

◆ **Playing cards, card playing, and card games,** especially bridge and whist.
  Bill Sachen,
  927 Grand Ave.,
  Waukegan, IL 60085

◆ **Photography books.** Old, out-of-print, or remaindered books on glamour photography, nude photography, or boudoir photography. "I'll buy single titles or collections, but **not** interested in other photography books." Jack asks you to set your price, but he'll send you a catalog of titles for $1. You might get his catalog and price yours at 50% of what similar books are sold for.
  Jack Qualman,
  Jax Photo Books,
  5491 Mantua Ct.,
  San Diego, CA 92124

◆ **Photography books and paper ephemera, pre 1900.**
  Ivan Gilbert,
  Miran Arts & Books,
  2824 Elm Ave.,
  Columbus, OH 43209

◆ **Photography or photographers,** and books with photographs tipped in (glued in) and photo albums pre 1900 only.
  Richard Rosenthal,
  4718 Springfield Ave.,
  Philadelphia, PA 19143
     (215) 726-5493

◆ **Journalism books.** Wants histories of newspapers and news wire services, American or foreign, but printed in English. No text books.
  Bill the Booky,
  PO Box 6228,
  Long Island City, NY 11106
     (718) 728-4791

Standard Bibliographic Information

Title, author, publisher, place and date(s) of publication,
number of pages, illustrator, and approximate number of illustrations.

Give the condition of (1) the binding, (2) the spine, (3) the pages, and
(4) the dust jacket. Note bookplates, writing, and other damage.
A photocopy of the title page will save lots of writing.

◆ **Sound recording history and technique,** pre 1930.
Steven I. Ramm,
420 Fitzwater St.,
Philadelphia, PA 19147

◆ **Fishing and hunting books,** but older, out-of-print titles *only*.
Robert Whitaker,
2810 E. Desert Cove Ave.,
Phoenix, AZ 85028

◆ **Thoroughbred horse racing** books and paper ephemera including KY Derby programs.
Gary Medeiros,
1319 Sayre St.,
San Leandro, CA 94579

◆ **All forms of harness racing, pacers, and trotters.** Also registers, year books, sire & dam lists, and horseshoeing. Also veterinary medicine.
Fred Rinker,
Harness Horse Books,
1168 Kaladar Dr.,
London, Ontario N5V 2R5,
CANADA

◆ **Horses and horse breeding,** including horse history, carriage driving and driving, breed registers, show yearbooks, stud books, and material about the Spanish Riding School, mules, and donkeys. Also veterinary medicine, but **no** *Diseases of the Horse*, books about betting, or books that are still in print.
Barbara Cole,
October Farm,
Rt. 2, Box 183-C,
Raleigh, NC 27610

◆ **Commercial aviation, U.S. or foreign, 1919-50.** No how to fly books, radio or navigation books or manuals, and no book club editions. Make certain to note condition of dust jacket.
Ron Mahoney,
Air Age Book Company,
Box 40,
Tollhouse, CA 93667
(209) 855-8993

◆ **Used and rare books, manuscripts, and maps.** "We specialize in books on the military, aviation, lighter-than-air craft, Ohio subjects, and **U.S. maps and atlases before 1870**.
Frank Klein,
The Bookseller,
521 W. Exchange St.,
Akron, OH 44302
(216) 762-3101

◆ **Aeronautics and airplanes.** Buys for resale.
Perry Eichor,
Keep 'em Flying,
703 N. Almond Dr.,
Simpsonville, SC 29681
(803) 967-8770

◆ **Boats and boat building, boat racing, yachting, marine engineering, and similar topics.** Buys for resale, but has strong personal interest in small boats, outboards, and canoes.
Robert Glick,
Columbia Trading Co.,
2 Rocklyn Dr.,
Suffern, NY 10901
(914) 368-3078

◆ **Paddlewheel steam river boat books** especially those that give historical or technical information. Wants 1st editions with dust jackets only. NO OFFERS.
Bill Warren Mueller,
Rt. 1, Box 262,
Middlebourne, WV 26149

◆ **Driving coaches and teams of horses.**
Donald Sawyer,
West Newbury Wagon Works,
40 Bachelor St.,
West Newbury, MA 01985

◆ **Marine history, whaling, sailing, yachting, steam, naval, engineering, and model building.** Also want ships logs, manuscripts, maritime charts, and letters about the sea or ship building. Out-of-print items only, please. A world famous "lifelong" dealer in the topic.
Samuel Lowe, Jr.,
80 Charles St.,
Boston, MA 02114
(617) 742-0845

◆ **Railroad technical reference books**, cyclopedias, dictionaries, and manuals published by RY Gazette, Simmons-Boardman, Moody, or Poors, pre 1950. No fiction.
Scott Arden,
20457 Highway 126,
Noti, OR 97461

◆ **Technical books and paper ephemera**, pre-1910. His wants list includes books on machines, trades, manufacturing, and technical processes.
Jim Presgraves,
Bookworm & Silverfish,
Box 639,
Wytheville, VA 24382

◆ **German books and magazines of all kinds.** Especially interested in pre 1920 cookbooks, topographical books depicting German and European landscapes and cities, trade catalogs, and children's books. Would love to find bound runs of magazines like *Jugend, Gartenlaube*, etc. Requests that you price what you have as she does not make offers.
Anni Waterman,
Colesburg, IA 52035

◆ **Fruit varieties before 1900,** including illustrated books, magazine articles, ceramic tiles depicting fruit, postcards, prints, folders, and greeting cards depicting apples. Especially books and paper with color plates or descriptions of fruit varieties. May be in any language. Also information about John Chapman (Johnny Appleseed). No tropical fruit, or anything later than 1940.
Fred Janson,
Pomona Book Exchange,
Rockton PO, Ontario L0R 1X0,
CANADA

◆ **Poultry,** but only books published pre 1930.
W.L. "Bill" Zeigler,
10 Lincolnway West,
New Oxford, PA 17350

◆ **Coins, currency, medals, tokens, or counterfeiting.** Especially wants scholarly books and auction catalogs on coins from any period or language. Chapman Brothers Auction catalogs between 1870-1920 will bring from $50-$2,000.
George Frederick Kolbe,
Drawer 3100,
Crestline, CA 92325
(714) 338-6527

EDITOR'S NOTE: All potential buyers of books are not listed in this chapter. <u>Always</u> check the index <u>and</u> the chapter in *I'll Buy That!* that covers the topic of your book.

Standard Bibliographic Information

Title, author, publisher, place and date(s) of publication,
number of pages, illustrator, and approximate number of illustrations.

Give the condition of (1) the binding, (2) the spine, (3) the pages, and
(4) the dust jacket. Note bookplates, writing, and other damage.
A photocopy of the title page will save lots of writing.

◆ **Negro history books and ephemera** including manuscripts, prints, and photos relating to the Black experience in America and worldwide.
Ron Lieberman,
The Family Album,
RD #1, Box 42,
Glen Rock, PA 17327-9707

◆ **Books and papers about the Cigar Makers' Union (CMIUofA)** or AFL President, Samuel Gompers. Wants all materials in any format, especially 1870-86. Normal single issues of the *CMIU Journal* are only worth $1 each, but commemoratives and special issues will bring premium prices.
Tony Hyman,
Box 699,
Claremont, CA 91711

◆ **Higher mathematics, mathematicians, and theoretical physics.** Also books on the history of science. No college texts.
Merlin Schwegman,
Merlin's Bookshop,
Box 1747,
Lompoc, CA 93438

◆ **Eyes or optics.**
Dr. James Leeds,
2470 E. 116th St.,
Carmel, IN 46032
(317) 844-7474

◆ **Science or medicine in any language** that are from before 1820.
Edwin Glaser,
Box 1765,
Sausalito, CA 94966

◆ **All aspects of palmistry or hands,** pre 1940. Buys fine condition only. Will pay $15-$20 for Sorrel's *The Human Hand*.
Geraldine Swigart,
12362 Kensington Rd.,
Los Alamitos, CA 90720

◆ **Teaching or operating schools.** Buys books or paper ephemera, pre 1920.
Tedd Levy,
Common School Collectibles,
Box 2217,
Norwalk, CT 06850

◆ **How-to books about picking locks and making escapes,** including but not at all limited to those by Houdini.
Joe and Pam Tanner,
Tanner Escapes,
Box 349,
Great Falls, MT 59403
(406) 453-4961

◆ **Occult and mystic science** including astrology, numerology, magic, alchemy, palmistry, spiritualism, pyramids, tarot, yoga, Atlantis, UFO's, ESP, and anything metaphysical. "I'll also buy art, posters, cards, games, antique crystal balls, and other mystical and occult ephemera as well as books on herbology, holistic healing, raw food, natural health, and the like. I'll buy one item or a thousand but only if they are in good condition."
D.E. Whelan,
Samadhi,
Box 729,
Newberry, FL 32669

Standard Bibliographic Information

Title, author, publisher, place and date(s) of publication,
number of pages, illustrator, and approximate number of illustrations.

Give the condition of (1) the binding, (2) the spine, (3) the pages, and
(4) the dust jacket. Note bookplates, writing, and other damage.
A photocopy of the title page will save lots of writing.

◆ **Pre 1970 crossword and other word puzzle books,** hard or soft cover, even if written in. Especially wants Simon and Schuster hardcover puzzle books 1924-60. Give the complete title, date, and series number, and tell how much of the book has been filled in. No crossword dictionaries, but does buy crossword puzzle magazines. Wants list sent for large SASE.
   Stanley Newman,
   American Crossword,
   Box 69,
   Massapequa Park, NY 11762

◆ **Atlases before 1900.**
   Shirley Sorenson,
   270 Sherri Dr.,
   Universal City, TX 78148

◆ **Encyclopedias published after 1984.**
   Lee & Mike Temares,
   50 Heights Rd.,
   Plandome, NY 11030
      (516) 627-8688

◆ **City Directories and telephone books** published 1860-1960.
   George Rinhart,
   Upper Grey,
   Colebrook, CT 06021
      (203) 379-9773

◆ **Cartoon books or collections,** hardback or paper, pre 1960.
   Leonard D. Dick,
   Box 3711,
   Bartlesville, OK 74006

◆ **Trade directories from the tobacco industry, 1860-1960.** Trade directories are hardbound books which list manufacturers and others involved in the tobacco industry. They come in a variety of sizes and publishers. Will buy <u>all</u>. Ship any tobacco trade directory for my check. Those before 1920 will bring $100 and the 1888 edition is worth $150. Directories from the 1920's and 30's are worth $30-50. **Please quote *all* tobacco related books, photos, and catalogs.** Especially wanted are catalogs of pipe companies, cigar companies, and wholesalers with a large line of tobacco related items.
   Tony Hyman,
   Box 699,
   Claremont, CA 91711
      (714) 621-5952

◆ **Catalogs of Oriental art goods including Japanese ceramics.** Wants to buy all catalogs on this topic published before 1942.
   Gardner Pond,
   62 Saturn St.,
   San Francisco, CA 94114

◆ **Baedecker Travel Guides.** "I'll pay $4 each for any pre 1945 in any language."
   John Slattery,
   352 Stanford,
   Palo Alto, CA 94306

Science Fiction
Horror & Adventure

◆ **Dime novels and serial story papers.** These were issued between 1860-1919, reprinted through 1933, and star such heroes as Frank Merriwell, Nick Carter, Buffalo Bill, Deadwood Dick, and many others. There are many he seeks, but especially Merriwell sports stories marked "Merriwell Football Stories" or "Merriwell Baseball Stories."
Edward LeBlanc,
Dime Novel Round Up,
87 School Street,
Fall River, MA 02720
(301) 951-0919

◆ **Detective and mystery 1st editions, hardcover or paperback.** Also reference, bibliography, and biography related to the mystery/detective genre. Wants Dashiell Hammett and Raymond Chandler 1st editions with dust jackets. His wants and stock are computerized for modem access.
Richard West,
West's Booking Agency,
Box 406,
Elm Grove, WI 53122
(414) 786-8420

◆ **Science fiction and mysteries.** First editions of fantastic adventure novels by authors such as Edgar Rice Burroughs, Sax Rohmer, and Talbot Mundy with their original dust jackets. He also wants **adventure and detective pulp magazines.** Include dates in your description.
Claude Held,
Box 515,
Buffalo, NY 14225

◆ **Horror, fantasy and science-fiction first editions.**
Merlin Schwegman,
Merlin's Bookshop,
Box 1747,
Lompoc, CA 93438
(805) 736-2234

◆ **Science fiction, fantasy, and horror rarities** including proofs, galleys, handwritten or typed manuscripts, first editions, signed limited editions, and the like. Know widely as a specialist in Steven King and Clive Barker. Not interested in common trade editions of most books, but will consider them as part of a lot that contains significant rarities.
Michael Autrey, Bookseller,
13624 Franklin St. #5,
Whittier, CA 90602
(213) 945-6719

◆ **Science-fiction, mystery, and detective paperbacks, hardbacks, and Digests,** British or American, 1950-80 and selected earlier science-fiction. No hardbacks without dust jackets. Values are surprising; some paperbacks can be worth $100 or more. Condition is very important. He does not want books "that show obvious signs of wear and age." No ex-library, no reprints, no book club editions, no condensed books, no Grosset and Dunlap hardbacks.
Leonard D. Dick,
Box 3711,
Bartlesville, OK 74006
(918) 335-2179

◆ **Paperbacks, Digests, and pulp magazines.** "The paperbacks we are most interested in are from the 1940's and 50's, though certain authors and publishers are collectible even into the 60's. The digests we seek are mystery, western, and sleaze. Any pulp magazines from the 1920's and 30's is wanted. We also want anything published by Bantam Los Angeles or Essex House." Wants original editions rather than reprints. Standard Bibliographic Information should include the book number assigned by the publisher (usually found on the spine).
John Gargiso,
Gorgon Books,
21 Deer Lane,
Wantagh, NY 11793
(516) 781-0439

index

index

BOOKS FROM TONY HYMAN

The World of Smoking and Tobacco

A GUIDE TO POPULAR TOBACCO COLLECTIBLES

Most comprehensive pictorial guide to popular smoking collectibles ever written. 184 pages, 1260 items seen in color or b/w, detailed historical annotations, full index, perfect bound. Created as a limited edition auction catalog and permanent reference. Its 100,000 words of text make it unique.

WHEN A SMALL PUBLISHER INTRODUCES A NEW CONCEPT IN AUCTIONS, AND CHARGES REFERENCE BOOK PRICES FOR THE CATALOG, IT BETTER BE GOOD.

THIS CATALOG IS BETTER THAN GOOD.

"This beautiful catalog is the best one I've ever gotten any time from anybody on any topic." (B. Roberts);

"I read every single wonderful word several times, and will again. Incredible piece of work." (M. McCain);

"The quality of information is phenomenal." (R.Munoz)

"Well thought out and easy to read." (T. Szold);

"From cover to cover, an excellent educational treat on tobacco." (B. Sutter)

"Absolutely superb." (C. Beyer);

"The catalog was perfect!" (D. Jones)

"It is a winner!" (G. Umberger)

See for yourself. But act fast. Copies of this valuable reference work are limited. Total printing less than 1,000.

ISBN: 0-937111-10-4   ©1989 $39.95 includes prices realized

HANDBOOK OF AMERICAN CIGAR BOXES

The fascinating story of the cigar box
History's most important retail package!

* 176 oversize pages...hardbound
* Printed to archival standards
* 45,000 words of well written text
* 190 large crisp photos
* Dozens of charts and drawings
* Thoroughly indexed
* All new info, available nowhere else
* Includes 1989 *Price Guide*

From 1865-1920 four of five men smoked cigars. More than 1,500,000 brands vied for attention by packing their cigars in colorful and unusual boxes.

A valuable guide useful to collectors, museums, package designers, historical societies, and all who want to relive the glories of 19th C. advertising.

By The National Authority on Cigar Industry History.

"The finest self published book to cross my desk in years," said the head cataloger at the Library of Congress.

"It's not often we rave about a book, but this one deserves every accolade," said the editor of the Tin Can Collectors Assn's monthly newsletter.

Total printing less than 3,000

ISBN: 0-932780-00-8   ©1979 $29.95 includes 1989 price guide

ORDER TODAY

Treasure Hunt Publications, Box 699, Claremont, CA 91711 (714) 621-5952

Changes in *I'll Buy That!* between August 1989 and July 1991

Americans are always on the move. Our listees are more stable than most people, but changes do occur. This is the most current information we have:

Page   New Addresses and Phone Numbers

17,78,81,102,109,267 Richard Bueschel has new phones: (708) 253-0791 eves (708) 980-3566 weekdays
18   Dottie and Dan Besant are no longer buying.
22,178,231 Vern Ward, Iron Horse Antiques, PO Box 4001, Pittsford, VT 05763
25,33   Charles Stapp, 7037 Haynes Rd., Georgetown, IN 47122 (812) 923-3483
31   Repinski has moved, leaving no forwarding address.
33   Herb Shearer has passed away.
36,53   Clark St. Waltz is no longer available.
37,53,67   Kevin Prediger has passed away.
43   S.Andrusier is no longer collecting.
43   L.C. Fisher, Silver Exchange, Rte. 8 Box 554, Huntsville, TX 77340   (409) 295-7661
47, 175   Darryl Rehr's phone number has been changed: (213) 477-5229
58,107,192,201,214 Sven Stau, Box 437, Buffalo, NY 14212
59   Bill Bege is no longer buying Fisher-Price toys.
62   R.E. Ziegler is no longer available.
65   Judaline McNece, 11270 Sirius Way, Mira Loma, CA 91752
66   Andrew Tabbat is no longer available
80,84,140,180 Jack Mattlack has passed away.
81   Tom Keefe, PO Box 464, Tinley Park, IL 60477
84, 85   Ray Brockman has passed away.
85   Ed Orth, a pioneer of world's fair collecting and editor of its newsletter, has passed away.
88   Hank Andrioni is no longer available
88,89   Gary Schneider: change city to Strongsville, all else OK
96   Dave Cook, 3900 County Line Rd. #23C, Lequesta, FL 33469
107   Les Paul, 568 Country Isle, Alameda, CA 94501 (415) 523-7480
108,115,129,189,205 Charlie Smith is no longer available.
118   John Buonaguidi, 540 Reeside Ave., Monterey, CA 93940 (408) 655-2363
121,281   Fred Rinker has passed away.
128   Lynn Munger, Potowatomi Museum, can be reached at Box 631, Freemont, IN 46737
132   Jerry King should not be contacted at this time.
132   Rolland Sayers, PO Box 629, Brevard, NC 28712
138,140   Dolph Gotelli, Box 8009, Sacramento, CA 95818 (916) 456-9734
146, 182, 196 If you can't get Harvey Boswell at the address listed, try: Rt. 4, Box 522, Wilson, NC 27893
166   Randy Liebermann, 211 E. 43rd St. #705, New York, NY 10017 (212) 972-2061
186   Glen Paruk, 4704 Woodburn Ct, W. Vancouver, BC Canada V7S 3B3 (604) 922-6759
200   Joani Blank's new address is 1210 Valencia, San Francisco, CA 94110
206   Steven Smith, Grandpa's Waste Basket, PO Box 5014, Ft. Myers Beach, FL 33932
209   John Pochobradsky's address should read 1991 E. Schodack Rd.
215   Harry Wigington has passed away, and will be missed by everyone who knew him.
217   David Beach, Box 2026, Goldenrod, FL 32733 (407) 678-6756
220   Steve Alpert's new phone number is (800) 332-2303
226   David Zdyb is no longer available.
227, 238, 260 Kenneth Rendell, Box 9001, Wellesley, MA 02181 (617) 431-1776   Fax: (617) 237-1492
237   David Compas is no longer available.
238   Michael Reese II, Box 5704, South San Francisco, CA 94083
250   Ron Ross's daytime phone is (415) 552-4543
253   Glenn Davis is no longer available.
274, 283, 285 Merlin Schwegman is no longer available.
283   Dennis Whelan, Samadhi, Box 170, Lakeview, AR 72642
285   Leonard Dick no longer buys any books or magazines other than science fiction.
307   Nick Koopman, 10600 Lowery Dr., Raleigh, NC 27615 (919) 870-8416

◆ **Designer furniture from the 1940's and 50's** by Herman Miller, Knoll, Eames, Nelson, Gilbert Rohde, Frank Lloyd Wright, Heywood Wakefield, Noguchi, Thonet, and other national and international designers. Most pieces are signed on the bottom. Primarily interested in bent plywood chairs, tables, couches, and case pieces and chrome furniture by Lloyd.
> Frank Novak
> PO Box 861333
> Los Angeles, CA 90086
>   (213) 625-0401

◆ **Arts and crafts period furniture and lamps,** such as those made by Van Erp, Roycroft, Limberts, Stickley, and others. These tend to be massive square oak pieces, often with dark finishes, visible pegs and hinges, and simple unornamented lines. Many people call it "mission oak." Lamps are often copper and colored glass. Send a photo or call if you think you have one of these pieces, as some can be quite valuable.
> David Rago
> PO Box 3592 Station E
> Trenton, NJ 08629
>   (609) 585-2546

◆ **Glass knives** are wanted in any configuration or color, especially with original painted decoration in original box. Values run from $25 to $100 or more. Send Xerox copy and describe color. She edits a quarterly newsletter about glass knives.
> Adrienne Escoe
> Box 342
> Los Alamitos, CA 90720

◆ **Victorian figural silverplate.** Anything small and figural including napkin rings, toothpick holders, card receivers, and similar items.
> Sandry Whitson
> PO Box 272
> Lititz, PA 17543
>   (717) 626-4978

◆ **Majolica pottery.** "Interested in all Majolica pieces." Claims to pay top dollar. Requests that you send a photo.
> Rick Kranz
> 702 W. Olive
> Stillwater, MN 55082
>   (612) 430-3016

◆ **Decorative and figural light bulbs.** Wants all unusual light bulbs including neon bulbs (a metal image inside the bulb glows when lit), Christmas bulbs (figural or bubble type), unusually shaped bulbs, and those made of colored glass (not coated) that have a standard base. Also wants display devices for bulbs and wired artificial Christmas trees. Prices range from $10 to as much as $600 for a Statue of Liberty bulb. A boxed set of Disney's Snow White and the Seven Dwarfs bulbs will bring $600. Santa bulbs are worth from $15-$150. Does *not* want Paramount brand Disney character lights or old utility, auto, or industrial light bulbs. Photo or sketch required. "I will beat any legitimate offer if it's a bulb I want."
> Joseph Kimbell
> 708 Bay Street
> San Francisco, CA 94109
>   (415) 346-8273

◆ **Figural cookie jars.** Buys figural ceramic jars and jar tops, but nothing cracked or repaired. Jars that aren't figural aren't of interest. **Also figural salt and pepper shakers.** She declares a photo to be essential. Describe all markings on the bottom of jars or salt sets. Make certain to mention every chip! Prefers you to price. Charges $10 per jar to do appraisals for insurance or estate.
> Mercedes DiRenzo
> Jazz's Junque
> 3831 N. Lincoln Ave.
> Chicago, IL 60613
>   (312) 472-1500

◆ **Electric clocks covered with colored mirrors.** Wants 1930's clock brands like *GE, Telechron,* and *Seth Thomas* covered with blue, peach, or green mirrors as long as the mirrors are not cracked or damaged. It's OK if the clock doesn't work. Give the brand, model, dimensions, and the color of the glass.
> David Escoe
> PO Box 342
> Los Alamitos, CA 90720

◆ **Beaded purses and bags.** Collector seeks pretty and unusual bags in fine condition. Color photos appreciated.
> Anne Foster
> 1913 Hyde St.
> San Francisco, CA 94109
>   (415) 776-8865

◆ **Embroidered items and stitchery.** Also buys quilt tops, crazy quilts, and other handmade items. Send good photo or photocopy.

    Linda Gibbs
    Heirloom Keepsakes
    10380 Miranda
    Buena Park, CA 90620

◆ **Hand painted ties** from the 1930's and 40's. Photocopy the bottom of the tie and also the label.

    Barry Pener
    9254 High Dr.
    Leawood, KS 66206

◆ **Cowboy theme dinnerware.** Sets or single pieces of pictorial pottery or china dinnerware which features cowboys or brand marks. Makers include *Wallace, Red Wing, Tepco,* etc.

    Frank Novak
    PO Box 861333
    Los Angeles, CA 90086
        (800) 727-4646

◆ **Early and unusual floor and desk fans.** Buys electric fans from before 1915 (check patent dates). Very interested in fans not propelled by electricity, such as wind-up, heat engine, water power, battery powered, etc. Some interest in ceiling fans. No interest in GE or later, mid 20's fans.

    Kevin Shail
    30 Old Middle Rd.
    Brookfield, CT 06804
        (203) 775-7017

◆ **Desk, ceiling, or pedestal fans** that are antique or unusual, especially mechanical fans not powered by electricity. Wants brands like *G.E., Westinghouse, Emerson, Peerless, Diehl* and others, but especially those made before 1920 or with unusual mechanisms. These early fans are usually cast iron and brass. Also wants literature, catalogs, ads and other information about fans and the companies that made them. No interest in steel fans made after 1940. Include the brand, nameplate information, number and dimensions of the blades, and what the various parts are made of. When describing condition, indicate if fan works.

    Michael Breedlove
    15633 Cold Spring Ct.
    Granger, IN 46530
        (219) 272-1231

◆ **Spiral bound church, community, or privately published cookbooks.** Will buy singles, collections, or multiple copies of the same title. Please indicate sponsor organization, number of recipes, quantity you have, the original retail price, and the price you want for them all wholesale. She publishes a newsletter for recipe collectors.

    Helen Jump
    PO Box 171
    Zionsville, IN 46077

◆ **American art pottery** by such makers as Overbeck, Van Briggle (dated pieces prior to 1904), Grueby, Marblehead, Newcomb College, George Ohr, Merrimac, Teco, Rookwood, Jervis, Pewabic, Robineau, Fulper, Brouwer, and Tiffany. The best of these pieces are quite valuable, and minor damage is acceptable. "We can either buy these from you or take them on consignment for our Manhattan auctions." This important pottery buyer emphasizes, "If you have any questions about something you feel is good, please don't hesitate to contact us. If in doubt, please call."

    David Rago
    PO Box 3592 Station E
    Trenton, NJ 08629
        (609) 585-2546

◆ **Architectural antiques,** including mantles, large chandeliers, garden statuary, gargoyles, gates, large quantities of iron fencing, stained glass windows and doors, and the like. Please send complete details and measurements.

    Architectural Antiques
    801 Washington Ave. North
    Minneapolis, MN 55401
        (612) 332-8344

    United House Wrecking,
    535 Hope St.
    Stamford, CT 06906
        (203) 348-5371

◆ **Antique doorknobs.** Loretta is editor of the club's newsletter and can put you in touch with collectors all over America who are interested in antique doorknobs and other door hardware. Send a good close up photo or a Xerox® copy.

    Loretta Nemec
    Antique Doorknob Collectors of America
    PO Box 126
    Eola, IL 60519

◆ **Cigar bands.** Small or moderate collections of inexpensive bands are wanted by a new collector.
>   Margo Toth
>   c/o Up Down Tobacco Shop
>   1550 N. Wells St.
>   Chicago, IL 60610
>   (312) 337-8505

◆ **Tin tobacco tags** are wanted, especially collections. He's in touch with other collectors, so is a good outlet for tags. Make a photocopy of your collection, if possible. Be prepared to send your tags for evaluation.
>   George Lincoln Barber, Jr.
>   PO Box 815
>   Jacksonville, TX 75766
>   (214) 586-9123

◆ **Cigarette and other insert cards.** Wants 19th century US cigarette insert cards, especially the *State Seal* series from Beck Tobacco and the *Wellstood Etchings* from Kimball. This 50 year veteran also wants cards from **Brooke-Bond Tea Company, Van Houten Cocoa,** and the **Liebig Meat Extract Company.** He will consider Liebig cards in any language, especially menu and calendar cards. Give quantities, and send photocopy showing sample of the front and back of cards.
>   Ron Stevenson
>   4920 Armoury St.
>   Niagara Falls, ON
>   Canada L2E 1T1

◆ **Cigarette silks** in fine condition. Also selected complete sets of early **cigarette cards.**
>   Charles Reuter
>   6 Joy Ave.
>   Mount Joy, PA 17552

◆ **Metal tobacco jars from before 1900** made of pewter, iron, lead, bronze, brass or silver. No tin cans or ceramics. He requires a clear photograph and a statement of condition. He is available to make appraisals but wants you to price your item. Some research may be in order since these are in the multiple hundreds of dollars.
>   Arthur Anthony
>   Mystic Valley Foundry
>   14 Horace St.
>   Somerville, MA 02143
>   (617) 547-1819 weekdays

◆ **Beer cans** from before 1960. Please don't offer any cans with pull tab tops. This veteran beer collector also wants beer advertising signs, trays, coasters, and bottles. Make certain to describe condition carefully.
>   Mike Miller
>   PO Box 1275
>   La Canada, CA 91012
>   1-800-882-2337

◆ **Golf memorabilia** of all sorts, including clubs, early balls, books, prints, paintings, photos, scorecards, tournament programs, trophies, catalogs, statues, ashtrays, china, desk sets...you name it, whatever it is, if it has a golf motif, he's interested. Does appraisals for a fee. Will consider consignments of certain items.
>   Richard Regan
>   3 Highview Terrace
>   Bridgewater, MA 02324
>   (508) 826-3537 days
>   (508) 279-1296 eves

◆ **Balloon tire bicycles** from the 1930's to 1960 are wanted. The most desired are boys' bikes with tanks, lights, horns, springs, and other accessories. "The more gaudy features, the better." Look for brands like *Schwinn, Road Master, Elgin, Shelby, Evinrude, Hiawatha* and *Western Flyer.* Bikes will usually have tires sized: 26 x 1.125, 24 x 2.125 or 28 x 1.5 and are especially desirable if colored. Will buy in any condition, but the value is determined by condition and accessories. Mike also buys parts, signs, shop fixtures, and literature relevant to this period of bicycles. No racing bikes, middleweights with 26 x 1.75 tires, or plain bikes. Photos and complete description important.
>   Michael Brown
>   260 19th Ave. N.
>   Clinton, IA 52732
>   (800) 383-0049

◆ **Black memorabilia** including cookie jars, older dolls, toys, kitchen items, prints, tins, historical items, Black folk art, Uncle Remus, advertising items, Aunt Jemima, Cream of Wheat, Amos 'n Andy, and "all items relating to Blacks in America. Will buy one piece or a collection."
>   Judy Posner
>   Box 273 W
>   Effort, PA 18330
>   (717) 629-6583 anytime

◆ **Rhythm and Blues or Rock and Roll 45rpm records from the 1950's.** Wants original recordings of groups like the *Flamingos, Robins, Wrens, Penguins*, etc. Will buy any 45's from race labels such as *Chance, Red Robin, Blue Lake, Harlem, Grand, Rockin, After Hours, Aladdin, Parrot, Flip, Allen, Rhythm, Club 51*, and *Swingtime*. Also buys *Vogue* **78rpm picture records.** Records must be clean and in excellent condition.

    John Widman
    3829 8th Ave.
    Kenosha, WI 53140
        (414) 654-6802

◆ **Movie memorabilia,** including lobby cards (especially from B movies of the 30's, 40's, and 50's), theater souvenirs, tickets, programs, photos of theaters, coming attraction pamphlets, studio promo material, etc. Will buy trade magazines such as *Motion Picture Herald, Box Office, The Exhibitor*, etc., aimed at theater owners, in any condition. Nothing made after 1960.

    Chris Smith
    26 Ridge Ave.
    Aston, PA 19014
        (215) 485-0814

◆ **Monster items** of all types including:
(1) **Gum cards, display boxes and wrappers** such as *Mars Attack, Outer Limits, Terror Tales, Spook Stories*, and *Flash Gordon*;
(2) **Plastic model kits** of Frankenstein's monster, wolfman, mummy, King Kong, Rodan, The Munsters, etc., built or unbuilt. Will buy some broken models for parts, and pay up to $50 for some empty boxes;
(3) **Toys and games,** puzzles, etc., featuring movie, TV, or comic monsters or creatures;
(4) **Halloween masks** of monster characters, especially masks made by Don Post;
(5) **Comics** by Zenith, E.C., and other 10¢ publishers of monster titles;
(6) **Magazines and record albums,** especially *Famous Monsters, World Famous Creatures, Monster Parade* and similar titles.

"I welcome any calls or letters, and am always happy to talk with anyone who has monster items." He requests your description include where you got the item. Don't forget your phone number.

    Joe Warchol
    5345 N. Canfield
    Chicago, IL 60656
    (708) 843-2442 days   (312) 774-1628 eves

◆ **Blues, jazz, and country 78 rpm records** especially on the *Paramount, Champion* and *Gennett* labels. Other labels of particular interest are *QRS, Autograph, Black Patti, Superior, Okey, Timely Tunes, Victor, Columbia, Brunswick, Bluebird* and *Vocalion*.. Many *Champion* and *Gennett* records are worth $100 each, and a few *Paramounts* can bring $1,000! "I particularly want 'hot' dance bands and rare guitar and fiddle vocals and instrumentals and will pay double what most price guides recommend and many times what most dealers pay." Condition is important, but will buy cracked records if very rare. Does not want reissues, opera, classical, swing, or pop records such as Bing Crosby. Include the label, record number, artist, and condition.

    Terry Zwigoff
    290 Mullen Ave.
    San Francisco, CA 94110
        (415) 647-5278

◆ **Comic, cartoon, and pop culture characters** depicted on *anything* in any form. Including:
    (1) **Lamps,** wall or table type. Values start at $250 and go up to $2,500;
    (2) **Paper dolls;**
    (3) **Empty boxes for any toys;**
    (4) **Cereal and food boxes and wrappers;**
    (5) **Halloween costumes,** 1930-70's, but only if in original box or package;
    (6) **Rubber monster masks,** especially those made by Don Post;
    (7) **Milk bottles depicting Disney characters,** for which he pays from $65 up;
    (8) **Model kits** of monsters, TV shows and movies if complete in original box;
    (9) *PEZ* **candy dispensers** and store displays are worth up to $150 each for rare ones. Give the serial no. when offering for sale;
    (10) **Disney silverware** by Oneida, International, or Rogers, but only if you have the box, toy, or stand that was sold with it;
    (11) **Star Wars toys** in original boxes;
    (12) **Character dolls,** including super heroes;
    (13) **TV and movie monsters and science fiction creatures.**

Condition is crucial. Note all damage, missing parts and if item is in its original box or wrapper since "that can make an item worth more." Photos are "very helpful." Does not buy reproductions.

    David Welch
    Route 2 Box 233
    Murphysboro, IL 62966
        (618) 687-2282

◆ **Plastic 1/25th scale model car kits**, whether built or not. Also buys dealer promotional materials, model car books and magazines, as long as they were issued before 1975. Does not want anything currently available. Give the name of the maker and the model number on the box. If you have dealer promotional models, give the color, condition, and whether the original box is present.

Rick Hanson
PO Box 161
Newark, IL 60541
(815) 695-5135

◆ **Metal vehicles** especially toy trucks from the 1920's and 30's. He'll buy cars, trucks, or construction equipment, but only those made of sheet metal, not cast iron. Send a clear photo and good description since condition is important. Include your phone number.

Calvin Chaussee
1530 Kenland Ct.
Colorado Springs, CO 80915
(719) 597-4000

◆ **Coin operated scales** in any condition and in any quantity are sought by this 10 year veteran dealer who also buys scale parts, literature, advertising, route books or maps, and "anything else" related to coin operated scales. Provide the brand name, model and serial number and describe the condition. Note whether the scale in complete. No interest in scales that weren't coin operated.

Bill Berning
PO Box 41414
Chicago, IL 60641
(708) 587-1839

◆ **Statue of Liberty.** Wants French bronzes of the statue, books before 1890, advertising depicting or satirizing the statue, bottles, lamps, medals and tokens, and other 19th century items related to Liberty or sculptor Auguste Bartholdi. Especially wants U.S. Committee models from early 1880's created to raise money for the pedestal. These pot metal figures come in 6" and 12" and have a tin base. He pays from $300 to $1,000, but wants early ones only. Photos or Xerox copies requested. No interest in postcards or centennial items.

Mike Brooks
7335 Skyline
Oakland, CA 94611
(415) 339-1751

◆ **Indian artifacts** including arrowheads, stone axes, celts, pipes, flint, ceremonial pieces, bannerstones, birdstones, baskets, beaded items, pottery, rugs, blankets, masks, wooden bowls, and any other Indian related items. He will pay high prices ($500-$1,000) for ancient birdstones he can use for his own collection. Please list what you have and make a drawing or photocopy, giving all measurements. If possible, please include both your home and work phone number. This forty year veteran holds 4-6 auctions a year of Indian artifacts and is always in the market for good items.

Jan Sorgenfrei
Old Barn Antiques
10040 S.R. 224 West
Findlay, OH 45840
(419) 422-8531 days;
(419) 384-3730 eves.

◆ *Colt* **pistols with factory engraving.** "I'll buy single action *Colts* in 95% or better original condition, if they predate WWII and have factory engraving. Give the serial number when you write, and if possible, a good close up photo of the artwork. Some newer single actions are also wanted. Also wants **guns from outlaws and lawmen** if they have proper documentation. All early memorabilia from the *Colt* company, including posters, advertising, and literature are also wanted, including *Coltrock* **brand products.**

Johnny Spellman, DVM
10806 North Lamar
Austin, TX 78753
(512) 258-6910 eves
(512) 836-2889 days

◆ **Fine quality cowboy clothing and gear.** Also other Western ephemera, including trail maps, brand books, wanted posters, and other items. **Also Artifacts, photos, and letters of Western personalities** including both lawmen and outlaws. Has particularly strong interest in **Samuel Colt, Sam Houston and Benito Juarez.** This active Western collector seeks "historically important" correspondence from any of these men and all items related to **the Mexican War.**

Johnny Spellman, DVM
10806 North Lamar
Austin, TX 78753
(512) 258-6910 eves
(512)836-2889 days

♦ **Wide range of fine and folk arts** including
(1) **Currier & Ives** on the subjects of yachting, riverboats, Western scenes, farm and New England scenes, and views of U.S. cities;
(2) **Paintings** of sports, Indians, North American mammals, river boats, the American West (pre 1920), Colorado mountains, Philadelphia, small still lifes, Hudson River, and those by 17th century Italian painters;
(3) **Autographs** of Presidents, signers of the Declaration of Independence, the Revolution or Civil War, scientists, movie stars, composers, dead ball players, and major US authors;
(4) **Maps** of America, or parts of America, including Canada, from the 1700's;
(5) **Books and sets of colored prints** depicting birds, animals, insects, fish, flowers, butterflies and other nature subjects before 1900;
(6) **Books** with fore-edge paintings or with particularly fine or unusual bindings;
(7) **First editions** of any literary classics;
(8) **Terrestrial and celestial globes** on stands;
(9) **Needlepoint pillows**;
(10) Carved or painted early **wooden boxes and other objects**, especially unusual;
(11) **High quality furniture** including 18th and 19th century English, French, and American, English Queen Anne, Georgian, Chippendale, Adam, and Sheraton, French empire, and Venetian painted furniture. Also furniture by Phyfe, Lannuier, Wuervelle, or Barry and sets of 19th century chairs.
Telephone, or send full details, including photos.
W. Graham Arader III
620 No. Michigan Ave.
Chicago, IL 60611
(312) 337-6033

29 East 72nd St.
New York, NY 10021
(212) 628-3668

560 Sutter Street, #201
San Francisco, CA 94102
(415) 788-5115

2800 Virginia Street
Houston, TX 77098
(713) 527-8055

1000 Boxwood Ct.
King of Prussia, PA 19406
(215) 825-6570

♦ **Tramp art** items made from cigar boxes or fruit crate wood which has been layered into edge-notched pyramids. Typical items include boxes, picture frames, doll furnitures, banks, wall pockets and small furniture. Especially wants large items, like chests of drawers, but will buy those only if they are in fine condition with a minimum of missing pieces. He will consider painted or gilded examples, though most are simply varnished. Original surface is important and documentation as to its origin (such as signatures and dates) is a plus. **He does not want** items made from ice cream sticks, clothespins or matches, nor does he buy items recently repainted or in rough condition. "A photo is almost essential," he advises.
Michael Cornish
195 Boston Street
Dorchester, MA 02125
(617) 282-3853

♦ **Bossons artware** including character heads, wall plaques and figures. "We buy modern figures that are still available, but are primarily interested in obtaining discontinued figures, which can be worth $85 and up, with a few rare ones valued at over $1,000." Only items marked "Bossons, Congleton, England, copyright" are sought. Slightly damaged figures will be considered, since Dr. Hardisty is a restorer approved by Bossons. He is author of the price guide to these popular British figures.
Dr. Donald Hardisty
3020 E. Majestic Ridge
Las Cruces, NM 88001
(800) 762-2263

♦ **Prints and illustrations**, including **yard longs, calendars,** and prints of flowers, children, beautiful women etc., including calendars and books before 1919. Also **illustrations by** Paulde Longple, Harrison Fisher, Francis Brundage, Newton Wells, Catherine Klein, Maud Humphrey, others. Also wants **magazines** with fashion prints and color pictures of women and children, such as *Ladies Home Journal, Women's Home Companion, Butterick, McCall's*, etc. Buys only color prints. Prefers unframed items. Must send photocopy. Note *all* defects. Will make approximate offers, but must see to determine condition before buying.
Linda Gibbs
10380 Miranda
Buena Park, CA 90620
(714) 827-6488

◆ **Checks autographed by any famous person** are wanted, especially bounced checks. He'll pay from $750-$3,500 for checks he especially wants from Henry Ford, Harry Houdini, Greta Garbo, Buddy Holly, President Taylor, Gerald Ford, Lyndon Johnson, Al Capone, Richard Nixon, Charles Chaplin, president Tyler, and others. "I want to know the condition, the date, whether the check is signed or endorsed, and the color of the check. If the seller has a price in mind, please quote it up front. If the seller has no idea of value, then I will make him a fair quote." Send a fax or photocopy.

Olan Chiles
1892 Avenida Aragon
Oceanside, CA 92056
(619) 724-2339 Fax: (619) 726-4964

◆ **National Geographic Society publications of all types.** Buys magazines, books, maps, article reprints, pamphlets, map indexes, school and news bulletins, advertising brochures, catalogs, invitations, announcements, autographs, slides, videos, postcards, and calendars produced by NGS. Also buys materials published by other companies with articles about the NGS, which spoof the NGS, are funded by the NGS, or in any way refer to the NGS. He is particularly interested in magazines before 1913, technical books such as that on Machu Picchu (for which he'll pay $1,000) and the complete advertising brochure sent to prospective members in 1888. He'll pay you $5,000 for a vol. 1, No. 1 magazine. **No interest in magazines after 1959.** Nick buys outright or accepts items on consignment. He encourages correspondence from buyers and sellers.

Nick Koopman
10600 Lowery Dr.
Raleigh, NC 27615
(919) 870-8416

◆ **L.Ron Hubbard collectibles** including books, photos, documents, pulp magazines, and other ephemera. This close personal friend of the author will buy virtually anything in fine condition, but does not want ratty condition pulp magazines or books printed after 1960 unless autographed. Send photocopy of smaller items and standard bibliographic information about books. Some autographed books are worth as much as $5,000 each.

Karen Jentzsch Barta
245 W. Loraine #208
Glendale, CA 91202
(818) 243-0125 fax: (818) 507-5702

◆ **U.S. Coins and paper money.** Wants estates, collections and accumulations of early U.S. silver and gold coins, paper money, and all other U.S. coins from 1793-1900. This nationally known dealer has been around for 40 years, and will travel to see large lots and better collections. Send a list and description. Photocopies OK.

Littleton Coin Co., THCC
253 Union St.
Littleton, NH 03561

◆ **Envelopes with stamps mailed in the Orient.** Buys all envelopes with stamps mailed in China, Tibet, Korea, Hong Kong, Nepal, Mongolia and Japan. Advisable to first phone or send Xerox, but will pay postage on items sent on approval.

Bridgewater Onvelopes Collectibles
680 Route 206 North
Bridgewater, NJ 08807
(201) 725-0022
(201) 707-4647 fax

◆ **Military items from the Coldstream Guards.** The museum wants to buy uniforms, equipment, badges, and miscellaneous items used by the British Coldstream Guards, especially from before 1900. Other British Army ephemera from before 1900 may also be of interest. No US items, though. A full description is requested, including dimensions, materials, and age. Indicate anything you believe to be unique. Donations acknowledged.

Ernest Klapmeier
Coldstream Guards Living History Museum
c/o Castle Keep RE
PO Box 334
Wayne, IL 60184
(708) 584-1017

◆ **Medically related advertising and memorabilia** especially tin containers, trays, signs, match holders, trade cards, advertising envelopes, calendars, old corked and labeled bottles, pinback buttons, mirrors, instruments, and the like. Among tins, he wants medical, dental, veterinary, talcums, prophylactics, etc. Fine condition items only.

Eugene Cunningham, MD
152 Wood Acres Drive
E. Amherst, NY 14051
(716) 688-9537

index to 1991 supplement